“YOU CAN HAVE CHIPS!”

“YOU CAN HAVE CHIPS!”

STEVE WIGNALL

FOREWORD by LOMANA TRÉSOR LUALUA

APEX PUBLISHING LTD

First published in hardback in 2009,
repinted and updated in paperback in 2016 by
Apex Publishing Ltd
12A St. John's Road, Clacton on Sea, Essex, CO15 4BP, United Kingdom

www.apexpublishing.co.uk

British Library Cataloguing-in-Publication Data
A catalogue record for this book
is available from the British Library

ISBN: 978-1-78538-527-8

Typeset in 10pt Baskerville Win95BT

Production Manager: Chris Cowlin

Cover Design: Siobhan Smith
Photograph: Kindly supplied by Colchester Gazette

Photos: Supplied by the author, Colchester Gazette and www.robertbluffield.co.uk

We would like to dedicate this book to our children, Thomas, Jack and Sally, and our grandchildren and great-grandchildren yet to come!

Anne and I love and are more proud of our kids than they will ever know.

FOR ANNE

The love of my life, Anne has always been at my side to encourage me in everything that I have done since we met as teenagers in 1970. Whether as a player, coach, manager or husband, her love, enthusiasm for life and drive have always inspired me.
I thank her for her help and input over many hours working on this book, which has proved invaluable and without her support I would never have finished it.

Recently I attended a function and was asked by a member of the audience,
"Who is your best friend?"
I answered without hesitation: "My wife Anne!"

CONTENTS

WITH THANKS

I would like to thank my wonderful parents, Peg and Arthur, for encouraging me to follow my dream. Sadly this meant that I have always been far from them in miles, but not in thought. People are often asked, "Who are your heroes?"

Mine are simply my mum and dad!

ACKNOWLEDGEMENTS

To all the players and others that I have not mentioned in this book, I apologise but it wasn't possible to name everyone. I must give a special mention, however, to Ian McDonald and Graham Brookland for graciously coping with my many phone calls to plunder their memories of certain facts that I couldn't recall myself!

FOREWORD

Steve Wignall was the manager when I joined Colchester FC after being spotted playing college football. I scored a hat-trick in my first trial game for the "U's" as a 17-year-old and was offered a chance to join their Youth Training Scheme to play in the youth team.

Steve always took a genuine interest in the young players at the club even when he had his hands full running the first team and doing all that the job entailed as a manager. He always encouraged me and showed great faith in my ability and rewarded me with my first professional contract. He also gave me my League debut at Chesterfield, which was my big chance and I scored my first senior goal within minutes of going on the pitch.

After Steve left Colchester I still kept in touch because of my friendship with his son Jack. I spent time at their home and Steve was always there to give me good advice regarding my career.

As a footballer you feel indebted to the manager who gave you your first professional contract and, as Steve gave me that chance, I will never forget him.

I always found Steve to be honest and upfront as a person. When I heard that he was writing his autobiography I knew that his book would also reflect him as a person. Honesty can be in short supply in football sometimes but not in Steve's case.

So this book is definitely a good read!

Best wishes, Lomana Trésor LuaLua

www.apexpublishing.co.uk

CHAPTER ONE

BAG BOX DAY TO SHANKLY'S WAY

I am not a great reader of books, so the thought of actually writing one myself was quite daunting. When I received a letter from Apex Publishing suggesting that they publish my autobiography, my immediate reaction was to put the letter to one side or even bin it! Why me? Who would want to read about my life and career, when there are so many more people of consequence and importance who have published work over the years?

However, my wife took a very different view. "Why shouldn't you write a book? You can say this; you can say that. It will be good fun! I'll help." Her enthusiasm for the task helped persuade me to give it a go. My wife has a great memory for detail, almost photographic at times, so going back over the years her recall would become invaluable.

Here's a little story to give you some idea of my wife's character. At junior school, if the curriculum for the day had been completed with ten minutes or so to spare, the teacher, not wanting the kids to be sat around idle or messing about would say, "Anne Parry [her maiden name, obviously], come out to the front and talk"! She would keep the class entertained and perhaps educated in anything she chose to speak about on that day. Nothing has changed after 32 years of marriage!

Regarding the content of my book, it will be as it was, with little sensationalism and not too much poetic licence, just honest everyday things that have happened and experiences that have occurred in my life as a professional footballer, coach and manager. Anne said, " Could you put the naughty bits in?" My reply was, " Let's wait and see." I have no intention of embarrassing anybody in my book, but at the same time most things need to be told as they were.

I have met some fantastic people in and outside football. I have also met some nuggets, back-stabbers, silly arses, big-time charlies, dicks and wannabes, etc. Oh dear, I'm sounding a bit cynical already and I've hardly got started!

I didn't play for England or in the top division of football but I still had a good career in a tough profession and came out of it in pretty good shape. People tend to take special notice when they read or hear something that a famous person has stated, or assume that if a foreign manager or coach at a high level says something in broken English it must be profound. What a load of cobblers! Having been in the game at a decent level, I can assure you it isn't all profound. Having been a manager in the Football League, I know that what is said in the dressing room at Colchester United or Manchester United will be very similar. One big difference is that you don't see many second-hand Vauxhalls in the players' car park in Manchester. The point I'm trying to make is that you don't need to be a household name before you have something worthwhile to say to people.

Coming from Liverpool I nearly always try to see the funny side of things, so there have been lots of comical events in my career as well as some not so funny moments. All in all I am a positive person and even now, at the ripe old age of 53, I try to be optimistic every day I get out of bed. My father always says, "You are a long time dead son!" and he is 88!

I was born in Liverpool in 1954, the fourth of five children with three older sisters – Carol, Lorraine and Pauline, and one younger brother - David. My brother David will appear in the book later, as he also was involved in professional football. In fact, we even played in the same team for a while. We lived in Tuebrook, Liverpool 13, only a bus ride from Anfield football ground.

Dad was born in Liverpool and mum was born in Llandudno, North Wales. My mum was a Wren and my dad served in the Army. They met during the Second World War, had a whirlwind romance and were married pretty sharpish before he was sent overseas. Five kids, seven grandchildren, four great-grandchildren and 65 years later, they are retired and living in Llandudno.

My father was a season ticket holder and still is to this day. In his earlier years he lived close to Melwood Drive training ground and used to watch the old Liverpool players such as Billy Liddle, Bob Paisley, Ronnie Moran and Jimmy Melia. At the end of one such training session, my dad wryly tells me of the time that Bob Paisley sauntered over to him still sweating from his exertions, retrieved a half-smoked ciggy from behind his ear and asked for a light! Unfortunately, my father had to decline one of his idols, as he was a non-smoker! Oh my, how the game has changed. I don't think the present Liverpool manager would be too happy with that scenario these days.

My earliest recollection of football is when I was about eight years old and I used to go down to a local field called 'The Red Wreck'. I would watch men's teams play with a real 'Casey' as we called them. This was basically a leather ball with a bladder in it and a laced-up slot. They were dubbined to try to repel the moisture that turned it into a huge brown bar of soap – no wonder the goalkeepers wore those big silly woollen gloves!

I used to stand behind the goal, which had 'real' nets. That meant to me in those days that it was a proper game of 'togger', as we called it in Liverpool. From behind the goal I would chase after the ball with half a dozen other kids whenever a shot went wide of the target. Most of the lads were older and bigger than me so I rarely got a look in. In fact I usually got pushed over and trampled on before I put a finger on the Holy Grail. I loved just being there though, and when I did actually get the ball I would give it the full welly back to the goalie without showing any kind of facial expression, even though it felt as though I'd broken my bloody foot! Those 'Caseys' were rock hard!

The real treat came in my ninth year when my dad first took me to Anfield with him. His season ticket was in the Kemlyn Road stand but I had to stand in the paddock on the opposite side of the ground. Kids could take a box or whatever to stand on, so I took mine in my haversack and worked my way to the front so that I could see. Of course, you are supposed to take your box out of the bag, but the manoeuvre seemed so awkward to perform amongst such a melee' that I actually stood on the bag instead, which consequently got all wet and filthy as you can imagine. Heaven knows what the 'wet' was; I shall leave that to your own imagination! I managed to see the game by just peeping over the wall. I got knocked off the box a few times when the crowd surged forward, but the men around me hitched me up by the scruff of my neck and dumped back on the bag box!

The atmosphere was unbelievable. It was scary, frightening, noisy and physical but I was hooked – not so much on the watching but rather my desire to get on the pitch and be one of them, 'A Footballer'. I wanted to wear that red shirt.

As I watched the game and everyone around me was shouting, cheering, swearing, singing and jumping up and down, I just stood there and took in all that was happening both on and off the pitch. When the players came close to the touchline where I was standing I could even smell them. The liniment or embrocation made the hairs on my neck stand up! I could feel my heart thumping, not in fear but just being enveloped by everything. When the players made physical contact I could hear the smack or thud of flesh on flesh and see the expressions on their faces. Fantastic!

When the game finished and the crowd began to move, I must admit I was a little concerned as how I was going to get out in one piece. I thought, if I fall over I will get trampled on and never get up, especially with this bag on my back, but I needn't have worried. In fact my feet hardly touched the ground. It was so packed that I literally got carried out of the stadium with my feet off the floor, totally compressed between others' bodies! I can't say that I enjoyed that bit and I was pretty relieved to reach the exit and meet my dad, who had left his seat a tad early so that he could get around to me in good time. My father has always been a Liverpool fan and from that day on I have been one too, always keen to discover their match results in a way that is different to my searching out the results of teams I was involved with as a player, coach or manager.

By the time I was ten we had moved across the Mersey River to The Wirral, which is still part of the Merseyside area. Some folk from Liverpool call people from over the water 'Plastic Scousers', but I was born in Liverpool city and as far as I am concerned I am a true Liverpudlian.

I started playing local junior football around this time and joined the Boys Brigade U12s. We did well at times to keep the score down to single figures; in fact, we did actually lose 27-0 in one game! From what I can remember I wasn't that bothered about the score, I was just happy to change into some kit and get my boots on. The boots were rubber-moulded studs (which were all the go at the time). I think mine were second-hand and they were a bit big for me but it didn't matter. The shirts were somewhat rugby-like and came down to your knees when untucked, or even nearly to the floor when wet!

Luckily for me, a man named Dave Bale was watching one of our games and he pulled my dad and me to one side afterwards. He asked if I would like to go training with one of his Junior Olympic teams, which he ran from U11s toU16s. Dave was and still is an unassuming bloke, very quietly spoken and not a brash or boasting type but quite persuasive. It turned out that Junior Olympic FC was a very well run outfit respected in the area and above all, for me, all the sides had full matching kit! Even better they played in RED. When I asked Dave in latter years why he picked me out of a team that was losing by double figures almost every week, he said, "You were the only boy in the team with your sleeves rolled up, you had a big bush of blond hair and you covered every inch of the pitch. You never touched the ball much but you ran your socks off!"

Talking of running your socks off, I can remember in some games when the pitch was saturated and like a quagmire, so if your socks were a little big for you they would slip down, get completely soaked and end up over your boots! It was like trying to run in sodden house slippers and, remember, they were at the end of thin white legs with knees that looked like knots in cotton. What a state! I still loved it though.

Believe it or not, I rolled up my sleeves in every game I can remember throughout my career, even if it was freezing cold. It was just my way and I felt comfortable with it.

While on the subject of being comfortable, how can you play a game of football in a pair of gloves? A lot do it these days. What a set of 'tarts'! They'll be playing in earmuffs next!

And, talking of ears, I will digress for a moment to recount a story that upset my wife when I told her some 20 years later!

I had not been in Wallasey, Wirral, for long and one cold day I was going down to the local park for a kick-about. On the way you had to pass some public toilets. As I approached them, I noticed a lad running out of them at some speed. He was only about my age and I didn't think too much of it, so I went into the loo for a quick pee before the game. However, when I got in there the floor was two inches deep in water and all the washbasins had their plugs in with the taps full on! Water was overflowing and flooding the whole place. My first reaction was to turn off the taps in order to try to stem the flow. As I grabbed a tap and started to turn it off, a big burly bloke came into the toilets and, before I could explain, he smacked me hard across the face and ear with his dinner-plate-like hand. It was the hardest I had ever been hit and I literally did see stars! The old survival mode clicked in and I legged it. He obviously thought that I was the perpetrator, but I wasn't going to hang about to protest my innocence and maybe cop another one! When I got to the park my mates said, "What happened to you?" Apparently I had a huge red handprint on the side of my face. I played for two hours or so with my mates until the redness had gone, so I could go home without my mum or dad seeing it. I didn't want them to know. I don't know why, but I just didn't want to tell them.

This was an early lesson in life for me, that there will always be an injustice in many ways and also that when you get hit properly it bloody well hurts.

There was worse to come. One morning my mum was talking to someone on the doorstep, so I nosed through the front window. It was him, the ear belter. He was only our milkman. Oh my God, I almost peed myself! I was torn as to whether to go and confront him with my mum at the front door, which could have been dodgy for him, as my mother (the eldest of six) can stand up for herself. He may have had to search for his 'Gold Top' in a place he could not imagine if she'd found out what he'd done! Having said that, he was only being a good citizen really and he didn't know I wasn't the culprit in the bogs. Anyway, I decided in those few seconds that discretion was the way to go - say nowt!

I avoided our milkman like the plague over the following months, but realistically he wouldn't have recognised me because on the day of the haymaker to the ear I was wearing a balaclava with just a slit for my eyes. It was kids' fashion at the time.

Can you imagine that red mark on my face without the cushion of the woollen material? I would've had to play footie for about four hours instead of two!

I played for Junior Olympic right up to the age of 14. We were very successful as a club locally. We even went on a mini tour of Ireland one year, which was a great experience. The ferry crossing was something in itself, as I can remember the weather wasn't good and our docking in Dublin was delayed. I had never seen so many sick people in all my life. Luckily I felt fine, but some parts of the ship were literally swimming in vomit! It was a real eye-opener.

In Dublin we went on a visit to the Guinness factory and at the end of the day we were allowed into the bar area, which obviously only served Guinness. Dave let us all have half a pint of 'the black stuff' if we wanted to try it. This was my first taste of alcohol at the age of 12. It tasted like sucking wet cardboard but I drank it. Most of the lads did, or attempted to. It did us no harm and to this day whenever I drink Guinness the memory of that visit fleetingly enters my mind.

It was during this Irish trip that I came up against some real aggression on the pitch for the first time. With a Welsh mother and grandfather and an Irish great-grandmother there is no shortage of the Celtic froth in my make-up, which will be more apparent later on in this book!

Junior football in England was competitive, as it always has been, but in the couple of games in Dublin it went a step further. I don't mean dirty or over-aggressive, it was just that the players seemed to have more of an edge to them. Some were absolutely fearless in their challenges. I played any position as a youngster, as a lot of kids do, but by now I generally played at centre half as it was known then. I stood up to the aggressors and actually handed out a bit myself. Perhaps this was a turning point for me. I probably saw myself as a good 'footballer' who tried to play at all times, which we were encouraged to do by Dave Bale. Looking back, he was ahead of his time in regard to how he handled the young players and the standards he set for his teams and football club in general. As far as I know, the football club still exists today, some 40 years later.

In the Irish games I found myself having to be mostly physical to compete with the players over there. There was still a lot of skill in the matches but much of the play was a battle and I think that I picked up more bumps and bruises in two games than I did in most of the season back home in England. In fact in one game an Irish lad overstepped the mark a bit and threatened to give one of our team a slap. In a flash a balding man, who had a bucket and sponge in his hand, ran onto the pitch and grabbed the aggressor. He slapped him around the ear and dragged him off the pitch. Obviously a genuine attempt to keep the peace! We were the visitors and they were fantastic hosts. Good old physical stuff was okay but anything above and beyond was frowned upon. What a difference from what happens on a regular basis today in junior football, where many managers', coaches' and parents' antics are worse than the players'!

I was now attending a grammar school after passing the 11+ exam the previous year. Football was not on the curriculum, only rugby. Luckily for me, however, the headmaster Mr Pettit was an ex-footballer with Stockport County. It was a very strict all boys school with the usual traditions. I had to wear a cap for the first two years. What a nightmare! Some of the 'Fags', as they were affectionately known, had their caps thrown on the bike shed roofs, booted around the school yard or even dipped in the toilets. At the end of the day some lads looked if they had oversized tam-o'-shanters on their heads!

I kept my head down over the first few days and stayed mainly unscathed, but some of the first years were given a pretty rough time. This was all new to me even though I could look after myself to a certain degree. Anyway, I worked the oracle and made friends with the right lads, ironically through football in the playground. We played with a tennis ball, as nothing bigger was allowed. It was great for practising your skills and I genuinely think that this period of two or three years with a tennis ball definitely improved my technique.

Within weeks of starting at the grammar school and for the first time I came across what could only be called cold-blooded violence. I made friends with a lad called Terry Kilty who lived not far from me and we used to cycle the three miles to school together. Terry was a game lad and we got on well. One day in the playground he was having a disagreement with a boy in the same year called Ray whom I didn't really know. This character was a loner with little to say for himself. I don't recall the cause of the problem but I'm sure it was trivial. I walked up and asked, "What's up?" Ray replied "Nothing important" or something to that effect. Terry was standing about three yards away when, in a blink of an eye, Ray took one step past me and punched Terry flush in the face, cool as a cucumber. Then he straightened his tie and jacket and just walked off! Terry, spewing blood from his nose, slowly picked himself off the floor with the help of some others including myself. I was totally shocked that someone so young could be capable of that. I thought: should I say or do something? I took a few steps in the direction that Ray had taken, but I think he must have anticipated this, so he swivelled around and said, "This doesn't concern you. He deserved it."

I never did find out why it happened. I felt sorry for Terry but never really clashed with Ray over the incident. However, in the inter-house rugby competition I was in Faraday and Ray was in Ruskin and our two teams inevitably met. He was upright in a maul and I crash-tackled him so hard that I felt his bones rattle. For a second I thought: oh dear! But he just got up, obviously in pain, gave me a wry look, smirked and just got on with the game. From then on we just said polite hellos to each other. He was perhaps the first hard case I had met.

I was a pretty good all-round sportsman at school, representing it at rugby, basketball, cricket and athletics. If you ask most footballers about their sporting prowess many of them will say that they were pretty much all-rounders. I actually won my 'full colours' for basketball, which was quite difficult to achieve. It was an award for excellence and came in the form of a different school tie for 'half colours' and a jacket for 'full colours'. I wore the tie with pride but never wore the jacket. This was for two reasons. Firstly, it was very expensive for my mum and dad to pay out in my latter school years and, secondly, it was a bit loud to say the least, so not my style really unless I was going to the Henley Regatta!

The rugby toughened me up a bit, to be honest. I wasn't keen on the old tackling; I could carry the ball well and kick it a mile but the contact, especially in the rucks, wasn't my favourite. I played stand-off, which suited me, and as the first couple of years passed I got more into it and started putting myself about a bit. My rugby teacher, Mr Burt, was a player himself and regularly came into school to teach with a black eye or cut lip or whatever. I used to look up to him and think he was a top man. Every other week we would play against a public school and literally we would take a beating, as they were excellent teams with players that were possible future Oxbridge candidates.

In one game I spotted the opposition number eight sneaking around the blind side of the scrum. I read the move and hit him as he picked up the ball, knocking him back. The ball spilled out of his hands and went into touch right next to where Mr Burt was standing. As I went to get the ball for our put-in, he whispered under his breath, "You are not chicken now,

Wignall, the penny's dropped." I was chuffed! Coming from him that was a great compliment. I enjoyed my rugby after that without any real fear. There were never many spectators at these games after school hours but one fan who always turned up in all weathers was my girlfriend, Anne. Nothing has changed!

I also competed in the athletic events for the school. During one sports day, one of our eight eighty-yard runners dropped out at the last minute through illness, so the housemaster asked if I would fill in. There were three runners from each of the houses, nine in all, and every runner gained points for their house. So even if I were to finish last I would still score some points. My main events were the javelin, the hundred yard sprint and the four-by-one-hundred yard relay. Hence my concern about what to expect. I decided to go off as quick as possible from the gun and just see what happened, so I set off like a train and just went for it. To my surprise I found myself about one hundred yards or so ahead on the first lap. I still had a bit left in the tank so I pushed on and won the race by a good margin. I couldn't believe it! The teacher said, "You've done that before." Breathing out of my bottom, I replied, "I haven't and I don't intend to again," to which he responded, "We'll see about that, laddie."

And guess what? He entered me in the inter-schools eight eighty-yard event. I didn't even get in the first four! It brought me down a peg or two. At the same meeting I did win the javelin and set a new school record, and my dad read in the local rag that my record was only beaten fairly recently.

I had found that I had a good arm a few years earlier during my time in the Boys Brigade. We had a junior cricket ball throwing competition. One of the officers took the whole troupe around the back of the church hall where there was a grassed area. It wasn't very big but was large enough to play small-sided games. He stood us at one end of the area with the junior officer and in turn we had a go at throwing the ball as far as we could towards him at the other end. I was one of the last to have a go. Most of the boys threw it about half the length of the grassed area and a couple nearly reached him. He marked the three furthest, as they would be the boys to throw for the troupe in the forthcoming contest. I was handed the ball for my go. I hadn't played much cricket with a real hard ball, only a tennis ball, and it felt quite heavy. I surmised that you wouldn't want that to hit you on the knuckles or anywhere else for that matter. I took a couple of steps back from the line, ran forward and chucked it as hard as I could. The ball flew … over the green, over the senior officer, over the hedge at the bottom and out of the church grounds! Running backwards to try to catch it, the senior officer shouted to the junior one, "This is only supposed to be the juniors throwing." "It is, sir," he replied. As he stopped at the hedge and peered over in vain to see where the ball had landed, with hands on hips he uttered, "Bloody hell!" Not really the kind of language you would expect to hear at the back of a church hall, but he was a little surprised so he could be forgiven for his lapse.

Another boy threw the ball after me and that also went out of bounds. His name was Gary Booth. I didn't know him very well but we were to become good mates in our early years. He was a very good footballer, achieving some success at youth level with Tranmere Rovers. We lost contact after my marriage, but little did I know that we would meet again some 25 years later.

Luckily, as I mentioned earlier, my headmaster was an ex-footballer and this turned out to be rather handy. The school had the power to stop you playing football on Saturdays if you were required to play rugby. Some lads tried to beat the system and play for their soccer clubs, but the school was having none of it and made it very difficult for them. I went to see the headmaster and told him that I would like to play football as well as rugby and that I was hoping to get a trial at a professional club. I asked him whether it would be possible for him to be flexible about it if I were successful. He was pleased that I had gone to see him and he assured me that if the situation arose he would consider it. This was my first lesson in diplomacy and it worked out very well in the end.

I wasn't bad academically at school, gaining seven GCE 'O' levels, or GCSEs as they are known now. Going to a grammar school wasn't really the normal route towards becoming a footballer in those days as most players went through the secondary education system at the time, where football was on the curriculum. However, I was determined that I was going to play football as well as rugby and have a grammar school education.

Another example of a grammar school lad that made the grade at professional level was a friend who was a year or so older than me. We both played five-a-side indoor football at the local boys club. His name was Marc Palios, who went on to play for Tranmere and Crewe. He had a good business career and went on to hold office at the Football Association, which has been well documented. I was sad to see how it turned out for him because he was always a nice lad and I thought he was a good choice to take things forward at the FA. It just shows how damaging the media can be to someone's career.

I was just coming up to 14 when Dave Bale asked if I would like him to put me forward for a trial at a professional club. He said that it wasn't something that he did often for his lads; he only did it if he genuinely thought that the boy might have a real chance. Over the years some of his boys did make it to the pro ranks. Anyway, the letter went out and we received a reply that I was to report to Melwood Drive training ground for a trial with Liverpool FC. I couldn't believe it - just going to the Reds training ground was a big deal to me! The thought of perhaps meeting one of the players was indescribable at that time, although why I thought there would be any pros about at a junior trial God only knows! I was pretty star-struck with the players at that age.

When I got to Melwood with my dad I think he was almost as excited as me. You can imagine it from his point of view: he had supported Liverpool from a boy and now his son was perhaps taking his first step towards becoming a Liverpool player. He must've been nervous for me even though he didn't show it. It was a feeling repeated years later when I took my sons to their first trials at professional clubs.

There were a lot more boys at the trial than I had anticipated, maybe two hundred or so. It was very well organised and we were put into groups and then teams of similar ages. There was probably only a year or so between the oldest and youngest there. They gave out some red (what else?) shirts to the team to which I had been assigned. It was a nylon round-necked type of shirt and I couldn't wait to get it on! It was a bit big, as you would expect it to be, and as I jogged about in the warm-up I imagined that maybe one of the first team had worn it at some stage. This was a possibility, as kit was passed down through the ranks for either training kit or trialist games much more back then than it is now. There were no names on the backs of shirts at that time. I rolled up the sleeves and took up my spot at centre half, which was my preferred position for the trial. Most of what happened in the two or three games that I played is pretty hazy to say the least, as I was caught up in the excitement and the importance of the day. I can remember enjoying myself, putting myself about and upsetting a couple of the opposing trialists with my physical challenges. This led to a comment from one of the coaches on the sideline: "Don't worry about them, lad, you're playing for yourself today, just keep doing what you're doing." I do remember vaguely that there were a couple of lads there a year or so older than me who were helping out and were already on Liverpool's books. Their names were Phil Thompson and John Gidman, both of whom went on to become England internationals and great players.

Some days later a letter dropped on the doormat with a Liverpool FC crest on it. I can hardly describe how I was feeling just before I opened it. For me, even at just 14, this perhaps marked a bigger turning point in my life than when I received my 11+ results and gained my grammar school place. When opened, it read, "You have been selected to train at Melwood Drive on Tuesday and Thursday evenings from the start of next season. This will include signing schoolboy forms for Liverpool Football Club," I was almost speechless. In the back of my mind was the thought: there's a chance here. I might make a player yet! I was absolutely flying.

I spoke to my headmaster as soon as possible, informing him of my acceptance. He was genuinely pleased for me and agreed to be flexible with my rugby and other school commitments. He also felt that it was a feather in the school's cap to have a pupil involved with a professional football club.

As I lived 'over the water' from Liverpool, I had to get a bus to board the ferry that crossed the Mersey to the pier head by the Liver Building and then catch another bus to Melwood Drive. This was about an hour's journey on a good night. It was tough - getting home from school, doing my homework, eating and then travelling over - but I was pretty determined to attend every training session that I could. It was even harder when the winter nights drew in and also there could be some dodgy characters on the ferry and return buses later on in the evening. Most sessions would run from approximately 7 p.m. to 9 p.m., which meant that I didn't get back home until 10 p.m. or later. As time went on and my workload from school increased because of looming GCE exams I was thankful for the support and library visits from Anne. Her research on several subjects was invaluable to me. Little did we know that this was just the start and she was on board for the long haul!

At Liverpool they had a 'C' team, a 'B' team and an 'A' team, and the next stop was the reserves. I started in the 'C' team and we played against some teams that were a little bit older than us. It was quite tough and when you put that red shirt on there was no quarter given by the opposition. We played most of the games at Melwood on good-quality pitches. There were designated coaches for each team on match days, but on Tuesdays and Thursdays a senior coach called Rueben Bennett, a red-faced uncompromising Scotsman with a deep gravelly voice, put us through our paces. From the two hundred or so boys at the trial only eight to my knowledge were selected. So I felt privileged to be at the sessions and Rueben was constantly reminding everyone of the standards expected at Liverpool FC.

In an early session I remember Reuben setting up a very basic passing routine: a ball between two players standing about ten yards apart in two parallel lines. He told us to pass the ball to each other with just two touches, one to control and one to pass side-footed. He let the session go on for a minute or two as he strode up and down along the outside of the two lines of players, hands behind his back, before all of a sudden bellowing, "STOP!" Everyone put their foot on the ball and stood still. He walked over to one pair and in his Scottish drawl said, "What the hell are ye two doin'?" The two lads, looking like rabbits caught in the headlights, didn't reply immediately but just froze. Rueben didn't give them much opportunity to respond anyway. "When I say pass it with the inside of your foot, I mean it, not the outside of the foot. If we wanted Fancy Dans we would've gone down to the girls school. This is Liverpool FC and we do things simple here, RIGHT?" "Yes, Coach," they replied. He set us off again and we passed the ball between us for about ten minutes as he watched over us. There wasn't a sound from anyone. It seemed a little harsh at the time, but the longer you were there the more the whole Liverpool way of simplicity rubbed off on you.

Bill Shankly was the manager there back then and all his coaches were as one. 'Get the basics right' was the core of everything. The staff in general were a pretty tough lot with the likes of Ronnie Moran, Joe Fagan, Bob Paisley and not forgetting dear old Rueben! Although there was a Liverpool way of 'passing' football, there was also a strong physical presence in the club, which came through the manager and staff and into the players. While I was there, from 1969 into the 1970s, Liverpool were a very successful club. It was no surprise to me, as they seemed to have it all just right. There was a feeling about the place that you could almost taste: supreme confidence in everything that they did.

I progressed quite well over the season and pushed myself into the 'B' team. We played against other clubs in the north-west such as Burnley, Oldham, Tranmere and Preston. They were always keenly contested especially as we were the reds, whom everyone wanted to beat for obvious reasons.

I remember one game away at Oldham on a fresh cold Saturday morning. It has stuck in my mind because I suffered some pain, which does tend to imprint itself on your memory! It was a tough physical match and the pitch was a little heavy. We were on the defensive a bit and I cleared a corner to about 30 yards out. The ball went quite high in the air, so I decided to charge out and press the ball. As I reached just outside the box, one of their lads volleyed it back at goal. It hit me full in the face and literally knocked me horizontal in the air. I came down flat on my back and I felt as if I'd been hit in the mush with a cast-iron frying pan! The next thing I knew the sponge man was sitting me up and saying, "You okay, Stevie?" (For some reason the staff at Liverpool always called Steves or Stevens 'Stevie'. To this day, you still hear them say, "Stevie Gerrard". Funny that, isn't it?) Anyway, he then sloshed a huge water-filled sponge in my face. There was a slight whiff of Ellermans Rub in that water - you know, that stinking white stuff you can smell on a Sunday morning recreation ground if the wind is in the right direction. He stood me up and said, "Away you go, it's their throw, you look fine." In actuality I felt like shit and couldn't feel my face!

Anyway, I got through the game and we forced a draw out of it. The coach was quite pleased with me and I noticed that he had a slight smirk on his face as he spoke to me. I thought nothing of it and was just pleased to get the praise that all footballers desire.

I showered but was still feeling a bit woozy after my make-up smudging collision, so I took a look in the mirror. I knew then why the coach had been smirking! I had a face like a pomegranate with bee-stung lips to match! My first battle scars! At least my mum still loved me when I got home.

Sometimes when more established or senior players were coming back from injury they would have the odd game in the 'A' team or even the 'B' team. This meant that I rubbed shoulders on the pitch with some very good players over the seasons. By the time I was 16 I had played a few games in the 'A' team with the likes of Phil Thompson, John Gidman, Hugh McCauley and Gareth Hughes (Emlyn's brother). The teams for Saturdays were usually typed out on individual team sheets and pinned up on the noticeboard in the changing room on Thursdays. I used to look at them all to see who was playing in which team, including the first team.

During the holidays we were invited to train at the same time of day as the pros. What an experience that was! To see the likes of Shankly, Paisley, Moran and Fagan first-hand was daunting and, as for seeing the first-team players, that was fantastic. We even got changed in adjacent rooms and you could wander around amongst everyone. I can remember there being lots of photos, books and shirts laid out on the treatment couch in the middle of one of the rooms. All the pros were milling around signing autographs on them before going out onto the training pitch. When the sessions got under way the youngsters would go off in their group. There was another group of apprentices and young pros and then there was the first team. I was still hopeful of an apprenticeship, as were several of the group I was training with, so the sessions were quite intense and competitive.

At the end of one such session we were walking back to the changing room and the first team had already finished. It was the Friday before a game so they hadn't trained for long - short and sharp, as they say. The other group were just finishing and Bill Shankly and his staff had set up a small-sided game. He was selecting some young players from that group to join in. It was virtually the staff versus young whippersnappers five-a-side on a Friday morning routine. We decided to hang about and watch for a while. I thought it would be a light-hearted knock-about - as if!

Shankly was bellowing his orders, Ronnie Moran was charging around like a bull and the young boys were running all over the place to impress. A few minutes into the game a penalty was awarded to the staff side, dubious of course, but there was little objection from the youngsters, just a few whispers under their breath. And guess who stepped up to take the penalty? Mr Shankly, of course. Hardly taking a breath, constantly talking and ribbing the other team that it was a foregone conclusion that he was going to score, he stepped up and hit a low shot towards the corner of the goal. There was no great pace on it; in fact it was a crap penalty! The keeper leapt across and saved the kick, pushing it out for a corner. The young boys gave a yelp and congratulated the keeper and then to their surprise Shankly shouted, "No, no, no ye cannie miss a penalty. Give me the ball." Taking absolutely no notice of muted grumblings from the kids - in fact the keeper's face was like a robber's dog - he replaced the ball on the spot and this time smashed it past the goalie! As he spun to jog off he turned to one of the boys and said, "That's the way to score a penalty, laddie," and the game just carried on.

I was told by some of the apprentices that those games were a regular occurrence and none of them could remember Shanks losing one. Some games seemed to go on longer than others until the correct result was achieved. We didn't stay to watch the rest of the game as Tony Waiters (ex-first team keeper), our senior coach, wanted us in and showered so as not to get cold. After all, we had our own big game the following morning. Tony was very professional and treated us as an important and integral part of the football club.

Crunch time was coming regarding decisions from the club as to who would be offered apprenticeships. My mind was resolute that, even though I had a good education and the chance of landing a decent job in Civvy Street, I still wanted to be a professional footballer.

When the time came I was called into an office at Melwood and sat down in front of the coaches. They said they liked me and felt I had a future in football but they couldn't offer me a place because they had their full quota of apprentices. This included Phil Thompson and John Gidman - some competition! They wanted me to stay on at school and continue to play in the 'A' team and if I progressed, as they thought I would, possibly in the reserves. I was gutted but not totally surprised. I had seen and played with most of the young lads that had been taken on and the standard was fantastic, as you can imagine. I needed to think about what they had said, talk to my mum and dad and then make a decision.

After lengthy discussions with my parents, we thought that it might be best to look at other options. Hard as this decision was, I still felt that I had something to offer and was prepared to put myself on the line at another football club. Through contacts I was offered a trial at Coventry City, which was a disaster. After travelling all the way to Coventry with a local scout, I was put in the wrong age group, a year below me, and I played in a game that wasn't of the best standard. The coach asked if I would like to return at a later date for another game. It all seemed a bit disorganised compared with my Liverpool experience, so I felt a bit deflated to say the least.

However, the scout that had driven my dad and me to Coventry said that there was an alternative. He knew a new manager in the lower divisions of the Football League who was looking for young players and he thought it might be worth my playing in a couple of under-18 youth team games so that he could have a look at me. The manager was Maurice Setters, who had just taken over at Doncaster Rovers. Maurice would go on to assist Jack Charlton in their very successful World Cup campaign with the Republic of Ireland some years later.

My first reaction was: where is Doncaster? At 16 and having not been far from the north-west coast, I didn't even know what county it was in!

Well, I decided to go for it and, although I didn't know it at that time, this was the start of a new life for me in a totally different place and the beginning of my football career.

CHAPTER TWO

PURPLE REIGN AT ANFIELD

Following my decision to pursue my footballing dreams at Doncaster, I went to see my headmaster to explain the situation to him. He was very supportive and could see why I had made that choice.

The Doncaster manager wanted me to play some youth team games, which would take place at Cantley Park in Doncaster. The kick-off times were at 11 a.m. on Saturday mornings and so, taking into account that it would be a two- to three-hour journey, it was clear that I would need to go the night before and stay over. The club agreed to put me up in a local hotel on the Friday evening before games so that I could be well rested and prepared for the matches. Mr Pettit, the headmaster, was fantastic about it all and let me leave school a little earlier so that I could catch the train from Liverpool Lime Street Station across to Yorkshire.

When the time came for me to travel over, to say I was nervous would be an understatement! It had been arranged for Jackie Bestall, one of the Doncaster scouts, to meet me at the station. It was autumn time and the nights were drawing in, so by the time I arrived in Doncaster it was pretty dark. I walked out of the station's main entrance and stood with my bag over my shoulder. The place was bigger than I had imagined and, being a mainline station, it was packed. I didn't know what Jackie looked like, so I just hoped that he would spot the lad with the lost look on his face. Almost immediately a very small, stocky, middle-aged man walked up to me and said, "Now then, are you Steve?" "Yes," I replied. "I'm Jackie. Maurice sent me to collect you. I'll drive you to your hotel."

I later learnt that Jackie Bestall was a local legend in so far as he played for, coached and managed Doncaster Rovers over the years. He was a true clubman and a great character. He was only tiny, with bandy little legs, very friendly and in his broad Yorkshire accent he never stopped talking on the way to the hotel. To be honest, I only understood about 50 per cent of what he said! He kept calling me 'yooth' and I thought: what the hell does that mean?

We pulled up at the Woodborough Hotel. It was right next to Belle Vue, the home of Doncaster Rovers FC, but I couldn't really see the ground in the dark, just the red lights on the top of the floodlight pylons in each corner. In my mind I had visualised a top hotel in the town or something to that effect, but reality kicked in as Jackie helped me with my bag as we entered the hotel. It was more of a large bed and breakfast place with a small reception in the hallway, a lounge-bar and a dining room. We were met by a portly lady who knew Jackie and was expecting us. She was very welcoming, which put me at ease. As Jackie left he said, "We'll see you at the ground at 9.30 in the morning."

I settled into my room and then went down for some dinner. As I walked into the lounge area I was greeted by a thin grey-haired man with a red face. "Hello Misterrrr, you joining us for dinner?" He turned out to be the husband of the lady owner who had met me earlier. He was a funny little man. He sat at the bar drinking a glass of lager and a whisky chaser all night, watching TV and chatting to guests while his wife ran around doing everything, and he greeted everyone with "Hello Misterrrr" as if he was going to say the person's name but had forgotten it!

After I'd eaten my dinner, the place started to fill up. There wasn't one woman among them, just men, and something else I noticed was that they were all very small! Most of them were on their own and sat separately and I thought: what have we got here? It gave me the jitters! They also had strange non-Yorkshire accents and I could hardly understand anything they were saying. In fact the only person that did seem to understand them was the funny little man at the end of the bar and he was half cut!

I was obviously having a complete shocker that evening, because when I woke up in the morning and looked out of the window there it was - DONCASTER RACECOURSE. The penny had finally dropped - they were all jockeys! Most of them were Irish, explaining the different accent, and there was a race meeting that day. Oh dear, what was I like?

When I turned up at the ground some of the apprentices were putting the skips full of kit, etc., into the backs of the taxis that had arrived to take us to

Cantley Park for the game, so I got a full interrogation from them. Who was I? Where was I from? And whom had I played for? The usual questions from young players, who always see a new face as a possible threat to their position at the club. Anyway, I played the game and did okay. In fact, I did better than okay, which brought further interrogation from a couple of the senior lads. They were mainly local Yorkshire boys and I was very much an outsider, but they were fine with me and tried to be as friendly as they could.

I caught the evening train home with my expenses in my pocket, which I thought was a good sign. There was no attempt to fob me off with the "We'll sort you out next week" routine.

Later in the week I got a call asking me to return the following weekend for another game. I stayed at the same hotel and, in the absence of any jockeys or race meeting this time, I practically had the place to myself. The old boy still didn't get passed "Misterrrr", though, and got the beer and Scotch down his neck again.

I spoke to the manager and youth coach after the second game and they told me that I was ahead of some of their apprentice boys in ability and they would like me to train full-time with them over a three-month period and then take it from there. I now had to make another big decision, this time regarding my education.

After discussing it with my parents I decided to take a chance. I spoke to my headmaster again and he said that if it didn't pan out I could go back to my education. After all, a three-month spell away from school wasn't going to affect things too much and if I returned it would be up to me to play catch-up.

The deal was that I would go into digs, which the club would arrange and pay for. They would also reimburse all my travelling expenses to and from the ground and my train fares for weekend trips home.

This was a big thing for me now. It is difficult to describe the feeling of leaving home and going to live with other people in a completely different environment. There was also a certain amount of pressure on me. It was different to someone going away to university to study, which of course has its own pressures. This was an acute situation where I had to adapt very quickly to being away from home, come to terms with the physical aspect of full-time training and perform in games to my optimum level all the time.

One injury could scupper everything, so I had to look after myself physically and mentally to make sure that I gave myself every opportunity. I was not only leaving behind my family and friends but also Anne, my girlfriend. I wasn't a million miles away, but 80 miles or so across the Pennines in the seventies was still a fair distance. You couldn't just pop home for a cup of tea and a bicky!

The day came to travel across and once again I was met by little old Jackie Bestall. This time he took me to my prearranged digs in Balby on the outskirts of the town. It was an end-of-terrace council house and a chubby blue-rinsed woman in her middle age answered the door. Jackie introduced me and then left me to get on with it. Her name was Eva but I always called her Mrs Hill, out of respect for your elders I suppose. Her husband, Horace (Ray), was an ex-quarryman with one lung and he worked at the ICI fibres factory in the town. He was also very short-sighted and had to wear very thick-lensed glasses. They were very down-to-earth Yorkshire folk; very warm yet very forthright in their opinions and ways. I was thrown in at the deep end in a way because as I walked in the living room with all my bags, etc., the place was full of family and grandkids. It was somewhat akin to a slightly upmarket Royle family (Jim Royle not the "Regal" lot!)

My bedroom contained two single beds but I was the only one in the digs at that time. Over the next four years there were several other players of all ages that would share the room with me; some would be short-term, some would be a little longer. As I went to bed that evening the landlord said, "Na then yooth, dos tha want sum snap tomorra?" I just nodded politely as I hardly understood a word he said. It turned out that he was asking if I wanted a packed lunch to take to work and I was glad I'd nodded, as a substantial lunch had been made for me. This was to continue, as I needed it. Mrs Hill looked after me well and there was always plenty of grub!

To report for training at Belle Vue I needed to catch the bus at the stop across the road from the digs, which took me straight to the ground and was about a 15-minute journey. The manager wanted me to take on the duties of an apprentice and help the other lads with their jobs, e.g., sorting out the kit, cleaning boots and general dressing room chores. We would train in the morning with the pros and sometimes a couple of afternoons a week on our own with the coach or manager if he had the time. Then when training was over we would get stuck into our jobs. The club had its own laundry under the main stand. This was organised by a lady who would wash all the training and match kit, dry it and lay it out in piles ready for us to put out first thing for the pros.

I had to learn pretty quickly who liked what and where it went, because if you got it wrong you could cop a clip around the ear. Or, if you were lucky, it might be just a verbal volley! The other lads tipped me the wink on the volatile characters as well as telling me about the more sympathetic ones. A sock missing for an old pro ex-Sheffield Wednesday player Colin Clish and you'd be threatened with some serious retribution, whereas Ian Branfoot would have a joke with you and give you a wink. Ian went on to be an excellent coach and manager at Reading and Southampton to name just two of his clubs. Colin went out of the game and became a copper. I don't think I'd step out of line on his shift!

The club had made decisions on a few of the young lads regarding their future and unfortunately some of them were told they would not be offered professional contracts. Most of them left the club either to look for a job or to try other clubs at home or abroad. That left me and a lad called Stephen Reed to do all the kit, boots and other jobs, but it was only to be for a month or two as other boys were due to come in as new apprentices.

Physically I found it hard going. For the first time in my life full-time training was taking its toll. With so many jobs on top, I was getting back to my digs at about 5.30 most nights. It was no more than a day's work for most people, but it was all so intensive and I was on trial, which brought its own pressure. If you compare my situation then with some clubs today, most these days have 16 apprentices who are not allowed to do certain menial tasks and they also have the opportunity to go to college a couple of afternoons a week. Their lot is definitely better than it was back then.

I must also say, from my experience, I have found that both the discipline and the respect for professionals and staff shown by many of today's youngsters are definitely not what they were! When I went to Southend as a manager their young players had no discipline whatsoever. They were lazy, unfocused and basically couldn't wait to get away from the ground. One morning when I walked through the front doors at Roots Hall one of the apprentices, or 'YTS' (Youth Training Scheme) as they are known now, walked past me and said, “Alright mate?” I stopped him and suggested he didn’t call me his ‘mate’ again - in my own way, of course! There was only one lad among the Southend apprentices that caught my eye. His name was Michael Kightly and he had a fantastic attitude. Where is he now? Wolves and worth £1 million plus! And where are the rest? Ryman League if they’re lucky!

Stephen Reed was a year younger than me, only 16, but he had already played a few games in the reserves. Standing six feet tall and weighing 12 stones, he played right back or centre half. Steve was a local lad from Edlington and his dad worked as a miner at the local coal pit. His family invited me over for Sunday dinner one weekend and his dad took us down to the working men’s club while Steve’s mum was cooking dinner. This was all new to me, as my dad didn’t drink and especially not on a Sunday afternoon!

The club was packed with local miners, all drinking pints. Steve’s dad asked me what I wanted and I didn’t know what to say. I had drunk the odd lager or whatever but I wasn’t a regular drinker and definitely not in the day! Sheepishly I said, “I’ll have what you’re having.” Three pints of brown and bitter later (half a pint of bitter in a pint glass with a bottle of brown ale on top) and I was feeling a little light-headed!

We walked back to the house, which was a small terraced pit-house. Steve’s mum was a big, jolly lady and she had quite a sweat on after tolling over a coal fire range in the kitchen. The place was immaculate with brasses on the walls and everything neat and tidy and in its place. The dinner was massive and I had to undo the old belt to make room for it all. The Reed family made short work of it!

It was a great experience for me, and later on when the miners’ strike was taking place I could relate to what sort of people were involved in it: a very honest and welcoming community in itself.

Stephen was a nice lad, a bit of a gentle giant. He wasn’t the brightest button in the box but he had a good work ethic and tried to do the right things. I remember one day when we had almost finished our jobs John Quigley, who was the first-team coach, pulled Stephen and asked him to go to the local shop for him. We used to run there and back in about ten minutes or so. John liked the odd fag and he had run out, so he gave

Stephen a pound note and said, "Reedie, get me ten Players son. If they haven't got Players get me anything!" (Players were an old make of cigarette.) So he set off running and ten minutes later he was back with a bit of a sweat on from the run. John was waiting and in his broad Scottish accent said, "Well done, Reedie son, I'm gasping!" A bit sheepishly Stephen said to John, "I couldn't get Players, so I got you a pork pie and a Wagon Wheel." This was followed by a moment of complete silence as John digested what he had said. I nearly wet myself laughing but John wasn't happy. I can't recall exactly what he said, but it wasn't complimentary you can bet! Who said footballers aren't the brightest?

John Quigley was an ex-professional who played for Notts Forest. He was a small, fiery Scotsman and together with Maurice Setters, the ex-Man United and Coventry star who was also very competitive, they made quite a pair, especially when playing in five-a-side games in training!

The time soon came for the boss to make a decision about my future. I had done well in the youth team and had progressed to the reserves. I felt that I had done myself justice during training and in the games and I had no regrets in terms of my performances.

The club had just signed some very good young pros in Mick Elwiss, Steve Uzelac and Stan Brookes, all local lads. They were all on the verge of playing in the first team, as the manager was trying to build a young side. Some of the other players were perhaps coming to the end of their careers, such as Chris Rabjohn Brian Usher, Howard Wilkinson and Colin Clish. All these players had played at a higher level than the fourth division (today's third division) and may have had an effect on the manager's budget that he probably had to address. There were other senior players such as Ian Branfoot, John (Nutty) Hazeldene, Archie Irvine and Glen Johnson, the goalkeeper, who had a bit more left in the tank and stayed around a bit longer.

A lot of what was happening regarding players coming and going went over my head, as all I was concerned with was getting a long-term contract, which was usually a year or two at the most in the seventies.

The manager called me into his office, which was in the main stand at that time (when I went back as manager my office was in a Portakabin). He sat me down and said that he liked me and saw me as part of his plans. He wanted a team based on young players with some experience mixed in. He offered me a professional contract even though I was still only 17, which was unusual as generally you had to wait until you were 18! He wanted me to train full-time with the pros - so no cleaning of boots, etc., with the apprentices! I was absolutely delighted and accepted the offer. It wasn't great money but it was a decent wage for a 17-year-old. I would be totally independent and I could get myself a car and the usual things young people wanted.

I couldn't wait to phone my mum and dad and give them the good news. They were so pleased for me and very supportive, as they always have been to this day. I also had to break the news to my girlfriend Anne, who may well have had mixed feelings about it all because of my being so far away for the foreseeable future. However, she didn't show it and was genuinely really pleased for me, which was a bit of a relief because after the euphoria of the offer of a contract reality had started to kick in a little! I had to face up to the fact that this could affect our relationship. One important thing it did tell me was that Anne was someone special who wanted me to live my dream before thinking of herself or her own feelings. I had dreamt of that moment when I would become a professional footballer from as young as eight or nine. Even though it wasn't my hometown club of Liverpool, it was still an achievement in my mind and I was 'made up', as Scousers say!

Mick Elwiss and Steve Uzelac made their League debuts in a Donny shirt on a Friday night - a game that I watched with great interest. These were two lads that I was now training with and they were only a year older than myself. They performed fantastically well and more than held their own. They were a breath of fresh air, with the crowd taking to them straight away. Steve was a tough, no nonsense centre half and Mick was a quick, strong striker. I could see that Maurice wasn't just someone who told you what you wanted to hear regarding chances in the first team, he actually put you in the team and let you get on with it. A first-team place was in my sights and this was next on my agenda!

I didn't have to wait too long before I was considered. I was just 18 when I was selected for a home game against Crewe, and I played okay even though we lost the game 2-0. Before the match Maurice had a quiet word with me. He said that I should try to impose myself on the game somehow and he gave me my basic instructions on what he wanted from me. As a manager he was a very good motivator and after his pep talk I wanted to do well for him as well as for myself and the rest of the team. I was always a committed player and Maurice liked that. I think that is why he gave me my chance at such a young age.

Early on in the game a ball broke in the centre circle about ten yards from me and one of the Crewe players, so we both went for it 50:50 you might say. I launched myself at the ball and so did he! Though he got there just before me, my momentum carried me right through him and the ball, which hit me in the chest. The ball then rebounded 30 yards or so back down the field and he was left in a heap a little worse for wear! I leapt up and got on with the game. The crowd loved it - I had broken the ice! I had imposed myself on the game and the opposition. It seems a small thing, but straight away the crowd took to me and I never really looked back in terms of support from the Donny fans.

Maurice was disappointed with the result but said that he was pleased with me. He also told me that the only way to gain respect in the game was by your actions, and he was spot on. Another nice touch to his management skills was when he asked my dad to come into the dressing room after the game. Once again it was only a small point, but it was very effective in motivating a young player. I never forgot that little gesture.

I had settled into the club quite well by now and had made good friends with some of the players. Mick Elwiss and I got on really well and we socialised quite a lot. His mum and dad, Pat and Walter, were very kind to me and welcomed me into their home as part of their family. My wife still writes to Pat to this day. I was fortunate to have good digs and another family for company, something that is very important for any young player away from home.

Returning to Maurice, he tried to be a father figure to his young players at times. He may have been tough but he also enjoyed life and he didn't mind his players enjoying themselves too, so long as it was done correctly, in the right place and at the right time.

On one occasion he pulled Mick and I into his office on a Friday after training. He wanted to know what we were doing out in Sheffield the previous night? Players were not allowed on licensed premises 48 hours before a game. We had apparently been seen in a pub on Thursday evening and someone had telephoned in to report us to the manager! It was our habit to go to the pictures on Thursdays and we told him that was where we were that night. Sadly someone had tried to stitch us up! We had gained a reputation in the town, which was created from hearsay. I guess that as Mick was a local lad most of the problem arose from pure jealousy. This was the first time anything like that had raised its head and it annoyed me, as one thing I prided myself on was my dedication to the profession. Thankfully, Maurice took our word for it and just told us to be aware that even at that level we were constantly in the public eye.

I was a good trainer and used to enjoy getting myself as fit as possible. Training could be a chore, especially in the depths of winter, but most of the time I enjoyed it. I tried to train as I played, at maximum level. You have to hold back a little at times to prevent injuries, but the adrenalin gets the better of you on some occasions!

On one such occasion we were having a 'keep ball' session. Two teams of eight or so were competing against each other to keep possession of the ball in about half the area of the pitch. This type of game can become very competitive, especially if one team is getting the upper hand! My side were getting the better of the other and the atmosphere was a little fraught. Sometimes the coaches would let it ride for a while to gain a reaction from some of the players - controllable aggression, they would call it. However, this was far from controlled!

A player called Archie Irvine was on the opposite side to me. He was a stocky, red-haired, fiery Scotsman in his early thirties and a very experienced player, previously with Sheffield Wednesday I think. I was just about 18 and full of vim and vigour. There is also red hair in my family from my dad and Irish roots from mum's side, so there was a good chance that we would clash at some point!

As we battled for a loose ball, he swung an arm across my face, catching me with his forearm. I retaliated by throwing an elbow at him, which scuffed him across the head.

And that was it! We set about each other. Much of what happened in the next few seconds is a blur but it was pretty nasty. Other players jumped in to separate us, as we had both completely lost it. Almost immediately after being separated, reality set in. I thought: what the hell am I doing scrapping with a senior pro? However, I was still annoyed and my blood was still pumping. Archie was also steaming and it took two or three players to hold him back.

The manager came over and told us, "ENOUGH!" He looked at me and said, "You had better go back to the ground and see the physio with that cut." Apparently I had a gash in the back of my head that was spewing blood down my neck. I was so psyched up that I couldn't feel the pain. Bill Gold, the old physio, stitched me up and had a little chuckle about the incident when I told him. He too was a Scotsman and he knew about Archie's reputation. "You could have fought with someone who wasn't quite so tough as him."

When the players returned after the session, Archie came into the medical room to see me. For a second I thought: here we go again, he's up for more! However, he had actually come to see if I was okay and proffered a kind of apology. I accepted what he said and told him that I had been as much to blame.

Once I was sorted and had showered, I spoke to some of the other young pros that had witnessed the altercation. Apparently a stamp of a studded boot had caused the cut to the back of my head. I had got a few digs in of my own though, they said, and they thought it was great that one of the youngsters had stood up to the senior lads! It wasn't the most sensible of things to have done, I know. It was all in the heat of the moment and even though it probably gave me a bit of 'cred', if you like, I can't say I was proud of that occasion and I'm sure Archie thought the same.

The next day I got a call from the manager to visit his office again. Maurice looked quite stern as he sat me down. Basically he read me the riot act about my conduct as a professional during that training session. I took the rollicking and was about to take my leave when his demeanour changed slightly and he said, "It was good to see you standing up for yourself though." Lifted by his final comment, I had a bit more of a spring in my step as I left.

I was playing regularly in the first team now. Although we were struggling in the League, Maurice still played the young players in whom he had great confidence.

At one point the back four comprised Stan Brookes, 19, Steve Uzelac, 19, myself, 18, and Stephen Reed, 16 going on 17. Playing up front there was Mick Elwiss, 19, and Peter Kitchen, 20. We were a very young outfit.

Maurice did bring in some experienced players like Graham Moore (ex-Welsh international) and Kim Book (goalkeeper). Kim is the brother of Tony Book who played for Manchester City. Peter Kitchen or 'Kitch' as he was known, was a natural goalscorer and went on to have a very successful career. Mick played up front with Kitch and would do a lot of the spadework, with Kitch often nicking a tap in or something and getting most of the headlines! It would gall Mick a little, which was understandable. They got on okay but there was always a bit of rivalry as you can imagine. Mick was forever ribbing him as he has a great sense of humour and would always be mimicking someone or generally taking the pee!

One day after training, with me tagging along, Mick as usual suggested we play a trick on Kitch. Peter drove a white Morris Minor at the time (a bit different to what you see in the players' car parks these days!) It was a bit of a rascal to look at and from a distance it looked like a local police car. So Mick got an old shoebox and wrote 'POLICE' on both sides, put a blue plastic cup on the top and placed the whole thing on the roof of the Morris. It looked surprisingly good! Great, in fact! He also managed to snaffle Kitch's car keys for a few minutes. We opened the bonnet and took the rotor arm from the distributor. Without it the car wouldn't start. We knew a little about engines as we did a mechanics course at night school together in our spare time. We put the keys back and waited for Kitch to come out.

We sat in Mick's Mini from where we could see the new-look Morris. We watched Kitch as he walked over to his car and at first he didn't notice anything different. However, by the time he'd put his bag in the back he'd spotted the box and he wasn't very happy. He ripped it off and lobbed it while muttering under his breath. Mick and I were helpless. He then got in the car and tried to start it up, obviously with no response, so he got out and lifted the bonnet. He was not a happy bunny! I said to Mick that we'd better give him back the rotor arm and Mick responded, "It's right in front of him." He'd stuck it in the little football boots hanging from his interior rear-view mirror! We thought it was funny anyway! Small things amuse small minds and those car mechanic night classes came in useful. We let him struggle on for a bit longer and then put him out of his misery. I don't think he ever really forgave us for that little prank! He was a decent lad though and he continued to score goals wherever he went.

Another local youngster turned up at the ground for a trial one morning. I don't know at what level of football he had been playing or whether he had been involved with any other professional clubs. He was of a similar age to me with tousled hair down to his shoulders, which was long even for the seventies. To add to that, he had a white headband on to keep it out of his eyes. I suppose he was a funny looking lad with bucked teeth and he had a really strong Yorkshire accent.

We used to have a game behind the Rossington end stand on Friday mornings after we had done our preparation work for the Saturday match, and it was in one of these games that this trialist was asked to play. Maurice and John Quigley also played in these battles. I say 'battles' because that is exactly what they were! They certainly weren't for the faint-hearted. The surface behind the stand was basically dirt and cinders and we would use an old ball, a bit like you would in the street. There would be tackles flying everywhere, full-blooded challenges in the air and you can imagine the banter, especially when it was sometimes young versus old. The goals were an old railway sleeper that you had to hit to score!

I looked at the trialist and thought: he has no idea what he's in for! This was a real test for him. He was an old-fashioned winger who loved to take people on with the ball at every occasion he could. At one point in the game, some of the senior players were virtually lining up to kick him. He could get past players in very tight areas, but as he did this there was someone else ready to have a bite at him. He was put on his backside several times, but he got up and still looked for more. The headband was like a red rag to a bull to some of the lads and they didn't disappoint him. His name was Terry Curran, or 'Ted' as we called him, and he was one of the gamest lads I have ever seen, with great skills to match.

Ted was another young player nurtured by Maurice who went on to become a local legend in Nottingham and Sheffield. Needless to say, the club signed him on and he was sold to Notts Forest a few seasons later. Brian Clough saw his potential straight away. When I linked up with him a year or two later at Notts Forest he'd had his hair cut a bit and his teeth done. He even had all the birds after him! Good on him, as he was a great example of a lad coming from nowhere to become a household name, especially in Yorkshire. It was done with total self-confidence and a great will to succeed. If I met him tomorrow and said, "Do you remember the years behind the stand at Donny?" he would probably be able to tell you in great detail about every player that tried to kick him. It was a steep learning curve for him, but one that he passed with flying colours.

The years behind the stand were also an eye-opener for me and other pros. It toughened me up no end, especially with my aerial challenges. Some Friday mornings I would go home with an egg on various parts of my head - and that was before we played on the Saturday. Some afternoons Mick and I would go behind the stand and practise our heading. Mick would be the first to admit he was not the best header of a ball but he wanted to improve so he worked at it. I could head the ball but there was always room for improvement, so we helped each other. Maurice would come with us on occasions. He was a terrific header of the ball even though he wasn't the tallest of players. His tips were invaluable to me and, although I was decent in the air, I definitely improved while I was at Doncaster with him.

Heading the ball is a skill that is much maligned by many people, especially with the progress of the modern game. The emphasis in academies and schools of excellence is technique on the ball and passing, etc. This is definitely the right way to go, especially if we are to catch up or get closer to the European and Continental players' skills. In my opinion, however, because of this trend players' heading skills have not improved. I watch premiership players with great athleticism leaping higher than ever to head the ball, but on many occasions the ball doesn't go where they intend it to go.

In fact some of them have what may be called 'three penny bit heads', as it comes off in eight different ways! We all want to watch attractive football played at ground level, but unfortunately the ball does end up in the air quite a lot and so it seems silly to me not to work on heading techniques from an early age as well. Mind you, on a purely sarcastic note, maybe they don't want to mess up some of those fantastic hairdos they have today?

Football people will always tell you ironic stories about incidents that have happened to them. I am no different and have had many such experiences.

One of them was about a year or so after I left Liverpool FC in the 1973/74 season.

We had won through the early rounds of the FA Cup and into the pot with the big boys. It was my first season in the League and my first experience of the greatest Cup competition in the world. The irony of the whole thing was that we drew Liverpool at Anfield. I was absolutely delighted, as you can imagine.

I had gone from playing at Melwood Drive for the 'A' or 'B' team to playing against the Mighty Reds on their home turf in front of 30,000+ fans over a period of 12 months or so. Fantastic! I was just 19 and there was a good chance that I would be given the task of marking Kevin Keegan, a Kop favourite already after his move up from the lower League with Scunthorpe. The other ironic thing was that Kevin was a Doncaster lad and, despite the two clubs being light years apart in the League, I'm sure he must have seen the draw as special in that he would be playing against his hometown club - especially as it was rumoured that Doncaster had rejected him as a youngster.

There was another uncanny connection involved in this situation. My landlord Horace and landlady Eva used to go down to their local, The Fairway. Sometimes if I looked a little lonely they used to invite me to walk down with them for a drink in the evening. I didn't drink alcohol in there, just soft drinks, but it was company. One night Horace said, "I want to introduce you to someone you might be interested in meeting." He walked me over to the other side of the bar where sitting at a table was a very smart, small, grey-haired man and his equally small wife with dark wavy hair. Horace spoke in his loud (because he was a bit deaf) Yorkshire voice, "Na then, I would like to introduce you to our young footballer who plays for Donny Rovers." I thought: oh my God, everyone is looking. What is this all about? The man stood up to shake my hand. Horace then said, "This is Mr and Mrs Keegan." I was quite shocked, but straight away I could see that Kevin was the absolute spitting image of his mum and dad. They were really lovely people and so very proud of their son. I had a good chat and they wished me well in my career. They kindly said, "Maybe you will play against our Kevin one day!" Little did I know then that some months later a draw would be made and I would indeed be meeting "our Kevin" at close quarters!

The time came for the Cup tie and, as you can imagine, everyone was excited at the prospect of playing one of the best teams in Europe. We were such a young squad and perhaps a bit naïve or even ignorant about the actual magnitude of the game. This may have played a part in what became a fantastic achievement for a club that was at the wrong end of the fourth division, as it was then. However, there was no fear in my mind, just immense anticipation of playing against my hometown club in front of my family.

I think about 20, not including friends, turned up to watch. I can't remember how many complimentary tickets I left on the gate, but it was never going to be enough! The local paper made quite a big feature of the fact that I would be playing against Keegan, him being a Doncaster lad and me coming from Liverpool. However, I was just pleased to be mentioned in the same sentence with such a great player. As for Maurice, he was like a dog with two whatsits! What a chance for some of his young players to perform against top-class opposition in such a prestigious competition.

So the day came to walk out at Anfield. I was so proud as we ran onto the hallowed turf. I felt ten feet tall! The noise was absolutely deafening as we came out of the tunnel. You could almost feel the noise, a bit like a shock wave. People say that they can feel the hair on the back of their neck standing up; well, I think every hair on my body stood up at that moment. I gave a quick look towards the paddock where I'd stood as a kid on my 'bag box' and I suppose it was quite a surreal, almost unbelievable feeling! I had another quick glance across to the stand to acknowledge my family, friends and my girlfriend Anne, but I couldn't make anyone out clearly; there were just too many bodies. I don't know exactly how they were feeling, but I'm sure they were happy for me and maybe more nervous than I was!

The only thing that I wasn't overly happy about was that we had to play in our 'minging' away kit, which comprised African violet (bright purple) shirts, black shorts and African violet socks. It didn't look great and I'm sure that the Anfield crowd thought: what have we got here? Dodgy kit, so probably a dodgy side too, no doubt! Well they were in for a surprise, as we more than gave them a game!

The match kicked off and within minutes a short ball was played into

Kevin Keegan's feet on the halfway line. I took a chance and launched myself into the tackle, getting a foot to the ball in front of him but clattering him at the same time. This left Kevin on his backside looking up at me as if to say "What the hell?" The referee gave a foul. Kevin didn't complain, he just got up and got on with it. The Kop weren't too happy with me getting stuck into their favourite son. I felt as though that set the trend for us. We were not just going to roll over; we were going to give it a go. I remembered Maurice's advice to me before my League debut about trying to make an impression in the game. I definitely did that, as all the team did on that day!

It was one of those classic FA Cup ties: the underdogs playing out of their skins and the top dogs having an average day. Somehow we managed to clinch a 2-1 lead through Peter Kitchen (I bet none of the Liverpool players drove a white Morris Minor) and big Brendan O'Callaghan. Brendan was 20 years old and stood at about 6 feet 4 inches. He was another of Maurice's young signings.

It was much like the Alamo after that. Just when we thought we'd pulled off one of the great giant-killing acts of the seventies, Keegan popped up with a neat header about eight minutes from the end to equalise.

With a few minutes left I think the Kop felt that their team could still snatch it, but it was actually us that nearly nicked it in the dying seconds. Kitch got in and lobbed Clemence only to see the ball bounce off the top of the crossbar. If that had gone in I bet you would've heard a pin drop at Anfield that day! It didn't and in that split second I thought: that was it, that defining moment when history could've been made but it wasn't and that moment would never occur again, even if there was to be a replay.

At the final whistle we were obviously pleased with ourselves - but if only! The Liverpool lads, although a little shocked about what had happened, were very gracious and congratulated us on our efforts. I had a quick word with Phil Thompson, who remembered me from my time at Liverpool. Phil was to establish himself in that fine side of the seventies alongside such greats as Emlyn Hughes, Ray Clemence, Alex Lyndsey, Larry Lloyd and Kevin Keegan.

After the match I came out to meet my family. I was a bit overwhelmed by how many had turned up: my aunties and uncles, close friends and, of course, my girlfriend Anne. I probably had one or two words with everyone

I could before we left on the coach for Doncaster. It all seemed to be over in no time at all. I was still as high as a kite after such a great experience. No matter at what level of football you play, those sorts of days are priceless.

I know it's a bit old hat to say enjoy it and take everything in, but it's only human nature for some of it to pass you by, as some of it did with me. Luckily, most has stuck with me to this day. It's in the football archives and I'm chuffed to be a part of that.

There was more to come, of course. The replay was scheduled for the following Tuesday at Belle Vue. This was at the time of the three-day week and the power cuts, so the game could not be played under floodlights, so it was arranged for the Tuesday afternoon - quite a unique situation. It was a sell-out with a 20,000+ crowd, and it seemed as though nearly the whole of Doncaster had taken the day off work to be there.

When I first joined Doncaster many of the locals told me that they were a big club at that level with good crowd potential. Our average crowd was probably around the 3,000 mark, so it was hard to imagine many more people coming through the gate. This game was obviously a one-off, but it did show that the fans were there and a little success would bring some more of the diehard core back to Belle Vue.

I'm not sure what was going through the minds of the Liverpool players as they turned up at the ground, but I can imagine they were a little apprehensive and definitely didn't want to be a giant-killing statistic! The first impressions of the ground might have been that it was a little run-down. The car park was similar to the surface behind the stand: cinders and dirt with the occasional pothole! The dressing rooms weren't quite up to the Anfield standard either - and the bath was 'cosy', shall we say!

One thing that was up to standard, though, was our pitch. Horace, the groundsman, did a great job on the playing surface. It was one of the biggest pitches in the country, which at times probably cost us some points, as teams used to love playing on it. In the seventies some of the pitches were dire, especially midway through the season.

You only have to watch some of the old clips from that period on the television to see how poor they were – and that includes some of the top clubs in the country. Horace would not even let you walk across it – and that included the manager. He would appear from nowhere and bellow, "Get off that f****** pitch!" It was his baby. Good old Horace!

It seemed strange kicking off on a Tuesday afternoon, but there was still a great atmosphere. The locals appeared to enjoy it even more, as it was a break from all the problems at the time with work, etc.

We started quite well and had a couple of early half chances. The scene was set to get a result but it didn't happen. The opposition were very clinical and went ahead through Steve Heighway, and they never really looked in danger of losing a grip on the game. Peter McCormack scored the second goal and that was that. We did okay and certainly didn't let ourselves down. I was lucky enough to get 'Man of the Match', which was great but the result took the gloss off it.

Our time in the limelight was over and it was back to the tough task of trying to push ourselves up the fourth division. Liverpool went on to win the FA Cup that year, beating Newcastle emphatically in the final. What might have been if Kitch's lob had dropped in? Never mind, eh!

This little Cup run of ours alerted some of the bigger clubs that there were a couple of decent young players at Doncaster. Mick Elwiss, my mate, came close to joining Liverpool some months later. I didn't know the reasons for that non-event but eventually he was signed by Preston for a substantial fee. He moved on again after doing superbly for the 'pie men'. Terry Venables took him to Crystal Palace to team up with David Swindlehurst up front. Palace was a club in the ascendancy with Venables in charge. Mick did so well that there were whispers that he may be heading for an international call-up. Unfortunately it all went wrong for him when he sustained a knee injury on tour in Europe. He had several operations and continued to play but eventually he had to call it a day and came out of the game. Mick was unlucky because he was hardly ever injured and never missed training or games. If he had sustained that injury today, the specialists would probably have sorted it out and he would have had a long and successful career in football.

Mick married a lady called Olive, whose father was the chairman of Preston for a while. They have two children, Oliver and Hannah, and I am Hannah's godfather. Living so far away means that we all don't have a great deal of contact, but if I picked up the telephone tomorrow Mick and I within minutes would be back to our silly ways, just as we were in the early seventies! He is one of the true friends I met in football. You don't meet that many - lots of acquaintances but not a lot of real friends.

Terry Curran also moved on, as did big Brendan O'Callaghan. I was being watched by two or three clubs, West Ham allegedly one of them. Nothing came of it, however. I think they took a player called Mick McGiven, who now may be on the staff at Chelsea.

Maurice had brought some other players into the squad before the Liverpool game to add a bit of experience to the young team. Alan Murray, a winger from Middlesbrough, was a good lad. We roomed together at times on away trips. He was a tidy, organised person, so that suited me down to the ground. As I am a Virgo, everything must be just right! Alan played with Graham Souness and they became good mates, working together at a few clubs such as Newcastle and Galatasaray.

In fact Alan took over in Turkey when Graham left. Can you imagine me saying to Alan over half a lager in the Salutation pub in Doncaster back in 1974, "Hey, maybe you'll be manager of Galatasaray one day"?! He would have got the men in white coats to come and take me away! Funny old game, as they say!

Alan introduced me to Graham one night in the Outlook nightclub in Donny while he was up for the weekend. I felt that he was a bit disillusioned at that time and he was very quiet, but it wasn't long before he took off as a player. The rest, as they say, is history. Alan went on to manage Hartlepool and Darlington and did very well. The last time I saw him he was on the touchline with Souness at Newcastle. He's got the old snow on the top and looks a little round for my liking! I'm sure he won't mind my saying that. 'Ruby' (after Ruby Murray the singer) is a genuine bloke. I also noticed that he never did get that nose of his fixed. He had it 'done' for him, if you like, by another player called Ray Ternant. Ray came up from Southend with Pete Woods. Ray was a tenacious and quick right back and Pete was a midfield player, a good-looking lad who never had a hair out of place.

I remember one day we were training as usual when out of the blue a bit of an altercation blew up between Alan and Ray. Alan was a quick winger, not a tackler or a physical player. Ray, however, was a bit of a Rottweiler! Both men fellow Geordies. I was standing close by the pair when words were exchanged between them. You know the banter: "Wey-aye yer bugga!" or whatever. All of a sudden Ray just butted Alan right on the nose!

I heard the crack, so as quick as a flash I and a couple of the lads grabbed Ray. Alan had staggered back but still wanted to know. It got a bit nasty but it was sorted. I felt a bit sorry for Ruby as he didn't ever really upset anyone, whereas Ray, though generally okay, did have a bit of a short fuse!

I was to find out just how short that fuse was a few months later when Ray and I clashed in a couple of tackles at a training session. They weren't too bad but things at the club were a bit fraught at that time. Results weren't great, the team was being chopped and changed, and so players were on edge. Ray had said something to me, probably something and nothing. I replied in my usual uncompromising way, especially when I'm a bit hot and bothered. Out of one corner of my eye I could see Ray walking towards me with old Rottweiler face on! I thought: "Eye-eye, watch out for the headbutt!" Sure enough he went for me with his head, but I saw it coming, fended it off and then grabbed him and started to try to give him a few slaps. Once again it was stopped and sorted by the coach and we were both sent in like naughty schoolboys. He was still jabbering away but we were kept apart by the staff - just as well really.

Kim Book was a very experienced goalkeeper who came to Donny. I think Kim was the poor old Northampton keeper who conceded all those goals against Manchester United. The clip of George Best sitting the goalie on his backside as he went around him to score is often shown. I bet Kim hates it!

When Kim first came to the club he stayed a few nights in my digs and, like several of the lads over the four years or so that I was there, shared my twin-bedded room. He teamed up with Graham Moore who was our most senior player. I think they knew each other anyway from earlier days.

One Friday night before a Saturday game we had some dinner together (or tea, depending on what part of the country you come from!) I went out to the pictures and Kim went out to meet 'Mooro', as he called him. I got back at about 10 o'clock had a bit of supper and then went straight to bed. There was no sign of Kim at that point. Anyway, I must've dozed off but I was awoken by a strange noise, which sounded like someone retching. This went on for a while and then I could hear a noise that sounded like scrubbing and the sploshing of water. It eventually stopped and Kim crept into the bedroom on tiptoe. I could see his silhouette from the landing light.

"Sorry to wake you up, Wiggy son," he said in his strong West Country accent. Or that's what it sounded like to me anyway. He got his head down and I just turned over and went back to sleep. In the morning my landlady served up a cooked breakfast as she usually did before games. We were just about finished when Kim appeared, looking a bit red-eyed but full of the joys of spring. He was a bit of a joker and would mercilessly pull the landlady's leg about just about everything.

While Mrs Hill was 'doing the pots' (as they say in Yorkshire) I said to Kim quietly, "What was all that noise last night?"

He replied ,"Had a bit of trouble. I was sick in the sink upstairs and had to unblock it with my fingers to squash it down the plughole! Sorry about that, mate."

I nearly brought my bacon, eggs, black pudding and tomatoes up there and then! "Bloody hell! Why didn't you go to the toilet downstairs?"

"I forgot there was no toilet upstairs and I was already being sick!" he answered. "What the hell had you been doing?"

"Just a couple too many with Mooro. Not to worry. Big game today, lad."

He was certainly a character, and if I remember rightly he played a blinder!

While I'm on the subject of my digs, I can recall a quick story about Horace, the old landlord. Yorkshire people are renowned for their thrifty ways with their brass (money) and Horace was no exception.

Colour televisions had been in circulation for a few years by now, but Eva and Horace hadn't succumbed to replacing their old black and white set. Eva eventually put her foot down and told Ray that she wanted a colour one. She got her way and the set duly arrived. The old set was put in the front parlour and the colour job had pride of place in the living room.

One afternoon when I came in from training, Ray was sitting watching an old black and white film. Nothing too unusual there, or so I thought until I noticed that the old black and white TV had been wheeled in from the front parlour and parked in front of the colour one. They were watching the old set! I asked what had happened to the new set. Surely it hadn't broken so soon?

"Nay lad," came back Horace's reply, "I'm savin' tha toob on tha noo set. Na point in watchin' a black 'n' waht film on tha colour set!"

Eva just scowled at him, whilst I think my jaw just about managed to touch the carpet. I simply responded, "Oh, right … I'm just going for a lie down"!

That was Horace for you - salt of the earth, but he could be as tight as a camel's backside in a sandstorm!

My by then fiancée Anne would travel over from the Wirral at weekends and Mr and Mrs Hill would give her digs too. It was on one such occasion that Eva asked Anne to help her get the house ready for Christmas. They always had the house decorated from top to bottom like Santa's grotto, with balloons and tinsel, etc. At the other end of the holiday, Anne quite happily took down all the bunting and was left with a handful of balloons on strings. As there were probably 20 or so of them she asked Eva if she should burst them. "No, you could let them go down the road. The kids will pick them up and have some fun with them." So Anne took them down the side street and let them go - loads of them!

An hour or so later, just before teatime, I heard the back door go and a bit of a kerfuffle. I assumed it was Horace back from his daily walk with their standard poodle called Honey, and I was right. But he was accompanied by a massive bunch of balloons, which he was struggling to pull through the back door. "Eva," he shouted with delight, "look what I've picked up. These'll do for tha grandkids!"

Oh no! Anne and I were helpless! Eva gave him short shrift yet again and ushered him and the balloons back out of the door.

By the way, the grandkids weren't due to visit for a few weeks, by which time I'm sure those balloons would've looked like Tom Jones's face (post-plastic surgery and orange) – sorry, Tom, just a joke.

Here's one last anecdote about Horace. He used to catch the bus over to the hospital to collect new batteries for his hearing aid each month. This was, of course, because they were free! The only thing was, taking into account the bus fare to get there, it came to the same amount as new ones would've cost if he'd bought them at the shop across the road!

That was Horace and Eva, but they were great and made Anne and me very welcome in their home.

Returning to the football side of my life, there were quite a few other players that came and went over that period. In no particular order I'd like to mention a few. Some you will recall some you may not.

One such player, who wasn't with us for long, was Ernie Hunt, ex-Coventry centre forward. He was to become a household name in the seventies for his sensational goal for Coventry, which was televised. It was a somewhat controversial goal as far as its execution was concerned. One of the Coventry players stood over the ball, with Ernie standing next to him, preparing to take a free kick from just outside the penalty box. He had the ball in between his feet and was facing side on to the goal. When the ref blew the whistle he flicked the ball up behind him by trapping the ball between his feet. Ernie, as quick as you like, volleyed the ball on the full and it screamed into the net! It's never been done since and it probably never will be! Ernie was past his best when he came to us, but what a great player. He looked average in training, but in matches he showed true class.

Chris Balderstone was a fine all-rounder: a professional footballer in winter and a professional cricketer in the summer. Chris was a real gentleman with a great manner about him. He wasn't a typical footballer to look at, more like a bank manager when you saw him in his match-day suit. He had a great left foot and read the game perfectly. He went on to play for England at cricket and eventually went into umpiring. Some years later, when I was manager of Colchester United, he came to visit me at Layer Road while he was umpiring at Chelmsford. He was his usual modest self and we had a few laughs about our Doncaster days. After all that he'd achieved, he only asked about how I was and how things were going at the club. Unfortunately he died not long after that meeting - a sad loss of a true gent.

Glen Johnson was the first-team goalkeeper when I joined Doncaster. He did a bit of wheeling and dealing with cars in his spare time and on our first meeting I thought that he was a lot older than he actually was - probably because he was losing his hair! Archie Irvine (with whom I had my little spat) was always clashing with him in training. I don't know why; perhaps they just didn't like each other. They did look a bit comical when the handbags came out though! Glen was about 6 feet 3 inches tall and Archie about 5 feet 8 inches. Glen also sold me my first car, a fiat. The bloody thing never did go properly! Never trust a car salesman - especially a footballing one!

He was a decent keeper and had a good career. The last I heard of him he'd bought a golf course and done very well for himself, so good luck to him.

Willie Watson was one of the funniest players I've played with and he was also very talented. He went on to play for Cambridge United when I was playing for Colchester. Even in the middle of a local derby at Layer Road he still had time for a joke, especially as I scored with a 'fluky lob' to deny them a victory in their promotion push one year. "I'll have you, Wiggy, if you've cost us, you bugger," he said. Though he always had something to say he was a real good lad.

Alick Jeffrey (senior) even tried to make a comeback while I was at Donny. It was a bit sad really, as he'd been a world-class player in his younger days. When he trained with us he worked so hard to get his weight down and regain his sharpness, but it just didn't happen for him. He had such humility and always said very positive things to me. He sadly passed away when I went back to Doncaster as manager. That was just one of several sad things that happened during my 18-month tender – more of that to come later in the book.

A couple of the younger players who were local lads but had totally different characters were Stan Brookes and Steve Uzelac. Stan was loved by everyone and he knew all the local kids. He made sure that he always had time for supporters and just about anyone who approached him. He was very mature for his age, which showed on the pitch, and he was a great talker and motivator. Stan married the love of his life, Sara, and moved to Belgium to play. Steve Uzelac was quite different from Stan. He was a tough, uncompromising player who liked a pint with the lads and the odd fag. He was a good, honest competitor in training, but he was always in my ear to slow the running down when he was in my group for laps!

There were others who passed through, but there simply isn't enough space here to include them all and I must move on, so apologies to any I haven't mentioned.

In the season 1974/75 Maurice unfortunately ran out of time and the club saw fit to let him go. I didn't know the circumstances or reasons at the time. From my own experiences, nothing would have surprised me! I was very disappointed. Maurice was the manager that gave me my first chance in professional football. He was also a great influence in the way I improved as a defender and a player. Just how knowledgeable he is was proved later when he assisted Jack Charlton in the World Cup with Ireland.

He also had a great eye for young players, and his ability to motivate is something you have innately as a person and it's not a skill that can be acquired as you go along.

So there was to be change at Doncaster Rovers ...

... and there was definitely going to be change for me.

CHAPTER THREE

MY "DONNY" DAYS ARE DONE

John Quigley was in charge for a short period; whether he honestly thought he had a chance of getting the job I don't know. He was in a difficult position, as all coaches are when the manager leaves. I got on okay with 'Quigs' and he liked me because of my attitude and commitment, as he was always telling me. He even took me to a reserve game at Everton one afternoon to look at some young players that may have been available. I saw that as a great compliment as I was only 20 years old and was still learning my trade as a professional. So for him to ask my opinion was quite something to me. John didn't get the job in the end, but he stayed on as coach under the new boss.

This was a first for me as a player. A new manager's arrival was imminent and I felt quite nervous. Maurice had signed me and had showed great faith in me, but what would the new man think? Would he like me? Had he seen me play? Would I like him? What was his background? Even though I was an established player in the first team, a change of manager is always an uncertain time for all the players at the club.

No matter how popular the manager, some players will always welcome a change, especially if they weren't the flavour of the month at the time. There are always mixed feelings throughout the club.

The new boss duly arrived. His name was Stan Anderson, a north-easterner and an ex-manager of Middlesbrough. He was an experienced boss who had also played at a high level. I was still very much a Maurice Setters player, but I tried to keep an open mind and be as professional about his arrival as possible. Oddly, however, when I first met Stan there was no real connection. I just didn't seem to take to him. It wasn't personal, just a feeling I had in my bones if you like. He'd come from a big club at a higher level and he seemed to have a bit of arrogance about him that I hadn't encountered before in my early career. Stan seemed to converse openly with most of the senior players and yet dismiss the younger ones at times. Maurice spoke to his older players regularly but loved his young lads too and gave them confidence.

So I already found myself comparing the two, which wasn't right, but it was so obvious to me that I was having negative thoughts about the situation within days of the new manager's arrival.

My fears were confirmed at a game at Sheffield Wednesday in the Hallamshire Cup.

I had been injured for a week or so and was on the bench for the game. Stan turned to the bench during the match, looked at me and said, "What position do you play?" I quickly replied, "Anywhere across the back four." He said, "Oh, right," and just turned back to watch the game. At that moment I thought: he hasn't even seen us play before he took the job! He obviously hadn't pre-planned anything and on top of that he'd brought in two defenders from Middlesbrough: right back Peter Creamer and centre back Brian Taylor.

The writing was on the wall and I had a fight on my hands to re-establish myself. Stan had obviously made up his mind that lads from his old club were better than what he had at Doncaster even though he hadn't seen us play!

Brian and Peter were good players and did what they had to do. I spoke to John Quigley confidentially about the situation and he was very supportive, but as I said earlier he was in a difficult position and wanted to keep his job. John took the reserves, which I hadn't played for in some time, but now I was in and out of the first team.

At one night game at Grimsby I was playing against a strong centre forward called Phil Hubbard. He was probably in his early thirties and was very experienced and battle-scarred. In fact his nose was like a dog's hind leg! From a goal kick I competed with him on the halfway line as the ball was in the air. Suddenly, he swung an elbow and hit me right on the nose. I heard a crack and woke up on my back with my eye sockets full of blood that was spewing from inside my nostrils. John came on with the sponge, sloshed it in my face, wiped the blood away and gave me some cotton wool to stem the flow. He chuckled and said, "You're not so handsome now, pretty boy!"

By now I had regained my senses. Phil was all apologies but he had definitely done it on purpose and I told him to look after himself for the next 60 minutes or so. He tried to soft soap me but I was having none of it. I chased him all over the pitch during the game and booted him at every opportunity (when the ball was there of course!) He was happy to get off the pitch at the final whistle! My nose was never quite straight again - git!

My younger brother David also played that night. He was only about 16 but was already playing reserve team football. Stan had signed him as an apprentice at the start of the season. Dave was a very talented midfield player who was at Chelsea from the age of 12 to 13 years, but travelling down to London from the Wirral was difficult so he signed schoolboy forms for Everton. It was quite ironic as we were an all RED household! He spent two years there and was very unlucky not to get taken on as an apprentice. He even had trials for England with the likes of Sammy Lee, who went on to be a full international.

Dave's progress at Doncaster was quite remarkable. He signed professional at 17 and he had played 50 League games by the time he was 18. His career looked on the way up, but by the time he was 19 he was given a free transfer by the manager only months after turning down an offer from Wimbledon who had just come into the Football League. It seemed a strange decision, but Stan made a few of those!

Dave had trials at Preston and Colchester, but it didn't happen for him and he went into the non-League with Southport and then Gainsborough. At Gainsborough he teamed up with a certain Neil Warnock, who was at the start of his long managerial career. Neil is a qualified chiropodist and he used to practise on the players' feet when they had problems. I don't think he has to bother with that these days!

Dave played a lot of games at a good level. Young players with whom he played, such as Barry Horne and Andy Jones at Rhyl, went back into the League and did fantastically well. John King, who excelled at Tranmere, was Dave's manager at Caernarfon and he even played for Tommy Smith (ex-Liverpool legend). Incidentally, he definitely was not as good a manager as he was a player! Dave ended his career with Llandudno where our mum and dad live. His two sons, Gavin and Ross, have made the town their home too.

Dave is a prime example of a player with the world at his feet but a set of circumstances that didn't go his way and lady luck seemed to desert him at a crucial time. He now has a successful business and has four grandchildren at the ripe old age of 49!

During his term at Doncaster Rovers, Dave took over my place at Mr and Mrs Hill's lodgings, as by now Anne and I were married and had a house in Armthorpe. Of course this meant that there were new tales to tell about Horace and I cannot move on without recounting one or two!

David needed a new battery for his car one cold winter and so Horace kindly offered to loan him the £8 to buy one. Dave assured him that he would be repaid in two weeks' time, on pay day. Ray quipped that it would be no problem as there would be an interest charge of £1 for the fortnight's loan! Dave paid him back ASAP! Our Horace would've made a good Chancellor of the Exchequer!

Another young lad called Mark Jones signed at the same time as Dave. He was a local lad and they got on very well together. In fact they are still good mates and still see each other regularly after 30 years. Mark is now a very successful businessman in Doncaster. They went everywhere together and Mark often went back to the digs with Dave and waited while he had dinner. On one occasion, they had been into town after training and for some reason decided to have something to eat mid-afternoon before they went back to the digs. What Dave was thinking of I'm not sure, because bang on 5 o'clock Mrs Hill would have an enormous dinner on the table for him. True to form there it was: roast rabbit and all the trimmings - potatoes, veg, gravy, the lot! Now he had a problem! Dave couldn't possibly say, "No thanks Mrs Hill, I've just eaten in town," as she wouldn't have been happy, so he sat down at the table while Mark sat on the sofa and watched TV. Dave started to tuck in but a sweat soon appeared on his forehead and he was really struggling to eat it, especially the huge piece of roast rabbit.

There would always be a pot of 'mashed' tea on the table at the digs, along with a plate of bread and butter (you were never left hungry in that house!) Mark could see that Dave was struggling by his beetroot complexion and beads of sweat! However, Mrs Hill didn't seem to have noticed and was just having a sandwich. As she got up and headed into the kitchen, quick as you like Mark got up, grabbed the piece of rabbit all dripping in gravy, stuck it in the teapot and put the lid back on. "There you go, that'll help you out mate," he said. Dave was gobsmacked!

Mrs Hill came back in none the wiser and said, "By 'eck, yoo must've been starvin' lad." She had brought a teacup from the kitchen for her cup of tea. To Dave's amazement she poured the tea and didn't notice that the teapot weighed probably twice as much as usual. However, what Dave noticed was the grease floating around the surface of the drink. Mrs Hill got up again and went out of the room. Mark was up like a flash and this time put his hand in the teapot, grabbed the rabbit and ran out of the back door with it. By now Dave was helpless. Mark came back in looking very pleased with himself, so Dave asked what he'd done with it. He said, "Oh, I've lobbed it in the hedge down the bottom of the garden." "Thank God for that," Dave said.

As Mr Hill did shift work he was due in at about six o'clock. Eva drank her tea while Dave and Mark watched TV. Horace came in promptly as always and ready for his dinner, which Eva had put to one side in the oven. He didn't used to say much after work, he would just go straight up for his wash, but this day he came in and said, "Eva, Eva, I can't understand it. Tha's a couple a dogs raggin' 'eck out of our 'edge down t' bottom of t' garden. Tha goin' berserk!" Dave and Mark had to get out sharpish before they burst into uncontrollable laughter. Then Horace said, "Pour us a cuppa, Eva, I'm parched." All the best they thought!

Stan brought in a few more players over the coming months: Ian Miller and Dennis Peacock from Nottingham Forest and Joe Laidlaw, who had played in the Carlisle team that made it into the top division in the seventies.

My relationship with the manager was, should we say, cordial by now. I always felt that he didn't really fancy me as a player. We had a few differences of opinion and his management style didn't fill me with confidence. At half-time in one game his team talk to me and Steve Reed was: "You two just knock it up field when you get it." We were playing as fullbacks, Steve on the right and me on the left, which wasn't my best position considering I was mainly right-footed. The team were having a bad time and we were all struggling. His attitude towards Steve and me was totally non-constructive and yet he took more time on other players. Our confidence was paper thin by now, just when you needed a good boss or coach to help you out. I could feel the confidence seeping out of me the longer I played for Stan.

The defining moment when I realised that I had to move on came at an away match. I can't remember the actual game, but I recall we were in a hotel having a pre-match meal three hours or so before the match. We were all seated around a large oblong table in a private room and the waiters served us as we all chatted. The usual banter by the usual suspects flowed, with plenty of mickey-taking and general good humour. We usually had tea and toast all round and a steak each, but on this occasion a waiter appeared with a large silver serving dish heaped with chips. He promptly started to serve someone at the opposite end of the table to Stan, who was busy chatting to one of his staff. It went a bit quiet as the lads looked up and saw what was going on.

All of a sudden, Stan shouted down the table at the waiter, "What's going on? No chips, no chips! These lads have to play in a few hours. They can't be eating chips, man!" His face was quite red, which indicated that Stan was not happy. "We didn't order them. Take them away." Stan didn't tell us who would be in the team until we got to the ground, so everyone's pre-match preparations were the same. Before the waiter reached the door, Stan stood up and shouted, "Hang on!" The waiter turned on his heels, still holding this huge platter of chips. Stan looked up and down the long table at all the lads and then he casually quipped, "Er, Wiggy, you can have chips," and gestured to a couple of the others as well.

For a second there was a deathly silence, almost an embarrassed pause. All the lads looked at one another, a couple emitted a muffled titter, and some put their heads down. I nearly died! It was the most humiliating way of finding out that you wouldn't be playing. I looked at Stan and thought: you BASTARD, I don't have to take this shit from you!" That was it for me. I had lost any sort of respect for him as a manager. I was an established player and he was treating me worse than a trialist! In fact you wouldn't treat a trialist like that. Needless to say, I declined the chips and I think the other poor lads did the same.

I learnt a valuable lesson in a few minutes that day on how NOT to man manage if ever I became a manager. At least treat a man with respect and dignity!

Afterwards, when chatting to some of the other players, most of them were supportive and sympathetic. In true football style, a joke was made of it and that saying of "YOU CAN HAVE CHIPS" took on the meaning that you were out of the side and it stuck for some time! It was only a small, maybe insignificant occurrence, but I would rather have Phil Hubbard break my nose again than be treated like that in front of my fellow professionals and mates.

Some weeks later we played the last game of the season against Scunthorpe at home and a local derby, which was always keenly contested whenever it was played. I had heard a little rumour that Brian Clough was coming to watch me. He hadn't long been in charge at Nottingham Forest at the time. Terry Curran, one of my old playing mates, was there and he had tipped me the wink that they were interested. Stan didn't tell me anything, as usual, and even put me on the bench for the game - no surprise there! My brother was in the side and doing well, having made his debut away at Torquay whilst still only 17.

During the match a ball dropped in midfield and my brother together with Richard Money the Scunthorpe centre back went for it. (Richard later went on to play for Liverpool and did very well for himself.) As they both went into the challenge, Richard went so high that he caught Dave in the groin in a bad tackle and our bench were on their feet, including me, to show our displeasure you might say. He was ticked off by the referee and everyone got on with the game. A few minutes later Stan told me to get warmed up as I was going on. I'll have some of that, I thought. When I came back to the bench he said, "Get your gear off and go on up front."

I had played a few reserve games up front and really enjoyed it. I could cause a few problems in the air and maybe just disrupt a few people. So on I popped and straight away Richard Money picked me up from our goal kick. The keeper took the kick and I jumped for it and got a flick on as Richard came piling in from behind. He ended up in a heap on the floor, holding his mouth as if I'd caught him. I hadn't done so intentionally, but he was steaming and went mad at me. The referee came over, gave us the free kick and ticked him off again. The free kick was knocked into their box and touched out for a corner, so I took up my position to attack the ball on the edge of the penalty area. The ball was floated in and I went for it hell for leather, got a contact on it but knocked Richard flying. It was just a strong challenge! He got up and went ballistic again, and this time he came at me throwing punches! Silly me reacted, ducked his efforts and then threw one back, scuffing him across the side of the face.

Players jumped in to separate us and it was sorted. The referee showed no hesitation and sent us both off! I was gutted. He had just lost it and I got sucked in. As I was going down our tunnel, one of the Scunthorpe fans threw a punch at me. His scarf was dangling down so I grabbed it and nearly pulled him over the wall, the prat, but his mates pulled him back. Everybody, including the press, thought that I'd gone onto the pitch to reap retribution for Richard's high tackle on my brother. This definitely was not the case; I was just being competitive as usual and Money lost the plot - maybe it was the wrong time of the month or something! No offence, Richard.

Believe it or not, I was only on the pitch two or three minutes. I think it was one of the quickest dismissals at the time. It was nothing to be proud of and, even worse, Cloughie was there to watch me! Stan didn't say much about the sending off. I think he realised I'd been drawn into the incident. Maybe there was quite a bit of frustration built up inside me that just came out at the first provocation after a long hard season of disappointments.

The season finished and so all the players would be called into the manager's office one at a time to discuss their future or perhaps lack of it at Doncaster Rovers. There was no 'Bosman Ruling' with agents negotiating contracts months in advance. You either had another year or so or your deal was up. You usually found out from the manager a day or so after the last League game. It was quite a nerve-racking time as you were never sure what the outcome would be. Most contracts were only for a couple of years and long extensions were quite rare. Some lads, even experienced players, would come down from the office, enter the dressing room where the rest of us were waiting for their turn and say, "That's me away. I'll just get my boots and be off." That would be that. It was very cut-throat, especially if you had a couple of kids and a mortgage. Basically you got the sack and had the close season to find another club or job before your wages were stopped in June, usually about 6 weeks' money.

Luckily for me I still had another year on my contract. Stan called me in.

There wasn't a lot said except an expression of some surprise on his part perhaps. Brian Clough had asked to take me on loan to Nottingham Forest, where I would join the team on its pre-season tour of Germany in July. Stan asked me if I would be interested. I hesitated for a millisecond and answered, "Yes." He told me that I would receive the itinerary in the following weeks. That was the end of the chat and I left the office with a smile on my face knowing that Stan was thinking Cloughie must've seen something in me that he obviously couldn't. I skipped down the stairs and told the other lads who were still waiting. They were chuffed for me.

As I drove back to the digs to pick up my gear for the trip home to Merseyside I wondered if things could possibly get any better. I was due to get married in a couple of weeks and then would be going to Notts Forest, with a chance of playing for a big club in a higher division.

I hadn't been home that much over the previous few months, as Anne and I had been saving for our first house, which we were buying in Armthorpe, Doncaster. Even though my future hadn't seemed that secure under Stan, I still had that other year on my contract and so we had decided the house would still be a good investment. Tony Phillips, the chairman of the club, owned a building firm and so he was able to help us with a new build at a bit of a discount.

A few of the lads lived close by, as you did back in those days. Not many sat in a car for two hours or more before training as they do today. Steve Uzelac, Joe Laidlaw, Brian Taylor and Peter Creamer all lived pretty local to us. We used to socialise quite a bit with Joe and Joan, who was pregnant with their son Jamie. Just recently I saw Jamie's name in a newspaper and discovered he was playing for a non-League team down south. He's in his thirties now, which is a sobering thought - how time has flown!

Our wedding day arrived - 29 May 1976, during the famous long hot summer! Getting married in May was not unusual for footballers as it was close season. We had a great day. As Anne has four brothers and one sister and I have three sisters and one brother, as you might guess we had many relatives present. There were over 150 guests during the day and the numbers swelled into the evening. My brother David was my best man and at the age of 17 he did a brilliant job of reading the messages in Welsh on several of the wedding cards from Anne's side of the family. My three young nieces, twins Isla and Sarah along with Louise, were our bridesmaids and Anne's sister Alison was chief bridesmaid.

When I went back to Forest in July, Brian Clough wanted me to do all the pre-season games with them, which included the tour of Germany. I travelled each day from Doncaster, which was a bit tiring, but we had only just moved into our new house and it was better than living in a hotel in Nottingham.

The training was very tough, harder in some ways than I had experienced before. That may have been down to the fact that I was now with better players, many of whom had played at a higher level for several years. I held my own in the running, as I had pretty good pace and stamina levels. When we did work in pairs I teamed up with Viv Anderson, who was a young up and coming right back. He had just come back following a dislocated kneecap injury sustained in the previous season. Sometimes he had to put the reins on me and haul me back a little, as my enthusiasm would get the better of me! Also there at that time were John McGovern, Ian Bowyer, Martin O'Neill, Tony Woodcock, Frank Clark, Terry Curran, John O'Hare, John Robertson and others.

After a couple of weeks' hard graft we left for Germany. This was my first football tour abroad except for my little jaunt to Ireland when I was a youngster. It was fantastic. We stayed in a nice hotel with a swimming pool, etc. I was involved in all the games we played and did okay. Peter Taylor, the assistant manager, told me that they were very pleased with my contribution and the other players made me feel very welcome. Having said that, they had very high standards and expected you to perform at optimum levels at all times. Cloughie and Taylor had a totally different style of management to the approaches I'd experienced previously. You hardly saw Brian - he just appeared on the training ground - as Jimmy Gordon or one of the other coaches would be taking the session. Late on in one such session we were playing a small-sided game when Brian and Peter wandered over and sat down on the grass as we played around them. They were obviously taking in more than they appeared to be. They continued to chat for a while and then got up and wandered off again.

Brian didn't ever leave you not knowing what was expected of you when you pulled on a Forest shirt. He could be very blunt and basic at times. His first team talk to me just before I took to the field was: "You should always be able to see the number 9 on that centre forward's shirt, lad … Go out and put him on his bottom a couple of times." There were coaching points in there somewhere.

Terry Curran had already been transferred from Doncaster where we had previously played together, so he gave me a few pointers as to how Cloughie worked. Terry had had a little bit of a run-in with him over not wearing shin pads in games. The wearing of them was not compulsory then, but the manager believed that everyone should wear them. As a sort of compromise, Cloughie made Terry wear them for every training session but not on match days! Terry obliged in a stubborn sort of way. I think it eventually worked, though, because I later played against him when he was at Sheffield Wednesday and he had them on.

Brian could be quite an odd character at times and a bit difficult to read even for the lads who had played with him over several years. There was one thing for sure -everyone was on their toes in his presence. I saw two different sides of him on tour. I remember on one occasion when the morning session was about to start at 10 a.m. on the dot and Brian and Peter got us together for a chat on the training ground. Cloughie began to speak and then all of a sudden his assistant, Peter, said, "Where's Robbo?" meaning John Robertson. It went very quiet for a few seconds and then somebody chirped up, "Er, I think he's still in his room, boss." Cloughie went mad. "Someone go and get him, NOW!" One of the lads scuttled off and we all stood shuffling our feet. Cloughie appeared to get more and more annoyed as we waited. After maybe five minutes had passed, Robbo appeared in the distance with the other player. They jogged over and as they got to the group a few of the lads were nudging each other as if they knew what was coming. I thought he was going to get a bit of a telling off and that would be that - WRONG! Cloughie and Taylor went ballistic and absolutely slaughtered him in front of everybody. They called him scruffy, lazy and just about everything else derogatory you could think of. They also warned him that he could be out of the door and even threatened to send him home. He was sent back to his room and wasn't allowed to participate in the session.

Robbo didn't do himself any favours. He was a bit laid back to say the least. He also looked less like a footballer than any I'd seen before. He seemed to be overweight and just generally unkempt. I'll tell you what, though, you put him on the pitch in competitive games and he was a genius on the ball. He could go past players in wide positions at will and was a fantastic crosser of the ball on the run. He went on to be a real quality player, so perhaps that rollicking marked a turning point for him. He was just an average first division player before Cloughie took over and later on he won European and title honours with Forest. The management had obviously seen John's potential but needed to push him on to better things by whatever means necessary.

Cloughie could be as cutting and ruthless as anyone I had met, and yet on other occasions he could be the utmost gentleman and a great motivator. After one of the tour matches we were all in the club bar when Brian walked in, sat down next to me and said, "Let me buy you a drink, young man. You did well today and deserve it." I had done okay, not brilliant, but he was clearly pleased with my contribution. He wanted to make me feel welcome in his own way. He was quite a complex man but his results were astonishing, especially as he had put together a team of players who had perhaps underachieved with youngsters who were untried at a high level.

Maybe subconsciously I learnt quite a bit about management from him - not all good, as he also had his annoying side which some players found hard to live with! One such example was during our preparation time at a local hotel prior to an evening game. I couldn't play as I had been suspended following my sending off in the Scunthorpe game at the end of the previous season. I had lunch with the lads at noon (PLEASE NOTE - NO CHIPS!) and they all retired to their rooms for a rest. I was collared by the manager, who said, "Young Steven, I need to talk to you. I'll see you in the lounge shortly." I went down to the lounge and waited. Three hours later he turned up with Peter, saw me and said, "Oh! I'll speak to you tomorrow morning at the ground." There was no apology or explanation. That was Brian Clough.

My three-month loan period was coming to an end, but unfortunately I hadn't been able to play in the early season games back in England because of my suspension. This may have had a bearing on the final outcome, but I will never really know. The manager and his assistant called me into their office and after quite a long deliberation they said that they had decided not to sign me. They felt that I would be good enough but needed a bit more time to adapt to what was needed immediately by them. I was disappointed to say the least. I had felt that this was probably my one chance to break into the big time. Instinct told me that the club, under their guidance, was ready to take off. Unfortunately I was right, because the achievements of that Notts Forest team over the coming years are legendary. I still look at a team photograph taken that pre-season and wonder: if only.

Brian and Peter went for a more experienced centre back that year in the shape of David Needham and later ex-Liverpool player Larry Lloyd. I was just 21 years old and felt that I would have learnt very quickly, but I respected their decision. I went back to Doncaster a different person. On the one hand I was gutted, but I was also full of confidence. I had played alongside some very good players and had learnt a lot in a very short space of time.

Stan was a little different towards me on my return and put me straight into the first team. However, I still felt uncomfortable with him and with my situation. My return to Doncaster was followed by a counter-loan, if you like, of a youngster called Tony Woodcock from Forest. He was a forward or wide man who was out of favour with Cloughie. Stan brought him in to give us a bit more pace in attack. Tony was a very quiet lad and was quite timid on the pitch and lacking in confidence when he first arrived. However, he had a great left foot and a nifty turn of pace. We got on okay, as we knew each other from Forest. He did well for us on the pitch but was called back after a month or so because of a bad knee injury to Terry Curran. Tony was totally out of the frame when I was on loan there, so he was a bit surprised and maybe worried that he was just going back as cover until Terry was fit again.

We often talk about turning points in someone's career coming as a result of another person's misfortune and this was a classic. Tony went back and they threw him in the team straight away. If my memory serves me right, he scored a hat-trick on his debut and the rest is history - European honours, England, etc. Doncaster could have had Tony for about £10,000 and if Terry hadn't sustained that injury then who knows in what direction Tony's career would have gone?

I never met Tony again until the summer of 2001. I was in Majorca with Anne and the kids at John Ryan's apartment. John was the chairman of

Doncaster Rovers, the club I was managing at the time. One afternoon I was sat by the residents' pool, which was used by only half a dozen or so people. Across the far side I saw a couple and spotted Tony straight away by the way he walked and his general mannerisms. He dived into the pool and swam past us. I said, "Tony." He looked up. "Steve, what the hell?"

We had a good chat. He had developed a bit of a German accent from his life in Germany as a player and then a TV and radio pundit. That change from a young lad on loan at Doncaster into an international star was incredible, but in many ways he hadn't changed a bit. He was still very grounded. One small coincidence was that, although we hadn't met in 25 years, he had a son of a similar age to ours and he too had named him Jack, which wasn't a common name in those days.

Not long after Tony went back to Nottingham, Stan called me into his office after training. He didn't really beat about the bush and just said, "A couple of clubs want to take you, one of which is Colchester United. Their manager Bobby Roberts has phoned up to ask if you would like to go down sometime this week for a chat."

My first thoughts were: where on earth is Colchester? I could remember playing against them at home but not away. Stan clearly wanted me to go. I think that he had been a little embarrassed by the interest shown from Forest. He had signed a couple of defenders on contracts before he had fully assessed my ability and perhaps he felt backed into a corner. I'm not one to blow my own trumpet, but I believe that I was one of his best defenders at the club. However, he had made up his mind and that was that.

I relaxed into my chair and cast my mind back to earlier that year when I was involved in a car crash. We had a little blue Mini and I was going to pick up Anne from ICI Fibres where she worked. As I stopped in traffic, an old boy in a huge estate car rammed into the back of me. The poor old Mini was a write-off and I hit my head on the back parcel shelf. I was knocked unconscious and sustained a deep gash to the base of my skull, which needed half a dozen stitches. I thought I was okay when I got home from the hospital, but Anne said I was talking gibberish for the next 24 hours - nothing new there then! The accident had happened on a Thursday and I went into training on the Friday. I didn't feel great but just got on with it. I told the physio about the accident and he informed the manager. His reaction was, "He'll be fine, he's playing Saturday." The match was away at Rotherham, or maybe Scunthorpe, I honestly can't remember. In fact on the Sunday morning I couldn't even remember much about the game. I obviously had concussion but Stan wasn't overly bothered. It was only my health after all, wasn't it?

I looked at Stan and told him that I would be interested. He said that he would finalise the details and let me know the arrangements. I found out later that the two clubs had already agreed a fee, which was about £10,000.

I went home and waited for Anne to come in from work. When I broke the news to her I wasn't at all sure what her reaction would be. We had only been in our new house for four months. However, Anne was her typical self. "Let's get the map out. Where was it again?" she asked. I responded, "Colchester. I think it's in Essex according to the manager." Anne was so positive about it. She knew that I'd been unhappy and so she was willing to move anywhere if it meant I could enjoy my football again. So I spoke to Stan the next day and he told me that Bobby Roberts would meet me at the station in Colchester.

When I checked out the League tables I realised that Colchester United had just been promoted to division three. Funny how Stan would let me go to a club in a higher division and yet couldn't find a regular spot for me at Donny!

Anyway, that's enough of me bitching ...

... I WAS OFF! Next Stop Colchester in sunny Essex!

CHAPTER 4

COLCHESTER CAPERS

I travelled down to Colchester by train on the following Saturday morning and Bobby Roberts met me at the station as arranged. Straight away I thought how young he looked. He was very enthusiastic and positive from the first minute he met me. I am sure he had plenty to be pleased about, because his team had just been promoted to division three of the Football League.

Bobby took me back to his house and made me some lunch and we chatted generally about football. He asked me what had gone wrong at Doncaster, so I told him briefly about the change of manager, etc., but I didn't want to come across as the typical moaning player who was out of favour. He said that he had been pleasantly surprised that I was available, because when Colchester United had played at Belle Vue the previous season he and the coach, Ray Harford, had thought that I was one of their better players and I had also caused Colchester all sorts of problems at set pieces in the air. I didn't really respond to that, but I felt pleased with his comments. In the short period of time that I was in his company he had already made me feel wanted as a player again!

Being 'wanted' is more important to a player than almost anything else. At any level, regardless of the money involved, a player wants the manager to show confidence in him. He needs him to show that he wants him to be part of his plans, however grand or small they are. This was another part of the jigsaw in the art of good management skills.

Bobby explained that Lindsay Smith, their regular centre back, was off to Cambridge United and they thought that I would be the ideal replacement for him. We talked briefly about the money and contract without my making any firm commitment. I made it clear that I would have to go home and speak to my wife before I could make a decision.

We attended the Colchester game in the afternoon. Bob got on with his job of managing the team and left me upstairs in the lounge. I was looked after very well and the local press asked for a photograph, to which I obliged. They also wanted some sort of comment from me as though the deal was already done. This time I declined politely.

I watched the game and was impressed with the way Colchester played: high tempo, pace and good organisation. They looked a better team than the one I was currently playing for. It was a much smaller ground than I was used to, as Doncaster had a wide-open arena with a massive pitch, similar in dimensions to the old Wembley. And I should know, as I had my tongue hanging out of my backside enough times chasing around the beggar for four years at Belle Vue!

The crowd were so close to the pitch at Layer Road. It was great and the supporters seemed to get behind the team right from the off. I enjoyed the game and a couple of the players caught my eye for different reasons. Ian Allinson, who was about 19 years old then, was very impressive with both feet, which is quite unusual even today. He took corners from either side, right- or left-footed - not bad at all! Steve Dowman, with his big Afro hairdo and no airs and graces, just headed it a mile and made tackles and Micky Cook, a bit like a Jack Russell, was up and down the line at fullback. I have only mentioned a few players here, but they just stuck in my mind on that first day.

I had to leave just before the end of the match so that I could catch my train back to Yorkshire. They were 1-0 up and still on top. I heard the final score on the cab radio: a good 1-0 win.

In my mind I had made my decision already, but I needed to discuss all the pros and cons with Anne. When I arrived home that evening, the moment I walked in the house Anne must have read the look on my face and said, "We're going, aren't we?" "Maybe," I replied. We discussed the move at length and decided that we would go for it. Anne seemed to be looking forward to it even though there was a lot to do.

Anne is a very organised person, so immediately her thoughts turned to the sale of the house, giving up her job as a research technician at ICI and sorting out the relocation. My main thoughts focused on attempting to secure as long a contract as possible if we were to commit to a move so far away. Security for the both of us was a priority.

In Doncaster we were living just two hours from our large families in the north-west whereas now we were facing the prospect of living six hours or so away in the south-east.

I travelled down to Essex a few days later to give the club my answer and I agreed to sign after a few things were ironed out. They put me up in the Marks Tey Hotel, which was very nice, but I didn't have a car at the time (after the crash in the Mini) and I had to travel to the ground by taxi. Living in a hotel is okay, but after a few weeks it can become a bit tedious and lonely at times.

Anne was able to follow me down after working her month's notice. We were quite happy there but felt a bit isolated without our own transport. After another three or four weeks I discussed the situation with Bobby Roberts and he suggested that we move into the town to be nearer to the ground. We were given a room in the Peverel Hotel on North Hill. Well, talk about Fawlty Towers! The main difference was that the owner was a woman. However, we were okay there and had a good laugh at times because of the antics of the staff and the weird clientele that stayed there at weekends! Say no more! It wasn't five-star accommodation but it was liveable and convenient.

Anne found herself a job at the Colchester Institute as a biology technician. We put our house in Doncaster up for sale but had no movement on it at all because of the late seventies recession. This meant that we were in the hotel for a further three months, which was costing the club. The possible solution was to put us in a clubhouse, but unfortunately there wasn't one available, except for the little detached property at the 'bar side' corner of the football ground, which lay almost derelict. So they arranged to give it a makeover. a lick of paint, courtesy of John Froggatt, the centre forward, who used to be a painter and decorator when he played part-time for Boston United; new carpets throughout; and two Calor gas fires, which were the only form of heating. The garden was so overgrown that one afternoon Anne came across a Japanese soldier who thought the war was still on!

It wasn't ideal in a lot of ways, but it was perfect for me in terms of being yards from the ground and Anne could get to work in ten minutes or so. We were only supposed to be in there for a few months while we sold our old house and found another, but in the event we were there for 13 months. That's how long it took us to sell the house in Doncaster.

We found a house in Great Horkesley, which back in the seventies was classed as living in the country! Micky Cook and his wife Wendy informed us of its availability as it was right next door to them. We were glad to get settled into our own place again, especially as the little house in Layer Road turned into an igloo in the winter. It was absolutely freezing. When we woke up in the morning the top cover of our bed was wet with condensation. We both caught the 'Red' flu, which rendered us absolutely helpless for about a week. We both huddled around one gas fire in the living room and took turns to make cups of tea in the below freezing kitchen. I lost about 10 pounds in weight and looked like a ghost. Who said a footballer's life is a glamorous one?

We used to have some of the players around sometimes and I think it was Steve Foley who nicknamed our abode 'the Igloo', which stuck and even to this day when we drive past that's what we call it. The building has been used in a few different ways over the years, such as club shop and commercial office.

While all these peripheral things had been going on I had settled into the side and was enjoying myself. We only had a small squad, which was usual then. The manager put together a good competitive outfit with an excellent mix of young and experienced players. The whole team seemed to have a different atmosphere about it from what I'd been used to at Doncaster. Most of the players had been there a couple of seasons or more and the team spirit was very good.

Everyone lived locally apart from a couple of lads. Steve Leslie was the furthest away in Chelmsford and Mickey Walker lived in Bures some nine miles outside of town. Compare that with today with some players travelling a hundred miles or so to train each day!

With the squad being so local, there was a thriving social life, with regular get-togethers arranged by the manager or the players. The team spirit definitely benefited from this and everyone got to know one another and their families very well. We had a wide range of characters, as with any club, but I got to know each individual much better than I did at my last club simply because of the nature of the set-up and the very close-knit community that encompassed the club and the town in a way.

My new manager Bobby Roberts was different in a few ways from my previous bosses too. Maurice was a terrific motivator and excellent with young players, and he could also handle senior players well in his own way. Stan was better with the older pros and expected players just to go out and perform, with not much of the 'arm around' stuff for the youngsters.

In fact Stan once dragged my brother David out of an upstairs bar (at Layer Road ironically) to play in the match after telling him he wouldn't be involved. The Colchester club doctor had refused to give one of the Rovers players a painkilling jab in his foot, which would have enabled him to play. By that time Dave had eaten a pasty and had downed a pint of shandy. Stan had the raving hump with the doctor so he just frog-marched Dave downstairs and told him, "You're starting, and you've got a few minutes to get ready!" There was no cajoling or pep talk for him! Funnily enough my brother got 'Man of the Match' on that occasion. Who said you need to prepare correctly for games?!

Bobby was a quieter type but very tactically astute. He did his homework on the opposition and explained certain players' strengths and weaknesses. Ray Harford, who had not long finished playing at Colchester, was also very good in his analysis of the opposition and what was required to get a result against them. Bobby used to talk to every player personally and tell him exactly what he wanted. He was also very good at half-time during games if changes were needed individually or tactically.

I learnt a lot from Bobby. On the training pitch his coaching was second to none.

Having said this, he was never really off my back for the four years or so I had with him. He expected very high standards from me, which I gave him because of my respect for him. His man management skills weren't as good as some, but I think that was just his character. He was more of a coach and a fine one at that!

Ray was also a good coach but I didn't get on as well with him as I did with the boss. Maybe this was because he was an ex-centre back himself. Steve Dowman and I were sometimes at loggerheads with him over defensive situations. Ray knew the game, though, and went on to bigger and better things with Kenny Dalglish at Blackburn Rovers. Eventually he took over there as manager, a role in which at times he looked uncomfortable, especially in interviews with the media. Ray died prematurely some years ago and I was saddened and shocked at the news. It just shows that even us lot in football are not immortal!

The team did well over the next couple of seasons, coming close to promotion into the first division, which is now the championship. Considering the budget and small squad at Bobby's disposal, this was a great achievement. We also had some decent Cup runs, one of the matches being against the mighty Manchester United at Layer Road.

There was a full house of over 7,000 for that game, which I nearly missed as I'd twisted my ankle in training earlier that week. It was black and blue but there was no way I was missing out on this massive event. I was strapped up pretty tightly, as that was the only way I was going to get through the match. The pitch surface was quite solid in parts due to the frost, which isn't ideal when you're carrying an injury.

Manchester United had the likes of Gordon McQueen, Brian and Jimmy Greenough, Sammy McElroy and many other stars in their line-up. However, we fancied ourselves to do okay, especially at Layer Road with the crowd behind us and the great atmosphere of an evening game. I didn't feel that we had many weaknesses in our squad. Mike Walker was a very experienced goalkeeper. We had decent pace at the back and generally a very good defensive record. In midfield we had a good mixture of hard work, strength and quality on the ball. Up front we were a handful for anyone whatever combination we played.

The game itself was a tight affair and we had our chances. Gary Bailey pulled off a couple of outstanding saves to keep them in the match. Andy Ritchie played up front for them and I had quite a battle with him over the 90 minutes. It looked as though we were heading for a memorable 0-0 draw and a replay back at Old Trafford. That would have meant a massive payout for the club: the monies probably would have funded our whole playing budget for the next season!

With minutes to go, United forced a corner and so we got ourselves organised defensively as the manager had instructed us to do. My job was to pick up Jimmy Greenough. Bobby liked to give everyone a specific task, so if you were a marker you were given a name and number to pick up and you were responsible for that man at all set pieces (corners and free kicks). So I got touch tight with Greenough at the far post on the six-yard line. I liked to help organise at set pieces, so I was looking around in general to see if everyone was where they should be. I noticed that Gordon McQueen was making a late run from the edge of the penalty box. Trevor Lee, our centre forward, was his marker but McQueen had got a head start on him and was arriving in the centre of the goal at pace as the corner was delivered. I made a split-second decision to leave Greenough and challenge McQueen, who seemed to be the danger at that second. We both clashed in the air and the ball went over both of us to fall at the feet of Jimmy Greenough who, cool as you like, knocked it in the net. Goodnight Vienna!

It had taken just one lapse of concentration during that 90 minutes and as a result we were out of the Cup. I felt totally responsible, as it was my man. Even though McQueen had looked like the danger at that moment, I should have stayed with Greenough. I still have regrets to this day. It was only a millisecond in time but represented a gigantic moment for Colchester United and the team, who deserved at least a draw on the night. The players and staff were sympathetic towards me but deep down I knew that they were gutted!

Most of the time when Bobby was manager everything was positive for me both on and off the pitch. Our first son, Thomas, had made an appearance in early September 1979, we were in our own place again and things were going well.

The squad had many colourful characters in it, one of whom was Colin Garwood, a great talent. He could rip a team to bits, create a goal or two and even score one, and yet still come off the pitch wearing a clean pair of shorts! 'The Gar', as he was known, was a real comedian and he also loved a good social event. He was usually involved in some way in organising or helping Mick Packer (the club red coat) with our little soirées in the bar above the main stand.

On one of these occasions Anne and I arrived a little early, around 7.30 p.m., because Anne had been asked to bring some food for the buffet. As we were walking up the stand steps, the bar door flew open and The Gar appeared with someone else whom I can't recall, carrying John Froggatt (The Frog) out by his arms and legs! I asked Colin, "Is there a problem?"

"Yes," said Colin, "there's been a problem with the drinks. Most of them have gone down Frog's neck!" Frog and The Gar had been responsible for setting up the bar, which they had done but obviously they had been checking the stock while doing so!

Frog was hilarious. It was like one of those comedy sketches you see on the TV.

He was slurring and laughing as his helpers manoeuvred him down the stairs. John wasn't a big drinker, so it didn't take that much to set him on his way. In fact when I was living in 'The Igloo' he was living in a clubhouse by the ground too. He used to say to me sometimes, "Call around tonight about 8 o'clock and ask me to go out for a quick half. Glenis [his wife] will let me go out if you call for me, she thinks you're sensible"! Poor old Frog had a few thumbprints on him over the years!

Colin got Frog home and out of sight before the boss and his wife arrived. It wouldn't have looked good having somebody carried out even before the buffet had been set up. These little do's we had were great little team-builders and were always done at the right time. We trained very hard and yet were able to enjoy ourselves as well, all in moderation of course.

Going back to John, he was a good old-fashioned centre forward who in my opinion never received the recognition he deserved. He took some knocks and handed a bit out. Any other forward who played up front with him always benefited from his physical presence.

There were other players over those years that also had their moments. Kevin Bremner, the brother of Des who played for Aston Villa at that time, came down from the Highland League in Scotland. He was a little overweight when he arrived, but Bobby and Ray soon got him into shape. As a player Kevin was as raw as they come, fearless and full of running, with limited ability at that level. Within a year or so, he was in the team scoring goals and more than holding his own. At times he was as mad as a hatter off the pitch. He would do anything for a bet or if someone wound him up regarding a dare or challenge.

We were on a pre-season tour abroad attending an after-match meal that had been laid on for us. One of the lads had been messing about and dropped a piece of food in a drink. Rather immature, but what's new? It got a bit silly and in the end there was a half-pint glass with a little beer in it followed by potato, broccoli, cigarette ash and a few more nasty morsels. Some bright spark, seeing an opportunity to wind Kevin up a bit, said, "Who dares to swig this down for a whip-round of a few quid?" There were no takers at first - most of the lads cringed, including me! Kev showed some interest, however, and piped up, "How much of a whip-round?" He liked a pound note, true to his Scottish roots. The lads quickly threw in what shrapnel they had in their pockets, which came to about a fiver - not bad back in the seventies! Kev paused and then said, "Give it here." With no hesitation he downed it lumps and all. "The lot," the lads reminded him as he came to the sticky bits at the bottom of the glass. There wasn't even a flicker from Kev, he just scooped up the dosh, belched and said, "Cheers lads!"

Another story about Kev, which came second-hand to me, relates to when he was living in the clubhouse next door but one to 'The Igloo'. He came home rather late one night and his wife had locked the front door, so he proceeded to climb up a drainpipe to get into an open upstairs window. The pipe gave way and he fell back onto the street from the second floor. No problem, though - he was in training the next day with a smile on his face!

Sometimes you would be shopping in town and he would zoom past you on a pushbike, "Okay, Wig? Can't stop, in a hurry!" God knows where he was going!

Kevin went on to play for Millwall and Gillingham. He also became Gillingham's youth teams coach for a while in the nineties. He was a great example of a lad making a living by sheer endeavour. Some youngsters should take note of that, and not just in football.

In a squad of footballers, as in many professions, the differences between individuals are incredible, but they all play their part in a team effort. It is the manager's job to somehow knit all those players together and come up with a winning formula. Bobby did this quite well in his own way.

An example of such differences would be to compare Kevin with Micky Cook. Mick seemed part of the furniture at Layer Road by the time I arrived in 1977. He was even on the bench for the historic win over Leeds under Dick Graham. Being the consummate professional and a qualified coach at an early age, he was someone who thought about the game in more depth than most. Cooky was super-fit and I nearly always tried to seek him out if

I wanted someone to compete against in sprints or anything that included levels of fitness or agility. I always felt that was the way to go to improve rather than take the easy option. Over the years we competed in Friday morning short sprints and I think that I can count on one hand the number of times I actually pipped him to the post! I would like to think he relished the challenge too. He was probably the quickest in the squad, so a close second to him wasn't bad!

As I have already mentioned, Anne and I lived next door to Mick and Wendy for a short while before they moved to Braiswick. Maybe it was something we said!

Who would have thought that some 25 years on I would employ Mick as my youth team coach at United and the youth system that we set up would finally generate millions of pounds for Colchester United?

Squads of players at that level were nowhere near as big as they are now. We had about 16 senior players and a couple of young lads who could come in if needed. This in a way made it feel more like a close-knit group. Also our geographical position meant very long journeys to many games up north or down to the south-west. This resulted in hours on end together on a coach or in hotels overnight - when the club could afford it, that is. So we got to know each other pretty well. I'm not saying it was all sweetness and light, but we all tended to tolerate each other's idiosyncrasies or whatever because it was our profession.

I have to admit that I hadn't really thought about how far we would have to travel to away games when I signed from Doncaster. Not that I had any regrets, but sometimes after a defeat at Hartlepool or Carlisle on a Tuesday night and faced with a six-hour journey back home I would wonder: why am I putting the key in the front door when the milkman is putting the milk on the doorstep? We would have the next day off, of course, but we would return to training on the Thursday, which was hardly ever a lively session as players were still recovering physically. It was even worse news for the lads who travelled with the squad all that way and in the end didn't get on the pitch or only played part of the match, as they were often needed for the reserve game on the Wednesday evening the following day after getting back as late as 4 a.m.! They would also be expected to train with us on the Thursday.

Top players complain today about having to play in Europe and then flying back first-class or sometimes even in private jets - I wish! They want to try Rochdale and back in a day with a fiver to spend in the motorway services at 2 a.m.!

Of course, the 'U's' supporters had the same distances to travel and I can vouch for one bloke who used to follow us everywhere on his little Honda 50cc motorbike. Our coach used to pass him in all weathers and he would give us a wave as he tootled along at about 50mph. We never did know his name but that is true support, isn't it? I suppose he did get plenty of fresh air and it was a cheap way of travelling, but apart from that it must've been a bloody nightmare!

We all had our ways of coping with the long journeys. Bobby Gough, Ian Allinson, Steve Dowman and a few others, including the bosses Bobby and Ray, would play cards for hours on end - not for money in any great amounts, I might add. Steve Leslie and Cooky would have a book and a pillow so that they could read or kip. Sometimes we would listen to music and in the latter years we watched videos. I could never sleep like some of lads so I would get pretty bored at times, especially in the last few hours of a long journey. I used to chat to the driver for a while or even just sit quietly in the front watching the miles go down on the signposts. There were no mobile phones then for idle chit-chat!

If we were really lucky we would be treated to a bit of light entertainment on impromptu stops for Frog. He occasionally got caught short and needed to do number 2s in the bushes at the roadside! He claimed that ever since he moved down from the north his bowels had never been the same and when he had to go, he had to go. On one trip home after a game he came lumbering up the bus and asked the driver to pull over whenever he could as he was desperate - almost 'touching cloth', 'tortoise-heading' or whatever you want to call it. We duly stopped and he leapt off and disappeared into the undergrowth in the darkness. He returned a few minutes later with a certain look of relief but apparently still in some discomfort. "Okay, Frog?" I said. "Much better after that, Wigs, but just look at me arse!" I dreaded the thought but instantly he dropped his pants to reveal bum cheeks covered in massive nettle stings. "I fell in the bloody nettles as I wiped me backside!" he said. Poor Frog, but it was funny and livened a few lads up from their slumber. The words 'leper' and 'the mange' were bandied about, quietly of course, as they didn't want to rile "The Frog" too much!

Nowadays, people say to me it's not like the old days, as there don't seem to be the characters that there were back then. I'm not so sure if that is quite right but there does appear to be a difference. Whether it's because of the inflated wages paid to all ages of players now, I don't know. Back in the seventies and even into the eighties there was some sort of pecking order with players. The older pros tended to be on the best salaries and younger players worked their way up over the years. Squads didn't change as dramatically as they do today. For instance, when I got the Southend United manager's job I had to let 13 players go and replace them in a matter of weeks - an almost impossible task without a big budget. Just an example of the constant migration of players in and out of football clubs these days. No one really seems to get to know one another now, as players aren't around long enough and don't get the opportunity to establish themselves as 'characters' in that club.

Colchester was a particular example of a club in an era when clubs retained players longer and changed their squads at a slower rate. We had many players in the squad who reached a ten-year and beyond association with the club and they were granted much-deserved testimonials. They were Micky Cook, Steve Foley, Micky Walker, Steve Leslie and Micky Packer. Considering that our squads only consisted of, at most, 18 players, this was some achievement. Apart from Micky Walker, who went on to manage Norwich and Everton, all the lads in that group still live reasonably local to Colchester.

Steve Foley was a local lad anyway and didn't move very far even when he coached at Norwich. He was a very talented player but had terrible trouble with injuries, which blighted his career.

Steve Leslie was a bit of an enigma to me. He seemed quite a serious lad who tended to sit in the background a bit and yet take it all in. He used to take unmerciful stick from some of the lads at times - nothing nasty, just banter. It was usually about his hair or general appearance and Steve took it all in good spirit. He was a totally different character on the pitch, however. He turned into a real winner and could be aggressive if needed or maybe just overenthusiastic. His room-mate on away trips was Cooky, which suited them both - a nice, quiet life! I think Steve made the tea or whatever!

Micky Packer was a different kettle of fish in the dressing room. He was always up for a laugh and taking the pee! When it came to the job, however, he took it quite seriously. He was a bit old school, if you like. He didn't suffer fools gladly and would kick his mother if she played for the opposition. In fact, he would probably even kick his grandmother! He had a great left foot, which could volley wingers almost as far as some could kick the ball. Only joking, Pack! We've kept in touch throughout the years and still socialise today with the 'old boy' and his wife Mary.

Micky Walker was a one-off really. Mind you, he was a goalkeeper and they can be a funny lot. We roomed together and got on well. We were both very tidy, so the room was always organised. Mick was a man of few words, but when he did speak people usually listened. A few of the boys mimicked him very well - when he wasn't in hearing distance, of course. He used to come to training in a suit most days and I've got to say he spent his fair share of time in front of the mirror. Everything had to be just right with his clothes, his kit and his hair. On the pitch he demanded high standards from you, especially if you were a centre back. He was a big lad and if you got in the way when he came for a high ball there was a good chance you would cop a glove around the ear. I still have a few lumps on my head to prove that point! During and after his success as a manager I saw him at testimonial games, etc., and I was a little disappointed; so, too, were a few of the boys. His attitude had changed and he'd lost that sense of humour that we all had in abundance back in the seventies and eighties. Even I, his old room-mate, didn't get much out of him. I guess we all change over time, but for me the banter between old teammates in football never dies. The old jokes and piss-takes are still the best!

Paul Dyer deserves a mention here. He was always on the fringe of the first team in the Bobby Roberts era. He was unfortunate not to play more games than he did. When he did play, though, Paul's enthusiasm for the game was second to none. He was always encouraging and geeing people up. What he lacked in ability he more than made up for with his presence on the pitch. We didn't get on all the time because of competitiveness in training, but I think there was a mutual respect for each other as players. He was very much a team player and still is, serving the club loyally over many years as a scout and covering thousands of miles all over the country, watching matches at all levels of football. He also runs his own business outside the game with his wife Carol, the daughter of the legendary Vic Keable, an ex-player.

Some new young players came through the system, one of them being Steve Wright, the son of the famous ex-Colchester United player, Peter Wright. Steve was a defender and quite different from the fleet-footed Peter who had played on the wing. Later Steve followed Bobby Roberts to Wrexham and also played for Dario O'Gradi at Crewe. Russell Cotton and Tony Evans were two more youngsters who broke through to join Steve Dowman and Ian Allinson, who had made the first team a season or so before.

Steve Dowman and I formed a good partnership in the centre of defence for a while after the departure of Lindsay Smith. Steve was a very confident lad and sometimes a little outspoken in the dressing room. His nickname among the lads was 'Soggy', and I couldn't quite work out why when I first arrived at the club. After a while I just had to ask how he came by that name and, as brutal as ever, they told me straight that it was because of his sweaty armpits! He seemed to 'chuck up' all the time according to the boys. Charming! But that's a football dressing room for you.

Nicknames do tend to stick in football and are usually transferred with you when you move clubs, as invariably someone at your new club nearly always knows someone at your old club. Football is an incredible grapevine, so you don't get away with much, believe me.

Ian Allinson, who went on to play for Arsenal, was called 'Blimpy' - a rather silly name he got from constantly looking around corners or 'blimping'. I'm not sure if the Arsenal lads kept it up, but I still called him by that name when I met him recently and he wouldn't expect anything else! Ian was only a young lad when I joined Colchester in 1977. To my knowledge, up to 2007 he was still involved in football, albeit at non-League level.

Ian was good mates with Bobby Gough, a northerner, who scored goals regularly throughout his career. Bobby is another player who has settled in the Colchester area, and the last time I spoke to him his son was a junior player at Colchester United. Bob and I didn't really socialise. In fact we crossed swords a couple of times - nothing too bad, just a bit of northern grit between us. He was one of the best in the penalty box, similar to my old mate Peter Kitchen at Donny. Bob definitely didn't drive a Morris 1000 though!

There were others who came into the squad over the coming seasons, so if I miss anyone out, my apologies. It's nothing personal, just old age or 'old man syndrome' as my sons say!

Talking of sons, when our second son, Jack, was born prematurely one Saturday in September 1981, unfortunately I was away for five days with the team, playing two games in the north. I received the news when I came off the pitch and it was a very expensive round for me in the bar later that night!

Bob Hodge came up from the West Country and did a great job on the pitch. He was a lovely lad who liked his motor cars. He always had a quality car that was immaculate. Eddie Rowles came down from Darlington and he and Bob teamed up off the pitch and worked together in their spare time. Bob was a chippy and Ed a painter and decorator.

Eddie was a centre forward and a nightmare to play against in training. He would challenge for everything and would leave the odd forearm in the way during aerial challenges at times. He took some stick as well, which was fair enough. That was Eddie, or 'Rowler' as he was known. He, too, along with his wife, Brenda, has settled in the area. I bumped into him a few years ago and he told me that he had just bought a smallholding in Ireland. Pretty shrewd, old Ed!

Trevor Lee signed from Millwall by Bobby for about £15,000 and after a couple of very good seasons was sold to Gillingham for about £90,000 - a good bit of business for the club. Trev was quite a shy lad but a great athlete with tremendous pace. I roomed with him on a pre-season trip to Germany and he was the perfect gentleman. His wife, Barbara, and Anne were good friends. Further down the line I played against him when he was at Gillingham and I have to confess I gave him a bit of a hard time physically, which was my remit, as he was their main danger to us up front. We needed a result and fashioned a 0-0 draw. Trevor didn't score so my job was done! Barbara was waiting in the players' bar and gave me daggers and she actually said, "I'm surprised at you," to which I couldn't really summon a reply. It wasn't personal. I was a professional and that was that. Sorry, Trev, but you still walked off the pitch so it wasn't too bad then, eh?

The late Ray Bunkell was a chirpy chappy from London. He was an ex-Tottenham player who was good mates with Mick Packer. Ray was a good passer of the ball and always wanted to get it down and play in midfield. He tended to invite a few kicks at times because of his reluctance to release the ball or just knock it forward as a lot of players did in our division. Ray just couldn't walk past a mirror without looking in it to see if his hair was okay or his clothes were just right. As you can imagine, he was teased about this but he didn't care. He would just laugh it off and then look in the mirror again!

'Bertie' (his nickname) decided to grow a moustache because it was the fashion and he liked to appear up with the recent trends. However, when it sprouted it came out a little lighter in colour than his hair. So, Ray being Ray, he wasn't happy that it didn't match his barnet and to remedy this he dyed the tash darker. Only Micky Packer knew he'd done this and none of the other lads even noticed. Anyway, we were all sat in the communal bath after training one day and Mick looked at Ray with a concerned expression, pointed to his own top lip and gestured to him that the dye had run! Poor old Ray panicked. With his hand over his mouth and tash, he scrambled out of the bath to get to the nearest mirror. 'Pack' was in hysterics as Ray came back into the bathroom a minute later with expletives galore vented in the direction of Mick! The dye hadn't run at all and now the squad were aware of Ray's little cosmetic effort! I liked Ray; he was a great lad. Anne and I were very sad when he passed away some years ago at no age at all.

I see most of the players I have already mentioned as 'characters' in their own way. The public may have imagined them as totally different in their own minds, so I hope that I haven't and won't spoil anyone's perceptions in this book.

Talking of characters, there was probably no bigger one than Roy McDonough. Roy was a good mate and I don't think that we ever had a disagreement in the couple of years that we played together. He was like a bottle of wine that seemed to get better as time went on. When he first signed for Colchester he was still a little disappointed at being released from Chelsea even though he did well at Walsall, his following club. With his size and touch he had most assets that a centre forward needed at that level. I felt that he lacked belief in himself at times even though he may not have admitted it. He was a very popular lad on and off the pitch, which led to a hectic social life. He won't mind my saying that, as basically he was a very honest lad who knew what it took to be successful.

Though many people said that Roy would never last in the game, they were made to eat their words as he continued to play well into his thirties. As I have already said, he became a much better player as time went on. We all gain experience and come to know the game as we mature, but I think Roy improved dramatically and became even more effective as a centre forward. He also went into management and did a fantastic job despite a few back-stabbers and vultures waiting for him to falter. What's new in football?

We played a few games together as twin centre backs when there was a glut of injuries to defenders. He did a fantastic job. He was strong in the air, decent on the ball and learnt very quickly, hopefully some of it from me. Roy loved his banter on the pitch and would often comment on how ugly the opposition forwards were - well within their earshot, of course, just to wind them up!

It wasn't all sweetness and light though. He hadn't made a mistake in the first few games and looked a natural, but in one match he left a back pass to the goalkeeper a bit short and the opposition got in and scored. As we walked back to the halfway line he turned to me and said, "Sod this for a lark," or words to that effect. His brief love affair with being a centre half was over and he couldn't wait to get back up front!

After the game he admitted that he didn't realise the pressure on defenders. "One mistake can cost you big time. If I make a mistake up front it is soon forgotten, unless it's an open goal, of course," he said. There are different pressures on all players and Roy definitely preferred the pressures of a centre forward.

Later on in the book I will mention the conversation that I had with Roy when I took over the manager's job at Colchester United. He was quick to inform me of some of those back-stabbers or problem people in and around the club. I always had time for Roy and I think the game definitely misses people or characters like him.

A different type of person completely was a player called Pat Sharkey. He was an Irish lad with a bit of a chip on his shoulder. I'm not sure whether he actually liked us English; if he did, he definitely didn't say! He was an excellent footballer and a bit of a rebel to boot. He always seemed dishevelled to me, on and off the pitch. I never really got close to him socially and the probable reason for that was that he did like a drink and could get a bit silly at times. He was a hard lad to fathom but a very talented player who could be a match winner. His heart was in the right place but he didn't appear to want people to know it.

Back in the seventies and earlier, the term 'physio', or 'sponge man', was a pretty ambiguous title. The care or medical side of things was pretty sketchy to say the least. In the worst case scenario the sponge man who ran on the pitch could have been simply an ex-player or someone with a first aid certificate at best. Your life and limbs were or could be in their hands! I have already mentioned the occasion when I broke my nose at Grimsby and John Quigley came on to slosh a sponge in my face, got me on my feet and left me to it. Well, that was basically it in the early days. Of course some clubs catered for their players better than others and it was usually down to finance in most cases. Thankfully those days have gone and a gradual improvement has been made in appointing qualified people across the board. Correct coverage for injured players is now provided in football. The FA set the rules and began to run courses in the treatment and management of injuries. I actually went on one of these two-year courses, which I will talk about later in the book.

While on the subject of physios, the man doing that job at Colchester United when I arrived was Ray Cole. He was a well-spoken middle-aged man who worked for Glaxo, the medical supply company. He did the job at the football club in a part-time capacity. Ray was a pleasant bloke and didn't seem to fit into the surroundings somehow. The lads used to take the pee out of him something rotten and he would respond in his own way, which was usually hilarious. He didn't seem to realise when the lads were serious or taking the mick and found it hard to grasp the joke. As you can imagine this made the lads worse. Mind you, there was always plenty of material for the lads to harp on about, as Ray often got things wrong.

On one occasion Ray was strapping a player's ankle up before a game while he was talking to someone else. Somehow his tie got entangled in the bandage and, as Ray stood up, it lifted the lad's leg off the bench and up into the air. The tie was literally part of the ankle support! It was unbelievable and he never lived that down - and probably never has to this day!

Ray also served as physio to the Essex cricket team. He did know his limitations as a physiotherapist and I am not criticising him, just pointing out the facts of how it was. Anne and I met Ray just recently. He is a sprightly octogenarian and definitely not as daft as some of the lads thought he was!

There were always comical moments in football and maybe some of these occurrences seem funnier to me than they actually were. As you know, I'm a Scouser and we'll laugh at anything!

One such event was something that happened to one of our young players in the eighties. Jeff Hull was a tricky little footballer from the Southend area. He used to travel up and down the A12 every day in his little Mini to and from training. At one of the night games we were getting changed when I noticed amongst his kit there was a loo roll in his bag, which seemed very unusual.

I asked him, "What's up, Jeff, got a cold?"

"No, I had a few problems last week on the way home," he replied.

I was intrigued and enquired a bit more.

He looked around and lowered his voice a little as if he wasn't overly keen on the rest of the lads hearing. "Well, you may not believe it but after the game last Friday night I was driving along the A12 on the way home in the pouring rain when all of a sudden I got awful gut ache and just had to go to the toilet."

A touch of the John Froggatts! The A12 being what it is I could picture the scene - a nightmare!

Jeff continued, "I just had to stop. I pulled over and got out next to a grassy bank. I decided to leg it up the hill away from the road and find somewhere to go sharpish. It was absolutely chucking it down when I suddenly slipped and slid down the steep bank."

I knew he must've been wearing his best match-day suit at the time.

He went on, "Unfortunately, I seemed to lose control and did whatever had to be done in my pants!"

By now I could feel a grin coming on, but I managed to stifle it, as Jeff was quite serious and not happy about the incident. Who would be? But there was more to come.

"When I reached the bottom of the bank, I just picked myself up and stood there for a second or two. I was covered from head to toe in mud and, even worse, what on earth was in my strides? I was in shock. I just got in my car and drove on!"

I said, "Oh God, how was your car seat?"

"Not good," replied Jeff. "When I got home and went through the front door my mum nearly fell over when she saw the state of me. Filthy all down my front and the stinking baggy-arsed look from behind. The stench was unbelievable. My mum asked me if I'd been mugged, so I told her, no, I just crapped myself!"

I had to apologise to Jeff, as by now I was definitely smirking; in fact I think I was laughing.

Jeff said, "That's okay, Wig. Not a nice experience though, mate."

That toilet roll was never far from Jeff's bag in the future. Mind you, toilet roll or not, if you got caught short and decided to leg it up a slippery bank in the dark I don't think it would make a big difference.

Most supporters probably think that a footballer's life is one of constant adulation, fun good pay and short hours, etc. They would be right to a certain extent, but what many forget is that they are just people with the same everyday problems and emotions that Joe Bloggs has.

In this respect, the case of our good friend John Lyons springs to mind. John came to Colchester United from Wrexham. He was an international centre forward with a good goalscoring record. He was the life and soul at a party, always having a laugh about anything. I got on really well with John as he had a similar sense of humour to me - a little wicked at times but good fun. Roy McDonough was very good friends with him too and they enjoyed a night out together most weeks. On some training days, however, John seemed a little short-fused; nothing major but noticeable to me. The next day he would be back to being an easy-going joker. John had everything going for him for a player in his mid-twenties: his own house; enough money; good career prospects. As far as I could see, he had everything to look forward to.

John's hometown of Bwcle in North Wales was a unique place in so far as the locals had their own accent, which was different from that of the people in the surrounding area. The famous footballer called Michael Owen comes from a nearby town called Hawarden.

Anyway, we played at home one Tuesday night. It was a close game and we scored late on to make it 1-0, so the opposition were desperate to get something out of the game. As the ball bounced into the stand close to the players' tunnel, one of their lads ran through the little white gate between the dugouts to retrieve the ball as quickly as possible. As quick as a flash John ran over, shut the gate behind the player and locked the bolt, preventing him from getting back onto the pitch quickly. This was typical of John - a great sense of humour. The crowd thought it was fantastic and gave him one of the biggest cheers of the night. The other team were none too pleased, but that was to be expected. We won the game and everyone was happy, none more so than John.

Roy and he were straight out on the town with a few others after the match.

The next day, on the Wednesday morning, Anne and I were in town doing general domestic chores. We were putting some clothes into the dry cleaners when who should walk past but John. He spotted us and came into the shop for a chat. He told us he was going to order the carpets for his new house and invited us round the following weekend for an evening. Then, as quick as he had appeared, he was off with his usual grin and some sort of wisecrack.

We never saw John again. He hung himself at his house in the early hours of Thursday morning.

For the first time in my life I felt bereft. A feeling of numbness and lack of speech overcame me as I was told the news when I turned up at the ground for training at 9.30 a.m. that day. Roy and a couple of the other lads were inconsolable as they had been out with him earlier the previous night. Talk about being brought down to earth. I can't begin to explain how we all felt. It just didn't add up and even today, some 25 years or more later, it still doesn't. What a sad waste of talent and humour and loss of a nice man. We couldn't begin to imagine how his family in Wales were feeling. There must've been more going on in his life than anyone knew.

This was probably the saddest incident throughout my 20-year playing career. God bless John and his family.

At this time Allan Hunter was our manager. He had taken over from Bobby, who had been relieved of his duties in the usual uncompromising way after seven years' service. I was upset when Bobby left as he had shown a lot of faith in me and I had definitely improved as a player under him. Ray Harford had left for sunnier climes, with Stewart Houston coming in as player/coach.

Stewart was a very experienced player who was at Manchester United and Sheffield United and he had also played for his country Scotland. He was a great professional and a very tough character. I also learnt a lot from him, as well as playing many games alongside him. Later, Stewart went on to coach and eventually manage Arsenal.

He followed George Graham to Leeds as his assistant and managed at QPR. I still see him occasionally at League Managers' Association meetings.

When Allan Hunter came onto the scene I got along with him straight away. Allan was a legend at Ipswich and a full international with Northern Ireland. He came as a player/manager and I was privileged enough to play in defence with him for a few games. Considering his achievements, Allan was a very modest man. His experience in management and coaching was limited as he was still playing, so he brought in Cyril Lea. Cyril was a very experienced man who had worked with Allan at Ipswich as one of the coaching staff. He was quite a tough nut and was definitely of the 'old school' way of thinking. They complimented each other in a way, as Allan was very laid back, yet Cyril was quite willing to wield the stick if necessary.

The boss played for as long as possible, but injuries were catching up with him and he began to struggle. In my opinion, managing wasn't enough for him. He wanted to carry on playing. Allan wasn't in the job that long and to my disappointment he eventually left the club. Whether the John Lyons incident had anything to do with his decision I don't know and I wouldn't suggest it. Someone would have to ask 'Big Al' as he was known. He was a good man who perhaps wasn't cut out for the uncertain and illogical job of football management.

Another privilege for me was when Kevin Beattie joined us for a short while. Playing alongside Kevin, or 'The Beat' as he was known, was fantastic. Even though he was struggling with his knees his ability was first class. Like Allan, Kevin had great humility and was always encouraging other players.

He was a top international and a prospective captain of England until his injuries caught up with him. You couldn't hope to meet a more down to earth lad. We formed a formidable partnership at the back and I can remember him saying to me in one game, "Bloody hell, Wigs, this level is tough physically mate." Kevin found that, no matter who you were, the players at the slightly lower level than he was used to didn't pull out of anything.

In the eighties there were still plenty of blood and guts games in our division, although not as many as in the seventies. Kevin broke his nose and gashed his knee deeply in two consecutive games. He wouldn't duck anything either, so there were bound to be some bone-rattling challenges along the way! He went off to play for Middlesbrough, but I don't think he lasted too long with his injury problems. Pound for pound, Kevin is one of the best left-footed centre backs this country has produced. If only his body had stood up to the rigours of the game, who knows what more he might have achieved? In today's market of inflated prices what would 'The Beat' be worth?

I haven't mentioned everyone in chronological order during the seven years that I was at Colchester. That would be a little too clinical for me and the book would be more of a football information one. As I write, more people and situations spring to mind, so I hope that any purists among you readers are not confused!

When Alec Chamberlain came into the side, he was very young for a first-team goalkeeper at that time. He matured very quickly, however, and became a top-class keeper. He went on to play for Everton and Watford. He has only just finished playing first-team football and is now coaching. Alec was a model professional and didn't have a bad word to say about anyone. My tip to any young goalkeeper who gets the chance to meet Alec is to listen to what he has to say, as it will be spot on!

Dennis Longhorn was another enigma to me. He came from Sheffield United as a midfield player but ended up being an excellent utility player. Dennis was a very quiet man. My wife used to say that he reminded her of the boy that sat at the back of the class at school and sniggered at the antics of others. He was a great footballer; he even played at centre back with me and did a great job. Sometimes he wouldn't say a word during games and then all of a sudden he'd come out with a tirade at someone, either on his own side or among the opposition. Dennis liked the game to be played properly and if he felt that a player wasn't pulling his weight or was shirking responsibility he would "'let them have it'. I haven't seen Dennis for quite a few years, but apparently he coaches youngsters at a local holiday camp these days. Watch out kids, Dennis is about! Only joking, Den. He was another good character to have in your team.

Phil Coleman came in from Millwall and could play anywhere across the back four. He was a good athlete and very young, and his versatility meant that he became a good asset to the squad. Phil was one of the quickest talkers I have ever heard. With his cockney accent and over-the-top comments some of the lads didn't know how to take him. He was loud and brash and had apparently seen and done everything already at the ripe old age of about 20! I wasn't quite sure about him to start with, but the more I got to know him and was able to strip away that brash exterior, the more I could see Phil as a person who had more about him than most people realised. He could be a bit of a loose cannon on the pitch too. He would go off on runs up the wing to support players or just go missing for a second or two when he should have been on your shoulder defensively. This was Phil, and it was all done very honestly and with enthusiasm. I needed to keep him on a leash most of the time, but he's an okay bloke. He's still a bit outspoken to this day and is now a teacher. Who would have thought?

Another centre forward came to us called Keith Bowen, or 'Goose' as he was known to the chaps. Keith was an odd shape for a footballer. He just looked a little awkward in everything he did. Having said that, he was very effective and scored some good goals as well as creating some for others. He had one of the longest necks ever, hence the nickname. We used to say that was why he nicked so many balls in the air, because of his telescopic neck! He was a smashing lad, always up for a laugh, very intelligent and a qualified accountant with it!

Perhaps one of the best that I must mention is 'The Red Rooster' or 'Tads'. These are just two nicknames for Tony Adcock. When I first saw Tony playing for our reserves as an apprentice he lined up as a right winger. I could see straight away that he had a certain quality and awareness. He seemed to glide past people with some ease and had a great touch. His red hair made him stand out and he didn't disappoint people, as he was good to watch. In training he was one of the best natural finishers that I had seen. Sometimes his awareness of the goalkeeper's position, even though he himself might have his back to the goal, was scary. I have seen him lift the ball over keepers from all angles, scoring some fantastic goals. Supporters and fans used to say to me, "He was a bit fortunate there," or "Did he really mean to do that?" and I could assure them that he did most of the time. Tony scored goals wherever he went and even came back and scored some for me when I was the manager.

Another redhead who started as an apprentice at Colchester was Perry Groves. 'Grovesy' as he was known originally came as a central midfield player. Right from the start Cyril didn't really fancy him in that position, so he stuck him out wide on the right. Perry was a good size for a winger or wide man. He had an unusual style in as much as he ran about constantly on his toes. He had terrific pace, which gave defenders nightmares in our division. Cyril gave Perry a hard time on occasions as he was always on his back regarding his diet, etc. When we used to stop on the way to games so that players could get something to eat, Cyril would watch the young lads like a hawk, especially Grovesy. If he bought an extra item and brought it onto the bus the boss would 'hammer' him if it wasn't totally healthy in his opinion. To be fair to Perry, he wasn't bad at looking after himself in the early days. I can't vouch for him later on, but he didn't do too badly at Arsenal. Unfortunately his career was cut short by injury.

I still see Perry now and again and it is hard to imagine him as that young tippy-toed apprentice back in the eighties with not a great deal to say for himself. Anyone who knows him now would not be able to accuse him of not saying much; on the contrary, try shutting him up! I think Perry is a good example of a lad who made the absolute most of his physical assets to be successful.

I must mention, of course, the famous Roger Osbourne. He was another ex-Ipswich player who played for the 'U's' and also had great qualities. He adapted to the slightly lower level very well. His energy and enthusiasm on the pitch were infectious and his discipline as a professional was a great example to all his peers. Having played alongside and socialised with him, his quiet nature and interest in others belied the fact that he himself was an

FA Cup match winner for Ipswich Town, scoring the winning goal at Wembley!

Having played with Hunter, Beattie and Osborne, it was easy to see why Ipswich was so successful over those years. Bobby Robson knew good players when he saw them and these were three of the greats. And that is coming from a 'U's' man through and through.

I got on okay with Cyril when he took over as manager after Allan left, even though he had a different style of management than I had been used to over the past several years. Bobby Roberts had been a good technical coach and had liked to change things around at times and try new methods in training. You had to be sharp of mind in Bobby's sessions, whereas most of Cyril's consisted mainly of hard work. There was nothing wrong with hard work, of course, but some of our warm-ups alone would consist of several 200-metre runs! One thing was for sure, we were never left wanting for fitness when Cyril was involved. Not that we were unfit under Bobby, but our team play mimicked our training. This was mostly physical, closing down the opposition, putting your foot in and a bit 'crash-bang-wallop'! I'm not criticising, because there is a need for that approach. However, you also need to have a little more subtleness to your play if you're going to win games on a regular basis. Cyril often became frustrated with the lads as he was used to being involved with better players at Ipswich and other clubs he had been at.

I wasn't aware of the fact at the time, but I was taking in more than I realised in terms of how things should and should not be done in the preparation of players and the team. It was seeping into those little grey cells for later on!

I was starting to feel a little stale under Cyril. Maybe it was just me after seven years at the same club or maybe there was more to it. I didn't see eye to eye with the boss all the time, yet respected him for taking the job on. He was inclined to be a bit 'acid tongued' at times, which looking back was probably down to frustration on his part.

Following a northern game we stayed at Lilleshall in Shropshire for the weekend instead of making the long journey back to Essex, as we had a game at Tranmere midweek. I had a stinking cold and just about managed to get through the Saturday game. By Sunday and into Monday I was in a bad way. In my own mind I had ruled myself out of the Tranmere game. Cyril wanted me to play if I could and was very persuasive, so in the end I succumbed and played. Stewart Houston was in defence with me that night and his encouragement and experience helped me a great deal. I was finding it hard to breathe in the game as the cold had gone onto my chest, but I did okay. The game was heading for a 0-0 draw, which wouldn't have been a bad result as we had drawn one each on the Saturday. One point was a good result before the 'three points for a win' system came in. There were only minutes to go and we really had our backs to the wall. They threw another free kick into our box. I didn't quite clear the ball well enough in a challenge, but we still had a couple of bites at it. They snaffled a goal and that was that: we lost 1-0 in the dying seconds.

We were obviously gutted and sloped into the dressing room with nothing to show for a gallant effort from everyone, especially in front of a partisan crowd at Prenton Park. Cyril was there waiting for us and his face did not look happy. He let fly at me and basically blamed me for the defeat. My immediate reaction was to bite back as I had given him my best when I felt only about 60 per cent or so fit and had done well to stay on the pitch. I could feel the sap rising and thought: I'm not having that! As Cyril was still going into one, I caught Stewart's eye and he was gently shaking his head as if to say, "Don't". I respected Stewart and so I held my peace and swallowed it. Nobody said a word. The manager finished and left the dressing room. You could almost hear a pin drop as we started to get our kit off. Stewart came over, patted me on the shoulder and said, "We know, don't we?" He was right, we did know. The boss was wrong this time and perhaps it was better to leave it that way.

After that I didn't really get on great with Cyril, just okay. My contract was coming up for renewal and I asked for a new three-year deal to take me up to ten years' service and a testimonial. However, the club said that they would only offer me a two-year deal. I was disappointed and decided that maybe it would be best if I left and looked for a new challenge. Deep down I didn't really want to leave, and also Anne and I had just put down a deposit on a new house in Wivenhoe.

Brentford came in for me and offered £25,000, which was a good fee for the club, especially as they'd had seven good years out of me. The deal was virtually done and dusted. I had been up to see Frank McLintock the 'Bee's' manager and agreed most of the terms. I just had to speak to Anne about the move. I couldn't believe it when Maurice Cadman, the chairman of Colchester, telephoned me the following day and said that I could have my three-year deal with a testimonial at the end of it. I was shocked and very disappointed that it had been left so late, as by this time Anne and I had let the new house go, taken Thomas out of school and made our minds up to leave. I thanked Maurice for his offer but had to decline as we had made our decision, I had formally accepted Frank's offer and so that was that. Sadly, this was the end of seven years at a very close-knit club.

Colchester and Colchester United will always be part of my family's life. Our boys were born at the Maternity Home, Lexden Road. Anne and I had not been married long when we arrived in Colchester, so it was a new beginning for us in a way. We had met some good people both in and outside the club and had enjoyed some great times over those seven years.

As a player most of my memories are positive, such as the Cup runs we had: playing against Manchester United; beating Aston Villa away in the League Cup 2-0 but losing on penalties after extra time; and scoring ten goals in one season from centre half. I also felt honoured to have won Player of the Year and Players' Player of the Year on a couple of occasions as well as being made the captain of the side. I was also very lucky to be liked by the supporters, which isn't always the case in football.

I had been privileged to work under the management of Bobby Roberts, Ray Harford, Allan Hunter and Cyril Lee and the coaching of Stewart Houston. All these people helped me in different ways to become an improved player and definitely gave me food for thought for the future, whether as a player, manager or coach.

CHAPTER 5
LONDON CALLING

The prospect of moving to London and my playing for a London club was a major issue for us. We were stepping out of the comfort zone of being at a provincial club such as Colchester on the borders of Suffolk and Essex. The move to Brentford also proved to be more of a problem logistically than I had hoped. We managed to sell our house in Colchester fairly quickly as the property market was quite buoyant. Unfortunately the houses in west London where we had decided to live were not staying on the market very long; in fact, some properties were selling within days of becoming available!

Of course when a player is transferred his move to that club is immediate, so I went to live in Chigwell, east London, with my mum's sister, Muriel, and her husband, Les. Naturally they spoilt me to death! Anne and I found it difficult to secure somewhere in Ruislip to coincide with our sale in Colchester, so after she had put the furniture in storage she took the boys, Thomas and Jack, to live with my parents in North Wales.

This was far from satisfactory for us all but we had no option at the time. I was in training at my new club and now had to try to find a house for us all while Anne was in her homeland.

The assistant manager of Brentford, John Docherty, was very helpful to us, as he knew the area of Ruislip very well. It was close to the training ground and only 20 minutes away from Griffin Park, the home ground of Brentford FC. Ruislip was a nice suburb of London and very expensive compared with what we were used to! The houses in that area were about a third higher in price than similar properties in Colchester and we knew that we would really have to push the boat out to afford a place that was a little smaller than our house in Horkesley.

The housing market was so busy that I literally had to view a house and then make a decision on the spot. I did just that and put in a bid, which was accepted. Anne hadn't even seen the place when she arrived some four months later with the removal van. The boys seemed to have grown since I'd last seen them. My mother-in-law, Joan, had driven them down and as they pulled up I was waiting at the front door, a little nervous about their reaction to my choice of house! I'm glad to say that Anne was pleased with what she saw and we ended up living there for the following six years.

I had not met Frank McLintock before but had seen him play for that great Arsenal side back in the seventies. He was smaller than I had imagined but he was a very confident character who had done a great deal in the game as a player. I had met his assistant, John Docherty, before when he was the manager of Cambridge United. The 'Doc', as he was known, had been a successful manager already, so Frank was lucky to have such an experienced campaigner alongside him. Frank didn't have to 'sell' the club to me when I met him at Griffin Park because it was one of the bigger clubs in the old third division with a good crowd base of six or seven thousand.

Doc knew more about me than Frank and briefed me on what they expected of me as a player. He told me that they wanted a steady centre back who would keep things simple and could organise the back four. They felt they were leaking too many goals at that time.

I knew very little about their squad of players, but looking at their previous results they were not pulling up any trees. When I was introduced to them at the training ground I was pleasantly surprised at the quality of players that were there. Chris Kamara, Terry Hurlock, Bob Booker, Terry Bullivant, Gary Roberts, Danis Salman and Francis Joseph are several that immediately spring to mind.

The whole atmosphere was different from the Colchester dressing room. Players travelled in from far and wide and there was a certain 'London' feel about the whole club that is hard to describe. Perhaps it's like comparing driving around the leafy lanes of the countryside with the hectic pace of driving around Piccadilly Circus.

The atmospheres in the two dressing rooms were that far apart! However, I needed to adjust to this pretty quickly if I was going to establish myself in the team and in the dressing room.

Most of the squad were from the south so I was an outsider to a degree. For some reason I think I was perceived as a bit slow on the uptake or even naive to the realities of certain things by a few of the players. I was happy for them to think that way to start with as it suited me. The reality was that I had played more League games than most of them - around 400+ by then. As I have already mentioned, I had also had a grammar school education. This didn't mean I knew 'the score', of course, but I had been through a fair amount in the football environment, seeing and learning about most eventualities. My perception of them was that they thought London was the centre of the universe and anything outside of that was definitely second best or behind the times. The fact that I came from 'up north' was a big deciding factor in their assessment. We all must have flat caps and ferrets, of course! There was often friendly banter on this subject between us.

I pointed out that you didn't often hear a southern accent in the dressing room of a northern club, and yet there seemed to be quite a few northern boys with their feet under the table down south. I commented that southern lads didn't like to get out of their comfort zone to ply their trade, whereas 'the ferret boys' would go anywhere to earn a crust. Their retort would be that up there the money was crap, the weather was shit and the people weren't the brightest! This was the eighties and not the forties, but even with a very large tongue in one's cheek there was a certain amount of truth in their comments as far as they were concerned. They did love their city and rightly so.

I wanted to demonstrate to them that I wasn't just there to provide some northern grit on the pitch and that there was much more to me than that. I intended to show them another side to us northern 'Lowry boys'.

Brentford wasn't Frank's first managerial position as he had previously been at Leicester. The Doc had plenty of experience in management and so I felt confident that we could be successful. The squad was made up of many talented individuals but the obvious question was whether the management team could mould a successful side from them.

First impressions are very important and mine were positive. However, within a few weeks I had some concerns regarding the relationship between the players and the management. The dressing room didn't seem to be totally as one. There are always little cliques or factions in a squad, but if you're going to get results on a regular basis you need all or most of the players to believe in what the management are trying to do. I felt that there were, perhaps, too many chiefs and not enough Indians, to coin a very old phrase. Some of the lads had been at the club for a few years and some, like myself, were quite recent signings.

Brentford was constantly in the shadow of much bigger clubs in London. One of the nearest, QPR, had plenty of success in the seventies and early eighties while Brentford had definitely underachieved for some years. But the fan base was worthy of a division higher for starters and, although the ground wasn't state of the art, it was still much better than most clubs in the lower divisions.

The chairman, Martin Lange, was a nice man who made me feel very welcome. My impression of him was that he tried to run the club correctly and do the right thing by people. I didn't get to know him that well, as I wasn't at the club long enough. He seemed to have a soft exterior, though how tough he was underneath wasn't apparent to me.

Playing for Colchester United had been a great experience. There is always a certain amount of pressure playing for any club, but I felt more pressure playing for Brentford. Perhaps it was the simple fact that there was a bigger audience generally in London! However, I coped with it very well and relished the new challenge. I did a good job for Frank and Doc.

Although I was only there for a couple of seasons and the squad didn't change that much, there were still a few comings and goings. The players were a very talented bunch, as I have already mentioned. One of them who was definitely a 'character' was the talented Terry Hurlock. His reputation as a tough player went before him. He was known for the wrong reasons, in my opinion, as he was perceived as a thuggish midfield player by many opposing supporters. Tel could certainly look after himself on and off the pitch, but people seemed to overlook his footballing ability. He was a great passer of the ball as well as being an excellent ball winner. When I played at centre back behind him, he was one of the best at regaining possession in front of the defence. He used to scare the living daylights out of some centre forwards who drifted off me into midfield with the ball. Tel would snap at them like a Rottweiler off the lead! I got on well with Terry and he treated me with respect.

One day in training, we were practising defensive corners when I headed one clear and Terry said, "Bloody hell, Wig, you should wear a boot on your head, you can head it as far as I can kick it!" I took that as a compliment coming from him. Terry was never at the front in the running sessions that we did but he was physically very strong.

We sometimes used to go up to Richmond Park in the club minibus, which was driven by Frank or Doc. On one occasion we were stuck in the London traffic as usual and Frank tried to manoeuvre the bus through a small gap between two cars. It didn't go well and we caused a bit more of a hold-up! As quick as a flash one of the drivers in the melee shouted out to Frank, "You were a better player than you are a bloody driver, Frank!" The lads wet themselves and Frank's reaction made us worse as he threatened to get out and chin the bloke – superb! We got there eventually and I think that the boss was still muttering under his breath about the punter who'd given him some stick!

If there hadn't been a little levity on that journey we would probably have travelled in almost deathly silence, as on previous occasions. The reason for this was that we all dreaded what was in store for us at the Park!

After a lengthy warm-up consisting of a couple of miles cross-country running, we would be put into small groups. Their aim would be to try to put lads of a similar pace together. Needless to say, I was one of the oldest but always seemed to be placed in the quick group. I still had decent pace and stamina but this was a killer! The remit was quite straightforward. We had to run up a 25-metre hill at full pace and get to the top within a specified time. The hill was a hell of a gradient; in fact, if you were out for a walk in the park and decided to go up this bank you would need to do it on your hands and knees to give yourself a bit more leverage. The Doc loved it, the little git! He would be at the top with his stopwatch barking orders out in his Scottish drawl, although mostly supportive and encouraging. There was nowhere to hide in this session. You were definitely out of your comfort zone. Terry used to say, "Wig, if you're going to be bad stay away from me or you will set me off!" What he meant was that if I was going to spew I should make sure it was nowhere near him!

On this particular morning there seemed to be more repetitions than usual, about eight as I recall! These would have been straight off again after just a short jog back down the slope as you rest. I was always a committed trainer and tried to do most things flat out if required. By the seventh 'rep' my head was starting to go and I knew what was coming. As I jogged (staggered!) down the hill for the final run, I began to retch a little but was determined to finish. We were the last group and so all the other lads were floundering around at the top. I could see Terry on all fours looking down at us. We set off and I gave it everything, virtually falling over the finishing line. Straight away I knelt down and started to spew up. Terry was right next to me and he whimpered, "No, get away," as he was struggling to hold back his own vomit! "F****** hell! No, Wiggy, you f*****!

I can't remember the next few seconds, but I can remember reeling about in the autumn leaves by one of the big trees on the brow of the hill. When you have sessions like those it's every man for himself and if you're bad you usually just want to be left alone to die in peace! As I was hoovering the leaves with my face, I was interrupted by a small dog licking my ear, with an old lady on the end of its lead. She asked, "Are you alright, young man?" With spit and sick dribbling out of my mouth I managed to mutter, "Yes thanks," but I don't think it came out like that somehow. God knows what she thought I was doing!

After a while we all sloped back into the minibus. There was no cool down or anything. This was the eighties and there was nothing as high tech as that! Mind you, I was just glad that it was over. I promised Tel that I wouldn't spew in the bus on the way back so long as he didn't fart!

I only played with Terry for just over a season before his £90,000 transfer to Reading. It was a bit of a surprise when he left us, as he appeared to be an integral part of the club, especially as he lived right next to Griffin Park. The move proved right for him, however, as he went on to do very well for himself. He even graced the Scottish Premier Division with Rangers, which only confirmed what I said earlier about his abilities as a player.

My first season at Brentford in 1984/85 was an eventful one. It started on a negative note for me as I picked up an injury in one of our pre-season friendlies. This prevented me from playing in the first four League games. This was rare for me. Maybe I was trying to impress too much and so put myself in situations that I wouldn't normally do. Once I got going, however, I settled in fine and felt comfortable with the situation, although I wasn't totally happy until my family joined me in our new home around the middle of November.

That season was special for many Brentford supporters, as we found ourselves at Wembley in the Freight Rover Trophy final. Our League form had been up and down but in the Trophy we played very well. The two games that stick in my mind (excluding the final, of course!) are the semi-final against Bournemouth away and the area final against Newport at home.

The Bournemouth game was great for the supporters, as some good football was played and five goals were scored. However, from a manager's or coach's point of view it was quite different. Goals from Robbie Cooke and Chris Kamara (Kammy) put us two up and totally in charge only for Bournemouth to pull back two goals. The game itself was quite physical and I ended up with the headache to end all headaches, firstly having clashed with Kammy when defending the edge of our box. I blamed him for that as he was always trying to do other people's jobs on the pitch, not in a bad way but more the actions of an enthusiastic 'jack of all trades'. He would try to win every tackle on the ground and every ball in the air! Unfortunately, on this occasion, my head got in the way.

I saw stars for the second time when late in the game their wide lad had whipped in a near-post cross. Their centre forward and I threw ourselves at the ball, but he got there a fraction before me and I headbutted him full on the side of the head. As I lay on the deck, our goalkeeper Gary Phillips (Stig) looked at me and said, "Any danger of you getting tight?" He had just pulled off a great save from the header and was showing me no sympathy. Incidentally, their centre forward was carried off on a stretcher unconscious, so I was the lucky one with just two golf-ball-sized lumps on my bonce!

Having already received no sympathy from Stig, there was also no compassion from Terry Hurlock either. He just quipped, "Get yourself up, it's only your head!"

When they scored their equaliser it probably looked odds-on for them to go on and win the game, but almost straight from our kick-off Robbie Cooke nicked another goal to put us 3-2 up. Then it was all hands to the pumps and hang on in there for the win!

Apart from the headache, I really enjoyed the competitiveness of the game, which suited me down to the ground. The fact that we had a great chance of playing at Wembley in the final never really came into my mind until we were on the bus home after the game. The forthcoming home game against Newport was something to look forward to, with the possibility of a big crowd. What a chance!

We took that chance and ripped them apart 6-0. It was unbelievable. Everything went right for us and it turned out to be a memorable evening. We had made it and Wigan were going to be our opponents. We were super-confident and were looking forward to the big day.

Then a strange decision was made and I'm not sure of the reason. The club took the whole squad away to Corfu a week or so before the final. It was a great gesture and we were obviously looking forward to the break. In my own mind, however, I could hear the alarm bells ringing. We had just won a magnificent area final at Griffin Park and we were flying, but I thought perhaps we needed to have our feet kept a little nearer to the ground.

Anyway, the trip went ahead and it was a great laugh. There were some training sessions while we were out there, of course, but I didn't feel it was the best preparation for the squad as a whole. I enjoyed myself as much as anyone, but I was never a big drinker and tried to be sensible. Some of the lads really let themselves go - and why not? After all, it was supposed to be a break for the chaps and some of them were unlikely to play in the final in any event.

The training sessions were planned for late afternoon or early evening when it was a little cooler, although it was still in the seventies. We couldn't do a great deal, as the facilities weren't that good. I had a very slight calf muscle strain, so I usually went for a straight run with one of the other lads who had a problem twisting and turning in a normal session. The whole trip was conducted in quite a relaxed way, with the players expected to act professionally. However, this wasn't quite the case at one of the sessions.

The lads arrived at the venue before Frank and the Doc. Jamie Murray, our left back who had come from Cambridge United, turned up wearing a massive sombrero with a brim wider than his shoulders and looking a little glazed around the eyes. Everyone appeared to be okay and in good spirits, but Jamie seemed to be a little happier! I thought that he was just messing about and would ditch the hat when the management arrived. I was wrong. He still had it on as we started the warm-up. Doc knew Jamie from when he was the manager at Cambridge, so I was surprised that Jamie had taken the liberty really. Frank and Doc saw the funny side at first, but that soon wore off when they realised that Jamie seemed bent on wearing the hat throughout the session.

We were knocking the ball about between us and Jamie was pretty lively with his sombrero bouncing about as they do!

Frank's voice changed suddenly. "JAMIE, GIVE ME THE BALL!"

Frank wanted to start the session properly and Jamie was dribbling the ball all over the place.

Frank shouted again. "JAMIE, GIVE IT TO ME!"

After what seemed like a minute or so, Jamie succumbed and passed the ball pretty firmly to Frank from about 20 yards away. All the players were trying to stifle their laughter at Jamie's antics, as Frank got more annoyed. As the ball arrived at his feet, Frank attempted to control it but for some unknown reason it bobbled under his foot and it rolled another 30 yards or so further on. Well, the lads just lost it and we had to turn away. How embarrassing for the boss! Frank ran after the ball, picked it up, ran back and with a face like thunder tore Jamie off a strip!

This kind of behaviour was out of character for Jamie. Why he decided to turn up a bit worse for wear on this occasion I don't know. Maybe it was just the heat that had got to him, or maybe he'd just had a drink or two!

Another funny occurrence on the trip involved my good mate Stig (Gary Phillips). He was as mad as a hatter - another one of the 'daft as a brush' goalkeeping fraternity! We nicknamed him Stig after the character from the book and TV series Stig of the Dump. He looked just like him so it stuck! Gary had not long joined us from Barnet but he had established himself in the side and was doing well. His kicking was some of the best I had seen in a keeper, and even though he wasn't the tallest I was always very confident when playing in front of him.

We used to go to a small bar just down the road from where we were staying in Corfu. Gary being Gary, he got to know the barman quite well and the usual banter and messing about went on. We'd gone out of season so there weren't many other people about, meaning that most evenings we had the bar to ourselves. There was usually a huge basket of fruit on the bar from which customers were invited to help themselves. To all the players this 'bowl' was mainly for display purposes, but for some reason Stig decided to select a large pineapple from the arrangement. It was a whole fresh pineapple and completely intact. He tossed it to me from about six feet away and said, "Catch, Wig." I caught it and then he said, "Shall we play American Football with it?" I threw it back to him and he took off across the bar with the pineapple in his hands. He dived over a low wall enclosing the area while shouting "TOUCH DOWN" and then disappeared from view as he lay flat out.

A few seconds later he slowly stood up with a strange look on his face. I walked over to him and saw that he was clutching one of his hands in the other tightly. I asked him what the hell had he done. He slowly opened his hand and there was blood gushing everywhere. He had gashed the palm of his hand deeply with one of the spines on the pineapple on 'touch down'.

After the initial concern about the injury, the reality kicked in for us both: we had a Cup final in a week's time, he was our goalkeeper, and he'd just cut his hand to the bone in a bar room prank! Stig was a tough old boot, though. The wound was stitched and he just had a strapping over it underneath his glove for the big match. It didn't affect his performance at all; in fact he did very well in the game. What a noodle, eh?

Robbie Cooke, another ex-Cambridge United lad, had scored quite a few goals for us that season. He was another of those natural finishers who always came up with the goods at every club he played for. Cookie wasn't a drinker as far as I knew, but one night he seemed to get drawn into a session with Terry Bullivant (Bully) and a couple of the others.

Terry was a very good footballer and pretty shrewd with it. He tipped me the wink when it started to look a bit dodgy for me just before I left to go to Aldershot. Terry went on to coach and manage at a good level as well as gaining his knowledge as a London cabbie.

Returning to Cookies' little session, at the point when he was downing shots of Tequila with the other lads I left the bar, so I wasn't privy to the rest of the tale first-hand. However, I saw him later that evening 'fast asleep' shall we say by the side of the road. The lads later told me that they had returned him to his room safe and sound!

I saw the state of him the next day. Cookie was very fair-skinned and some of the boys used to rib him about the suncream he used to put on, asking him if they could borrow his Factor 75! Or they would ask him if he had a tan or whether his freckles had simply joined up! Anyway, when he came down to the beach that morning his face looked like a crumpled-up grey paper bag. What a mess he was in! He must have felt like shit! In contrast the other chaps, including Bully, looked quite chipper and reasonably fresh.

What they had done to poor Cookie I don't know. Maybe he just wasn't up to stomaching the Tequila or maybe he was downing pints of the stuff as opposed to the shots they were drinking. Who knows? However, he did well in the final and scored our goal. The last time I spoke to Robbie he had joined up with David Moyes at Everton. They played together at Cambridge and are good mates.

The trip itself was successful in so far as there was no trouble. It was good for team spirit and a great laugh. As I have already said, I wasn't convinced that it was the correct preparation at that time and it is still a point of conjecture in my opinion. I am not criticising Frank or John, as I don't know the full circumstances surrounding their decision to organise that trip and hindsight is a wonderful thing. However, I knew that if ever I went into management I would not be taking players away before big games.

The big day arrived and, as is par for the course, it was absolutely boiling! It was one of the hottest days of the year. I was really looking forward to the whole experience. Anne and the boys as well as several other members of our family came down for the game. Even my father-in-law, Tom, who has sadly since passed away, made the trip from North Wales to Wembley.

Everyone in the squad looked very smart in their dark jackets and grey trousers. I tried to take in as much of the atmosphere as possible. It wasn't an FA Cup final or anything as grand as that, but it was still a tremendous occasion and an achievement to be proud of. I'm sure if anyone were to ask Frank McLintock how he felt on the day he would say that he was just as proud then as he was when he stepped out at Wembley as a player with Arsenal. A manager's feelings about such an achievement are different to a player's, as I would experience for myself on a couple of occasions in the future.

I enjoyed every minute of the preparation for the game. I wasn't particularly nervous because I felt that the day was a massive bonus for me and I was confident that I wouldn't let anyone down, including myself. I also had confidence in the players who had been lucky enough to be selected for such a big game. Even though we had been away and had let our hair down a little, I still thought that we had enough ability in the squad to beat Wigan.

There was one player in the squad who had the right to be nervous with such a big game approaching and that was Keith Millen. He was a young 18-year-old centre back and he played alongside me. Whereas I was in the autumn of my career, you might say, he was definitely in the early spring of his! Keith was quite slim for a defender but he was a brave lad and a quick learner. He read the game well and conquered the problem of inconsistency that can plague young players. He made a lot more good decisions than bad ones, giving him the chance to become a good defender. He is a genuine lad with a very supportive family. He went on to have an excellent career and the last I heard he had a coaching roll at Bristol City.

At any new club you join, you always come across one player who appears to 'know everyone'. From the man on the gate to the chairman, they seem to be on first name terms! Danis Salman, our right back, was that player at Brentford. He was a very nice, amiable bloke who had time for everybody. Danis was unbelievable at times and he would drive some of the lads mad, as he would pick up little injuries and as a result missed quite a lot of the training sessions, especially in pre-season. He could miss a week or so with a strain or some other minor ailment and yet still be at the front in the running exercises on his first day back. The boys would give him some stick as he left them in his wake! Danis was very much what I would call a 'confidence player'. If things were going well for him, then he was as good as anyone. If he made a mistake that gave the team a problem, then he could quickly retreat into his shell and would struggle to regain his confidence. However, that was Danis and I had a lot of time for him, as did many people in and around the club.

Vying for the right back position was Bobby Fisher, the ex-Leighton Orient player. 'Fish' was a good technical player with a good laid-back way about him. Nothing appeared to fluster him on or off the pitch. I once said to Fish in training, "I've never seen you with a real sweat on." "A sweat on? Why would I want a sweat on?" he replied. He then just strolled off back into the session at his own pace but with an air of quality about him! On our break in Corfu, Fish would be the one with his earphones on listening to soul music or similar while reading a good book, whereas most of the other lads would be jumping about in the pool or the sea like lunatics! He was a real laid-back Mr Cool!

One freezing cold night when the team was away at Rotherham, Fish was playing at right back and I was alongside him at centre back. The pitch was half frozen, as there were areas that the sun hadn't been able to reach due to the shadow cast by the stand. The other half of the pitch was quite soft but unfortunately there was a covering of snow, in some places a few inches deep. Under today's guidelines the game simply wouldn't have gone ahead. Most of the players were wearing studded boots to grip the softer areas of the pitch. Unfortunately, the frozen parts were impossible to see, so players were going down all over the place! It was a farce and almost comical to watch and yet quite dangerous to take part in!

Fish was wearing two undershirts as well as his team shirt. He'd also donned a pair of big black woollen gloves and, with his socks pulled up as far as they would go, he didn't exactly strike fear into the opposition's forwards! Poor Fish really did feel the cold quite easily and was always complaining about it; in fact he hated it. His slightly Afro hairdo also appeared to have a top layer of frost on it, so Bobby was not happy!

At one point in the game, three or four of us chased the ball into the corner of the pitch and one by one we all went down. It was just like a slapstick comedy! The ball trickled out of play. Fish came across to me as I got up, laughing his head off, and said, "Wigs, what are we doing here? What am I doing here? This is a farce!" He jogged off, shaking his head, and continued to make dry comments about the game as he played on. Bobby was never really in love with the game, so I think that trips such as these may finally have cast doubts over whether he would continue to carry on as a pro at that level. Fish is still a good friend and he did some work for me at Colchester United and Southend United when I went into management. I shall mention his contribution in more depth later on.

Chris Kamara was quite a strong character and had a certain ruthlessness about him when he needed it. I remember during one training session he went right through me in a tackle. I wasn't best pleased considering it was my first full session in a month because of a groin injury! Kammy just shrugged his shoulders and grinned. Ten years earlier I would probably have waited and then hit him with my 'tool bag' and everything in the next tackle! However, experience had taught me just to count for a little longer and not take it too personally!

Kammy and I got on well and actually roomed together for a while. He had been at Brentford for a time and was a fixture in the side. From what I'd seen there wasn't a better pairing in central midfield throughout the division than Kamara and Hurlock. Kammy left for Swindon after my first full season in 1984/85. He was travelling in from his hometown of Swindon every day and so it was a good move geographically for him. Chris went on to do well for himself in football. He even dabbled in management at Bradford and later on he went into media work with Sky TV. When I took over at Southend United as manager Chris sent me a fax welcoming me back into the game and wishing me good luck. I was pleased to receive it, as I hadn't seen him for a few years.

I am sure that all of us were looking forward to the day ahead at Wembley and we were ready to digest as much of it as possible. It was my first appearance at the home of British football, as it was for most if not all the other players. Even though I wasn't feeling nervous as such, I didn't know how I would feel when I actually walked into the dressing room of the famous venue!

The lads were reasonably lively on the bus ride to the stadium, with plenty of banter, but there was certainly no feeling of overconfidence. We had murdered Newport in the area final and had beaten Wigan in the League at our place. We had also drawn 1-1 at Wigan, so we felt that we had the measure of them. However, this was a Cup final and, as everyone knows, anything can happen!

We piled into the dressing room and in a strange way it went a little quiet. Maybe the reality of the situation had kicked in, I'm not sure, but there was a definite change in the atmosphere. Personally, I was just trying to imagine all the famous players who had changed there. Before we got our kit on for the game we walked down the tunnel to take a look at the pitch. I could only imagine how the England players must have felt as they walked out for the World Cup final back in 1966. The atmosphere must have been electric. I was 12 years old then and watched the match on the family's black and white telly back in Liverpool, dreaming of course of walking down the same tunnel!

As I walked out into the baking sunshine, the stadium appeared much smaller and more compact than I had imagined. Even though most of the fans hadn't arrived, with probably only about 10,000 supporters already in their seats at this point, there was still a unique and mesmerising atmosphere about the arena. The players wandered over to the side where most of the Brentford supporters were located. To my surprise and delight, Anne and our two sons, Thomas and Jack, together with Anne's dad, Tom, had made their way from the stands down to pitch level and so we all had a chat, which was a real bonus!

The heat down on the pitch was stifling. There was no wind and the temperature was in the high eighties. As a result we didn't stay out too long, but by the time I returned to the dressing room my shirt was still completely soaked with sweat. I did start to wonder to myself whether I was fit enough to cope with such temperatures. In fact I hoped that all the lads were!

When we got changed for the game I noticed that some of the boys didn't follow their usual routine; nothing dramatically different, just little idiosyncrasies. The occasion had got to a few of the lads already but this was bound to happen. Doc appeared to be a little more relaxed than Frank. Both were confident and tried to project that to the players. This was also a great day for them and so I shook the two of them by the hand just before we went out and wished them good luck!

We lined up with the Wigan lads in the tunnel prior to going out onto the pitch. When we played League matches the players very rarely stood alongside one another in this way. We didn't look each other in the eye directly as we stood waiting for the go-ahead to walk out of the tunnel. A few shook hands briefly because they knew each other, mainly as they had been opponents before. I spoke briefly to Roy Tunks their goalkeeper, whom I knew from his Preston days with my old mate Mick Elwiss. Then we got the okay from the official and Frank led us out into the sunshine.

The noise was something special! The walk from the tunnel exit to the halfway line in front of the royal box in the main stand was indescribable. The hairs on my neck most definitely were standing up! I felt a great deal of pride for myself and for my family. I am aware that this may sound rather soppy and it wasn't a World Cup final, but who cares? There aren't many people on this planet that get to walk that walk and I was one of the privileged few. I loved it!

We lined up alongside the halfway line as usual. I glanced up at the stands and was lucky enough to catch a glimpse of Anne and the boys again. So I gave them my usual pre-match wave, but this time I felt a bit of a lump in my throat. I thought: bloody hell, I'm going to blub here if I don't watch it and we haven't even kicked off yet!

Fortunately I regained my composure as we were introduced to the dignitaries and the guest of honour, Watford chairman Elton John. Then, formalities over, we kicked off!

For whatever reason, Wigan were able to get into gear more quickly than us. We were 1-0 down and I don't think that I'd touched the ball. We went 2-0 down before half-time and were left with a mountain to climb in the second half. I felt that I'd been doing okay as an individual and I'd had a good battle with young Mike Newell who was playing up front. They had an experienced side and made it very difficult for us to get any sort of grip on the play. I can't say that I enjoyed the match as such. We had to chase the game for a great deal of the time after they scored. The heat was horrendous to play in, and even though the pitch was like a bowling green the groundsmen hadn't watered it so the surface was rock solid.

We were glad to get in at half-time and hopefully sort out a few problems. Most of the lads were in a state of shock. We hadn't performed. We were having to chase the game after going 2-0 down and, if you look back at the statistics, I don't think many teams have come back from 2-0 down at Wembley to win the game! Frank and Doc tried their best to get our heads up, as some of the boys were struggling not just psychologically but also physically because of the heat. The main theme of their advice was to remain positive, as we had nothing to lose.

We went out for the second half and, to be fair to our supporters, they really got behind us. They realised that we were struggling and just wanted us to give them some hope. We did just that in our first decent attack of the half when Cookie volleyed one in to make the score 2-1. The crowd went mad! It was short-lived, however, as they went down the other end within minutes to score a spectacular third.

There was still enough time left to get back into the game, but realistically that was that. We huffed and puffed and gave everything we had, but they just played the game out and were the worthy winners.

It was a horrible feeling at the final whistle, especially having to watch them celebrate with their supporters. I was a bit bruised, battered and absolutely drained physically, but I was reasonably pleased with my contribution. It didn't really matter how I felt, though. In the end we had lost a Cup final that on paper we should have won. We did the customary lap of honour and our supporters were fantastic. I'm sure that they had a great day, although I'm also certain that they would have had a much better one had we won!

The whole occasion was a terrific experience and it had been a once in a lifetime achievement just to get to Wembley. The competitive nature of the players involved was such that I'm sure everyone in the squad that day felt a tinge of sadness simply because we had lost the game. There is still a difference between a fantastic day and a perfect one, and we didn't quite achieve perfection that day! After the match we had a great evening get-together at a hotel. All the wives and girlfriends stayed overnight and a good time was had by all.

It had been a good first season for me, culminating with my Wembley appearance, and prospects looked good for the coming season. Even though I had a steady run in the side before the final, I had still picked up more injuries than I would have liked. However, I was lucky compared with my old mate Francis Joseph (Joe). Joe had broken his leg against Wigan and missed the whole season including our final, ironically against Wigan! It was a big loss for us when Joe got injured, as he was a real threat up front for the team. He was a quick, strong player and could score goals as well.

I remember the moment when Joe snapped his leg on a previous occasion during my first season. He'd gone to volley a ball on the edge of the opposition's box when the big centre back, Walsh, put his foot up to block the shot. Joe didn't appear to see him coming and just followed through with the volley, connecting with the centre back's boot. Joe went down in a heap and I knew straight away that he was badly hurt. The break was so bad that he had to have a nail inserted into the whole length of his tibia (shin bone).

Joe was out for over a year after that and to be quite honest he never really regained the sharpness or the form that he had shown before his bad luck.

His younger brother Roger came on trial as a centre forward originally but somehow ended up playing at right back. He was a lightning quick player and, even though he was limited technically, he made a very accomplished defender. Roger went on to play for Wimbledon and did very well.

Remembering the Joseph brothers brings to mind the occasion of Danis Salman's wedding. Danis held his reception in the main bar at Griffin Park, which was not unusual as it was available for private hire. Almost all of the lads and their partners were there and we had a good do. As Danis was a Turkish Cypriot, the food was a little different but still fantastic. There was a free bar for the evening and most people took full advantage of it shall we say. Even the single boys turned up despite weddings probably not being their thing, which was another testament to Danis's popularity. The proceedings even included a traditional belly dancer, which went down extremely well as you can imagine! The Doc turned up to wish the couple well and was on good form too.

Anne and I were enjoying the evening and were standing at the bar near Terry Hurlock and a mate of his. Joe was talking to them and all seemed fine. Then, in a split second, Terry's mate appeared to poke Joe right in the eye, which Joe didn't take too lightly! The pair started to grapple with each other and immediately the whole atmosphere changed. Terry tried to intervene and get between the two but they were having none of it! A few other people got involved and it all turned into a bit of a bun fight.

Doc came over to Anne and asked what the hell was going on. On hearing the answer he was determined to put a stop to the fracas. He turned towards the bundle and then seemed to get 'hoovered up' into the melee! Anne and I stood and watched, more in shock than fear or anything else. What I can remember, though, is Doc disappearing over tables and chairs, being dragged in the horizontal position about six feet up in the air! The last glimpse we got of him was the soles of his feet melting into oblivion! It was a wedding, for God's sake, and it was a shame that the rumpus had broken out at all. However, I must admit that Anne and I couldn't stifle our mirth at poor old Doc's Superman impression. Fortunately the bride and groom had already left, along with many of the guests, so it hadn't spoilt the day for them.

Eventually Doc emerged largely unscathed, with just a dishevelled-looking appearance. As he walked over to us he was straightening his collar and tie, which had somehow been wrenched around the side of his neck. "Time to go, Stevie boy, I think," he uttered in his broad Scottish accent, and then he was gone!

The problem spilled into the street between Joe and this geezer. I don't know to this day who he was or what the scuffle was about, but we all decided it was time to leave. As we went outside we could hear the distant sound of police sirens, so somebody must have called the Old Bill. Joe's brothers turned up to sort out the problem for him so we left sharpish. I'm not sure if Danis found out about this little altercation and it was never discussed later on. Funny about the Doc though!

Another player who joined the club around the same time as me was Rowan Alexander. Rowan was a centre forward from Scotland for whom Frank paid a transfer fee of about £25,000. This was a bit of a gamble for a lad who hadn't played at Brentford's level before. He reminded me of David Speedie in terms of his abilities in the air considering his size. I think that the whole move for him and his wife was a real culture shock. Coming to a London club at any level can be difficult for most players and even more so perhaps for a player from the Scottish League. Rowan was a wholehearted lad but didn't score as many goals as he would've liked, which is obviously a problem for any centre forward. I didn't really get to know him very well; in fact I don't think many of the lads did. I was very surprised just recently when I read that he was the manager at Gretna in Scotland. He did a great job there, gaining a couple of promotions. To be honest he appeared to me to be one of the last players in that dressing room who would go into management, but what do I know?

One player that I really liked was Bob Booker. Bob was definitely a part of the furniture when I arrived. He was used to playing in a few different positions and was what you might call a utility player. This went against him in some ways, as he would fill in when someone was injured, either up front or midfield. For me, Bob had more promise than he was showing and he looked like a lad that needed to move to another club to fulfil that potential. And that is exactly what happened, as eventually he moved to Sheffield United and performed superbly. He played consistently at a higher level for some time, which surprised a few others but not me. He has also stayed in the game in a coaching capacity and most recently I heard that he was the assistant manager at Brighton.

Frank also brought in two players from the Army: midfielder George Torrence and centre forward Steve Butler. George was an industrious midfielder with fantastic fitness levels, and Steve was an athletic lad who could look top quality one minute but appear to be very average in ability the next. They both found the transition from Army to League football quite difficult. George settled in a little quicker and played more games, while Steve played very well in some pre-season games but couldn't produce the goods on a regular basis. Both of them dropped back down a level after a couple of seasons. Steve came back very strong and played in the League again at Watford and other clubs, whereas George went into business.

I had settled into the team and in my second season I was playing well and feeling fit. At the end of November 1985 we travelled up to York City. York were doing very well, just as we were. Both teams were in the top seven of the division and only one point separated us.

The weather was freezing and it had been snowing in Yorkshire. The London boys were not happy when they saw the state of the pitch, as there was an inch or so of snow covering the surface. One positive point was that it was soft underneath, which made it just about playable. York had two lads up front who had scored 23 goals between them already and it was only four months into the season. Keith Walwyn had bagged 15 of them. He was a real handful at about 6 feet 3 inches tall and weighing 15 stone. I had played against him before and usually needed plenty of ice packs for my battered body afterwards! He wasn't a 'dirty' player at all, just big and strong and very committed.

The game, as you can imagine, was far from a classic because of the conditions, but with the likes of Terry Hurlock, me and big Terry Evans, who was playing alongside me, it was always going to be quite a physical game. We more than held our own throughout the first half and started the second half strongly. Terry and I were shackling Dale Banton and Keith Walwyn well, so it looked as though we were heading for a clean sheet. Not many teams would manage that at Bootham Crescent that season.

Late in the second half a loose ball dropped in midfield between Walwyn and me. Most centre forwards would try just to nick the ball as the defender flew into the tackle, but not Keith. He competed for every ball with anybody. It was a 50:50 ball so we both launched into the challenge. Unfortunately for me, my back foot slipped on the dodgy surface and I arrived a little too early on the ball. His momentum and his weight carried him through the ball and my leg, which bent back the wrong way, opening up the knee joint. I knew the second we made contact that I was in trouble and the initial pain was bad. I lay there in a heap waiting for the pain to go as the physio ran on. When I got to my feet, I knew that I couldn't carry on. My knee felt totally unstable. Terry Hurlock came over and geed me up, saying, "You ain't going off ,Wigs, you're okay." I tried to run about but it was a waste of time. There wasn't long to go but I was just a passenger so I went off. York scored in the dying minutes to beat us 1-0. I felt guilty in a strange sort of way for bailing out. It was rare for me to come off in a game. I'd been sent off in a few matches but that's a different story.

In the event, the injury kept me out until February, as I had torn my right medial ligament. This is the ligament on the inside of your knee that helps to stabilise the joint. It was the longest that I had ever been out due to injury in 500 or so appearances.

Sod's Law was such that I returned to the side playing away at Rotherham (Bobby Fisher's favourite place) on 1 March and then away to Swansea the following Saturday.

Within a few minutes of the start of the Swansea game, I was defending a corner when someone jumped for the ball and came right over the top of me, trapping me underneath. My left knee was locked and the weight of the player on me caused it to rotate! I felt it grind with a very sharp pain. The pain disappeared quite quickly and so I just carried on playing and didn't think too much about it. I completed the game, which unfortunately we lost, but I felt okay. As I was sat in the dressing room listening to Frank giving us a bit of a rollicking, I could feel my knee stiffening up. By the time I had finished showering, my knee was a completely different shape. It had swollen dramatically and I could hardly get my tracksuit bottoms on. After being out for so long with my previous injury, I felt gutted! Any player will tell you that rehabilitation involves a lot of hard work in the gym, etc. I had visions of another lengthy lay-off.

I went to see a specialist in London and his diagnosis was that I had torn the cartilage in my knee joint. This was another first for me on the injury front. He said that I could have surgery straight away but this would mean that I would miss the rest of the season. The alternative was to play on with reduced training and have the procedure in the following close season. Frank asked me to carry on playing for him, which is what I agreed to do, and I saw the season out as the captain of the team because of the departure of Terry Hurlock.

It was great to be named as skipper, so I wanted to be a playing captain and not one who was sat in the stand with a knee brace on. Playing on definitely didn't do my injury any good, but when I finally did have the operation everything went okay and the surgeon was quite pleased with his work. What he did add, though, was that I had also partially torn my cruciate ligament (this also stabilises the joint). He felt that with constant exercises my knee would be fine and that it was up to me to put in the necessary work.

Earlier I mentioned Terry Evans and his role in the York game briefly. Terry was a big 6 feet 4 inches centre back whom Frank had brought in from the non-League. He was very raw but physically strong and he had a great attitude. He saw this opportunity at Brentford as his big chance to prove himself in the Football League. Terry did just that, but not without a massive setback.

We were playing a friendly at Bisham Abbey on the AstroTurf. Terry went to make a tackle but caught his toe on the plastic surface and ruptured the cruciate ligament of his right knee. He was out for months and that's how I got to know him quite well, as we did some of our rehab together in the gym. When we were both fit there were signs that we would've made a formidable partnership as twin centre backs. Unfortunately that did not happen for reasons that were beyond my control!

Close season came and went and I reported back for pre-season training. My rehab had gone well and the knee was almost back to full capacity. I wasn't at peak fitness but, given time, I felt that I could regain the form of the previous season and have a good campaign as the new skipper.

There had been a few changes in the squad. Andy Sinton, another of Doc's lads, had come in from Cambridge United. He cost £25,000 and was only 19 years old. Many people had questioned the move, especially as he had come as a central midfield player. He wasn't a Terry Hurlock or a Chris Kamara but he was a very talented player who needed nurturing. His best position was out wide and that is where he established himself as a very good player, culminating in his playing for England! So not a bad signing by Frank and Doc.

Years later, when I was on holiday with Anne, I met Andy walking along the front in Puerto Banus, Spain. We had lunch with him and his wife in one of the restaurants on the quay. Anne's brother, Philip, and his wife, Lynne, lived in Spain for some years in that area and on another visit in the same restaurant our paths crossed with Peter Shilton. We had a short chat with him. He was very grounded and respectful, which is typical of the older top players.

There are a couple of other players that were in the squad when I first went to Brentford that I would like to mention.

Keith Cassells, or 'Rosie' (after the tennis player), was a centre forward from Southampton. I had played against him when he was there and he was one of the nicest blokes that you could meet. Keith wasn't the biggest or the quickest, but he was a clever player and scored plenty of goals. He moved on to Mansfield and I heard that when he left the game he became a policeman.

A completely different character was Gary Roberts. A Welsh international, Gary was a good wide player with great skills. His nickname was 'Gaspin' because after every game he would always come into the bar and say, "I'm gaspin' for a drink"! An alcoholic drink, I might add! He could be as daft as a brush at times but was pretty good in the dressing room, especially when the banter was flying about. Gary had to retire prematurely through injury. He also went into the police force, which I thought would be the last job in the world that Gaspin would go for! I saw him recently when he was managing Cambridge City FC in between shifts.

Another Roberts at the club was Paul Roberts. Robbo was a real London boy and he used to travel right across London on the tube every day for training. I wouldn't dream of calling Robbo a spiv, but if you didn't know him personally you might!

He was almost hyperactive physically and verbally - loud and in your face! He could be an acquired taste but I got on okay with him. I think he was a little underrated as a player by a lot of people. I'm not certain what his best position was as he was a jack of all trades in midfield or at the back. He was a good competitor and definitely knew how to rub the opposition up the wrong way! In my opinion, if he had looked after himself better off the pitch he could have done even better for himself on the pitch.

Just recently Anne was on a trip to Newmarket Races and whom should she meet but Robbo. He hadn't changed a bit even though it was over 20 years since she had seen him - at the post-Wembley party. Paul is a London cabbie now, which I'm sure suits him down to the ground.

Ian Holloway moved to Brentford from Bristol Rovers, but we didn't play that much together. He was a real live wire on the pitch but didn't really settle and moved back to Bristol. From there he did very well for himself and he eventually went into management. He is well known for his eccentric manner, which comes as a bit of a surprise to me as he was reasonably quiet at Brentford. He has had some hard times in his private life and if anyone deserves success it's 'Hollers'.

A real old character, who was the physio when I first arrived at Griffin Park, was Eddie Lyons. He was of the 'old school' if you like. Whenever he met anyone he would shake them by the hand and nearly break every bone in their fingers! He had a grip like a vice and a heart of gold. When I had my bad knee injury he gave me 'frictions' on the ligament every day for weeks. It brought me out in a cold sweat and nearly drove me to tears. All it brought out in Eddie was a grin! Bless him!

The 1986/87 season was now under way and the Doc left to take over as the boss at Millwall. I think John was happier as manager. He went on to do well there over the next couple of seasons. And guess who was his assistant a year later? Frank McLintock. They reversed roles at the Den and it worked very well for a while.

Before his move to join Mr Docherty, Frank needed a new coach or assistant at Brentford and so he drafted in Terry Mancini, the ex-Arsenal player. They had played at Highbury and QPR together, so Frank knew him quite well. I liked the Doc and was sorry to see him go, but it wasn't a problem for me. I was looking forward to working with the new man, especially as he was a defender. I was still learning at 31 years old and looked forward to gaining further experience from him.

Unfortunately, it didn't quite work out like that. A few alarm bells rang in the old head after a couple of Terry's half-time talks. In one such talk he was brandishing a brush pole or something similar that he'd found in the dressing room. We hadn't performed in the first half and he was having his say before Frank gave his assessment. All of a sudden he 'appeared' to lose control. He smashed the pole down on the top of the physio table. Perhaps it was to get our attention. He was renowned for his bald head, even when he was a reasonably young player. On this occasion, his pate and face were crimson and his eyes were bulging out of his head! It was all a bit of a show and the lads spotted it straight away. I caught the eye of a couple of the experienced boys and they looked far from impressed with Terry's antics. You can't get away with much in a football dressing room, especially if there's a core of experienced players. They will see straight through you if you're not genuine and this was a case in question!

I was on my guard after that little rant. I wasn't sure now how to take him, so I just kept my head down in training and decided to see how things panned out. My initial suspicions were to be proved right within a few weeks.

We were training as usual and Terry was taking a session that involved pattern of play with the first team against the rest. The play started and our left fullback rolled the ball to me. I opened myself out and switched the ball with a firm pass to Andy Sinton wide on the right. The ball went straight to his feet but unfortunately he let it go under his foot and out of play. The coach, Terry, turned to me and had a right go about being sloppy and that I needed to show more quality. Andy tried to explain that it was down to him but Terry was having none of it. I responded by saying, "You what?" which wasn't like me but this was ridiculous. He just glared at me and we got on with the session. Experience had taught me that something wasn't right. A couple of days later Terry Bullivant pulled me and said, "Watch your back, Wigs." Bully was a very experienced player who had been at Aston Villa and he went on to manage and coach at a high level. He had also sussed the problem with Mancini and perhaps he had heard a whisper?

Within the week, one day I was sat at home with Anne and her mum, Joan, who had come to visit us from Wales, and the phone rang. It was Frank and he said, "Aldershot have made a bid for you and they would like to speak to you tomorrow."

I wasn't totally shocked but I was disappointed. I didn't even have a conversation with Frank, as there didn't seem to be any point. I just said, "Okay, what time do I meet them?" He told me and that was that.

I put down the telephone and turned to Anne and said, "It looks as if I'm on my way to Aldershot."

My mother-in-law was almost dumbstruck at how quickly things can change in football, but Anne just shrugged her shoulders and asked, "Can you travel or will we have to move again?"

I wasn't sure and told her that we would just have to wait and see how I got on the next day.

I tried to be as positive as I could in front of Anne and her mum, but deep down I was disappointed with the situation. I liked Frank and I know that he liked me. I also liked the club and felt that with a little luck we could have progressed that season. Terry obviously had different ideas and plans and I wasn't to be a part of them. That's the way football is, all about opinions!

I spoke to Frank a few weeks later and, reading between the lines, I think he'd had second thoughts about my departure but the decision had been made. Managers live or die by their decisions and I know that Frank didn't have a ready-made replacement for me, which I felt was a mistake at that time.

I enjoyed my time at Brentford. The club was definitely in the shadow of many other higher-placed London teams but I always felt that they were a bigger club than many of the clubs in their own division. Perhaps one of the reasons we underachieved in the League was the 'too many chiefs' theory that I mentioned earlier.

Frank was a nice man; maybe he was too nice. Doc was a little more ruthless in my opinion. Perhaps that's why they did so well together when they switched roles at Millwall.

Anne and I travelled down to Hampshire the day after the phone call from Frank. We met up with the manager, Lennie Walker, at the 'Rec'. It didn't take us long to make a decision and the deal was done and dusted within 24 hours. There was no point in any delay.

I wasn't wanted at Brentford and that was that!

CHAPTER 6

A SHOT AT THE FINISH

Len Walker didn't have to work too hard to convince me to sign for Aldershot, as the financial package was okay and the two-year deal definitely suited us at my age. It meant more security for the family, which was a major factor. The journey from west London, where we were living, to Hampshire wasn't too bad. We had done it in about 50 minutes that morning, so it was do-able, as they say! The travelling wasn't going to be ideal, obviously, but we had only been in our house for two years and our young boys had just settled into school. It was probably just as well that Anne and I had that clear run through on the M25 and M4 on the day we met Len, as we might have had second thoughts otherwise!

I was dropping down a division, which hadn't been on my agenda, but the way things had panned out at Brentford I just wanted to go to a club that wanted my services. I didn't know too much about Len's team before our meeting, but once he had given me a list of all the players in our squad I was surprised at the number of quality players he'd put together. I wasn't familiar with some of the names, but the likes of Andy King (ex-Everton), Bobby Barnes (ex-West Ham), Tommy Langley (ex-Chelsea) and Ian McDonald, who was one of the best left-footed midfielders in the division, were definitely known to me. Aldershot looked as though they were 'having a go' that season, as we say in football.

Another plus for me was that I would be reunited with their coach, Ian Gillard, who was an ex-QPR and England player. Gilly and I had met at an FA coaching course some years earlier when I was a Colchester player. I liked Ian's enthusiasm and commitment and had got on with him quite well over those two weeks. The manager, Len Walker, was a quiet man who spoke plainly and didn't try to bullshit anyone, which I liked.

Everything that we had discussed in the meeting sounded satisfactory and so we drove home in a positive frame of mind. I would be 32 within the week and the contract would take me past my 34th birthday. This wasn't a bad thing: 15 years as a pro already and still going strong. At that time the average length of a professional footballer's career was about seven years, so I was almost an antique in the game!

The knee problem that I had sustained at Brentford had settled, but if I am totally honest it was still giving me some concern, as I still had some swelling in the area and couldn't get full flexion of the joint. When I had the medical at Aldershot the doctor had pushed the knee into a fully flexed position, which was painful to say the least, but I just smiled and tried to ignore the agony. He didn't notice that my eyes almost popped out, as he was too busy looking down at the mechanics of the joint! He passed me with flying colours and said that I had the body of a 25-year-old. Perhaps he'd drunk a glass or two of sherry with his lunch that day!

I went straight into the side and felt very comfortable with the players around me. After a couple of games, my very quick assessment of the team was that we could do well if we steered clear of too many injuries to key players. I was playing alongside a young lad called Darren Anderson at centre back. He was a big strong player with good ability. Len had brought me in to help organise the back four, which was comprised of quite young players on the whole. Barry Blankley at right back and Paul Friar at left back were of a similar age but were much younger than me.

Colin Smith, who was more experienced, usually played at centre back but he had been out for some time with Hodgkin's disease, which is a form of cancer that affects the lymph glands. Once Colin got back into training and we had a chat, he refreshed my memory as to where we had met before. It was at Notts Forest when I was there on loan back in 1976 and he was an apprentice at the time. We swapped stories of the great Brian Clough: some good, some not so good! What was plain to see, though, was that Colin had certain qualities as a player that were picked up at Forest under the guidance of 'Old Big Ed'. Colin had come through a life-threatening illness, got himself fit again and was put straight back in the side alongside me at centre back. Darren had done well but the manager ultimately went for experience.

I settled in fairly quickly and started positively in my early games. It always makes it easier to be accepted in the dressing room if you are performing on the pitch. I am quite a strong character in any dressing room without being loud or brash, so I had to impose myself again at my new club.

Andy King was very dominant in the squad. He had played at a high level and was a very lively lad. You might say he ruled the roost! I had no problem with this at all so long as he didn't try to rule the roost over me! Kingy was a great player. He would accept the ball in any situation and take responsibility for getting the team playing. He could be a bit of an old woman on the pitch at times but I could tolerate that, as I knew he wanted to do things the right way. He wasn't the most physical of players; in fact, he couldn't tackle my mum! But give him the ball and he could pass it short and long. He could also create opportunities for others in the final third of the pitch.

In training Andy would sometimes get frustrated with other players because they were not on the same wavelength as him. He would get a bit silly and throw his toys out of his cot. This would give me the hump at times. My reaction to this would be to rattle him with a couple of strong challenges. I would also have a word in his shell-like and tell him to stop being a silly arse!

Andy turned to me one day and said, "You are the only one who speaks to me like that, Wig."

"Well, you deserve it!" I replied.

"Fair enough, you're right," was his answer.

He was a fantastic player and a great character and he was essential to our success that season. He was also the life and soul off the pitch and was forever taking the pee out of anyone and everyone. Lenny and Gilly got it too sometimes.

I got myself into trouble on a couple of occasions trying to help Andy out on the pitch. He didn't just take the mickey out of his own teammates, he also slaughtered some of the opposition, especially if they were 'meat heads' or 'hammer throwers', as he would call them.

On one such occasion at Hartlepool we were getting a rum deal from the officials, which wasn't unusual up in the north-east, and Andy was taking a bit of a kicking in midfield. They knew our team could play a bit and with Andy's pairing with Ian McDonald, another excellent footballer, the only way to stop them was to be physical.

The Hartlepool boys didn't disappoint them. We had just had a blatant penalty on Mike Ring, one of our forwards, turned down and feelings were running high. The ball dropped in the middle of the park and, as usual, Kingy brought it down stone dead. Two of their lads came in at him, one from each side, and absolutely 'mullered' him. They hit him so hard that they almost smudged his eyeliner - only joking, Andy! Kingy reacted and squared up to one of them, and for a second I thought Kingy was going to hit him with his handbag. I ran forward about 20 yards and for some unknown reason I right-handed the lad that Andy was confronting! I caught him in the mouth and knocked him back a few paces. He didn't come back at me, however. In fact, everyone seemed to freeze and I was left standing there with my fists raised like one of those old-fashioned boxers back at the turn of the century. The referee came over and sent the player with my fist print on his teeth and me straight off! Pathetically, I tried to plead my innocence when the reality of what I had done sank in, but the ref was having none of it. After the game Kingy thanked me for sticking up for him, which was fine but I was facing a suspension for both unprofessional and stupid behaviour. I was in my thirties, so you would think that I would have learnt by now! The old 'red mist' was still there.

Ian McDonald was similar to Kingy in so far as not being a physical player, but on the ball he was above the standard we were playing in. Ian had been at the club for a few years and was loved by the supporters. He lived in the town and knew the club inside out. Everyone knew 'Macca', and our families got to know each other very well over the years. Ian and his wife, Glenis, had two daughters, Kirsty and Kimberley, who were almost the same ages as our boys, Thomas and Jack. Our friendship became closer as the future of the club changed in the years ahead.

Bobby Barnes was another player who on paper should have been playing at a higher level. Bob was an ex-West Ham boy who had played in their first team. He was very much a Londoner and used to get a little giddy on away trips if he couldn't see a red London bus! The whole world revolved around the capital as far as Bob was concerned. I had experienced that syndrome before when I was at Brentford, so I took all his banter with a pinch of salt. He was a bit of an old-fashioned winger who could be a match winner as well as a provider. He had a great change of pace with or without the ball and on his day could torment the opposition's defenders. Bob used to amuse me when we travelled on long away trips. Sometimes after games, if we had played well or gained a good result, the management would let the players have a couple of beers on the coach - definitely not the ticket these days, I know. Kingy and some of the chaps would get a case of lagers between them to swig while they played cards, but Bob would buy a good bottle of red wine or claret and sit at the back on his own. We used to give him unmerciful stick! The lads reckoned that he had his smoking jacket on and a Times newspaper, joking that he was reading it wearing a little monocle! Bob didn't care; he just did his own thing and didn't do anyone any harm. He has now got a good job on the staff of the PFA (Players' Football Association). He was pretty shrewd, our Bobby.

Tommy Langley was a centre forward who had played in the Chelsea first team. He had many good qualities, both personally and as a player. It was also fortunate for us that he was able to score a few goals! Lenny Walker had been pretty shrewd with his signings by the look of things and I was becoming more excited about our prospects for the season as we went along.

Gilly took most of the training and, with limited facilities, kept it as interesting as possible. The manager would sometimes join in at a Friday morning five-a-side. He would still show on some occasions that he could get stuck in - that is if he could get close enough to anyone!

I remember one morning we were playing a small-sided game across the first team pitch, which was a bit of a treat for us especially with the groundsman, Dave Tomlinson, prowling about! Gilly would ask Dave's permission first, of course, but he wasn't ever really happy about the pitch being used between games as it was his 'baby' and it belonged to the council, his employers.

That day the boss joined in and we had a trialist with us for the week. It wasn't anyone noteworthy, just somebody on recommendation. The lad wasn't quite up to it as I recall, but he was keen and ran about a lot, as you would when you're on trial. The game wasn't going Len's way and he was getting a tad pissed off. He went for a 50:50 ball with this trialist and in that split second I thought: just let the boss have it, mate. Unfortunately, he flew in for it as honest as you like. Lenny, being a very experienced old pro, went for it studs up, catching the ball on the top, and followed right through into the lad's shin. It was virtually 'over the top of the ball but in a clever way'. I would call it a 1970s tackle, if you get my drift! The trialist gave a bit of a squeal as he went down and the boss just carried on with the game. The youngster picked himself up and looked down at his leg, which was sporting three parallel lines down the full length of the shin. Luckily his foot was off the floor so there hadn't been any danger of anything much worse happening!

I asked the trialist how he was and he nodded an "okay thanks". I could see that he was upset and a little shocked that this could happen on a Friday morning just 24 hours before a match day. Nothing further was said, obviously because it involved the boss, but I felt at the time that it had been out of order. However, looking at the incident now, I can see that the manager may have been stressed or preoccupied. Perhaps that tackle was the result of other issues and it happened in a split second.

After all, who was I to criticise anyone for their actions on a football field?

One player who caught my eye immediately on my arrival at Aldershot was Martin Foyle. I knew very little about him, but I could see that he had very few weaknesses in his game. He was very young and, with all due respect to Aldershot, I wondered why he was there rather than playing at a higher level. After talking to him, however, I got my answer. Originally, he was at Southampton, who rated him very highly but unfortunately he sustained a serious back injury that needed major surgery. Lenny had decided to take a chance on him and had brought him back to fitness. This was a piece of very good management. Martin was quick and good in the air. He had a great first touch and on top of that he could score goals. 'Foyley' was a great lad who played the game with great enthusiasm both in games and in training.

Whenever I got the chance to go up against Martin in sessions, I would jump at the challenge. We would regularly play attack against defence and I would man-mark him at times. Although we were always very competitive, there was no great physical rivalry between us. He used to liken me to a limpet because he couldn't shake me off!

It was a great test for me as well, because I knew that I wouldn't come up against anyone as good as Martin in our division. Those sessions kept me on my toes and, even though I was much older than him, he told me that I also tested him to the full. Just how long we could keep hold of him was foremost in my mind. As it turned out it wasn't for very long, as would become apparent later on that season.

The squad that the manager and Gilly had put together on a small budget was developing with plenty of potential. One player showing great promise was Mike Ring from Brighton FC. He had pace to burn, he could play wide or up front and he was a great alternative player for us if Bobby Barnes, Martin Foyle or Tommy Langley were missing. Mike was one of the quietest blokes I had ever come across and wouldn't say boo to a goose in the dressing room or on the pitch. However, his 'street cred' went up a notch when we were on one of our away trips.

We had booked into our hotel at about midday for our usual pre-match meal before a Saturday game. The hotel was better than most of the usual establishments we frequented and the large dining room had a big grand piano in the corner. We all piled in ready for our meal and sat down at the tables that had been set out in readiness for our arrival. The staff at the hotel started to serve us with our pre-ordered food and everything was as it should be with the lads in high spirits before the game. I was just about to dig into my scrambled eggs on toast when the whole room went quiet. Dulcet tones of classical music were floating over from the grand piano in the corner. I thought to myself: that's a new one - a bit of culture for us philistines! I had presumed that it was a professional pianist hired by the hotel. What a shock! It was Mike Ring tinkling away on the ivories and he was brilliant! Everyone, including the waiters, just stopped what they were doing and listened. What an amazing talent and prior to that nobody at the club had a clue he could play. That was typical of Ringy though, as he was a very modest man who didn't say a great deal. After a couple of minutes he finished with a flourish, stood up, closed the lid on the keys, walked back to his place and sat down as calm as you like. The whole room broke into spontaneous applause and Mike just smirked.

The season was going well and we were getting results on three fronts. Our League form was decent, FA Cup results were good and we were progressing in the Freight Rover Trophy. As I have already mentioned, I had played in the final of that competition for Brentford just over 12 months earlier.

In the third round of the FA Cup Aldershot were drawn at home to first division Oxford United. The match was given more publicity than usual because it was John Aldridge's last game before his move to Liverpool for £750,000. Our chairman, Colin Hancock, had also put up the admission prices for the game, which went down like a lead balloon with the supporters. I'm sure that Colin had his reasons for this; perhaps it was because of the club's financial position. We were apparently £250,000 in debt and he was looking to make a bit of a killing from the game. His relationship with the supporters was probably damaged beyond repair following that decision' however. We only attracted a crowd of just under 2,000 spectators for the game, which was counter-productive as far as creating an intimidating atmosphere for our first division opponents was concerned. In fact the crowd was one of the smallest in history for a third round clash in the FA Cup!

We had a great surface to the pitch at the 'Rec', but because of the state of the pitch that day the game itself only just went ahead. It was January, the weather had been freezing and parts of the pitch were quite solid. This didn't really bother us as much as it might have bothered the Oxford boys. Being the usual 'underdogs', we had nothing to lose!

The main talking point was obviously that it was John Aldridge's last game. The press were suggesting that he might not fancy it too much with his big move pending, as the last thing that he would want would be to pick up an injury on a dodgy pitch. As I would be directly up against him, the local and national press wanted me to back them up in regard to this theory. I didn't want to go down that road, however, and just tried to be diplomatic. John was a top-class striker, so I was going to have my hands full anyway!

When it came to the day of the contest we had a couple of problems regarding the selection of the team. Kingy was out with a knee injury and Martin Foyle went down with the flu on the Friday night before the game. They were two of our key players but we still had a decent squad. Admittedly we only had 17 or 18 players, but they could all play in the first team without any problem. Mike Ring came in up front and Glen Burvill (Burve) came in to replace Kingy in midfield. Burve was another ex-West Ham player who possessed exceptional skills. The crowd had been giving him a bad time, so this was a good opportunity for him to showcase his ability.

The game got under way and we tore into the opposition right from the off. They looked very hesitant as they played. I had noticed that when some of their lads were warming up they had seemed to be more concerned about the surface than the actual warm-up. Colin Smith headed us into an early lead after six or seven minutes - a great personal achievement for him after all his earlier health problems. We controlled most of the first half, with Mike Ring's performance being outstanding. Everyone else on the pitch was finding it difficult to keep their feet on the icy surface, but Mike just appeared to glide over the grass at full pace, giving their back four nightmares. After about ten minutes of the restart, Burve crashed a 30-yard shot past their keeper. Again this was great for Glen and would silence his hecklers. Any fight that Oxford had seemed to ebb away after that and we went on to win quite comfortably. Barnsy stuck a third one in for us late on, which made our victory even more emphatic.

Smithy and I had dealt with John Aldridge well enough. To be fair to him, the way the game went meant that he received minimal service throughout the 70 minutes or so that he was on the pitch. When he was substituted we shook hands and I wished him well. He was obviously upset with the result and perhaps the way he finished his Oxford days. It definitely wasn't the ideal send-off for him, but I'm sure that within weeks the memories of that day were long gone - especially when he pulled up at Anfield to enter one of the greatest football clubs in the world. The rest is history. He didn't do too badly, did he?

We were ecstatic with our win and for the first time in a while Aldershot were in the national papers. It was all good news!

On the very same day my brother, Dave, was playing for Caernarfon Town in the third round against Barnsley. John King was the manager of the 'Canaries' and it was a great achievement for them to get as far as they did considering that they were a non-League outfit. John went on to manage Tranmere where he was also very successful. I was eager to find out the outcome of Dave's match, so I was asking people in the dressing room if they had heard any other results. I discovered that they had drawn, which was a good result on the face of it. A replay had been arranged for the following week, which would be after the fourth round draw.

The irony of football is such that after the draw that week we came out of the hat to play the winners of the replay between Barnsley and Caernarfon! Also, it was to be played at the 'Rec', which would be a real bonus for us. There was a distinct possibility that I could face my brother in the fourth round of the FA Cup, but, alas, Barnsley beat Caernarfon 1-0 at Oakwell and it wasn't to be.

We met Barnsley at home in the next round and it was a little like after the Lord Mayor's Show compared with our outing against Oxford. We did okay and should have won the game as we were given enough chances. I felt that we had let them off the hook really. The replay at their place was a tough game and we lost it 3-0 as we didn't have quite enough on the night to win.

The club did pick up a few quid from the Cup run but nowhere near as much as we could have done if we had put Barnsley out at our place and then drawn one of the big boys. We had played well in the competition; I would say just as well as any previous Aldershot side for many years.

One player that I haven't mentioned yet is Georgio Mazzon. George, as we called him, had a nose like a dog's hind leg. I'm not sure whether it was because of one really bad break or several mediocre ones. Looking at George's face you would expect him to have a deep gravelly voice, as he appeared a real tough character. In fact he was one of the most softly spoken lads that I had ever met and a very nice fella. He had some pedigree from his days at Tottenham and was an extremely useful player in the squad because of his versatility. Lenny would put him at fullback, centre back or midfield and we also used him as a man-marker on rare occasions. Whatever George was asked to do, he just got on with it and did a fantastic job for the side. I didn't really get to know him socially, as I would shoot off back to London after games or training. He was an impressive signing by the manager and a real gentleman.

Another utility player who had been at the club for a while and had also played for Brentford like myself was Paul Shrubb. Shrubby was only short but was a very good player who, like George, would just get on with it if asked to do a specific job. He also had his own window cleaning business, which was his afternoon occupation. How he had the time and the energy to have four daughters is beyond me! Nothing was too much for Paul and he would do anything for you. That is one of the reasons I got him involved years later with the new Aldershot Town. Last time I saw Shrubby he wasn't very well at all but I'm sure the girls and his wife, Judith, are looking after the wee man.

We were out of the FA Cup but still had plenty to play for. I thought that we had enough in our make-up to get into the play offs. We also had enough about us to do well in the lower league Cup competition, the Freight Rover Trophy. We had progressed to the southern semi-final and were drawn against Swindon away. It would be a very tough game, and at that stage of the competition supporters and clubs were beginning to take it very seriously. I knew first-hand, having been at Brentford when we played Wigan at Wembley in front of a 40,000+ crowd, that there was money to be made for the clubs and great days out to be had for the supporters!

There were about 8,500 at the Swindon game, which showed how serious these stages had become. We played okay in the first half but found ourselves 2-0 down at half-time. Two of the best strikers in their division, Jimmy Quinn and Steve White, had scored the opposition's goals. It looked all over for us until Foyley got in behind them and was battered by their keeper, Fraser Digby. The referee made a very brave decision and sent Fraser off. Lou Macari, their boss, was not a happy bunny, which was understandable. The keeper was their last man and so the ref had deemed it to be a 'professional foul'.

By that time there were about 35 minutes to go, so we gave it all we had. Kingy nicked a half chance and scored after the substitute keeper, Jimmy Quinn, couldn't hold a shot from Ian McDonald. Then the 'classical pianist' Mike Ring scored a cracker in off the post to set the game up for extra time. I was having none of that though and crept up for a last-minute corner from Macca. He whipped it over and everyone seemed to miss it. I just steamed in and prodded the ball in the net just in front of Kingy! Everyone went mad!

I think I actually celebrated that goal, which was unusual for me. What a result to come back from 2-0 down. Winning that match was testament to the types of lads we had in the squad that season. Even though the turning point had been the sending off, we still had to show composure and the ability to score three goals in the final half hour or so.

My old mate Chris Kamara was in the Swindon side that night, along with Quinn, White and Colin Calderwood, who is the present Nottingham Forest manager as I write. They had a strong outfit, which made our victory even sweeter.

This competition was becoming one of my favourites! I had a chance of playing in a second Wembley final within a couple of years if we could beat Bristol City over two legs in the southern area final.

With only a matter of weeks until the end of the season we were still in the Freight Rover competition and had a fair chance of making the play-offs, yet the amount of games we were playing were really racking up. I think that we had already played 40+ by now and I had been involved in most of them. Not bad for an old boy with a supposed 'dodgy' knee!

My knee had settled down and was pretty stable by now, but I still had to look after myself with regard to over-training. With so many competitive games coming up, Gilly was brilliant as he regulated the sessions for everyone. We didn't overdo it, especially when we were playing two games a week.

There was a five-a-side pitch, if you could call it that, behind the stand at the Rec. Although it didn't have a good surface, compared with that cinders and rocks pitch behind the Doncaster stand that I played on as a youngster it was Wembley Stadium! Even so, Gilly would let me give it a miss on a Friday morning and I used to do my own thing around the edge of the pitch. I would usually end up talking to Dave Tomlinson, the groundsman, after my session and someone would have to come and wake me up while he was in full flow! Sorry Dave, only joking mate! I wasn't really bored, just tired!

In an earlier round of the Freight Rover we had quite an interesting time of it against Fulham at home. We were locked at 1-1 after extra time and therefore the tie went on to penalties. This was the second time that I had been involved in a marathon penalty shoot-out. The first time, as I have previously mentioned, was playing for Colchester United at Aston Villa in the League Cup. On that occasion the result went to 8-9 in Villa's favour, but this time around the result was 11-10 in our favour! Apparently there were 28 spot kick attempts that evening, which was a British record at the time. It was a crazy experience and a real roller-coaster ride for everyone on and off the pitch. I'm pleased to say that I scored my penalties in both shoot-outs, much to my relief!

In the southern area final we faced Bristol City, who had beaten Bolton 3-0 in the final the previous year. They were the favourites in many people's eyes. Terry Cooper, their manager, was having a good season as they were also chasing promotion from the third division, which was one division above us. They also had a great fan base and following. The previous year's final against Bolton had attracted a crowd of over 55,000 - what an achievement for a lower league competition.

Our first leg against Bristol City didn't go our way. Again we had our chances but they were a strong and well-organised team. You could see why they were pushing for promotion from the division above us. We felt that we needed at least to go down to their ground, Ashton Gate, on level terms. We lost 2-1, which wasn't an ideal situation, especially with Bristol having a 15,000+ home crowd behind them in the return leg.

By now we had lost Martin Foyle to Oxford for about £140,000. The sale of Martin at that stage of the season, when we looked like a decent bet for the play-offs and we were doing well in the Cup competition, appeared to be a strange decision to many.

If you looked at it as a business decision then it was a good move. Lenny had paid a small fee for Foyley so he had made a good profit on the deal for a club that were obviously struggling to clear their debts. Gary Johnson came into the squad to replace Martin and did a very good job, scoring some vital goals for us in the final part of the season.

The second leg at Bristol City was always going to be difficult for us. It was a real test for me personally, too, as I was up against one of the best centre forwards on his day in the game. He may have been in the autumn of his career, but Joe Jordan was a real handful. He scored one of their goals at the Rec in the first game and literally gave me a bloody nose. Joe was a great professional, going out onto the pitch long before the other players to do his own warm-up, which was quite extensive. I had played against him on a couple of occasions and he usually drew blood – mine, of course! He didn't disappoint me in this game either. A corner came in and my remit was to mark Joe. I got to the ball first and headed it back out for another corner. As I made contact with the ball, Joe came in from behind and either nutted or elbowed me! All I felt was this crack on the back of my head. The ref wasn't far from the incident so I went mad with him, pointing out that I was fouled and it should be our free kick and not a corner. He just waved me away and said, "He didn't touch you." I put my hand on the back of my bonce and then showed him. It was covered in blood! Joe had done me like a kipper again! The ref asked me if I wanted treatment and I told him politely to "BUGGER OFF!"

We lost the game 2-0 and that man Jordan scored again along with Alan Walsh, who was a tall, elegant, left-footed midfielder. They deserved to go through over the two legs and we had no complaints even though we were gutted.

I trudged off the pitch feeling a little sorry for myself. I was bruised and a bit battered. I had to go to the physio's room to have my scalp looked at as it was still bleeding profusely. Their man had a look and told me to get showered, changed and then come back to his room. He said that he was off to look for the club doctor to tend to me. I went back later and as promised the doctor was there, looking a little flushed. He sat me down, had a good look at the injury and said, "It looks quite straight forward, and two or three stitches should do it."

So I just sat there while he got his stitching gear ready. He stood above me and started to sew me up. I hadn't been given any local anaesthetic so it was a bit painful and he seemed to be taking ages doing it with quite a lot of huffing and puffing! "Just relaaaaax," he kept repeating. "Just relaaaaax." I had started that journey sitting upright in the chair but by now my head was between my knees with the doc digging away at the wound on the back of my skull. Eventually he stopped and let me up from my 'aircraft crash position'! "All done then?" I asked. "Er, not quite. The needle's blunt. I haven't got it in yet!" I had a right 'dab' on by now and I could smell drink. He may well have had a whiff of the barmaid's apron, I thought. It was turning into a really bad day, so I asked him just to get on with it, preferably with a sharp needle. He did so and the physio proffered a cup of tea. I declined and was away on my toes within five minutes!

The Bristol City defeat was a big disappointment for everyone concerned. When you get as close as we did to a Wembley appearance it can be a bitter pill to swallow. From the players' point of view, most of the lads wouldn't ever get that chance again. All the staff at the football club and the supporters had also lost a once in a lifetime chance of having one of the best days out that they could imagine. However, there was still plenty to play for in the League, as it was the start of the play-offs era and we were still in the frame.

We managed to steer clear of too many injuries in the squad considering how many games we had played. As I have mentioned, our training schedule definitely helped me on a personal level, so I am positive that the younger players would have benefited from it too. I wasn't the oldest in the squad though. Ian Mac was a year older than me so we both had to keep our callipers well oiled for the final run of games!

One crucial game that I recall well was against my old club Colchester United. We had already beaten them three times that season in the League and Cup competitions. They were probably sick and tired of the sight of us – and it wasn't going to get any better for them!

You always enjoy going back to your old clubs to play or manage. Sometimes you may think that you have something to prove or perhaps you just want to put one over on them for a different reason. I had neither of these thoughts in my mind, however, as I had done very well for Colchester and I hadn't left with a flea in my ear. Just going back meant seeing a lot of the people that I had got to know well, including both playing and club staff, which was nice for me. The crowd also gave me a good reception and that pleased me more than anything. We won 1-0 and Mike Ring scored the winner. I was happy with my performance defensively. It was another clean sheet, which always pleases a defender!

It was all getting tight at the top of the table. There were still three or four teams in the shake-up for the last couple of play-off places: Colchester and ourselves, with Leyton Orient and Wrexham still in there with a shout. The results panned out our way and on the final day of the season we finished in a play-off position. This was a hell of an achievement for us considering our success in the FA Cup and our run in the Freight Rover Trophy, not to mention the fact that we had lost our top striker to Oxford midway through the season. It just showed how well the boss had done with the limited financial resources available.

From the players' point of view, we were pretty pleased with ourselves. We felt that we had nothing to lose now. We could take the kid gloves off and express ourselves. Our opponents were to be Bolton at home and then away.

If we could beat them, we would then go up against - yes you've guessed it - my old club Colchester yet again! How ironic was that?! Or we would face the mighty Wolves, the team that had hammered us 3-0 earlier in the season. Nowadays the play-offs final takes place at Wembley Stadium, so the only disappointing part of this for us was that back then it comprised two games played home and away.

Bolton Wanderers finished fourth from the bottom of the third division, so they needed to win both the play-off rounds just to stay in their League. We finished in the last play-off position of the fourth division and therefore we had to play the team from the higher division (Bolton) first.

There wasn't much respite after our last League game of the season. The following week we were at home to Bolton playing on a very heavy pitch. It was rather a dour battle but the pressure was all on the opposition. They were managed by Phil Neal, the old Liverpool and England fullback. He also played in the match, which was a tough job for him. Gary Johnson scored the only goal of the game for us, which was great for him, as replacing Martin Foyle had not been easy and that goal definitely endeared him to the supporters.

The pitch was so heavy in that match that I can remember getting cramp in both calf muscles when I jumped for a high ball. Getting cramp in one leg is bad enough, but both is not good at all and I was walking around like Douglas Bader for the last couple of minutes or so. For the first time after playing 50+ games that season, I think that I was beginning to feel the pace!

We felt that one goal might not be enough, but in this competition away goals would count double if teams were drawing after extra time. Bolton did not have an away goal, which could be decisive.

The second game at their place was a tense affair. Their crowd was very partisan, which was to be expected. Tony Caldwell scored a penalty for them early in the second half and their fans went ballistic! They could smell blood and really got behind their team. We weathered the storm and, all credit to our boss, Lenny threw big Darren Anderson on, who came up trumps and scored the equaliser with about 15 minutes to go. Then that lad Caldwell scored again for them very late on and sent the game into extra time.

At that stage we didn't have to score to go through, as it was 2-2 on aggregate and away goals counted as double at the end of extra time. To sit back and just defend would have been a mistake, however, so we tried to take the game to them and it worked, as Glen Burvill scored for us just before the end of the first period. We then killed the game off in the second period and came out worthy winners.

Unfortunately our victory meant that we had condemned Bolton to relegation into the fourth division for the first time in their 110-year history. As you can imagine, their fans were not a happy bunch and the atmosphere became quite hostile around the terraces. Our team got off the pitch sharpish and left them to it!

Our thoughts could now switch to the final and to who would be our opponents. I preferred my old club Colchester, for obvious reasons, as did many of the other lads. After all, we had beaten them on our previous four meetings. However, it wasn't to be, as Wolves brushed them aside and were looking impressive. Their striking force of Steve Bull and Andy Mutch probably made them the best pairing in the division.

Being the competitive person that I am, I was relishing the clash even though we were definitely going to be the underdogs. This suited us and the lads had come a long way in a hard season, so we weren't going to be fazed by their reputation as a 'big' club.

Our manager and Gilly did a good job on us. They were positive in everything that they said and did, which I felt was very important.

The first leg was at the Rec and some people thought that this was a disadvantage. Their theory was that if the game went to extra time at Molineux then they would have the advantage of their 20,000 crowd behind them. We didn't see it that way, however. Our reasoning was that if we could get our noses in front at home then it would be up to them to take it away from us at their ground!

The evening of the game started badly for me personally. Anne and I and the boys were travelling along the M25 as usual when there was an unbelievable cloudburst. The rain was so bad that the car windscreen wipers could hardly cope with the challenge. The three lanes of traffic came to a virtual standstill and we were stuck for some time, maybe half an hour. We always left in plenty of time for games, so we had some leeway. We began to move slowly as the rain eased off, but with still some way to go I was getting a wee bit worried. We had bought a nice Escort XR3i after my move to Brentford, which could be fairly nippy if required, so I put my clog down a touch. I didn't want to miss the biggest game of the season so far because of a bit of water! There were no mobile phones then, which probably seems unthinkable to the younger generation now, so we couldn't let the management know that I might be a tad late.

In the event, I drove up to the Rec gates at just before seven o'clock, which didn't give me much preparation time for the match. And – would you believe it? – by whom was I met at the gates but Mr Jobsworth! Who he was I have no idea, but he was playing it by the book. Usually as the players approached the gates the guys opened them and allowed us to pass through into the car park. No such luck today, however. This fellow left the gate firmly shut and slowly wandered over, gesticulating with his arm for me to wind the window down. I did so as quickly as I could and with a certain air of panic!

"Yes, can I help you?" he enquired deliberately.

I stated my name in the hope that it might mean something to him and he would let me in.

"Yes," he said.

"I play for Aldershot," I screamed at him.

"Who are these people?" he uttered, pointing at Anne and the kids.

This was too much. "Just open the bloody gates, you idiot!"

I think he realised that he'd picked the wrong man at the wrong time to be pedantic with. Panic over and I'd just made it. The team sheet was in and my name was on it. Lenny and Gilly were more confident of my making it on time than I was!

There was a great atmosphere in the ground. Wolves had a fantastic following and at last a big Aldershot crowd had come out to support us. I say 'at last' because late in the season, even when we were chasing a play-off place, we were still only getting 2-3,000 for home games. In contrast, Wolves were getting 10-20,000 for some matches.

When I went to have a look at the pitch before the kick-off I was surprised at how much water had settled on the surface. The rain had stopped but it had been so intense that the pitch had become waterlogged very quickly. My immediate thought was that it could become a lottery early on in the game and there could be mistakes made because of the conditions. Lenny just told us to be positive from the off, to take the game to them and to see how they reacted. We were instructed to get the ball forward because of the conditions and to be as uncompromising as possible in every position.

We started like a house on fire and put them under pressure. In one of our attacks the ball stuck in the water and was only half cleared. It sat nicely for Ian McDonald to smash a low shot at goal, which appeared to gather pace and skip off the wet turf. It flew into the corner of their net, giving their keeper no chance of saving it. What a great start for us and I loved it!

Bull and Mutch were a real handful. It wasn't just their movement and ability that were difficult to deal with, it was the fact that they both had a fierce will to win as well. They weren't giants in stature but they were very physical and also both had a bit of a nasty side to their playing character. They were prepared to scrap for every ball with anyone. Smithy and I did a decent job on them physically and tactically, however. Put it this way, I don't think that we were on their Christmas card list after that game!

We scored a second goal from a penalty after one of their back four stuck his arm up in the penalty box and handled a cross. They were a little shell-shocked to find themselves trailing. We needed to show some courage and resilience to keep them out for the remainder of the game. There were some close calls but we deservedly won the match 2-0.

All the bookies had put Wolves as the hot favourites but we had other ideas and this was a great confidence booster for the second leg at Molineux. Later that week some of the bookmakers were still backing Wolves to turn us over as we had lost there 3-0 earlier in the League and the betting men must have seen this as a distinct possibility again. From my point of view, all that sort of speculation served to do was to motivate me even more!

The day of the return game was a nice sunny one. It should have been, seeing as we were nearly into June. There was a big crowd and the ground looked fantastic. I was feeling a touch nervous, which was good for me. I knew that we were in for a very physical encounter and that the whole team would need to perform well to gain the necessary result. If we had any passengers in our ranks we were going to struggle.

Colin Smith and I knew exactly what to expect from the terrible two up front, Bull and Mutch. We felt that if we could shackle those two for as long as possible then our team had a decent chance of winning it. There were another nine players out there who also needed to win their individual contests, but the two front lads for Wolves were the darlings of the home crowd. In my opinion they were quite capable of scoring goals against anyone in all four divisions!

Within a few minutes of the kick-off, a ball bounced awkwardly into our box. It popped up and hit Colin Smith on the top of his arm, almost on the shoulder. The Wolves players and the crowd appealed for a penalty to Keith Hackett, the referee, who was only yards away. He was having none of it and waved for everyone to play on. Their lads went mad with him and likewise the terraces. However, it would have been very harsh if a penalty had been given.

Football can be a very strange game at times when you are actually involved in a match. For me, the moment he didn't give the penalty I felt a wave of total confidence come over me. People talk about defining moments in games and in my mind, even though the match had just started and there was plenty of time to go, I just felt that it was going to be our day.

We slugged it out with them for the next 80 minutes. They bombarded us with an increasingly desperate stream of attacks and Steve Bull was like a man possessed at times. He probably kicked, elbowed, slapped or grabbed 80 per cent of my body surface over the 90 minutes! Mutchy wasn't any different. There was also this constant wind-up banter from both of them, directed at either Smithy or me. We kept our composure, however, and didn't rise to the bait, as we needed to keep all 11 of us on the pitch to get something from the game. Time was running out for them and they threw everyone forward. After about 85 minutes, and for the first time in the match, we managed to break out and get behind them. Bobby Barnes, who had finally managed to have a kick against David Barnes, scored with a cross shot in off the post to put us 3-0 up on aggregate! Steve Bull turned to me on the halfway line, shook my hand and said, "That's it, you've done it mate." That was the only cordial contact we had over the two games. We had bashed each other about for 180 minutes or so and yet, to be fair to him, he showed true respect and sportsmanship with that one small gesture.

They were obviously gutted as a team. I shook hands with Andy Mutch, who was almost inconsolable. He was another great competitor and little did I know then that the next time I would shake his hand would be 16 years later when I would offer him a position as my chief scout at Doncaster Rovers when I was the manager there.

What a great victory it was for us! We had won 3-0 on aggregate against a team that had finished many points above us in the League. What an achievement! We celebrated on the pitch and at long last our supporters had something to cheer about. They had played their part on a difficult day for us. We'd had an outstanding season performing at a good level for 60 games or so with an average-sized squad. The manager and coach had done a marvellous job fashioning the squad and getting the optimum from the players. John Anderson, who was one of the 'old school' trainers, had also done his bit in assisting Gilly.

I was absolutely drained at the final whistle and after the usual hugging we all gathered together for a team photograph. The photographer suggested that we put our arms in the air to signal our victory. When I lifted mine it felt as if I had a covering of chain mail all over my body. I was so tired, I could hardly stand up! What a lovely day though, and by the time I'd had a cup of tea and a sandwich in the dressing room I felt a lot better and the adrenalin started to flow again.

Gary Johnson appeared to have plenty of that after the game! He had sustained a cut to the back of his head in a challenge and it needed a couple of stitches. The club doc came in to attend to him and wanted to give Gary a jab in the cut to deaden the area so he could sew it up. Gary, a big strong lad who was brave on the pitch, wasn't happy at all, as apparently he couldn't stand needles! Nobody was aware of this, so we were all surprised when he jumped up onto the benches to get away from the doctor and refused to have the jab! Two or three of us had to grab him and virtually hold him in place for the job to be done. He was no worse for his trouble but it was hilarious at the time, especially as we were all in such high spirits.

On the coach journey home the realisation of how big a club Wolves was really sunk home. As we passed people in the streets of Wolverhampton, almost to a man or woman, they either shouted abuse at us or stuck two fingers up, or made even worse gestures with their hands that I'll leave up to your imagination! We passed a few pubs that had supporters outside drinking at tables. They stood up as they saw our coach and gave us a right mouthful. It appeared that the whole city had the right hump with us for beating their beloved team.

I enjoyed the moment for what it was, but in the back of my mind I knew that in a few years there was a good chance that they would leapfrog us and leave us behind.

No official celebration party or get-together had been arranged for after the match. I had boarded the team coach at Luton with a few of the other lads who lived in or around London. There was a hotel just by the M1 where we had left our cars, so the chairman decided that we should stop off there for a few drinks. I'm not a great drinker and was also driving, but although I was unable to join in with the drinks I wanted to savour the moment and let the reality of the day sink in. The lads were absolutely buzzing, especially the younger ones. Mind you, Kingy was flying - nothing new there! When I managed to have a chat with him he admitted that he was the most nervous he had ever been before a game in the dressing room at Wolves.

Bearing in mind that Andy had played in Liverpool v. Everton derbies and other big games, it was strange that he found it difficult to control his nerves before a lower league play-off game. It just goes to show that, at whatever level you play, circumstances and situations can still have an effect on you.

The lads who were driving gradually drifted away, myself included. We all said goodbye to one another and after a very long season it was all over. In due time we would receive our letter from the club informing us of when pre-season would start. Perish the thought. I had just played in about 55 competitive games over a period of nine months or so and I needed a good rest.

Anne and I had arranged to drive up to my mum and dad's place in North Wales the next day for a week's holiday. I only had a few hours' sleep so that we could get an early start, because it was about a five-hour journey from Ruislip. My parents lived right on the beachfront, and so by 11 o'clock that morning, within 24 hours of the game, I found myself relaxing on an almost deserted beach fishing with my family in the sunshine.

While we were fishing, a small balding bloke walking a little dog strolled up and my dad introduced him as one of his neighbours. To my surprise he said in a broad Midlands accent, "Bloody hell, you didn't do my team any favours yesterday, did you?" Can you believe that the first person I met the following day on a deserted beach miles away from the game was a Wolves supporter?!

The only dampener after that glorious win for the club was that three of the lads had an unfortunate accident. Darren Anderson, Glen Burvill and Georgio Mazzon were involved in a car crash on their way home from the Rec after being dropped off by the coach. It had been a very misty night and they hit a tree on a country lane in the early hours. The car was a write-off but luckily they escaped with relatively minor injuries considering the state of the motor. Burve broke his arm. Darren cut his eye and George, who was travelling in the rear of the vehicle, suffered some internal and back injuries. They were lucky to be alive.

The close season came and went very quickly. I only had about four weeks' total rest before I started doing some conditioning work. We didn't finish until the very end of May and most pre-season training usually commenced within the first two weeks of July, depending on the start date of the season. I never go into pre-season without some kind of preparation of my own, one reason being that it lessened the chances of picking up soft tissue injuries such as strains or pulls during the first week or so. How much I would do would depend on the manager or coach that I was working with. For instance, if it was my old Colchester manager Bobby Roberts, I would do less preparation as I knew that he would be sensible and let the sessions build up gradually. He was in some ways ahead of many coaches at that time because he was always looking at different methods in pre-season. If I were with another Colchester manager, Cyril Lea, then I would do much more preparation because he would go into it hell for leather and I would need to accustom my body to the rigorous methods that Cyril used. Lenny and Gilly were somewhere in between: not quite as innovative as Bobby, yet not as gung-ho as Cyril. After all, the boss was well aware that we had just had one hell of a physical season. Having said that, however, we had just been promoted and would be playing in a very tough division with the likes of Bristol City who had beaten us in the Freight Rover Trophy. So the staff had to get their preparation right for the new challenge.

There had been some activity in the close season regarding the movement of players at the club. The boss would have already started to plan for the next season within hours of our victory at Wolves. That is how management is. You don't get much time to sit back and smell the roses in football management. Lenny had made some difficult decisions that in his mind would strengthen the squad so that we could compete in the higher division. I must admit I was a little shocked when I heard of some of the changes. I was still only a player and was glad to have been able to tuck my tongue back in my backside after one extra long season, so the fact that the squad needed changing hadn't really entered my head during my rest period.

When I clocked in for training there was obviously a buzz about the place because of what we had achieved. We had gone our separate ways quite quickly after the match at Molineux and so we were keen to discuss the game.

Paul Friar had been released, Barry Blankley had been given a free transfer and young Colin Fielder, who could play in several positions, was another casualty. And in came young Paul Holsgrove, a tall midfield player whose dad was an ex-professional. The more experienced Gary Howlett also joined us as a midfield player. The left back spot went to an old mate of mine, Ian (Mad Max) Phillips. 'Phippsy' or 'Max', as we called him, came from my old club Colchester. He was a strong character and he was also physically very strong as a player. His legs were like tree trunks, and bowed ones at that! Ian was a great talker on the pitch and we knew each other so well that I was looking forward to playing with him. The tag 'Mad Max' probably came as a result of his Scottish antics, although he wasn't as mad as Kevin Bremner who shared the same label!

Ian was travelling from Colchester every day for training, which was difficult for him. Even then, in the late eighties, things had changed in that players were travelling further to their jobs at football clubs. Squads were changing around more and players were not prepared to move their families on the back of the contracts that were being negotiated. I had been travelling some distance for about ten months by this time and I still hadn't really got used to it; in fact the bloody M25 was doing my head in!

Another addition to the squad was an old teammate from Brentford, Paul Roberts. Robbo was useful as he could play in a few positions for us. One thing was for certain, he was going to add to the dressing room banter! I was looking forward to him and Kingy trying to outdo each other! I had an advantage over the other lads, as I knew exactly what to expect from the crafty cockney. David Coles, our other keeper, came back into the squad after an 18-month absence due to a broken leg. Tony Lange had been in the team the previous season and had done very well, so David had a job on his hands dislodging him.

The older I became the quicker the new seasons seemed to come along. My break that year was short but it was worth it because of the success that we'd had. As a family we still managed to fit in plenty of outings together. Apart from our week or two in North Wales, where both sets of parents lived, we took the boys out as much as we could. My parents would also come down and stay with us, as we hardly got to see them or Anne's mum and dad throughout the playing season.

My father was a keen fisherman and if the opportunity arose he was keen to give it a go. Be it freshwater or sea fishing, he was always up for it. What I must say at this point, however, is that I usually spent more time unravelling birds' nests of fishing twine than I did fishing. Thomas and Jack were only eight and six respectively, so you could understand them getting in a bit of a mess at times with their rods and reels - but my dad? He had more birds' nests than a Chinese restaurant! The problem was that he had fingers like sausages. Well, if you tried unravelling a complete tangle-up with ten saveloys you'd get some idea of what I mean! Also, he wouldn't wear his specs, so that didn't help matters either!

Mum and dad came to stay that summer and we decided to take a trip out to Rickmansworth Lido. This was a Sunday favourite of the family. We took a picnic with us, which was more like a banquet - typical of Anne. We liked our grub and as the boys were youngsters they were constantly eating something. The Lido is a huge, rambling place with a very large lake, fantastic wooded areas, a canal and lovely walks. It was a sunny day and we soon found ourselves a nice opening by the lake so that we could all fish quite comfortably. Mum and Anne had put the big blanket down, as you do, and set out the picnic. We'd even brought fold-up chairs to add to the ladies' comfort!

Our dog, Ralph, a scruffy-looking fella, was also with us. We had found him at Battersea Dogs' Home as a pup and bought him for Thomas's fifth birthday. He was a 'Heinz 57' breed, a mongrel, and the best type of family dog in my opinion. He was certainly well loved in our household and went with us every weekend on our family outings. He had watched me load the car in eager anticipation on this particular Sunday, and while I was walking back and forth with rods, baskets, blankets, wellies and food, etc., he was bounding alongside me thinking: wow, where are we going today? Although my initial idea was that he would be staying at home today! We could NOT have left him behind! I had suggested that we did, only to be shouted down by the wife and kids. "We are not leaving him here?" they begged, and that was that.

When we arrived at Rickmansworth the dog had his run about and then we tethered him with a long lead to one of the chairs so that he didn't wander off while we were fishing. The two boys, dad and I were quite contented, peacefully fishing from the bank next to the picnic and mum was having her usual fag while sat chatting to Anne. It was the idyllic scenario - or so we thought, as all of a sudden all hell broke loose!

A terrier dog came scurrying out of the bushes at a rate of knots, jumped on a sleeping Ralph and attacked him. As Ralph was tied up he couldn't escape or even fight back. The two dogs became entwined in the long leash and mum and Anne were caught in the middle of the whole fracas. The picnic was taking a right hammering as you can imagine. The chair that Anne was sitting on became upended and mum was waltzing around the entire affair!

This all happened in a matter of seconds. I dropped my rod and jumped into the melee to try to separate the dogs. By now the owner of the terrier, a middle-aged woman in a pink velour tracksuit, had also got involved with our dinner and was attempting to detach her pooch from the throat of ours! At the same time as apologising profusely for her dog, she was successfully trampling all over a Cadbury's chocolate sponge and a packet of sausage rolls! Then, unfortunately for her, she lost her balance and fell back into the undergrowth!

I tried my best to pull the two animals apart with my bare hands, but lost the fight pretty quickly and was wary of being bitten by this terrier and so I resorted to the tools of my trade! I just volleyed the dog and it literally flew through the air and landed about ten feet away. The little sod got up and came back for more, but this time I managed to grab it by the collar and restrain it. In the meantime, Anne and mum had helped the lady to her feet. She was shaken but quickly managed to put the devil incarnate on its lead, still uttering profuse apologies. Her pink tracksuit now looked as though she'd been dragged around a muddy field by a horse! She tootled off with the dog, which was still foaming at the mouth and making a vain attempt to return to Ralph.

I surveyed our former idyllic setting, which now looked as if a bomb had hit it. Ralph was just lying there still on his lead attached to the chair, which was on its side. Mum was standing up, still with her fag in her hand, and gave a rather understated summary of the situation: "Oh dear, that wasn't good was it?" Anne, who can usually look immaculate at any time in any circumstance, looked like some mad woman with her hair all over the place. Even worse, she was holding up her brand new white summer jacket, which now resembled a dirty old dishrag! I looked over at the boys, who had put down their rods to watch the commotion. Dad, however, hadn't budged. Rod in hand and still fishing, he turned to me and said, "Everything okay, son?" Enough said!

We managed to settle down and I untangled a few more reels. I had the hump a little bit but peace had returned to the camp. The ladies had rescued some of the picnic and poor Ralph was recovering from his ordeal. He was relatively unscathed, with just a few tufts of fur missing here and there. Dad was happy, the boys were set up with their rods again and I was just about to cast mine out. Mum had lit another fag and Anne had resigned herself to the fact that her new designer jacket would now be relegated to being used for cleaning the car in future! At least peace was restored, or so we thought!

Believe it or not, before we knew it another dog came out of nowhere and launched a second offensive on Ralph! It was a much bigger animal this time, and it meant business. Well, I just went into one! I dropped my rod and ran at the dog, grabbing it by the collar. Close behind was its owner, a woman in her thirties.

"Oh, oh!" she said, "What's going on?"

"I'll tell you what's going on, missus, I'm going to volley your dog if you don't get a grip of it!" I replied.

"Don't you dare touch my dog! We all know about your 'type' of people. Why don't you and your family go and jump in the lake?" she suggested.

Well, I lost it completely at that point and threatened to dispatch both her and her dog into the water immediately.

Her female friend appeared on the scene and helped her get the still growling mutt on its lead and they walked off still muttering about us. She even turned to inform me that her husband was waiting in the car park.

"Bring him over here," I shouted, "and I'll throw him in too!"

My head had well and truly gone by then. I looked at my lot, all wide eyed and opened mouthed!

"Right, that's it, we're off!" I snapped. I'd completely had enough.

So we packed everything up, trudged all the way back to the car park with our stuff, piled into the car and left. On the way home I must admit that we started to see the funny side of the whole episode. One observation by my mum was that when I volleyed the terrier into the air, I had only narrowly missed the head of the lady in the pink tracksuit as she floundered about in the long grass! Now that would have been a totally different story!

That 1987/88 season was a real test for us. At times we more than matched the opposition and then at other times we fell short. The simple reason for this is that, although going up a division may on the face of it appear to bring few significant changes, there are subtle differences. In the lower divisions you could find some very good players in four or five positions, whereas in the next flight you may find seven or eight. In some cases, the higher up you go in the leagues, the better the managers and coaches. However, it is also true that some bosses produce miracles on minute budgets and simply don't get the chance to be tested at a bigger club with more money available. The fact is that it is not always obvious why some teams are better than others, but at the end of the season the teams' finishing positions will reflect how good or otherwise they are.

We had a decent squad and it had been strengthened slightly. Lenny didn't have much money to spend, so I'm sure he did a lot of wheeling and dealing behind the scenes.

From what I could see, Lenny had to make a big decision for himself. He had just had an unbelievable season as manager alongside Gilly. He must have weighed up his options over the summer and, putting all his loyalties and sentiment aside, I was surprised that he didn't go for a bigger job. This is only my opinion, however, and it does not signify any disloyalty on my part towards Aldershot FC or their supporters.

The manager was in as strong a position as he would probably ever be, so now was the time for him to promote himself and his coach, Ian. There may have been little additional funding on offer as we moved into the next division and it was going to be one hell of an effort to stay up. I didn't know Lenny well enough to talk to him about such things, although I was very surprised when he stayed and didn't even appear to be linked to any other clubs. Then was the time for him to branch out, as it didn't make any difference to me as a player. I liked Lenny and Ian, but in the end business is business and he should have filled his boots!

We had stayed up by the skin of our teeth that season, which in many ways could be viewed as a success. From a player's point of view, it was more difficult than the previous promotion season. Chasing games every other week and the team having to perform at a good level just to survive was hard. Even though we were playing at a higher standard, having to accept that the team was struggling was not pleasant. There was an almost palpable target the previous year, but this campaign was most certainly about keeping the club at this level in the Football League. The alternative was relegation and going back to where we'd started from 12 months earlier.

I did okay and played as well as I had in the past, but we had been spoilt the previous season and so I can't say that I was as happy as I had been. The outcome was successful even though it was a little tight at times.

The manager had plenty to think about in the close season regarding how to improve the squad with probably very little funding. He had brought in Mark Ogley, a defender from Barnsley, and Glyn Riley, a forward from Bristol City. Glyn had actually played against us in the southern area final of the Freight Rover Trophy competition. He played up front there with Joe Jordan and did very well, but I felt for him a bit at Aldershot as he just couldn't get on the score sheet enough and took some stick from the crowd. I think that expectations were high because he had come from a big club like Bristol and so he had a hard time of it.

A lad called Steve Berry also came to us from Northampton. He could play in a number of positions and was good on the ball but a bit of a lightweight. He was one of the first players I had met who told me he didn't like to stay at any club too long. He preferred to move about almost at will. I presumed that this was mainly for the money. That wasn't my way of doing things, but who was I to say he was wrong?

Little did I know that the 1988/89 season was going to be even more of a struggle for us. After our survival season in the third division, I was optimistic that we would add more quality to the squad and maybe make a bigger fist of it this time. It was a very tough division and the addition of some better players in certain positions was crucial. I wasn't being arrogant in my thoughts, just honest. The present squad comprised a nice bunch of lads, but as I had already played in a team at Colchester that had competed at the top of this division for a couple of seasons I knew what we needed to be up there.

One decision that did confuse me was that Tommy Langley was given a free transfer during the summer break. Tommy had scored many vital goals for us the previous season, 1987/88. I wasn't privy, of course, to what he was being paid or the nature of his contract, but it seemed to be a very strange release to me. We will never know whose decision it was either: was it the manager's or was it taken out of his hands?

We had lost Andy King due to a bad knee injury, so that meant that two quality players were missing for a start. Tommy and Andy had more than enough quality for the third division.

The manager had gradually tried to change the squad for the better. David Barnes was already with us. He had come from Wolves and was in the side that had lost to us in the play-offs. Barnsey was good mates with Andy, and what a pairing they made. They were both as daft as a brush at times, especially when they got together. They were a 'double act', you might say. David was probably one of the best left backs in the division. He could also play wide left, which also gave us another option. The only snag was that he was experiencing ankle problems that kept him on the sidelines at times.

Kevin Brown came in at right back from Southampton and he was the consummate professional. Kevin was always on time and never missed training. He was immaculate in the way he dressed on and off the pitch. What I mean by 'on the pitch' is that he even looked pristine in his kit. This may sound silly, but I'm afraid that some lads always looked scruffy on the pitch even though they wore the same kit as everyone else! My old mate Kevin Bremner couldn't quite cut the mustard in anything he wore for some reason, but you could dress Kevin Brown in a sack and he would look good!

Dave Puckett also came over from Southampton. He was a renowned goalscorer at a good level. Another player that had played at a higher level was Ian Stewart. Ian, or Stewie, had played in the World Cup for Northern Ireland and he had played at QPR and Newcastle. He was an immensely talented footballer with great experience and was very much an old-fashioned wide man. Ian lived not far from me in London, so for that season we shared the driving into work. I therefore got to know him very well. He was very softly spoken with a very distinctive Belfast accent. Ian told me that he felt his best days were behind him because he had contracted glandular fever a year or so earlier. He was still a very fit lad but he thought that he had lost his edge after that. On his day he was almost unplayable, however. He could go either way against fullbacks, using both feet to dribble with the ball. Sometimes in training you just couldn't get the ball off him. On other days he appeared really off the boil and a little disillusioned. I'm sure he won't mind my mentioning it, but this was also reflected in his driving! Some days he would pick me up and just cruise along at 60-65mph on the motorway down to Hampshire and on other days, even if we had plenty of time, he would clog it at 80-90mph constantly all the way there! I didn't say a word to him about it; I just let him get on with it.

I remember one away game at Southend when Stewie picked me up. It was absolutely peeing it down and the motorway was just one mass of spray. He'd got a new car, a SAAB 900, and it was rapid! I don't think we travelled below 90mph all the way around the M25! I was transfixed in my seat as Ian chatted quietly to me. I couldn't see more than 30 yards in front of the car because of the water, so how he could I just don't know. However, we arrived at Roots Hall in one piece, which was a great relief to me. I'd already got a sweat on before we even warmed up on the pitch. Stewie, as laid back as you like, just strolled into the dressing room. We played the game and drew1-1, scoring late on when I headed down a free kick for Glyn Riley to bang it in the net. Stewie got 'Man of the Match' and they presented him with a case of the sponsor's beer.

We all congregated in their clubhouse afterwards and I was talking to a couple of our players. Stewie's name cropped up in regard to how well he had played and as we chatted I happened to mention his driving and how I had been almost stiff with fear on the way down. What I didn't realise was that he was standing right next to us and must have heard every word. I caught his eye but he didn't say anything and just walked off. I felt bad about it, but at the same time I was hopeful that he might decide to slow down on the way home!

We set off with his case of beer on the back seat. The rain had stopped and it was a nice sunny evening, so I was looking forward to a pleasant, leisurely journey home. Wrong! Stewie drove just as fast as before. The only difference this time was that I could see the road ahead. We discussed the game and he was quite pleased with his performance, especially his nice little crate of beer.

The A40 took us into the area where we lived and, although it was a dual carriageway for most of the way, we were still flying along. When we came over the brow of a hill the traffic ahead was at a standstill at a set of traffic lights. As we were travelling at about 80+mph, Ian had to slam on the brakes. In fact he braked so hard that the spoiler scraped along the ground and it was clear that we were going to smash into the car in front of us. Stewie spotted a gap in the inside lane and in a split second swerved to avoid the car, missing it by inches.

The lights changed to green and as we approached the actual junction we had slowed down enough to cruise through at a leisurely 20mph behind the inside lane of traffic. I was in total shock and I don't mind admitting it! I think my hands were stuck on the windscreen like one of those 'Garfield the cat' characters with suckers on their paws! I didn't say a word; well, I don't think I did! Funny squeaking noises may have emanated from somewhere about my person as we hurtled towards the car, but I was definitely mute at this point! Stewie turned to me and said quietly, "That was a wee bit close, eh? Is that beer okay? I think it's rolled off the back seat." Rolled off the back seat? He was lucky that we weren't wearing the bloody stuff! That was Ian, so laid back he was almost horizontal.

Another one of Lenny's additions was a very young Adrian Randall, who had come to us from Bournemouth. Adrian had tons of ability but was one of the quietest lads I had played with. He didn't say much on or off the pitch. 'A bit of a loner' would probably be the best description for him. Sometimes before training he would juggle a ball with his feet all the way around the perimeter of the pitch without it touching the ground. I hadn't seen any player do that before and he just did it as part of his warm-up or for a mess about. What an incredible talent to have. He eventually went off to Burnley and did quite well at a higher level.

One character that I must mention is Steve Claridge, or 'Worzel'(from the children's TV programme Worzel Gummidge), who was a real one-off. He originally came to us on loan from Crystal Palace. On the pitch he was in a world of his own, or so it appeared, as trying to get through to him or get any sense out of him was a waste of time. He had a really eccentric talent. Some of his actions on the pitch were totally instinctive. He could score a goal out of nothing but would also 'take the lace out of the ball' as we say and not pass it to anyone. He thought that he could do it all on his own. Some would say he was a bit of a nightmare to play with and to coach but great to have on your side.

Steve had his own fruit and veg stall as well as playing full-time. We used to put orders in with him and he would bring them to training the next day in the boot of his car, all boxed up. He was a nice lad but could be very strange at times. On match days he had some funny routines that he used to go through. I am presuming that they were routines. All the lads would watch him and yet he appeared totally oblivious to everyone and just got on with it. Steve always had a big kitbag with him that appeared to contain several pairs of boots. Some didn't match; some didn't have laces in; some were dirty and some were clean. He would try out lots of different combinations in the dressing room before he went out for the warm-up. Then he would try more on before he went out for the kick-off. Sometimes he would still be doing this as the boss was giving his pre-match talk! Lenny would blank it at times but if the atmosphere was a little tense he would shout out, "WORZEL, FOR F***'S SAKE MAN, GIVE US A MINUTE!" I would have to look down at the ground when that happened as it made me giggle.

At one away game, I had come in early from my warm-up for some reason. A few of the other lads in the dressing room had spotted something in Worzel's wide-open bag on the changing bench. It was a black mouldy sandwich in a small see-through plastic bag! Heaven knows how long it had been there. The kitbag was full of mud, dirty old socks and, of course, boots! For a bit of a laugh we found a piece of string and tied it around the sandwich bag. We didn't dare open the bag, as the sarnie inside was absolutely rancid. We strung it up from the ceiling and left it suspended over the physio's table in the middle of the dressing room. Then, like a bunch of naughty school kids, we waited for Worzel to come back in. We were dying to see his reaction.

Steve returned in his usual pre-match quandary as to which boots to wear, so he didn't notice the execution site straight away. In fact, I think one of the boys gave him a nudge to bring his attention to the hanging butty. When he spotted it he recognised it instantly, but not a word was said. He just grabbed it, ripped it away from the ceiling and silently put it back in his kitbag! Surely most people would have chucked it in the bin? Everyone shared the joke but not Worzel. He just sat there and waited for the bell to tell us it was time to go out for the kick-off.

Steve also liked to play with his socks down, his boots undone and his shirt out. He looked a right 'two and eight' at times! However, he was a very talented player who went on to play at a much higher level, scoring many goals. He has experienced both management and coaching and now he has succeeded as a football radio and television personality.

Just for a minute I nearly felt guilty about our 'mouldy sandwich' incident. Sorry, Worz, there are no regrets - that's football for you!

Our physio was Jim Lange, who was a retired captain from the British Army. Jim was German by birth and had quite a strong accent. "Viggy, my boy," he would say to me, and I got to know him well over the seasons. This was probably because at this stage of my career I was forever picking up little niggles here and there and was always asking his advice. His usual response was, "Just pack in ze game, you old git!" That was typical of him! I was about 35 by then, however, so I suppose he wasn't far wrong.

I was always interested in anatomy and some might say that it's no wonder in view of all the injuries I'd had. I was lucky in some ways that I'd sustained very few really serious injury problems compared with some pros. I had been playing for some 17 years by now and had probably injured nearly every part of my body to some extent. I can remember seeing a magazine article about George Best. There was a double-page spread in it and a picture of him wearing just a pair of shorts. They had used make-up to replicate all of his injuries to date and his body was covered from head to foot: contusions, stitches, bruises, strains, pulls, breaks and tears. Besty wasn't very old when that was published, but I tried to imagine what a similarly labelled picture of me would look like at my age - a bit gruesome, I think!

Jim encouraged me to take an interest in his work and we used to have some informative conversations from my point of view. He would sometimes have me stand in when he was examining one of the lads and then ask my opinion on the injury. My thoughts were very limited compared with his expertise, but I think that he quite enjoyed teaching me, if I could call it that.

Physios are renowned for their moody demeanour at times and Jim was no exception. Sometimes he was a pain in the backside first thing in the morning, so I would give him a wide berth. God help you if you caught him on a bad day and dared to moan yourself! He would turn the interferential machine, which worked the muscles through electric waves, right up and when he did this you would have to be scraped off the ceiling!

Jim and I became quite good friends and he encouraged me to go on a two-year FA course at Lilleshall for the treatment and management of sports injuries, which would result in the minimum qualification needed to go on the pitch as a physio. You could also treat and rehabilitate players, so it was a very comprehensive course. For too long just about anyone had been able to run on the pitch and treat people, so the FA had quite rightly been determined to improve standards of care. Jim was very supportive and helped me a great deal, and at the end of the second year I spent a week away doing practical and theory exams. Fortunately I passed and became a qualified sports therapist. This was the second time that I had combined education with my football career, as when I was at Colchester United I had studied at Colchester Institute along with Mick Packer and Steve Leslie and had gained a certificate in recreation and leisure management.

My optimism for the season ahead was proved wrong. Even though the manager had replaced some of the lads with what appeared to be better players, it just didn't happen for us. By now there was only me, Colin Smith, Glen Burvill, Tony Lange and Ian McDonald left out of the original promotion side from 1986/87.

We were relegated to the fourth division, which was very sad for everyone. All that hard work on and off the pitch to get into the next tier of the football pyramid seemed wasted at the time. That may have been my initial thought, but it became easier to take once the financial situation at the club became clearer. As a player you don't normally take too much notice of idle gossip about matters going on behind the scenes. You come to the club, do your training and go away, especially if you have to travel a fair distance. Sometimes you don't even read the local newspaper, unless it's got great news all about you in it! I'm being a little flippant here but I guess you get my point.

Our achievements a year or so earlier had put the club in a reasonably strong position, or so I had thought. We had performed well in the Cup competitions and the play-offs. We had also sold one of our top assets in the form of Martin Foyle for £140,000. Surely this must have been one of our largest incomes over one season for many years? This may have been the case, but there were more deep-rooted problems than people realised.

The next season, 1989/90, was another difficult one for everybody. It just proved how quickly situations could change in this uncertain industry. We struggled in the bottom half of the division and my old club Colchester were relegated into the Conference League. Only two years earlier we had been promoted to the third division and Colchester had actually finished above us in the League but had lost out to Wolves in the play-offs. It was a sad time for them and for me, as I still felt affiliated to the club after being a player there for seven years. Aldershot had only finished seven points ahead of Colchester. I suppose the one positive of the season was that we hadn't fallen through the trapdoor into the non-League too!

An old favourite of the club, Dale Banton, came back. Dale had been a huge success at the Rec a few years earlier. He had then moved on to other clubs, scoring plenty of goals. He may have been past his best as he'd had a bad knee injury while he was away and had lost a yard of pace but, understandably, the crowd probably expected too much from him.

The whole season was a frustration for everyone, including me, and some of our training sessions became a little fraught at times. When there are underlying problems at a club this sometimes happens and even the best of mates or colleagues can fall out, albeit briefly.

In one such session we were playing attack against defence on the main pitch. Gilly liked putting on this type of exercise and would usually wind the defenders up a bit to get them at it in order to create more realism. I had the hump for some reason and I was crashing about the pitch. I should have known better at my age but old habits die hard. The ball was laid up short to Dale and I went right through him, taking the ball and everything. It was not a good challenge and he rightly reared up and grabbed me. For a split second I wanted to take his head off. David Coles, who was in goal at the time, ran about 20 yards, pushed me away and gave me a rollicking. He was spot on and I was out of order! I quickly apologised to Dale and we just got on with the session. Gilly, being the experienced coach that he was, quickly wrapped up the exercise. I was settling down as a player but it had taken 17 years!

There were a few other incidents like that in the squad throughout the season, which could have been linked to the overall frustration that I have mentioned.

Someone else who was probably more frustrated than most at that time was Ian McDonald. He had been phased out of the side and had taken on the role of youth team coach. Macca kept himself fit by playing in the reserves and he also kept his League registration going just in case he was needed. We definitely missed his quality on the ball in the first team and I know he would have been spitting feathers watching us struggle week in, week out, while he was not able to get on the pitch and do something about it.

One clear memory I have of that term is a game at Cambridge United. They were a decent outfit, finally gaining promotion that season via the play-offs. Jon Sheffield, a fine young keeper destined for better things, was in goal for us. Cambridge knocked a long ball over our back four, which I chased along with their centre forward. The ball bounced just outside our box and sat up a bit, so I stretched to head it back to Jon. Their lad, who was right on my tail, just nudged me in the back as I headed it. I went flying and hit the ground like an arrow, with my shoulder taking the main impact. The moment I made contact with the turf I knew I was in trouble! The ball fell short for Jon and the centre forward chased it down and lunged for it, with Jon trying to get his hands on it first. Jon got clattered! The ball squirmed out of his grasp and rolled out for a corner.

Afterwards the lads told me that both challenges were fouls, but you didn't get much from referees at Cambridge in those days!

We were both laid flat out. I was in agony and I knew something wasn't right so I didn't move. Poor old Jon was laid prostrate with blood gushing from a gash above his eye. Jim Lange came strolling on, took a quick look at me, felt around my collarbone area and said, "Oh, Viggy, zat doesn't feel vrite!" He then ran over to Jon and started treating him! I managed to sit up gingerly and by now their physio was walking towards me. Jim just blanked me and got on with patching up the keeper. Their man got me on my feet and told me to cradle my arm myself in whatever position was the most comfortable. This wasn't easy as it was bloody agony!

It turned out that I had dislocated my clavicle (collarbone). Jim had realised this straight away and, knowing that he was not going to be able to keep me on the pitch, he had gone to tend to the keeper first! Jon did stay on the pitch and was able to play on, so it was a good decision by Jim. I was slowly walking off when he finally caught up with me. He didn't say a lot, but then what could he say? He just immobilised the arm and shoulder with a sling and that was it. Jim wasn't a 'pamperer'. I guess with his Army background he had seen a damn sight worse than a dislocated shoulder!

I had travelled to the game with Ian Stewart, so you could imagine what thoughts were going through my mind regarding the drive home! I was in absolute agony and the idea of Stewie driving like a bat out of hell on the M25 made me feel even worse. To be fair to him, however, he was superb and drove as smoothly and as slowly as he could.

I was out for about six weeks and even now, on a very cold day, the old shoulder still gives me a bit of gyp. Over that recuperation period, I spent more time in the company of Jim in the treatment room in order to further my knowledge of sports injuries. We got on well and he generally enjoyed a joke. One weekend he and his wife kindly invited Anne and me over for dinner. The evening was going very well and Jim was regaling us with humorous tales from his Army days. They had a lovely old dog that was at that age when they are unable to settle and it kept bumping into the coffee table and in and out of our legs. Jim adored it, but one example of his dry sense of humour was when, during one of his stories, the dog again decided to decamp and Jim shouted in his German/English accent, "For God's sake, lie down! You're like a vandering Joo!" Anne and I just cracked up! He hadn't meant it in any kind of racist way - far from it, I can assure you!

The season finished with a few exciting games but only because we were trying to save our League status. Those games brought a different pressure to bear. This was nail-biting stuff at times, as there were still three or four teams in trouble. Halifax, Wrexham and Doncaster were involved until the last couple of games. We had more than enough quality in the side but we still made it difficult for ourselves. Fortunately we were able to retain our status.

I needed a good rest in the close season of 1990, as I was having a few problems with my groin and hamstring. Jim thought that I could have a deep-seated pelvic strain or similar problem. I was still as fit as a flea, but after some of the latter games of that season I struggled to get out of bed the next day. Jim recommended a really long rest to see if it would settle over the summer.

Behind the scenes the financial situation at the club had become desperate and we had not been paid on time for some weeks. At that level of football not everyone is as financially secure as people might think. Some of the younger players were really strapped for cash and were struggling even to fill their cars with petrol in order to get to training. It all may sound a little dramatic but I assure you that it is fact!

Believe it or not, Anne and I were in the process of moving home from Ruislip to Aldershot. I'd had enough of travelling as it was affecting my health and I simply didn't want to do it anymore. Four years up, down and around the M25 was more than enough! Even though I was close to my 36th birthday I still had another year of my contract to go and maybe an extension beyond that if I could stay fit. We couldn't have predicted what was to happen.

We signed for the new house literally 24 hours before a winding-up order for the club was due in the high court. We had received virtually no pay throughout the summer. The Professional Footballers' Association provided a little one-off payment for us but only after we had suffered for some weeks. On top of that, we had also had an addition to the family with the birth of our lovely daughter, Sally-Anne, that April in a London hospital.

Talk about pressure! I had no income as such at that time; the club could have gone out of business, taking my job with it; we were moving home; the boys needed to move schools; and we had a four-month-old baby. Apart from that everything was fine! Talk about walking on the edge! We must have been mad putting ourselves and the kids through all that, but circumstances took over and it was all in the lap of the gods, as they say.

When we moved into our new home we found that the previous occupier had left us a 'calling card'. We had never met the gentleman but he certainly had a sense of humour. On the doorstep was on old, well-used, deflated football!

Colin Hancock, the chairman, had managed to keep the club going throughout all the problems, including the winding-up order from the courts. Our losses were estimated at about £2,000 per week, which in 1990 was quite a few quid. Colin couldn't possibly continue to finance Aldershot in its present state and so he appealed for help. He even went as far as appearing on television. In the end he got a response from a young man called Spencer Trethewy, who was reportedly only 19 years old and apparently, to quote Colin, "had a few bob". Trethewy came up with the £200,000 to satisfy the courts and consequently the winding-up order was dismissed.

It all seemed rather strange to me but to be honest as a family we didn't care who had saved the club. The main thing was that Aldershot had survived and I still had a job. Ultimately our move had made sense as now we had a bigger house for our expanding family and I could be at the ground in ten minutes - heaven!

From the players' point of view, we just wanted to get on with playing. Without wanting to sound too mercenary, at that stage, so long as our wages were going into the bank regularly and the club appeared stable, that was all we wanted.

Personally, I had my doubts about the way that this young man had ridden up on his white charger, or should I say his white stretch limousine. The reason I mention the limousine is that at our away game at Scunthorpe in January 1991 young Mr Trethewy turned up at the game in one such limo and got out with two girls. They were blonde twins and he was 'wearing' them, one on each arm. What was that all about? I'll tell you what it was about - a load of 'bullshine'!

My reasons for saying the above relate to my first encounter with Spencer

Trethewy. We were all called to a meeting with him not long after he had supposedly stumped up the money to save the club. Players and staff, including the office workers, were summoned to the ground and we all sat in the lounge upstairs eagerly awaiting the arrival of the young saviour. The chairs had been placed against the walls of the room, creating a sort of 'central stage' in the middle.

Trethewy strolled in to address us. He was as young as had been rumoured, he was quite a good-looking bloke and he appeared pretty confident. Standing slap bang in the middle of the room, he introduced himself. His address began well, with the usual stuff about being there for the right reasons and that he was glad the club had survived, etc. As his speech continued, however, the whole thing started changing into a motivational oration. He banged on about what we were going to do in the future in an incredibly adolescent way to all these experienced professionals! Then the swearing started, with a liberal peppering of f*** this and f*** that every other word! It was embarrassing and everybody began to squirm in their seats, especially the ladies present. The lads were glancing round at one another and thinking: what on earth have we got here? I know he was young but this was something else and all was not well in my mind.

Apparently, Trethewy had agreed to pay £100,000 up front in return for becoming a director and receiving shares in the club. Another £60,000 was to follow in a matter of weeks, with a further £40,000 within the year in return for a sponsorship deal. These facts were detailed in the press for the public to see and, on the face of it, it seemed quite straightforward. In fact it all appeared too good to be true but, as I have mentioned, we just wanted to get on with trying to get results on the pitch!

We had a few new faces at the club. Mark Ogley came in from Barnsley. He was mainly a defender but could also play as a holding midfielder. Mark Whitlock joined us from Southampton. He was an experienced centre back who had played at a good level. Leigh Cooper came in at left back. He had a silky left foot and was a good footballer. Charlie Henry came over from Swindon and was an all-action midfielder who could also play up front. A youngster called Paul Coombes also came into the squad. Coombsy was a centre forward with good pace who was just starting his career.

What all these new lads made of the situation at the club heaven only knows. Lenny must have got his old silver tongue out to persuade lads to sign for us when the whole future of the club looked in jeopardy.

We kicked off the season away at Rochdale, which wasn't exactly a glamorous fixture for what you might call a 'revamped' club - no disrespect to anyone at Rochdale. Anyway they 'mullered' us 4-0, so who am I to say anything?

One observation I did make that day was that of the 13 players on the team sheet I was the last surviving player from the great 1986/87 promotion side. Glen Burvill came in at Southend, our next game, so then there were two of us. No disrespect to the 1990/91 team, but that old side would definitely have given the new lot more than a game!

I wonder what the manager was thinking at that time? I felt it in my bones that there were going to be changes at the club. I wasn't sure what these would be but something was afoot.

There were some changes around the corner for me personally. I was having trouble with my groin and hip. Once I got myself warmed up, I was alright and could get through training and games. However, I was finding it increasingly difficult to recover in time to train on the Monday following a Saturday game or the Thursday following a Tuesday match. Eventually, I hardly trained at all and just took anti-inflammatory tablets to help to dull the pain, which enabled me to play in games. I still loved playing and my enthusiasm never waned.

Jim Lange was concerned that I had a very deep-seated problem in my pelvis, which was causing me what is called 'referred pain' in my groin, hip and leg. After matches I noticed that I was starting to drag my left leg a little. Jim decided to send me for a special kind of X-ray called a 'Stork' view. I had to stand on one leg with a weight in one hand as they took pictures of my pelvis. Jim explained the results to me; in fact he actually showed me the problem. I had damaged my 'symphysis pubis'. In plain terms, where your pelvis joins at the pubic bone there is a cartilage and I had damaged this, resulting in movement of a normally stable joint. I was having all sorts of problems because of this instability and Jim gave it to me straight from the hip, so to speak. There were two options. Option one would be to have an operation and have a metal plate inserted over the pubic bone to strengthen and stabilise the joint, which would require a rehabilitation period of 8 to 12 months, if successful. And the second option? That I packed it in altogether!

I was absolutely gutted. The operation wasn't really an option for me at 36 years of age. I would have been getting on for 38 before I could play again even if it worked out okay. And it wasn't a very pleasant operation according to Jim. I won't say that I was shocked, more disappointed. I always thought that the end would come when I wasn't up to the job, but the facts were that my legs hadn't gone and my stamina was excellent. My desire was also still there but that bloody injury wasn't going to go away with basic treatment or rest. However, after 700 or so competitive games I should have been grateful that I hadn't suffered many really serious injuries and that I had played constantly for nearly 20 years.

I knew that I was finished as a professional footballer and had to accept the verdict. The pragmatic side of my nature took over almost immediately. My contract was up at the end of the season and any monies that I could claim for having to finish through injury were not going to go far, so I had to look to the future pretty quickly!

The FA sports injuries course I had taken was an option, as I would be able to stay involved in the professional game in some capacity with that qualification. Jim helped me a lot by getting me more involved with the injured players. He even opened a private practice away from the ground and asked me to do some work for him on a Sunday with his clients. It was great experience for me. I was learning so much from him. There is nothing like practical involvement to learn quickly, especially in the area of sports injuries and rehabilitation.

To my surprise, Lenny called me into his office a short while after my retirement as a player in early April 1991. He told me that a couple of clubs had enquired if I would be interested in going over to them to work on the physio and rehab side of things.

Brian Little was at Leicester at the time and he wanted me to go there as their second physio to work with the injured pros on their rehabilitation and fitness work. He told me that he wanted an employee that the players could relate to more than a medical man, if you like.

It was a positive offer and one that I discussed at great length with Anne. It would mean moving house again and we had only been in our new home for a matter of months. Considering the financial package on offer, a move just didn't seem viable for us. I wasn't looking a gift horse in the mouth. It was a good job at a big club, but we had to survive financially and it would have been a massive wrench for the kids again. Anne was incredibly supportive, as ever, and left it up to me to decide the final outcome. She would go anywhere and make the necessary arrangements so long as we were all together.

Not long afterwards, I was approached by Swansea with a similar package on offer. I turned them both down in the end, but it was nice that people within the game wanted to employ me.

Although I had my own concerns to worry about, Lenny Walker had even more pressing business. Just before I retired, the end was nigh for him in the season even though he was due his testimonial game. I wasn't privy to what went on behind the scenes, but Gilly had gone and Lenny was to follow. John Pollard, our secretary, had also gone and so too had the chairman, Colin Hancock. And as for Spencer Trethewy, he appeared to have disappeared off the face of the planet! Macca was hanging on to his youth team coach job, but apart from that it looked like all change.

What else could possibly happen to this club?

Once again everything was up in the air and I'm sure some of the players' bums were tweaking a bit at the thought of who or what was next!

CHAPTER 7

A DEAD CLUB WALKING

We were soon to find out what was going to happen next. There had been speculation that a certain manager or a group of people were going to take over. However, all speculation stopped when Brian Talbot breezed into the club. I have deliberately used the word 'breezed' because he definitely made a few folks windy with his arrival!

With some assistance from me, Macca, who was officially the youth team coach but technically also the caretaker manager, had looked after the team for a few weeks. Then suddenly, even though it was only a matter of days, I was on the other side of the fence for the first time in 20 years. I was officially no one, just a player who was on the verge of retiring giving Macca a hand.

Anyway, Brian came in and appeared to be very autocratic and organised. He marched around the club with us both and pointed out things that needed doing - from the dressing rooms being tidied to finding a place to hold a meeting with all the staff at a specific time. He was laying down the law straight away, if you like. My first impressions were not particularly great. I thought he came over as a little arrogant and smug. Mind you, he was well clued up, as he knew all about us both! Someone had obviously briefed him, but whether it was positive or negative we weren't sure. His whole demeanour was that of somebody who knew exactly what he wanted from day one.

Brian was well known in football, not only for his exploits on the pitch with Ipswich and Arsenal but with his work in the PFA. He had also managed West Bromwich Albion where he'd had a bit of a rough ride. Perhaps that was why he was so forthright when he came in. Had he wanted to stamp his authority straight away?

Brian took Ian and me into his office for what we thought might be the third degree on everyone, but all he wanted to know was if we would work for him. He wanted Ian to be known as 'coach' and me to be the club's 'physio/coach'. He wanted me to treat and rehabilitate the players, as well as helping out in training by setting up sessions and carrying equipment, etc. Macca was doing a few jobs too, helping with the first team and reserves. Basically, we would be doing the sorts of tasks you do when you start at the bottom of the ladder. Brian didn't bring any of his own staff with him.

It was more than likely that there was no budget for him to do that. I was still being paid as a player and I think that Ian also had a contract, so in effect he had a ready-made pair of dogsbodies for want of a better word.

A new chairman, Mike Gill Anderson, and board took over along with a new secretary, Steve Birley. It looked as though a whole new package was taking over the club. However, the old actor, Mr Arthur English, was still our president. Arthur was a lovely man and a real gentleman. He used to sponsor my kit when I was a player and he was always there with an encouraging word. He remained loyal to and involved with the club even when he became ill. Sadly he is no longer with us but there are many at Aldershot who will remember his support at that time.

As Brian was a big name in football his arrival was viewed as a positive move by the club. From Brian's point of view, he jumped at the chance to manage in the Football League again after his departure from West Brom. He didn't talk too much about his time there, but he was clearly stung at the way it had all finished and felt that he had been let down by some people, or even stabbed in the back, you might say!

Ian and I used to meet with Brian in his office every morning at 9 o'clock. He insisted that we were both clean-shaven and on time for work. After being a player for so long and only shaving a couple of times a week at most, this was something that I had to get used to! However, it didn't take long to get into the swing of it and I have shaved daily ever since. Someone in our house was well pleased with a smooth face on a regular basis - and it wasn't the dog!

Every morning for a few weeks, without fail, Brian used to say to us, "You're both with me, aren't you?" and we would answer in the affirmative every time! Ian and I are very loyal people. As far as I was concerned, if I worked for someone they would get my total commitment and loyalty. That doesn't mean that I intended to spend my day with my nose up the manager's backside, far from it. If I felt that something wasn't right then I would air my opinion to him in private and he could pick the bones out of it. I would not undermine him behind his back, especially not to players, in fact not to anyone.

Brian was still wary of people he didn't really know, which was understandable. However, the more we got to know the boss, the more relaxed he became with us and he soon trusted us enough to start delegating tasks. In our morning meetings he would inform us of exactly what we would be doing that day on and off the training field. I also had to give him a complete rundown of all the injured players' fitness levels and who could or could not train that day.

Monday morning meetings were quite long, as Brian would map out the whole week for us: what games we were to go to either for scouting or assessment purposes, times and duration of sessions for each day, and anything else that took his fancy. He travelled in from London Colney, not far from Arsenal's training ground, every day and was in for work most mornings by 8 o'clock. His work ethic as a manager was similar to when he was playing. If you have seen him play, you will know what I mean. He was a non-stop midfield man.

Brian could come over as a little arrogant and quite loud, which unnerved some of the lads, especially the younger ones. However, the more I got to know him, the further away from that description I found him to be in reality. If anything, I felt that he was a little insecure sometimes, perhaps due to his previous management experience. So, although my first impressions of Brian had not been great, by now I liked him and got on with him very well, as did Macca.

I wasn't totally convinced that the club was financially secure for the foreseeable future. I knew that Brian was involved in a lot of wheeling and dealing to keep things going. He was a great organiser and he appeared to know just about everybody in the game. His phone would ring in his office while Macca and I were there and he would ask us to wait outside for a while so that he could take the call in private. This was only in the early days of his taking the reins. Later on he would take any calls at all when we were together in his room. I suppose that he had decided that he could trust us by then. Ron Atkinson would phone him quite often and Brian would rib him unmercifully at times. Brian was acquainted with lots of high-profile people, but how many of them did him any real favours in football terms I don't know.

The boss asked us to play in the reserves on a few occasions. Ian was still quite fit and I was okay for the odd game in the 'stiffs'! When he saw us play he asked us what we thought of playing in the first team again. I told him that I had taken my retirement money and couldn't but Macca hadn't officially retired through injury and was still registered to play in the League. He asked me if I would consider paying the money back so that I would be available to play. I explained my injury problem to him and he reluctantly accepted the situation. In no disrespectful way to the players at the club, Brian felt that Ian and me were better even at 38 and 37 years respectively than what he had in the team. Ian was ready and able and so Brian threw him into the team a few times. He added some quality on the ball that was lacking and definitely didn't embarrass himself.

Brian's style of management with the players meant that he could be brusque at times, but with his staff he could be quite the opposite. Ian and I, along with our wives, were invited out to dinner with Brian and his wife, Sandra. He wanted to get to know Glenis and Anne and wanted them to get to know him and his wife too. It was a clever move, as he would be demanding of us as staff over the coming weeks and wanted our spouses to know that he was trying to do the job properly. He also came up with a nice touch at the meal, producing a small gift for each of the ladies. They were little trinket boxes, which the girls loved. Sandra didn't even know anything about them. It was both a genuine gesture and also a great way of setting off on the right track with our wives. Anne has still got her present to this day and is very fond of it.

The finances at the club were always at the back of my mind. Listening to the boss on the phone at times opened my eyes to the realities of running a football club. I hadn't been privy to any of that side of things as a player and had only received second-hand information or heard rumours. Any official information handed out by the club had probably been edited anyway. Now I was in a position where I could hear some of the problems first-hand and it was a little unnerving. I watched as Brian worked so hard just to try to keep the place going, and that was before he put on his kit and got down to the everyday coaching and managing of the players.

My job as club physio and coach was very interesting at times. Jim Lange stayed on in a consultative role. He would treat players if required and I would refer lads to him if their injury was something major. Brian would throw me in at the deep end sometimes and give me four or five 'out of favour' pros who needed extra work in the afternoons. I can assure you that this is one of the hardest tasks for a coach! The players are usually peed off because of their lack of involvement with the first team and to put on a session for as few as five lads and keep them interested isn't easy. The senior professionals would test you out right from the start to see what you were made of. Sometimes some of the lads were there because the boss wasn't happy with their performance during the morning session, so I was left with the task of doling out what the players perceived as a form of punishment!

I was more than ready for them in these sessions, however. I had no intention of rubbing their noses in it, but at the same time I wouldn't tolerate anyone taking the piss or being disruptive in any of my routines, even if they did seem meaningless to both of us at times. I think that I had the respect of most of the players just because of my experience in the game. I needed them to respect me as a member of staff now and that was my target. My mindset had to change quite quickly. I wasn't one of 'the boys' anymore, yet I wanted to be able to join in the banter and give out some stick as well as take some.

I found that being the physio was difficult sometimes because the lads might on occasions open up and say things to me that they wouldn't say to the boss. Whether it was their way of getting their gripe or problem over to the manager through me, I couldn't always tell. What I didn't want to be was a 'stool pigeon' or a 'grass', so most of what was said stayed with me and I tried to help that player in any way I could. If the problem was something major, then I would edit the conversion slightly and mention it to the boss.

Everyone wants to be liked by other people in any walk of life and I was no different. Now for the first time in my career some people were going to dislike me just because I was doing my job. I was not going to run to the boss every five minutes to tell him things just to get in his good books. I was also not going to go against the manager just to keep in with the lads in the dressing room.

I would go home and tell Anne about anything that was giving me problems at the club. She was great and gave me her opinion on the matter, and we usually came up with a very similar solution. One thing's for sure, she would never 'bullshine' me for the sake of my ego - I got it straight from the hip even if I was wrong about something!

I was enjoying my first couple of months on the staff, but I was quickly realising that it was much easier to be a player. If only I could just buy myself a new pelvis!

When the season petered out Lenny had his testimonial game against Arsenal and did alright out of it. I felt for him as he'd done a fine job at Aldershot under very difficult circumstances over many years. As is often the case, it is sometimes quite a few years later before some supporters realise just how well a manager did during the time of his tenure, by which time a very good boss can be long gone - and I don't mean dead!

My first close season as a staff member and not a player arrived. I must admit that it was good to relax my body completely and not have to be too concerned about everything that I ate and drank. I didn't become a 'porky' - I was probably too vain for that! Anyway, I needed to maintain a certain level of fitness to take some of the pre-season running with the chaps.

Brian, Ian and myself were probably as fit as any team of staff in the country at that time. Brian used to do a 12-minute run around the perimeter of the pitch at the Rec after training. He would clock up about ten laps, which was as good as any of our fittest lads in the squad. Macca and I weren't far behind at about nine and a half. There was still a little left in the three 'old gits'!

Brian briefed us with the pre-season schedule he had set out. After the initial first week of running we were going down to Exeter University for a week. The campus was empty for the summer exeat, so he had negotiated a good deal for the squad to stay there. We would play a couple of games locally and train every day at nearby facilities. Initially I thought that we would be going down by coach, but discovered that we were actually travelling by minibus - and I was given the task of driving the bloody thing! As I had never driven a minibus before in my life, that prospect somewhat tempered my excitement at the thought of going away to do some decent work with the team at a nice location. With 15 professional footballers crammed in for about four hours, the trip seemed quite daunting!

Brian was taking his car and would be following us, and Macca was to stay at home with the youth team and mind the fort. Brian had organised this trip on a very tight budget, but it was better than slogging away at the same venue day after day for six weeks or so. That is why I was now driver, physio, coach and player on the bench if needed.

On the way down I came in for plenty of stick, which was par for the course. However, I managed well enough and got us all there on time and in one piece. My driving 'cred' went up a few notches with the lads, as we managed not to get lost and we had some good 'sounds' on as the minibus rattled down the M4.

The boss rolled up in his motor later that evening. All the lads were sorted and paired off in their rooms. It definitely wasn't the Ritz but it suited our purpose for the week. The boss was always lively and full of enthusiasm, which impressed me. He was very professional in everything he did and yet he still enjoyed a beer and a laugh.

After dinner Brian lay down the law to everyone in terms of how he expected them to behave. There was to be no drinking, they were to be in their rooms by a certain time, and all the usual dos and don'ts that went with our trade. The players dispersed, leaving just Brian and me in the canteen.

The moment the last player had disappeared around the corner, he said, "Do you fancy a beer?"

"What, here in front of the lads?" I said.

"No, we'll go down the road and find a nice country pub!"

I wasn't sure whether he just had a great sense of smell or he knew the area better than I thought!

We got in the car and he just drove out of the town into the sticks to this lovely old pub. We had a couple of pints and a laugh, swapping stories about football. It may sound a bit sad, I guess, but they weren't anorak-type stories, they were the sorts of tales Joe Public wouldn't get to hear about - unless you wrote a book, of course!

A couple more players had come into the squad and some had left. Youngsters Peter Terry, a midfielder, and Jason Tucker, a defender, came up through the ranks. Alex Fisher, another young defender, also progressed. These three lads bulked up the numbers but would only be on the fringe of the first team. Richard Dunwell came in on trial and showed some promise, but he was a very inexperienced wide man or centre forward and he too was only a fringe player.

Brian had a hard job putting together a squad that could do well in the fourth division. I didn't know the size of his budget, but I could tell from the way he was trying to balance his squad with some experienced players on decent money and youngsters on not so good contracts that it wasn't a great deal.

Keith Bertschin was one of the senior players who came in. Bertsch was still very fit and just as game as ever. Mark Rees also arrived with Keith from the Midlands. He was a quick winger and was very experienced. He reminded me of my old mate Alan (Ruby) Murray at Doncaster - a bit of a twinkle toes down the right-hand side, and he even looked like him. Big John Flowers, something of a gentle giant really, was a centre back who came from Northampton. He was a nice lad and did a decent job as a defender for us but he was limited on the ball. Peter Hucker, a very good goalkeeper with an excellent record, joined us from QPR but he lost his place to John Granville.

John was black, and I'm only pointing out this fact as you didn't see many black goalkeepers in the League back in the early nineties. He was a big, strong lad who could kick the ball a mile out of his hands, which were bigger than dinner plates!

Most of these players were on the pre-season trip down to Devon. They had trained well and the games had gone okay. We had been pleased with their conduct too and had decided to give the lads a day off to do whatever they wanted. You could get to the coast reasonably quickly from the university, so some of the boys took full advantage of the good weather and headed there for their day out.

Brian and I drove down to the seafront and took a walk along the promenade. It was really warm, so Brian suggested we have an ice cream. We soon found a kiosk and with our 'Mr Whippys' in hand we found a couple of adjacent deckchairs on the grass verge and took up residence. We just sat there in silence, Brian in his 'Eric Morecambe' knee-length shorts, polo shirt and sandals and me in tracky bottoms, T-shirt and trainers. The old ices were going down well as we gazed out to sea.

As a bit of fun I turned to Brian and said, "Do you think that we look like a pair of queens sat here?"

He sat up and said, "NO … we don't, do we?" Then he leapt up and added, "Best be on our way!"

So we got up and walked on. I couldn't help but laugh at his face as he quickly left the deckchair still licking his ice cream. I don't think Brian had quite grasped my Scouse sense of humour yet!

The season got under way and the more we became acquainted with Brian the more he would tell us in regard to the state of things behind the scenes. He was having trouble with the finances and at one meeting he told Ian and me that if at any point he couldn't pay the players their wages at the end of the month then he would go. This was serious stuff. Ian and I had already been through an awful lot over the last year and the prospect of a similar scenario happening was a nightmare that we didn't want even to contemplate. Perhaps everything that Brian had been promised when he'd taken the job hadn't been put in place. He didn't discuss that with us, but reading between the lines I think that he was let down by the powers that be. It may not have been their fault, of course, but I know Brian was disappointed. His frustrations came through on some occasions while he was in charge.

One such instance happened when Tony Hopkins, a left back with a good left foot, was with us. He was from Newport in South Wales and came over as a bit flash. He was always tanned (even in winter!) and he would sometimes wear a white tracksuit, which looked somewhat out of place. His general attitude made him seem a little above his station. However, when I got to know him better I realised that the bling and brashness were mostly pure bravado. He was a decent lad who wasn't quite up to the standard required to play in the Football League.

At an away game Tony had been left out of the starting eleven. I don't think that he was even on the bench. Tony being Tony and wearing his heart on his sleeve, he showed his displeasure, as many players do, by huffing and puffing around the dressing room. What I had learnt already was that once the boss had announced the team it was always best to clear the dressing room of the other squad members. The reason for this was so that the players involved in the game could focus on the task in hand and not have any sort of negative influence around them before the kick-off. This doesn't mean that every player who is left out of the squad is negative, but it is more professional to clear the decks.

Tony did leave the room but for some reason he reappeared for a minute or so eating a meat pie! He was chatting to a couple of the lads while at the same time taking huge mouthfuls of pastry. I thought: oh my God, if the boss spots him he's in for a bollocking! Brian had popped out for a minute and I was just about to intervene when the door opened and in he walked. Straight away he clocked the lad with gravy around his mouth. Here we go, I thought, but the boss didn't say a word. Tony was on his way out anyway. "All the bethd ladth!" he spluttered with a gob full of pie!

Brian didn't say a word about this to me or anyone else so far as I know. I knew that Brian wasn't a happy man with some of the warning signs at the club. I didn't feel that the incident was worth harping on about and thought Brian had just let it go. How wrong could I have been?

After the game, in the very next session Brian called us all in for a chat on the training ground and we stood in a circle on the pitch. Brian would sometimes do this to explain the morning's format to the players, so we all presumed that this was one of those briefings.

Brian said, "Tony," and looked directly at him.

"Yes, boss," Tony replied.

Brian then reached into an inside pocket of his tracksuit top and produced an envelope. "There you go, son, that's a free transfer." He handed it to Tony in front of all of us. "That's because of your behaviour on Saturday," he added.

Tony's face was a picture. I don't think that he could speak. Anyway, Brian didn't give him a chance to respond as he just turned away and we got on with the session. I hadn't seen that done before but there was always a first time! Do you think the boys were on their toes after that little beauty? You bet they were!

Brian saw the writing on the wall and decided to look after Macca and me by offering us new contracts. He wasn't to know what was actually going to happen at the club, but he attempted to secure our future, if there was to be any chance for Aldershot at all. In the event, Brian left at the end of November 1991. It was a sad day from my point of view, as I felt that he had worked very hard to try to keep the club going. Unfortunately, the financial restrictions made that task almost impossible and, as he had already told us, he wasn't prepared to carry on if people were not being paid. I presume that he was not willing to mislead employees regarding their wages if he knew damn well that the monies simply weren't there. I had learnt a lot from Brian. I didn't agree with all of his methods, but his drive and determination were commendable.

I had many sympathies with our secretary, Steve Birley, at that time. Poor Steve was even sleeping in his office at the ground some nights because of his workload. He obviously didn't realise that he didn't have an ice cube's chance in hell of making any real difference to what was eventually going to happen.

Macca and I were on our own now. Ian was made caretaker manager and my role was to assist him. We took the jobs with some hope in our hearts that something would materialise on the financial front that would give us the chance to run the place professionally.

Trevor Gladwell was the new chairman and we had been paid up to the end of November. However, there were no guarantees that anyone would be paid after that. Most of the squad stayed with it - they didn't really have any other choice! There was even the undignified fact that the police had visited the club premises to investigate possible 'financial irregularities' in previous administrations.

In the beginning, certain empty promises were made that money would be forthcoming to the players. We didn't tell the lads any untruths; we just relayed the information that was given to us from the powers above. Talk about being thrown in at the deep end! Ian was now an unpaid manager of a League club with an unpaid assistant. He had to put out a team of unpaid players and play in the side himself at times as well. We both had limited experience in managing a squad, so we had no idea how they were going to react to this difficult situation.

The players all had contracts that technically had to be adhered to by both parties. They would be entitled to free transfers if the club didn't pay them what they were owed within weeks. Some of the players were capable of getting other clubs to take them on; some, however, were not. Without being disrespectful, we didn't exactly have a squad of players that were worth a great amount of money. If we'd had any real assets, other clubs would have cherry-picked them for a small fee because of our situation. Also, anyone worth a couple of hundred grand would have been sold already to pay the bills.

We had a meeting with the players and one thing was for sure: we were all in it together. Macca and I weren't getting any pay either. The lads knew this and also realised that we had no control over payment or non-payment of wages. This was a unique situation because it meant that people tended to speak more freely in front of one another. Ian may have been the manager but because we were all in the same boat the players felt that they could say how they felt in front of him just as if he were another player. Most of the players were prepared to give it a go. They would have their own separate meetings as well, which was understandable as Ian and I were still 'staff'. To start with most of the lads came to training and things went along as normally as possible.

By the second week in December 1991, we hadn't won a game in 16 attempts. Our opponents at the next home game would be my old club Doncaster Rovers, who were 93rd in the Football League, just one place below us. The game was a classic nightmare resulting in a 0-0 draw. How much lower could we go? Results are always important to professionals. In this case, however, it was pretty irrelevant as we were just happy to be able to field a team of 11 players for the game!

Some of the lads were struggling to pay for their fuel to get into work, so they trained at home and just came in one day a week if they could, or just for matches. You can imagine what our team preparation was like at this point: virtually non-existent. More rumours and counter-rumours came in by the day - a 'mystery backer' here or a 'fairy godfather' there! The only reality was that time was running out for all of us. How long could we keep persuading the lads to play for nothing so that we could fulfil our League fixtures?

Supporters and other clubs were sending cash into the club office and this was distributed in the best way we could to the players. These were fantastic gestures even though the monies represented only a tiny fraction of what was needed. George Berry, our centre back, was a member of the PFA committee and he was an excellent mouthpiece for the players. He used to speak to many groups of supporters to explain the situation from the players' point of view. I think he also helped with communication between the PFA and the squad when needed.

On a lighter note, George was a real character. He could sometimes be a bit of a rascal in training and come over as disruptive if we were doing something he didn't fancy. He tried it on once in one of my sessions, but I clamped down on him straight away and just made him get on with it. If I had shown any weakness he would have eaten me for breakfast from then on! He had just been testing me out and we got on very well after that as it all had been a 'game' to George. Brian had brought him in and knew him very well, so George had toed the line for him.

At home games Anne and I always brought our kids. Although Sally was still a little young to appreciate them, Thomas and Jack used to enjoy the matches. On one such occasion, as we drew up to make a right turn into the ground, George pulled up alongside us in his Escort XR3i going in the opposite direction. He stopped and rolled his electric window down to ask me a question, sticking his head completely out of the car. Somehow he must have pushed the electric button that operated the window and it shot up, so George ended up with his head stuck as his neck was trapped! A traffic jam of cars waiting to go in and out of the ground ensued, providing many witnesses to his rather embarrassing predicament! Our children thought it was hilarious as George was one of their heroes. Coughing and spluttering, George eventually located the correct button and managed to release himself. As he would often play to the gallery, both intentionally and unintentionally, I wasn't sure whether or not this little performance was for the pleasure of his captive audience, our children in the back seat! He was a great chap.

Christmas wasn't the most celebratory of times that year and by January nothing had improved on or off the pitch. The kit was being washed by none other than our wives, Anne and Glenis. They were getting a small amount of cash for their labours, which just about covered the cost of the washing powder. Doing full sets of kit in industrial washing machines is hard enough, so you can imagine how tough it was doing it all in a domestic one. Anne used to have to scrub the socks with a toothbrush to get some of the mess out of them - and that brings me to a point of conjecture.

We were all getting fraught with the tensions at the club. We couldn't win games, we had no money and we were having our hopes built up one day only to have them dashed the next. The whole affair was a nightmare.

After one game the lads were getting changed and I was sorting the kit into piles so that everything could be counted. We couldn't afford for anything to go AWOL as we didn't have any replacements. It was then that I noticed that Dave Puckett was cleaning his boots with one of the socks! Dave was a good professional and typically he was looking after his tools of the trade straight after the game. The pros at this time were looking after all their own gear except the match kit.

I caught Dave's eye and said, "Don't do that, Dave, it ruins the socks, mate."

He didn't really respond and just kept on rubbing off the mud with the white sock. I had visions of my wife slaving over that sock in order to get the mud and polish out and restore it to its former glory for the next game.

"Dave, don't do that," I said again.

"Why's that then?" he asked.

For a split second I was tempted to grab him by the throat and throw him around the room like a rag doll! It felt as though all my frustrations were about to boil over – and all because of a sock. Just then Dave threw the sock down and sort of relented. I think he thought that I was going on a bit, so I explained my reasons for asking him not to do it and he appeared to see my point of view. We were all a little tense, so seemingly small things like that could develop into a big deal very quickly.

Problems had snowballed so much that, on the day of our match at home to Gillingham in February 1992, a man from the Electricity Board came to the ground and demanded that we pay our outstanding bill of about £1,200 or the 'lecky' would be switched off. This happened in the afternoon, just hours before our evening kick-off. By now I was expecting Jeremy Beadle to jump out from somewhere or pull off his 'lecky man' disguise! Fortunately, as usual Steve Birley did an amazing negotiating job and gained us a few days' grace, so the game went ahead.

It was at this time that the board of directors resigned and apparently waived any claim to money that they had already invested in the club. This was supposed to open the way for a potential backer to come in and save us all. We had heard it all before, of course, and most of us treated the news with contempt.

While this was all going on, a lot of people had forgotten that poor old Macca was supposed to be celebrating his testimonial year. How unlucky could you get after ten years of great service?

Considering that the top League was in the process of negotiating a possible £500,000,000 television rights package, it didn't seem fair that all this was happening to people at the lower end of the scale in the same industry. Football is and always has been a business, but this differential seemed obscene to me.

We were as low as we could be and the writing was on the wall; in fact, it was almost carved in stone. On the frontline, of course, was the team but the supporters were going through a torrid experience too. The genuine supporters who really cared about the football club kept turning up and paying their money week in, week out. Even some of the not so diehards were turning up on the terraces, because even their slightly cynical view concerning the demise of the club was now a possible reality and they felt that their support was now needed.

One really top-class supporter was Mary Sweet. She had seen Aldershot's first ever game back in 1926 and had only missed a handful of games home and away since. She was the nicest lady you could ever hope to meet and she never had a negative word to say about the team or the club. Whenever she saw my children she would always give them a sweet or two and if she saw the team in the final days there was always some cash handed over to get the lads a drink. You can imagine how bad she must have felt with her beloved club in a right old mess.

By now I was feeling totally drained and I am sure that Macca felt the same. We had become close friends, as our families had been through a lot together. At times, we had even eaten together as one big family to save a few quid! Our boys and their girls were of similar ages and became good mates too.

Our day at the high court eventually arrived and everyone was there, including the media. This was a big story; after all, bad news sells! We were possibly set to become the first club to drop out of the Football League since Accrington Stanley back in 1962, 30 years earlier.

Even though it looked like curtains, in the back of my mind there was still a little voice saying, "Don't worry, something will turn up"! As with anything in life, if you are given more time then there is always hope, and as I am the eternal optimist I still clung on to that one-in-a-million chance.

After all the hype before we went, then the journey down and the media circus that awaited us outside, we all squashed into the courtroom. I could hardly see a thing; just a few wigs bobbing up and down Muppet-style. Then there was a deathly hush as our case was read out briefly. Within 60 seconds the top man had wound us up! There was no emotion in his voice and he didn't falter. That was it – off you pop, job done! We were gutted with the outcome and it was also devastating to think that a 60-year club history, not to mention all the supporters that had watched and all that had been done to keep the club afloat, could be effectively swatted like a fly in seconds by the judiciary system.

Technically, we had a week to find someone to come in and finally rescue the club. The chairman, Mike Davey, who had taken the reins from Trevor Gladwell, felt that he could still save the "Shots". By now, however, although I wouldn't say that we had given up the ghost, we were mighty close to it. I don't want to sound too melodramatic, but all our emotions had taken an incredible pounding over the previous three months, with little hope and no pay. Some of us had been through it all before, so we were virtually at the club's wake already.

We managed to put out some sort of team for what was to be our last game in the Football League at Cardiff City. The whole experience for me was very strange and almost surreal. Over 6,000 turned up for the match and our lads gave a decent account of themselves considering all that had been happening during the previous week. I can't say that any finer details of the event have stuck in my mind, possibly because of the emotions that surrounded the occasion. The ordinary man in the street might shrug his shoulders on hearing of our demise, and who can blame him? Football supporters everywhere are more concerned that it could be their club next if they are outside the elite few at the top.

Everyone was feeling pretty sorry for themselves and quite rightly so. Someone who had more right than most to feel down was Macca, as he still hadn't had his testimonial game. The council actually locked the gates of the ground at the end of March, and those padlocks on the front of the Rec spoke a thousand words. Ian managed to get the council to promise that, if he could get a top side to come down and play against an Aldershot eleven, they would unlock the gates and allow the match to be played. That was nice of them, wasn't it? He eventually persuaded Southampton and their superstar-to-be, Alan Shearer, to visit the Rec. However, the game had to be played midweek and in daylight, with a 6.30 p.m. kick-off, as the health and safety certificate had expired. This obviously had an adverse effect on the attendance figure, which was just under 2,000.

The players went their separate ways to join other clubs. Looking at the situation from a positive perspective, I suppose you could say that their experiences over those last few months would make them stronger people, but the Football League is the only place to play for most professionals. If they lost that privilege because of what had happened then they would look at the whole experience as an expensive nightmare! Sadly, most of them did not play in the Football League again.

That was it for us. With no money for 13 weeks, a family to look after and the mortgage to pay, I felt as though I'd been shafted from every angle!

I rang Macca to ask him if he knew where the dole office was situated and suggested that we could go down there together.

CHAPTER 8

JOINING THE "MAD HOUSE"

The agony of a 'Dead Club Walking' was over. Personally, I needed to get a job soon for obvious reasons. Even at this early stage of the club's demise there had been rumours that a couple of local non-League football clubs had made enquiries about playing at the Rec. At first I thought the idea ridiculous, as the attendances for such a large stadium would be very small. On the other hand, it would be even more ridiculous to see a great surface and stadium go to waste. I wasn't part of the club anymore and so I had to get used to all the speculation in the local press about the fate of the Rec and live with it!

A local businessman called Terry Owens came forward and suggested that the club could be re-formed as Aldershot Town FC. To be honest, when I first heard this I was a little sceptical, but could anyone blame me after all that had happened previously?

I didn't know too much about Terry's business background, but we had met on quite a few occasions because of his involvement with the old club. He had always been positive about Aldershot FC and had loved to meet the players for a chat. I am going to be kind to him and say that he always looked younger than his years. 'Quite a dapper sort of chap' might be the right description and we always called him 'Tel', as he preferred the more informal title when mixing with the lads.

After one game, I saw him outside the dressing rooms and he was wearing a shell-type tracksuit. The style was a little young for him maybe, but it looked okay.

Tel asked me, "What do you think, Steve?"

"What about Tel?" I replied teasingly.

"My tracky. Do you think I look like one of the players?"

I hesitated for a millisecond and simply responded, "No."

Poor Tel, his face was a picture!

"You look good though, Tel mate! See you later," I added, and I was off.

That's how I saw Terry - a bit off a jack the lad maybe, who wanted to be seen as something he really wasn't. This had been my initial impression of him anyway, but as I got to know him better what I did realise was that he definitely had the best interests of the football club at heart.

Terry, in conjunction with the Supporters' Club, called a public meeting to discuss the possible formation and proposed infrastructure of a new club, Aldershot Town. No one knew how many people would turn up after all the traumas that the old club had faced but, to everyone's surprise, some 600 people arrived at the venue. This proved that the enthusiasm in the town for football to be played at the Rec was still there.

Terry and Graham Brookland, the chairman of the Supporters' Club, were successful in getting nearly 6,000 people in the town to sign a petition in favour of football on the club site, and, after a lot of hard work, they managed to get the local council, Rushmoor, to grant them a three-year licence to play at the Recreation ground. All this had been achieved within a month or so after the demise of the old club.

Graham's brother, David, became the club's financial adviser and he helped set up a financial structure for the new venture. There was an unbelievable amount of work to be done if the club was to be formally established, up and running with all systems go by August 1992!

Although all this was going on, I was mostly unaware of it. Macca knew more than I did and he was just as wary. He told me of their ideas but realistically it all still looked unattainable. Time didn't seem to be on their side, and even if they did manage to set up the infrastructure and get the finances in place, at what level of football was this new club going to start?

We drifted into May and I cast my mind back to the couple of offers that I'd had to ply my sports therapy trade at Leicester and Swansea the previous year. Even with all their logistical problems and lower salaries, both of those opportunities looked appealing to me now. Ian was offered a management position with Millwall reserves under Mick McCarthy, which he accepted. I would have dealings with Mick later on in my managerial career.

Terry and Graham were appointed chairman and director respectively of the newly formed company and Peter Bridgeman was the company secretary. All they had to do now was appoint a manager, who would have about two months to put a squad together for the coming season.

Terry called me and asked if I would like to go over to his house for a meeting with him and Graham. I accepted his invitation and went with an open mind. They didn't know as yet which league and at what level the club would be playing, so I was totally in the dark at the time. It was a nice day and so we sat in the garden at Terry's place. Graham looked a little nervous to start with but soon relaxed as the conversation went on. Tel did his hard sell on me, telling me all about what had been achieved and what their ambitions were. As Terry was speaking, I must admit that I was still not convinced that this was all going to work. What Terry said was excellent, but even with the best scenarios in the world, this still looked like a massive task for a manager, especially in the non-League environment, which was almost totally alien to me. He even threw in his target of a return to the Football League in ten years! That comment coming from Terry at that time seemed almost ridiculous. I couldn't get my head around anything of that sort at that moment.

So the club, or Terry and Graham, offered me the position of manager. How could I refuse? Their enthusiasm for the new adventure was more than infectious. I accepted and within about two minutes my brain went into overdrive. Whenever I decide to take on a project, I start planning immediately.

We wouldn't know if we were in the Diadora League until the second week in June, which was still a couple of weeks away, but I still had to start recruiting players ASAP! I also had to get my staff together - if there was to be a budget for them! Oh my God, my head was hurting already. Also I needed to go home and tell Anne that I had joined a fraternity called 'The Mad House', or Football Management as it is commonly known.

Anne, as usual, was very philosophical about it all. The fortunes at the club had brought changes for us before, from having no income to washing the kit. That had been a culture shock and Anne had dealt with it superbly. There'll be no more of them, I'd thought, but I was wrong again. There would still be many culture shocks for me to come, from washing the dressing room baths out myself to pumping up the match-day balls. I was determined that we were going to have a nice, new, well-run club, and that would only happen if everyone did their bit and got their hands dirty.

Initially, I even had thoughts of playing - and then I woke up! I had a word with myself, which went along the lines of: you silly beggar, you're too old and you're going to need every ounce of energy just to get this team off the ground, so playing is a definite no-no. I had actually had a couple of offers to play in the Conference when I finished but had declined, as I didn't want to go into non-League football. I had enjoyed my career in the Football League and wanted to leave it at that.

Another meeting took place, which resulted in the formation of the board of directors, which comprised John McGinty, Karl Prentice, Peter Bloomfield, Malcolm Grant and, at a later stage, Kevin Donegan. The new club emblem was chosen and quite rightly it was a phoenix rising out of the ashes. Some people might have thought that the choice was a little dramatic, but after going through the dreadful demise of Aldershot FC I am sure that anyone involved with the rebuilding of the new Aldershot Town saw the emblem as quite poignant.

Most of the necessary background work was done now. The council had agreed to unlock the gates of the Rec, we had a football club in stature and structure and all we needed now were some players to kick the ball around the pitch, win games and attract lots of supporters. Easy-peasy!

My networking began and I put out all my feelers. I needed to talk to people who knew the level of football at which we would be competing, even though we didn't actually know what league we were in yet. One player had already agreed to join us and that was Chris Tomlinson, the son of Dave the groundsman. Chris was a decent, honest defender with a good attitude. I knew he wouldn't let me down whatever league that we joined. He had actually played in Aldershot's last League game against Cardiff City, where he acquitted himself very well. So it was one down and only 15 or 16 left to find!

I knew that there wouldn't be a shortage of lads waiting to play for such a big club at this level, but it was essential that I only signed players that I felt were capable of handling everything that would be thrown at them. I use the word 'thrown' because they would be entering an environment that was totally different from anything they had experienced before. I had my own ideas as to how I was going to tackle this situation, but at the same time I was very open-minded and prepared to listen to individuals who had greater experience of this standard of football.

I received information that a player called Keith Baker might be interested in joining the club. Keith had an extensive history of playing in the non-League at a good level and I had seen him about on a few occasions at Junior County football matches where his son Neil played. I was there because my eldest son, Thomas, also played for the County and I always tried to go and watch both of my sons play whenever possible.

I telephoned Keith to ask him if he was interested and the conversation went well. Even before meeting him, I felt comfortable in my own mind that he would be a valuable member of my staff and when I did meet him he came over as articulate and confident, which impressed me. I offered Keith the job of player/coach and he accepted. This was a coup for us as he had played 300+ games for our local rivals Farnborough and was now leaving them to join Aldershot Town. He would not only be valuable in terms of his knowledge of local players, but also he was an extremely good footballer. Another bonus was that Keith was a left-footed defender and good ones were like gold dust!

I needed to see as many potential players actually demonstrate their playing skills as I could. It was all very well going on recommendations from someone, even Keith, but I needed each team member to play a specific role, so I organised trial games. I wanted to watch the lads in action, taking particular note of their physical shape, their body language and how they handled the whole experience. I didn't have a great deal of time, so I needed to make decisions quickly as to which players to take on.

The trials were an eye-opener for me because I didn't have a 'scooby' what to expect from these lads. Some of them looked like scared rabbits caught in car headlights even before they took to the field. We had trialists of all ages, from about 17 to 30+ years old. Many of them were local lads, which was good. In my mind I wanted to have at least a core of local boys in the line-up. I hoped that these fellas would really want to play for the club, and if they had previously stood on the terraces or sat in the stand watching Aldershot FC then all the better!

I had to keep my comments and expectations to myself, as I didn't want to come across as a 'big-time charlie'. The standard was obviously going to be much lower than I had been used to during my career, so I had to adjust very quickly and be realistic.

At the top of my agenda of qualities to look for were passion and enthusiasm. I've always had time for players who put themselves on the line. They won't win you anything on their own, but mix them with some slightly more skilled players and you've got a chance. As one of my old playing mates used to say, "Some players carry the piano on their backs while others play it"! That's something that will never change.

I spotted a few possibilities at the trial, but one lad stood out because of his total physical commitment and that was Stuart Udal. He was very limited technically but he was a good athlete and totally fearless. I marked him down straight away as a possible squad member who could play in three or four positions. He also came from a sporting family. Sean, his cousin, was a fine professional cricketer and so there was definitely quality in that bloodline.

Some other candidates came to see me in my office at the ground. Incidentally, it seemed really strange to be sitting in the manager's chair looking over the desk from the other side. That scenario hadn't even crossed my mind a couple of months earlier! It only seemed like yesterday that Lenny Walker was sitting in that seat talking to me about my proposed move from Brentford in 1986 as a player.

One lad who walked in was Mark Butler. I had received some information about him and was aware that he was local and could score a goal or two. I knew from the moment he entered the office and sat down that I was going to sign him. There was something about him that I felt was just right. His eyes were alight with expectation and, although his body language showed a nervousness in my presence, he was confident in his own ability. You could see that he couldn't wait to pull on the red shirt and get out on that pitch at the Rec! I took to 'Butts' straight away. I now had one goalscorer and just needed to find another.

Terry had set an approximate playing budget for me and we used to 'number crunch', as he liked to call it. Some of these lads, in fact most of them, would be offered less in remuneration than they were getting at their previous semi-professional clubs. There was no real debate regarding the finances, as we all knew what could happen if the budget was not tightly controlled at all times.

So it was my job as the boss to produce the best possible team with the money allocated by the football club. The fact that we were a big club, had a fantastic pitch and hopefully would be attracting a decent following was going to play a major part in enticing good players to come to us. I would also like to think that my vision for the future of the team and the club helped them to make their decision. The standards that I had set for myself had seen me through more than 700 senior games and I was hopeful that these players would allow me to pass on that experience and inspire them to become better players and, with that, achieve success.

Getting used to the rules and regulations of the non-League was a necessity and Peter Bridgeman, our secretary, was always on hand to explain what we could and couldn't do in regard to players on contracts and non-contracted players. I was fully aware that if a player was not on an FA contract then he could be the subject of a seven-day approach by another club, i.e., he could leave after the end of seven days! We could use this rule to our advantage during the playing season, but at the same time other clubs could use it to their own advantage, against us. My dilemma with this was whether to place players on contract, which would then commit the club to wages for the duration of that contract, or to take the chance and put them on non-contract, which could be discontinued in seven days by either party.

I had to play it by ear to start with and wait for us to get under way before making some decisions for the benefit of the club.

The squad was growing and by mid-June 1992 we were formally accepted into the third division of the Diadora League. I was informed that the average attendance at a game the previous season for that division was 92 - including pets! As you can imagine, I wasn't overly impressed by this statistic and thought it best to omit that fact from my presentation to potential new players! Surely the statisticians had got it wrong and they had missed a zero off the end?

Another recruit, Dave Osgood, turned up in my office and I later found out that he was related to the great Peter Osgood of Chelsea. Here was another lad with genetic connections to a quality sportsman. Dave appeared quite confident, with fire in his eyes, but I could tell that he wasn't quite as confident as his portrayal. However, I thought him a formidable lad who liked a bit of physical stuff. I took to him and I think he took to me too. As he was leaving the office I noticed that he wouldn't be able to stop a pig in an entry with those bandy legs! He definitely looked the part physically and had the gate to go with it!

Brian Lucas had started at Aldershot FC as an apprentice and had gone on to play professionally for them. Now aged 31, he had come back to sign for Aldershot Town FC. He had put on a little weight but he still had some great qualities that could only benefit us. He was one of our 'senior citizens', but, compared with Keith Baker, or 'Bakes', who had reached the grand old age of 37, he was a mere stripling!

Another signing that I made was Kev Parkins. Kev was a fullback who had made many appearances for the Army and the Combined Services. He was still serving and was as fit as a fiddle. Kevin was very regimented, as you would expect, and he was also a very honest and straightforward man. Kev fitted nicely into the jigsaw of the team that I had envisaged. I knew that we would probably clash at some point in the future but that wasn't a problem, as I would get the best out of him until the team reached a certain level of football.

The progress of the club was gathering pace. Terry and the directors were working hard on the infrastructure, e.g., the stewards, office staff and match-day officials. They were also negotiating the commercial and sponsorship deals. Anne was also working for the club now in the commercial department. She dealt with the running of the lottery and sponsorship alongside Norman Penny, an ex-paratrooper who had been with the old club for years. Norman was great to talk to and would always tell you how the natives felt about what was going on at the football club. So it was very much a family affair. In fact, the whole club really was like that now, with the likes of Rosemary Aggett in the office, who was almost part of the furniture. Everyone, from Terry the chairman down to the groundsman Dave, was doing their utmost to make the club a success.

My squad was taking shape and I was pretty happy with my signings so far. Some luck came our way with the unfortunate demise of local club Farnham Town. The core of their side was possibly up for grabs, so I wasted no time in contacting them. I reckoned that centre forward Steve Stairs, centre half Steve Harris and midfielder Shaun May would fit into my plans just right if

I could get them.

Steve Harris had previously been on trial at Aldershot FC and had played in a couple of reserve games. He was a big, strong lad who was dominant in the air, which was exactly what I wanted. Steve Stairs was like an old-fashioned centre forward to me. He wasn't the quickest player but he was strong and resilient and he could score goals. In my mind I could see Stairs and Butler being a real handful for any defence at that level even though I wasn't really sure what to expect from my own team let alone the others! Shaun was a very quiet, skilful player on the ball. He didn't get around the pitch as much as I would have liked, but I was determined to get him fitter if he agreed to join us.

After some persuasion, all three players joined Aldershot Town along with their left back Steve Buckingham, who only actually played in one game for us.

I was now close to having my first ever team of my own choice and our pre-season games had been arranged. I now had to get this lot fit enough over the coming weeks as well as moulding them into some sort of team shape. Many of the lads had never even met before, so there was still a lot of work to do.

One very important position was proving a problem to fill. I didn't have a goalkeeper, so Tim Read from Woking came in on loan. He was a very quiet lad for a keeper but had a good physical presence. I knew that his experience at a higher level would be invaluable to us. I felt that having a decent-quality keeper would give us that final piece of the jigsaw and help to achieve a solid backbone for the side.

I was reasonably happy with the make-up of the team, although we were probably short of another quality midfield player. However, we were ready to roll and give it our best shot.

The employment of non-playing staff was new to me too and I approached this in the best way I could. My job under Brian had covered the physio's role, so with my experience in that position my intention was to appoint a qualified physiotherapist who would hopefully get the players back on the pitch as quickly as possible. Jim Lange was a great help as he introduced me to Ginger McAllister, an Army captain and head of the Accident and Emergency Department in the local Army hospital.

Ginge was a good character to have at the club. He had seen it all in the forces and his medical and physiological knowledge was fantastic. He was someone that the lads would respect and listen to as well.

My jigsaw didn't just apply to getting the team right, as I also needed to put the pieces together correctly in regard to the staff. If I got it wrong in that department then it could have a detrimental effect on everything. Even choosing the right match kit was something that I wanted to be involved with.

A major problem for me was providing a decent training facility for the players. This was another important aspect, especially now that we were only part-time. Most of our training would be during the evening two or three times a week. Apart from the floodlit first-team pitch or the all-weather pitch behind the stand, there was nowhere available for us. In reality we couldn't possibly train on our pitch, as it would kill it as a decent surface for first-team games. I had to resign myself to doing the best I could with what we had. I suggested to people within the club that we would need a floodlit facility, as it would take some time to become a full-time club again and only at that point would training in daylight hours be feasible.

By July 1992 I had put together a reasonably balanced squad, appointed a good assistant/coach in Keith Baker and brought on board an excellent man in Ginge McCallister as physio. The kit was sorted for the first team and my intention was for the club to provide for a reserve team downwards to junior level. My plan was that we were going to build a club and not just a first team, although that team was my immediate priority. I had no intention of diluting my management of that team by getting involved with all aspects of the junior teams, but I still wanted to have some input in terms of who would be running them and their structure and training format. It was important to me to have the right sort of player at the club whenever possible and also to have the right choice of staff all the way down the line.

With a couple of late additions to the squad in the shape of Koo Dumbaya, a quick wide lad, and Steve Benitez, a midfield player, we started our pre-season games. We entered the Simpsonaire Trophy Tournament at nearby Camberley and to be honest I didn't have a clue what we were going to come up against. What I did know, however, was that we were reasonably well organised and fit for the challenge. More people than I had imagined turned up and, for the very first time in my football career, I found myself slightly nervous in a way that I had not experienced before. The situation had completely changed for me. This was my team, I had been totally responsible for picking it and I would also be accountable for their actions on the pitch. The feeling that I used to get in the pit of my stomach as a player was different from the feeling I had on that first day at Camberley. As a player, it was more of a competitive anticipation than nerves. As a manager, the anticipation came from a different perspective. I had so many more things to think about and I had to rely on other people to perform, rather than myself.

A few days earlier a journalist had interviewed me and one of his questions had been, "Do you think you will enjoy being a manager?" My answer was, "I haven't a clue. Maybe you should ask me after my first game"! I was being totally honest, as I really didn't know if I would enjoy the role at all. I had been excited that a new club was being formed and had enjoyed putting together a squad, but the bottom line was going to be when match day came along and a ticket-paying public was watching and anticipating good football on the pitch. I knew that the supporters were just glad to see their club, although under a new title, back in business, but I also knew that there had to be some sort of quality product there to be sold to them. They needed to see something positive after all the negativity of the old debacle. Fortunately, they didn't have to wait too long.

In our first game in the tournament at Camberley, Mark Butler volleyed in our first ever goal within two minutes against Fleet! The moment that the ball hit the net, I knew we had managed to get something good going. For some people reading this, you are probably thinking that it was only a pre-season goal against Fleet (who?) in front of a couple of hundred people. However, it was much more than that to everyone connected with the club. It was almost an announcement that we were back - back from the dead! The few hundred supporters went mad, as though it was a massive relief to everyone. We won the mini-competition that day, which was a nice boost for the players seeing as it was their first ever get-together in a competitive situation. 'Butts' was a hero already and we hadn't even got down to the real stuff yet.

Even in my most creative thoughts I couldn't possibly have anticipated that within six months we would attract a home crowd that would number one thousand more than a division two fixture between Wigan and Reading - and where are those clubs today? Around the same time, Wimbledon's Premier League game against Everton nine divisions higher would only pull in 166 more fans than our game. What an achievement for a club who had a lid on their coffin well and truly nailed down only months earlier.

Our first League game in division three of the Diadora League arrived and it was fortunately to be played at home. Our opponents were Clapton and, although I wasn't entirely sure where that was, I was told that they were ironically the oldest Isthmian League side and were founder members in 1905. I suppose it was a big day for them as well, seeing as they were coming to compete at an ex-Football League ground. The script definitely didn't go according to plan early in the game. We found ourselves 2-0 down in half an hour. Nearly 1,500 people had turned up to see us and anticipation was high. The coach in me told me that we were playing okay and doing things the right way. I just needed to get them in at half-time and make a few minor changes. I was confident that we could still win. The manager in me told me that we had attracted 1,500 supporters, which was more than our final Football League game at home, but I also wondered how many would come back the following week if we lost that game. These are the sorts of thoughts you have as a manager, both positive and negative.

The script changed in a flash when that man Butler got us a goal and suddenly the floodgates opened! Stairs then nicked two goals before the half-time whistle to put us 3-2 up. My half-time team talk was slightly different from what was in my thoughts at the half-hour stage and in the end we went on to win 4-2, with another goal from Butts. It was a good start even though there had been a few blips. Realistically, however, this was only to be expected from a comparatively new team. One thing I did know was that I had two lads up front who could score goals and that gives any team a chance at all levels. The most important part of the day was the fact that we'd had a good crowd for our first ever game and they had left pleased and hopefully pleasantly surprised about what was on offer at the new club.

My analysis of the game was that Clapton would not be one of the better sides in this division. I came to that conclusion not just by my own observations but also in discussions with my assistant and players, as they had more experience of playing at this level. Watching the game from an ex-pro's perspective, I thought that some of their players were very poor technically. They gave their all up to a point, which was something that we would have to get used to, especially at our home ground. No team was going to come to the Rec and throw in the towel in front of big crowds. I felt that our fitness had been a deciding factor against Clapton, yet we would probably need to be even fitter if we were to play at the tempo I had planned for them.

I was a full-time manager now and there was no turning back - not that I wanted to. I was probably the only full-time boss at that level, as other managers had full-time jobs outside of football and only managed teams as a 'glorified hobby', for want of better words. Aldershot Town were very different to the likes of Clapton, of course, and had to be run as an ongoing business. I well and truly had my manager's head on now and I found myself doing some things automatically. I would cast my mind back to my old bosses or coaches and think: that was a good idea, or that method was effective. Basic experience was helping me but I wanted to stamp my personality on my team, which I don't think some people I had worked with had done. I hoped that my players would reflect the standards, discipline and commitment to the game that I had shown throughout my career. This wasn't an egotistical aspiration; I just felt that if my own work ethic was mirrored by the team we would be successful.

Our next game the following Saturday against Horsham was also at home. They looked a better outfit than our previous opponents during the warm-up. They did provide stiffer opposition but we controlled the game better this time. We should have been out of sight but let them back into the game after giving away two sloppy goals. As you can imagine, that sort of slack play drove me mad, especially as I was an ex-defender. However, we won the game 3-2, with Butler and Stairs getting the goals again. They had scored seven goals between them already in just two games. The crowd had increased by a couple of hundred, which was a good sign.

The first two games were done and dusted with six points in the bag and everyone was happy. For me the next game was the real test. Playing Collier Row would give me an insight into how these lads were going to cope with this division. Big Steve Harris was brought into the line-up, as I knew that height and strength would be vital in this away fixture.

I wanted us to look as professional as possible on these away trips. We travelled by coach together and I liked the players to wear club tracksuits or smart suits, whatever the destination. These were just the basics that many teams at this level didn't have. We were there to be shot at and that was the way it was going to be, so why not look the part?

When we arrived at Collier Row's ground, it was a real eye-opener for me. The ground itself was always going to be what I expected but the pitch was a real shocker! It was very early in the season and so I had expected something half decent. However, the grass was very uneven, some parts with tufts up to six inches high and other areas completely bare, and it reminded me of an overgrown garden at a house that has been empty for a few weeks. Any plans that we would to try to pass the ball around them virtually went right out of the window. This was even more of a test for the boys than I could have imagined. I had been briefed that Collier Row fancied themselves to do well in that division and that they were no mugs. By the look of the ground surface they probably had a game plan that almost certainly involved less than two concurrent passes!

Around 300 or so Aldershot supporters turned up, which was a great following for a midweek game at that level of football. The total attendance figure was 444 and their average for the season was usually only 83! As I had expected, we had a right old battle with them. They scored early on and then had a lad sent off, which was inevitable considering some of the tackles that were flying about. This may have changed the game for us, and, after drawing level in the second half through Mr Butler, we nicked it in the dying minutes, much to the pleasure of our travelling band. Butts yet again had done the business!

After a game I would usually reflect on most aspects of what had taken place on the pitch. I would go through everything in my mind, from each individual's efforts to the performance of the side as a whole. Also I tried to analyse what the opposition had done that had given us problems. It may only have been something small but to me everything counted.

There was also a possible problem with some referees. These chaps had usually only presided over low-profile games and now they were under more pressure than they were used to, especially at the Rec. We needed to keep them sweet on the pitch and not put them under even more pressure.

My directive to the players was to be as disciplined as possible, even in the face of provocation, as we couldn't afford to lose key players for any match due to suspensions.

Overall I had to be happy with our start. Keith Baker had been fantastic on the pitch, as he possessed more all-round quality than most players in our division. He was also invaluable in terms of his knowledge of the non-League scene. Bakes was a full-time air steward and he used to travel all over Europe. Sometimes he would fly in from Barcelona to Heathrow and then drive straight to the Rec just in time for a game. For a bloke of his age he did an incredible job. Despite all of this, however, I still felt as though we needed even more input with a possible addition to my staff.

I managed to persuade my old mate Paul Shrubb to join us as a player/coach. Shrubby was another good egg, with extensive knowledge at all levels of the game. He also knew the club very well due to his former playing days there. Around this time I also brought in a new left-sided player called Andy Nunn. Nunny was always smiling even when he was running up and down the left flank like a lunatic!

One player that I haven't mentioned yet is Tony Calvert. Keith Baker originally told me about Tony when discussing a number of players. Some had said that I wouldn't be able to handle him because he had been at so many clubs previously and hadn't stuck around very long. I bore this in mind, but having looked at him in training I still decided to take him. In my opinion he had certain qualities as a player that many of the other players didn't possess. I've already mentioned jigsaws and I thought that he would fit in well. The major problem was that he had to serve a ten-match ban, which he had picked up playing local Sunday League football. Some managers might have steered clear on learning that, but I was sure that I could get the best out of the talented Tony.

Tony became available in mid-September 1992, so it was like signing a new player and, as I felt that we were short of a creative midfield man, it was now up to him to establish himself in the side. He had to bide his time a little but once he broke through he was there to stay. Ironically, on his debut we lost our 100 per cent record by dropping two points at home to Bracknell. It was a local derby and some of their lads played out of their skins. They deserved the draw on the day and it showed the fans that we weren't a machine that just had to turn up to record another win. However, it was pleasing to me that we bounced back within days with a fine 6-3 win away at Flackwell Heath while Bracknell lost their next game 9-0 at Thame. What does that say about players? I was happy with my lot, as they had shown me that following their first disappointment of the season they could turn it around almost immediately.

By now I was beginning to get into the ribs of a few boys. The honeymoon was over and we were just a team with a professional job to do in an amateur league. Our crowds were hitting the 2,000 mark and expectations were higher than ever. I began to test a few of the boys out in training by demanding more and more from them. I was clamping down on any sloppiness whatsoever. If they were late for training I would fine them and let them know I wasn't happy. I generally squeezed them on most things until the pips nearly popped out. Some of the chaps were finding it hard going but from their point of view everything was rosy: we were winning games, the crowds were great and they had never had it so good.

For me this was a dangerous time as the players could lose their focus on why everything was going so well. My standards and ideas had helped us set the trend so far and there was no way that I was going to jeopardise that by compromising on anything. I'm probably sounding like a bit of an old woman here and I'm sure they felt the same. In fact I think that a few of the lads started to dislike me a little. I was pushing them to certain limits, not just physically but performance-wise too, that they may not have attained before. They all had full-time jobs, so I knew it was very hard for them, but I wasn't there to compromise and I was going to make a success of it my way. I wasn't a total idiot in so far as realising that these lads were not full-time professionals, but I was aware that this squad of players, regardless of their occupations, could still achieve high standards.

I found out that some noodles in my squad were also playing on Sundays for their 'muppet' teams. I told them that if this didn't stop immediately then I would sack them without question. When I heard about this I was steaming and I knew that I had to change the whole mental outlook of these players if they were going to stick the pace for the whole campaign!

Come November it was time for Tim Read, our goalkeeper, to go back to Woking after his loan spell. Tim had done well for us when he was needed.

Mark Watson had been waiting patiently in the wings for his chance and now he could have it. Mark was a friend of Keith Baker and also worked as an air steward, leading the rest of the lads to refer to them affectionately as 'the trolley dollies'! A young utility player called Nathan Fealey also joined us from Reading. He had some very good qualities and could play in a few positions for me.

About this time we came up against one of the most reputed teams in our division, Thame United. The game was as their place and I felt in my water that we were in for a tough old time. We were still undefeated so far, which was a great achievement. The game had been built up as a grudge match, but I'm not sure why as we had never met before. Many things had been said about us being 'big time' and 'above our station' -the usual green-eyed garbage!

Thame was a nice little club and the people there were welcoming, but I just sensed that there was a slight undercurrent from the moment we arrived. Occasionally an opposition manager or official would whip up the local press out of sheer desperation to beat us. However, they played very well and we found ourselves two goals down with about ten minutes left to play. For the first time in the season I decided that I needed to make a change if we were to stand any chance of clawing our way back into the match, so I threw on Brian Lucas and Nunny and just went for it. Luckily it paid off. Ozzie got a goal almost immediately and Brian scored in the last minute to equalise. We had got out of jail against one of the better teams away from home. On reflection, I thought that Thame would be close to us come the end of the season.

The game also stuck in my mind for another reason. At the final whistle I walked over to where our supporters were standing to applaud them for their support and then I turned to cross the pitch and make my way to the dressing rooms on the far side. Their manager and staff were almost halfway across the pitch by now. As is customary, both managers usually shake hands and so do the staff. I caught up and offered my hand to their boss (his name escapes me) and he shook it in a limp sort of manner and said, "What's the matter? Are you too big time to shake hands with the likes of us?" He had clearly copped the needle about our scoring so late on and the undercurrent we had felt on arrival had got the better of him! In fact some of his comments during the game had been like comic cuts at times. I had been patient but this just topped it! As I let go of his hand I felt the old red mist rising for the first time in a long while. "You cheeky prat!" I said. "I happened to be applauding our fans if that's okay with you." He just waved his hand and tried to dismiss me as if I was nothing. I could feel myself losing it. Their physio stepped between us and ushered the manager away while apologising for his behaviour. That tempered the atmosphere, but what an idiot! I had a good memory and so I was looking forward to our return match in April at the Rec! Perhaps he would care to put on the number 9 shirt and I would wear the number 5. I would enjoy that!

We kept the bandwagon rolling right into the Christmas holiday period. I had asked the players to look after themselves as best they could. I suspected that most of our opposition would probably overindulge, as is usual at this time of year, so if we could just take it steady it might give us more of an edge. My lads probably thought that I was going on again but that was my job. Whether any of them took any notice, I don't know, but we bagged nine points from three games over Christmas.

It was a different story in our first match of the New Year. Clapton, whom we had played in our first ever League game, were our opposition. Their ground, which was called the 'Spotted Dog', was probably one of the most run-down places that I had been to. We had to get changed in a boiler room that was only 12 feet square. This was a real test, especially on 2 January and a freezing cold day.

We created enough chances to win the game, taking the lead through Stairsy, but they equalised and then broke away late on to score with a lob from outside the box. We huffed and puffed but couldn't manage to force an equaliser. The final whistle marked the first time that these lads had tasted a League defeat in an Aldershot shirt. I wasn't happy at all but I congratulated their manager and bench on an historic win for them.

As I walked back to the boiler room, I was thinking about what I was going to say to the chaps. My pride had been dented because of the nature of the defeat, but I needed to put it into perspective. After all, it was only a defeat in division three of the Diadora League at Clapton FC in front of 500 or so fans. However, I also knew that the players felt embarrassed having experienced, possibly for the first time, playing for a 'big' club and, with no disrespect to Clapton intended, losing to a 'minnow'. This was not a nice feeling for them.

I chaperoned my lads into the shoebox of a dressing room. Even my staff had their heads down and were looking at the floor. You could hear a pin drop. I had already handed out a few rollickings so far this season and, although we had an unbelievable record, what the supporters didn't realise was that a lot was still said in the dressing room after matches and it wasn't always sweetness and light just because we had won a game. I let very few things go and if I felt something wasn't right I would have my say irrespective of the score. On this occasion I could have carpeted a couple of them and I think that they were expecting it big time! However, I decided to go down the opposite route and congratulated them on a magnificent run of results from August. Basically that was it.

They didn't see that coming! Dare I mention his name? Cloughie would have been proud of me, as that was very much his style - totally unpredictable sometimes. I am fiercely competitive but I think my reaction did me some good as my heart rate probably dropped much more quickly by doing it that way.

We had already tasted defeat back in December against Hendon during the Diadora Cup. They were a couple of divisions higher than us so it wasn't totally unexpected even though the players were still desperately disappointed, which showed just how far we had come in a short period of time. The Cup games were a good test for us and they didn't seem to have a detrimental effect on our League results, which was our main target. Some of the teams, for instance Leatherhead, Hampton, Chertsey and Worthing, were in higher divisions but we still gave them all a good game. It also gave me the chance to look at my players' prospects for the future. How many of them would be able to take us forward over the coming seasons? I was very pleased with what I had seen and the core of the side wasn't bad at all.

There were some exciting matches in these competitions, but one that really stood out was our Hampshire Cup semi-final against our old rivals Farnborough Town. Farnborough were in the top tier of the non-League pyramid, four divisions above us, so realistically it should have been a walk in the park for them. The local press thought so, reporting that if 'Borough took it easy they should still manage to rattle in four or five goals, but if they decided to turn it on then they should manage seven or eight! My initial reaction to the report wasn't favourable, of course, but what it did do was provide a great motivational team talk for my lads. There was enough rivalry between the local clubs already so this spiced up the tie even more! This competition was usually treated with a certain amount of contempt by many of the clubs in Hampshire. It was seen as just another couple of games to be squeezed into a busy season. This was a one-off game that had attracted a lot of interest.

On the night it turned out that the locals saw it as a massive game! Just under 6,000 fans turned up at the Rec and were treated to a fantastic match. The atmosphere was the best I had seen by far since our play-off game against Wolves back in 1987. Now we were just a Diadora division three team, so it was a great achievement.

The early part of the game didn't go well for us as they took a 2-0 lead. There were probably a few smug faces in the press box when their second goal went in, but that changed just before half-time as Brian Lucas stuck one in for us. My half-time team talk was quite simple really. I just told the players to relax a little. The whole occasion and the wind-up by the local press had pumped some of them up too much. We needed to go about our normal game, still keeping that competitive edge to it but in a more controlled way. Chris Tomlinson equalised 20 minutes into the second half and from then on the game was anyone's. Alas, David Leworthy notched their winner on 85 minutes. However, we had more than held our own against a good Conference side.

Our product had been on show to a huge audience, who could see how far we had come in a very short space of time. The players had attained good standards now and there was no turning back. They had shown their supporters and me what they were capable of. Anything below that would not be good enough.

Promotion was within our grasp by now and I had got to know the individual players quite well. Some of them had come right out of their shells and some had stayed pretty much as they were when they had joined us. The likes of Shaun May and Steve Harris were still quite reserved, whereas Mark Butler and Steve Stairs were lively in the dressing room. Ozzie was more confident in his role as skipper and, as for Tony Calvert, what a character he was! For me, he was rather like Gascoigne. He even looked a little like him. I think that I spoke to him on the telephone more than anybody. He was forever calling me to tell me he couldn't make training for one ridiculous reason or another. Most of the time it was just a wind-up and he would be at the session as usual. I already knew that he had a reputation as a practical joker, as Bakes had primed me early doors. The problem was that you couldn't always read his frame of mind or tell what the next prank might be.

On one occasion, he apparently went to his young daughter's sports day at her private school. His wife Jo had suggested that he didn't attend, for her own good reasons I'm sure! However, Tony had reassured her that he would be on his best behaviour. Everything was progressing nicely on a peaceful sunny afternoon until Tony took it into his head to go up behind one of the lady teachers organising the kids' races and pull her shorts down around her ankles in front of everyone! Needless to say, the Calverts left shortly afterwards, Tony wasn't just an instinctive player, he also had an instinct for doing outrageous things!

In training one night he arrived a minute or so late without his trainers. This was a problem because we were doing a road run that evening. If there wasn't a midweek game we would do a two-mile-plus run around the Army base and back to the ground. I had already set the lads off when Tony came dashing out of the dressing room wearing a pair of Wellingtons! As usual I thought: what the hell is he up to now? He flew past me saying, "These will do, no trainers!" He was yards behind the rest of the lads but I just let him go. Some 15 minutes later the boys started to arrive back with the usual ones up front - and who should be among the leading pack but Tony! Even in a pair of wellies he had managed to beat most of the others in a high-paced road race. I was almost speechless! For all his messing about and silly arse stuff he still produced a high standard of stamina and determination. Tony was a tougher lad than the supporters realised.

After the disappointment of the Farnborough result we bounced straight back by crashing six goals past Camberley in our next League game. Then we finally clinched promotion to the second division in our game at Tring Town in Hertfordshire. I didn't realise it at the time, but apparently we were the first team in the country to gain promotion that season, 1992/93. It was a great day for everyone. Initially I didn't have a clue where Tring was and I didn't imagine I would ever go there again. However, 13 years later our daughter, Sally, attended an audition and gained a DADA scholarship to study Dance full-time at the Arts Educational School there, so Anne and I found ourselves visiting Tring rather often over the next two years.

We secured the championship at home against our close rivals, Thame United. When we had played them earlier in the season I had predicted that they would be close to us at the end of the campaign. Even though they were 18 points behind us they did finish in second place. Collier Row, who had given us a hell of a game at their place on that dreadful pitch, finished in third spot, the final promotion place.

The scenes at the end of our game were exceptional. The 2,500 supporters had witnessed their team actually winning a championship. The lads went crazy too, which was understandable after all their hard work. I got dumped in the bath with all my gear on! Who knows, maybe a couple of them wanted to drown me after the almost impossible demands I had placed on them?

There were a few players that had come in and out over that season and all of them had done a great job whether it was for a one-off game or for the whole season. What I call the main core of the side had been quite consistent and that is why we had won the division title. Consistency from the majority of the players had been the key to our success - and the 62 goals that Butler and Stairs bagged between them helped a little too!

The chairman and the board of directors were very pleased with everyone's efforts and I was happy with the support from the boardroom. We had made a profit from the first season, which was almost unheard of at most levels of football. It wasn't a massive amount of money but it was a start.

It had been my first season in football management and I couldn't possibly have anticipated that it would go so well. I had appointed some staff that I knew well, such as Shrubby. I had known a little about Keith Baker and he had been a huge asset on the pitch. Ginge, our physio, had been recommended by Jim Lange, and our reserve team manager, Andy Meyer, was well known to Shrubby. That old saying "We were all singing from the same song sheet" was a fact and my initial brief to all of them was just that. I didn't want any mixed messages going out to the players. There was one way we were going to tackle the campaign and that was my way. I was pleased with myself and everything was sweetness and light. After all the problems of the previous seasons perhaps I had needed a bit of luck and some good times.

Something that opened my eyes to the reality of management in this game was a letter that I received at the end of the season. I had been sent many cards and letters of congratulation - not just to me, of course, but to the team and everyone else at the club. I had won the Manager of the Month award three times over the season and I was lucky enough to win Manager of the Season too. On top of that I was very honoured to collect a Rothmans Football Yearbook award on behalf of the club in London. Alex Ferguson was also there to collect Manchester United's award for the season. So from my point of view it had been an almost perfect season - but not according to this letter! I can't even recall the name of the sender of the letter, but they were local. It consisted of ten pages basically telling me everything that I had done wrong! I couldn't believe what I was reading. I didn't know whether to frame it or lob it in the bin. I showed it to Anne and she was gobsmacked too.

Significantly what this brought home to me was the fact that no matter what you do someone will always see it differently, especially in football management. I realised that I was now in a job that was almost impossible to do at times as you were always going to be criticised no matter what decisions you made. Whether players, directors, office staff, coaches, the media or supporters, you were going to be their target at some point. Don't get me wrong, I had been in the game a long time and wasn't naive in thinking that you're ever beyond criticism, but to be questioned in quite such a blatantly unjust manner was something quite different and something that a manager has to get used to. You can't ever know what it feels like to be a club manager until you are one, no matter how closely you have worked with one in the past. I'd had a tremendous first season at the helm but deep down I sensed that the vultures were only in hiding for the time being.

Terry and the board had done a great job with the budget. The key to any club's future is a controlled budget. I was privy to what went on in the boardroom; everything was completely transparent and that was essential if the club was to be run successfully. We could not afford to go down same old road as the previous club. Our first season had been a roaring success in so far as Terry and the board getting great support from the Supporters' Club and many others. People had stepped forward and given their time for free on many occasions. Stewards, gatemen and general helpers had cost us very little that season, but we were well aware that it wouldn't be possible to continue in that way for much longer. Our second season budget would have to be revamped to allow for all these costs. All this was good experience for me. I was seeing all the workings of a football club first hand. I was also making sure that I had a large input in terms of the club structure, from the first team down to junior level. We were like a runaway train at times but it was important that we all kept it on the tracks!

It was interesting to hear that some of the players among the opposition throughout the season had made comments about our players being on big wages, so no wonder we were successful according to them! This was a complete fallacy, of course, as my lads were on very similar wages to most other players in the division. In fact, some lads had taken a drop in their money to come to us. We had no intention of paying out big wages to anyone. Pure hard work and organisation brought us our success that year, with no small amount of skill on some occasions.

The club rewarded the players with a close season tour in Portugal. I was pleased with the gesture, as the players really deserved it. My only reservation was from a personal point of view. I had been on several trips before as a player, but this would be my first trip as a boss. Four staff, including Keith Baker, would be accompanying me, which was a relief as it can get quite lonely as a manager on an away trip. Also Terry Owens and John McGinty tagged along, so the players just had to be on their best behaviour!

A game had been arranged against a local Portuguese side on the Algarve and I had wrongly presumed that it would be played on a grass surface. Instead, we played on an all-weather pitch that was very much like red ash. As some of the lads had been unable to make the trip due to work commitments, just about every member of the tour party made a match appearance, including me, Shrubby and reserve manager Andy Meyer! I think even physio Ginge made a cameo appearance at one point. The referee was about 14 years old and seemed to adhere to a totally different set of rules to the ones we used. If we made any sort of physical challenge he wanted to give a foul against us. The opposition were a set of local farmers and workers who were pretty large and tough looking, but when it came down to bodily contact they didn't appear to know how to handle it. It was a real culture shock for us, as they just wanted to fanny around with the ball and make pretty patterns all over the pitch! In contrast, we got stuck into them right from the start, friendly or no friendly, and then tried to pass the ball about. We won the game even with us old crocs in the side, but they weren't overly happy. I think they saw us as a bunch of nutters running around like madmen in the heat.

It was a very good PR exercise for the new club and, even though things became a bit fraught in the game, they made us very welcome afterwards with a nice buffet and drinks. John McGinty hired a minibus, which he drove around all week just like a local - rather like Ian Stewart on the M25! Terry loved the trip and spoke to everyone in a broken English/Portuguese accent for the duration of the stay! He loved the 'crack' as he would say.

Within hours of our memorable season finishing I had my manager's head on again. I was reasonably happy with most of my players, but when the hullabaloo had died down I needed to meet with my staff and analyse the performance of every player throughout the season. I needed to make decisions in terms of who could take us to the next level again and who couldn't. It wasn't a huge step up but there was a difference, as we knew only too well after playing against a few division two sides in the Cup competitions. We weren't looking simply to survive in division two, we wanted to win it.

As usual the close season went much too quickly and we were back in action pronto! The squad needed strengthening to make competition for places keener, and three or four additions would do it as the season progressed. That is how it panned out, with the likes of Danny Holmes, Darren O'Neil, Tony Cleave, Mark Frampton and Darren Angel coming into the squad. Phil Burns, a big goalkeeper and an ex-Army lad, also joined us. Chris Hollins, the son of the ex-Chelsea and England player John, played several games for me too. He showed great qualities as a footballer but instead returned to university and chose a career in the media. He is now working for the BBC as a top TV sports reporter.

My spies told me that Chertsey and Newbury were the boys to beat in the division. Newbury were set to go full-time. The club had been taken over by a supposed millionaire who had links with Reading FC and he was determined to put them on the football map.

In the event, my players once again did a fantastic job. It was almost a carbon copy of the first season except that we didn't quite dominate the top spot as we had previously, as Chertsey and Newbury were also flying. We were the three best teams by a mile. We gained promotion with 97 points in third spot. Newbury and Chertsey had 103 and 102 points respectively. The nearest team to us was Barton Rovers with 83 points. Once again our success ratio in games had been phenomenal. Of the 57 League and Cup fixtures played, we had won 51 of them. Butler and Stairs had done it again with 62 goals between them. We also hit new crowd records for the division of 3,000+ for the Chertsey and Newbury games.

I hadn't imagined that we could top the previous season, but we actually had from my point of view. We didn't win the title but we were only just pipped in the final few games by two very good sides at that level. Newbury won it but what pleased me was that we did the double over them in the League. Our away fixture was one of the highlights of the season.

The Newbury ground was undergoing extensive work, so we played them at Basingstoke's ground. Newbury had brought in the great Don Howe, ex-Arsenal and England coach to work with the team. That's how serious they were even at this level. It was a good opportunity to pit my wits against a true great in the football world. They were paying their players big money, going great guns in the League and now they had Don on board as their coach!

The match went like a dream for us. We outfought them and outplayed them for most of the game and came out 3-0 winners. It was a great result for us! It was probably my best result as a manager up to that day. The outcome didn't have a major impact on the season, but from a coach's point of view it was massive. I was like a dog with two dicks when I went into the clubhouse after the game! I was introduced to Don and he was reasonably magnanimous in defeat. Perhaps I was hoping to hear him say something profound; but he didn't; maybe he was still raw or maybe he was just human like me!

While we were performing very well in the League we also managed to progress in the FA Vase. When we entered this competition I thought that the squad might just be good enough to go all the way. I didn't tell anybody that, however, especially not the players. We progressed well through the early rounds, scoring 17 goals and only conceding one.

Our opponents in the quarter-finals were a team from up north called Atherton Laburnum Rovers. We were completely in the dark in terms of how they played, but their results and League form were impressive. In fact their results were very similar to our achievements in division two. I didn't intend to go into a game as important as that totally blind, so I decided to drive up to visit my parents in North Wales and then go along to one of their games midweek. Unfortunately, on the night of the game it snowed heavily and I had to turn back halfway to the ground. As a result, I was unable to get to see them play before our fixture and that worried me a little as I am a great believer in fate!

At least we went into the game with the advantage of being on home soil and we were a decent outfit. I knew they would be a handful just by looking at their pen pictures. Their keeper had kept 26 clean sheets in 42 League games the previous season for a start. Also in their team was Andy Feeley, the ex-Leicester and Brentford player with over 350 Football League appearances. Their skipper was Jimmy Evans, who used to play for Blackburn Rovers, and their midfielder Paul Burrows had been an apprentice at Bolton. Atherton's two strikers had also notched up 45 goals between them and it was still only February!

As we did our warm-up before the game, I glanced over at their lads. They were a bit of a scruffy-looking outfit; you might even say unkempt. Appearances can be deceptive, however, and I got the distinct impression that it was going to be a difficult match physically. They had a lot more experience in some positions than us, but I was hopeful that we might be the all-round fitter side.

When the game got under way, they used every ounce of that experience to con the referee, waste time, wind people up and put their foot in all over the pitch. I was disappointed at the officials on the day, but the game was still there to be won and we just couldn't get that all-important goal. There was a great atmosphere with a good crowd of 3,000+. From Atherton's point of view, they did an excellent job on us. Not many teams had prevented us from scoring at the Rec but they had managed to do it by any means they could and they had got away with it. A 0-0 draw was a great result for them.

The prospect of a trip up to Atherton was quite daunting, but if we wanted to win the Vase then we had to go up there in a confident frame of mind. I had a picture in my head of what we would be up against and I would be proved right.

When we pulled up at the ground in the middle of a council housing estate, I could see that some of the lads were less than impressed. It was a cold wintry afternoon in a run-down arena. There was very little grass on the pitch, the floodlights looked as though they were operating on 60 watt bulbs and the natives looked pretty hostile! I also knew that the Atherton lads in their dressing room could smell blood. They had already got away with all sorts at our place, so they probably fancied their chances back home in Manchester.

We knew how they would set their team up and what they were capable of, so I decided that my team talk would be mainly motivational. I intended to wind them up as much as possible because that was going to be the only way that we would get something up there.

That is how it was as we battled it out with them. We defended magnificently and almost nicked a goal in the dying minutes, but it ended in another stalemate. For the first time in my career, it would be down to the toss of a coin to decide who had the home advantage in the second replay. It was a strange way of doing things but those were the rules. Skipper Steve Osgood and I joined their captain and manager in the referee's room. The referee tossed the coin and it came down in our favour. Ozzie and I were obviously chuffed but we remained quite calm as we left the ref's room, showing a fair bit of decorum. When we threw open our dressing room door Ozzie rushed in screaming at the top of his voice, "YES, YOU BEAUTY!" The whole room went ballistic. They could obviously hear all this in their room next door and were not overly pleased! Anyone would think that we had just won the game. Extra time had taken its toll on both sets of players and they would have to travel down to us once more in midweek, which put the ball back in our court. It was up to us now.

On the way home a few of the lads collared the chairman on the coach to try to get him to commit to taking the team away again at the end of the season. Their angle was that they would draw another big crowd for the second replay and this would bring in additional monies on top of the planned budget, wouldn't it? After the previous trip Terry didn't really need much persuasion and he agreed to sort them out with something. The players were delighted and at the time I was okay with it too, as it seemed a positive gesture considering the players' efforts.

The third game soon came around and anticipation at the club was high. Atherton turned up looking a little jaded as they stepped off the team coach. Once again, however, appearances can be deceptive. In the event, they did a smash and grab job on us. They man-marked Tony Calvert for 90 minutes and demonstrated all their experience to stifle us as a team. I tried to change things around on the pitch as the game progressed, but nothing seemed to work as I would have liked. If I'm totally honest, a few of the lads 'choked' on the night, which was disappointing for me. Perhaps too many of them thought that the hard work had been done up at Atherton and they had been rewarded with a nice little trip come June.

I was gutted because I felt that if we had gone through then there would be nothing to stop us getting to Wembley. We would have played Diss over two legs and I was confident that we would have been too much for them. However, it wasn't to be, and the atmosphere in the dressing room was different after that game than at any other time since we had re-formed as a new club. You could almost feel the disappointment. Maybe it was because the players knew me quite well by then and I knew them better than they did themselves!

I didn't go down the "Well done, you've had a good run" road when I addressed the squad. Instead I pointed out a few home truths and told some of the players that they had 'choked' at the vital moment. This may have sounded a bit harsh but unfortunately it was the truth. I sensed that a couple of the lads resented my comments but that was their problem. If they wanted to become all-round better players then these were acute situations in which they needed to look at themselves and accept criticism. Big games always show you as a manager which players are your best assets. The demands of such matches strip away all the crap and highlight who you need to keep at the club for as long as possible.

One player with whom I did have a few problems after this game was big Steve Harris, our centre back. I had to have words with a few of the lads on an away trip. They used to like to play cards at the back of the coach on the way to games, which on the face of it wasn't a problem, but on one occasion it came to my attention that they were playing for money. Huge sums weren't involved, but enough; let's say their football money for the week. I wasn't happy with that on the way to games as, no matter what your temperament, if you lose a reasonable amount of dosh on the way to a game it will affect your frame of mind. We were an established club again now, albeit at a lower level, and were still perceived as professional. I voiced my opinion on the matter and basically banned any money changing hands on the way to games. If they wanted to lose their mortgage payments on the way home that was up to them!

Steve Harris voiced his objections to my ruling, which was his prerogative but I told him to his face I had made my decision and that was that. I had a feeling that he might jump ship at some point. At 6 feet 3 inches tall and weighing 14 stone, he seemed as though he would be one of the last to throw his toys out of the cot. I thought: someone's bottom is going!

Steve, or Harry as he was known, was a lovely lad who gave everything. I watched him carefully after our few words and his body language changed towards me. Ironically he would be joint Player of the Season with Keith Baker. Anyway, Harry came to see me in my office a little later in the season to tell me he wanted to leave the club. I had expected it so it was no surprise. I wasn't happy about it, as he had done a good job, but at the back of my mind I reckoned it was all getting too much for him - not physically but psychologically. I had dug him out after the Atherton game and the 'card school' situation, which he wasn't pleased about. He said in the meeting that he didn't like the way I spoke to players and he expressed a few other gripes, but in all honesty he just wanted out.

I knew that Steve had been talking to his old manager from Farnham, Ernie Howe, who was now manager of Basingstoke. What Steve really wanted was to go to Basingstoke and play in front of two or three hundred people instead of staying with Aldershot and playing regularly in front of two or three thousand. The money package would be no different to what he was currently getting. At the time I just couldn't get my head around it. He eventually got his wish, as the whole issue went to a tribunal and we received £2,000 for him.

Paul Chambers, a very talented and experienced centre back, came to us from Basingstoke for £5,000, which was also set by a tribunal. They tried to fashion a deal whereby we virtually gave them Harry for £500 and yet they wanted £12,500 for Paul. Sorry, Ernie, but that was taking the piss, old chap! It was strange how some players went about things in the non-League. They would sometimes rather play with their mates or for someone that would spoon-feed them than strive for success in a tough environment. I had to get used to that fact and accept it more readily.

A close season trip was again arranged and this time we were set to play a game in Malta at their National Stadium. This trip was organised by Terry, as promised when the lads had collared him after the away game to Atherton in the Vase. Once again it was a good team-building exercise and the players really enjoyed themselves. They obviously felt relaxed after a very tough season. In fact they were in such high spirits that two of the cheeky blighters, Mark Butler and Stuart Udal, crept into my room one night at God knows what time, tipped me out of my bed and threw the mattress and bedclothes on top of me! I was fast asleep and only really started to wake up when they were virtually out of the room. At the time I wasn't sure who the culprits were, but they both owned up in the morning. They weren't sure how I was going to take it so they were a little sheepish. I just laughed it off, of course, and put it down to high jinks! I had been on their case all season, so I suppose they were allowed one little 'pop' at me.

The match was switched to one of the peripheral pitches at the National Stadium, which was a disappointment for us. They made some sort of excuse at the last minute that the main pitch had been reseeded. The temperature was in the high eighties and Ginge was concerned that some of the lads would very quickly suffer from dehydration, especially as we had already been there a few days. Ginge, being the professional that he was, made the whole squad rehydrate for 24 hours prior to the match. He monitored all the players closely and told them that he wouldn't allow them to play if they hadn't drunk enough water. On the day of the game we took literally litres and litres of water with us. It was a real struggle for the lads against a young Maltese side who were all used to the heat, but we battled away and came out as winners. Even though it wasn't an important game, the players still wanted to win. This was part and parcel of what I had been trying to drum into them for two seasons!

I had quite a good relationship with the players, especially the lads that had been with me from the start. That didn't mean that I acted more favourably towards them ahead of new signings. It was just that they understood me and would only push their luck to a certain level, be it with a practical joke, banter or even in a team talk.

My second season was over and I was learning all the time about the job. How much better could it get? When I looked at it logically, my conclusion was: not much. I'd had two seasons of success on the pitch with basically the same bunch of players. There had been a few additions but no drastic alterations. This was going to change, however, as I now had to put together a squad capable of getting out of the first division and into the Diadora premier division. Towards the end of the season I had already started doing my homework in terms of some possible adjustments. There had to be changes, there was no doubt about that: some would just happen; others would involve my making hard decisions without sentiment.

The new season was upon me again and more quickly this time, or so it appeared. 1994/95 was without doubt going to be even more of a challenge than the previous two seasons. The feeling around the club was good and even though everyone knew that this could be a real tester for us the mood was positive.

I made the decision to strengthen the squad with a few additions. Jason Chewins, a very talented left-sided player, came in from Wealdstone. Mark Biggins from Woking joined us but needed some knee surgery over the summer. He would fit into the midfield and would be joined there by David Bass, another talented player on loan from Reading. Andy Russell, a big, strong centre back, came to us from Kingstonian and Darren O'Neill left us to go the other way. I replaced him with Stewart Mitchell from Marlow. In fact there were more comings and goings of players now. We had so many fixtures to fulfil in the League and several Cup competitions, which required a larger, more flexible squad.

Pre-season had gone well, but I was then notified of a new initiative that the Diadora Committee had decided to bring in for our division in League matches. I was totally in the dark about this until our squad was virtually finalised. The powers that be had decided that you could now also 'kick' the ball in when it went out of play as well as the normal 'throw in' and, not only that, you could not be offside from the kick either. To be honest, I thought they were having me on when I was told this. It was going to have a major effect on a lot of teams - positive for some and negative for others.

I was having nightmares in my mind relating to the consequences of this silly experiment. For a start, if I had known earlier that this rule was definitely coming in then I might have adjusted my squad accordingly. On top of that, this rule only applied to League games and not Cup competitions, so it could effectively be in force in a Saturday League fixture and then not so in the following Tuesday's Cup match. Talk about confusing! In my opinion, it was an absolute farce!

We were going to need every ounce of luck and know-how to gain promotion from division one, but now we had to contend with this lunacy as well. I was gutted and deep down I knew that when the bad weather came and we had heavy pitches then this was going to give us a problem. Average sides would be even more difficult to beat, as this rule would be a great leveller. I was imagining an away game on a glue-pot pitch, with the opposition launching balls into our box from 30 or 40 yards away and seven or eight bodies thrown into our penalty area. It would be a bloody lottery! I know it was the same for everyone, but we had a very good reputation as a footballing side so this rule could only go against us in the long run. However, we had no choice but to get on with it.

There was a positive start to the new campaign with a 1-0 win over Billericay. Udal, Baker, Osgood, Stairs and Butler were in the starting line-up, as well as Tony Calvert. These six lads from the original team that had started over two years ago were still going strong. That wasn't bad considering they had been literally thrown together in a matter of weeks. Results were becoming harder to achieve. It was a tougher league, there was the new ruling, and we seemed to hit a glut of injuries early on in the season. There was a disappointing outcome to our first venture into the FA Trophy.

I had signed a lad called Solomon Eriemo from Kingstonian. Solomon was a big, strong boy with pace who could shore up the midfield or play in the back four. Our club did everything correctly and he had been signed within the seven-day limit stipulated by the FA. Solomon played on the Saturday in a 1-1 home draw against Rothwell and the replay was set for the following Tuesday night. On the morning of the return game we were informed that there was a problem with his registration and the match had to be postponed while the FA looked into the situation.

In the end, we were basically thrown out of the Trophy competition because we had unwittingly fielded an unregistered player. It was confirmed that we had done all our paperwork correctly but 'apparently' (and I say that because they hadn't been happy about his move) Kingstonian had failed to cancel his registration, which was their responsibility. So technically we hadn't done anything wrong but we were still required to bow out of the replay. To this day I have not quite figured that one out! Kingstonian messed up and yet we were punished. I will leave it up to you to judge whether they failed to de-register him on purpose or whether they were simply totally incompetent.

Whatever the reason for the administrative error, it showed how intransigent the FA could be at times. We were not even allowed an appeal and yet, if my memory serves me right, Tottenham were thrown out of the FA Cup for a so-called breach of the rules but were allowed back in after an appeal. Not much has changed right up to the present day: one rule for the big boys and another for us serfs, or that's how it appears!

By now we had accumulated lots of injuries and suspensions and our third season had not been without incident. Our disciplinary record had been excellent for the first two seasons, but this year the officials seemed to clamp down on us for the slightest misdemeanour. Perhaps I was becoming paranoid, but in some of the games I got the distinct impression that we were being put in our place, not just the players but also me and my staff.

In one such game I had words with a referee during the first half at a home game. At half-time, as he was walking off the pitch, he collared me and said quite calmly, "If you want a word, come into my dressing room now." I accepted his offer. My lads had been incensed with his performance, so I settled them down, went to his room, knocked politely and we had a reasoned conversation. He let me have my say and then he had his. There was no abuse or finger wagging from me. I remained quite controlled even though I was steaming inside. There didn't appear to be a problem, although I did speak honestly to him and to a certain extent he listened. I left his room and got back to the lads just before they went out for the second half. I informed them that I had spoken to him, that he had listened and that they should maintain their discipline and just get on with the game. There was a marginal improvement in the referee's performance during those 45 minutes, and that was that as far as I was concerned. Matter closed – or so I thought. Unfortunately, within the week I received a letter from the FA fining me for my "Ungentlemanly Conduct" towards the referee. He had stitched me up! What a snake!

From that day on I knew that I would never trust a referee again. It may be a sweeping statement but that's how I saw it. And that's coming from a player who was never booked for dissent during 20 years of playing. I wasn't into abusing officials and I wasn't going to start then. I didn't know how someone could blatantly lie in that manner.

Although the seasons were serious affairs, there were still lots of lighter times and laughs along the way. One such occasion, during the 1994/95 season, was on our overnight stay in Guernsey when we played a team called Sylvans Sports in the Hampshire Cup. From the moment we arrived at the airport for the flight, Tony Calvert, the joker in the pack, was like a one-man comedy act! He had everybody in stitches with his one-liners and general banter. The stewardesses were unmercifully put to the sword. Somehow he had the ability to slaughter people while making them laugh at the same time.

The game was important, as it brought much needed income to the club, but there was also an element of fun in it for the lads. None of them had flown to a game before and, even though it was only Guernsey, they wanted to enjoy the trip.

We checked into the hotel after the game, which we had won 3-2. It was a hard-fought victory, especially as Mark Butler and Dave Osgood were sent off. It was totally out of character for both of them, but the refereeing left a lot to be desired to say the least!

At the hotel most of the lads let their hair down and had a few drinks. I went to bed and left them to it, confident that they would behave themselves as my assistant Keith Baker was around somewhere keeping an eye out.

Spirits were high anyway but, with Tony about, anything could happen!

I was watching TV in my room when there was a knock on the door. My manager's head thought: eye-eye, what's occurring? I opened the door expecting to see the hotel manager or an underling, but there was nobody there. I looked up and down the corridor and there was no sign of anyone. Someone was playing silly buggers! As I shut the door, I happened to glance down and there on the carpet right outside my doorway was what looked like a small plastic bag with something inside it. I hadn't ordered room service, so I knew it couldn't be that. I bent down to check it out and, to my horror, it was a transparent sandwich bag containing a large turd! Thank God it was nicely presented and sealed!

My immediate thoughts were: Tony, you git! What the hell was I supposed to do with half a pound of crap in a bag? I picked it up gingerly with two fingers at the sealed edge and, holding it at arm's length and with what was probably a very contorted face, I made my decision. I walked across the corridor to the lift directly opposite my room. Then, looking both ways to make sure nobody was coming, I pressed the button, expecting the doors to reveal the culprits inside waiting for my reaction. The doors opened and to my disappointment the lift was empty. Thinking that some stranger would be along any minute and catch me with said item, I just wanted rid of it pronto. In a split second I plonked the bag of doo-doos on the floor of the lift and pressed the down button. Sod that for a lark, I thought, and went back to my room. Heaven knows what happened to the faeces, as there were no repercussions the next day!

I went down for my breakfast in the morning along with a few of the lads who had managed to vacate their pits and I looked around to see if there were any signs of a giggle or a nudge in my presence. There wasn't a whimper. In fact some of the lads were feeling a little delicate after the night before. Others didn't even make an appearance until we were ready to leave and catch our flight home. When it was time to depart we all assembled in the hotel foyer to do a head count. Some of the boys looked as if they'd had a reasonable night. I caught Tony's eye and he just giggled as usual. I had a word with him about the phantom excrement deposited outside my room but he just giggled even more and denied all knowledge of it! Well, what did I expect? We caught our flight and some of the boys were turning green as we were buffeted about in the tiny plane. I think Butts was one of the first to "YewEEE" into a sick bag followed by a few others. Maybe something in their breakfast had upset them?

As the season progressed my team talks and tactics remained the same, yet we were having players sent off. Holmes, Butler and Osgood had been sent off within a few weeks. It seemed to me that every problem you would encounter as a manager manifested itself in the first few months of this very important season. I probably learnt more as a manager in those months than I had in the previous 18 or so, not about football issues as such but more to do with the peripheral matters that can indirectly affect the results. I know I'm sounding negative about the 1994/95 season, but there were also many positives.

We had beaten Dorking 7-0 in the League and we had been victorious over our rivals Basingstoke in the Cup and Trophy, but it appeared that there was always a price to pay around the corner. David Bass sustained a bad knee injury, as did John Humphrey who gave us tremendous pace up front.

The honeymoon period was well and truly over for the team and me. This was a real test for us now and the majority of our supporters and staff knew it. There was a minority in the crowd that were starting to get a wee bit restless. I had some feedback from a couple of the players that some of the supporters over the far side of the ground opposite the dressing room were abusing them. There had been the odd shout of disappointment the previous season, which is only human nature, even though we had won 51 out of our 57 matches. This was different though. Some of the lads that had been with us from the start were not exempt from the abuse. They felt let down by this treatment, as they had played out of their skins for two seasons and produced a fantastic set of results.

I still lived in the real world, but in view of what had happened and the recent history of the club I still found it quite incredible. I didn't think that people realised or wanted to take on board that these lads were still only part-time footballers with full-time jobs outside of football. We were also up against teams that were paying their lads more than we were forking out.

As results became more inconsistent, or maybe hit a more realistic level, a few more of our fans began to have a go at us. The euphoria of the past was over and reality had kicked in for everybody. There would be no more 'walk in the park' seasons. We were now in a better-financed league with better players and better managers and coaches. We all had to put up with that bloody 'kick in' rule as well! We weren't feeling sorry for ourselves, far from it. Some of the boys were geed up by it and wanted to shut the 'boo boys' up, which was the right way to look at it. Personally, I hadn't had much direct criticism from the fans until we played an away game late in December.

I think the fixture was at Barton Rovers and the pitch was an absolute disgrace. It was literally inches deep in mud and playing football was nigh on impossible. The game was a complete lottery and the opposition used the 'kick in' rule at every opportunity just to smash the ball up the pitch or into our penalty box. The result could have gone either way but we lost the game. As we were walking back to the dressing rooms one of our supporters, a bloke of about my age, looked straight at me and said, "You haven't got a clue what you are doing, have you?" I just looked at him with contempt and decided not to bite back, even though inside I felt totally frustrated with the game and its outcome and really wanted to jump the barrier and chin him. There would have been venom in that right-hander! To get to the dressing rooms we had to walk past the majority of our travelling fans behind the goal to our left. Quite a few of them voiced their displeasure to the lads and me as we went in. They were quite rightly frustrated too, but the old days when Aldershot FC were in the League were back and there to stay as far as I could tell.

Not long after this, I was sitting in my office when my phone rang. It was a journalist wanting to know if I had shown any interest in the vacant Colchester United manager's position? I had to disappoint him and confess that I didn't even know the job was available. He told me that George Burley, their manager, had walked out on them and gone over to Ipswich. We chatted for a while and he told me that a few people had mentioned my name as a possible candidate. I was flattered but didn't give it too much thought at that point, as I had enough on my plate trying to get us into the top three in our division.

When I got home that evening I mentioned the phone call to Anne and we had a long chat about it. As with me, experience had taught her not to take too much notice of journalistic speculation. However, despite our cynicism, we decided that it was worth checking it out and so I decided to follow up the phone call to see if there was a genuine possibility of the job going to someone like me.

I telephoned my mate Micky Cook, who was now working with 'Football in the Community' at Colchester United. Mick didn't work directly for the club but I knew he would be well versed in the present situation at Layer Road. It was good to talk to Mick again after quite a few years. He had seen how well we had done at Aldershot and was genuinely pleased for me. He confirmed that George had left Layer Road and told me that it had come completely out of the blue. The two clubs, Ipswich and Colchester, were at loggerheads because, despite still being on contract, George had walked out to take over at Portman Road, just as I had been informed. So the 'U's' were actively inviting applications for the vacant position of manager. Mick thought that I had a real chance of getting the job because of my success as a player there in the past and also because of the job I had done at Aldershot.

Part of me thought that it would be a big jump, but I had played at that level and above so why not? I was full-time at Aldershot but the players weren't, so this would be a good opportunity to get back into full-time football. I must admit that the thought of once again working with the players day in, day out, appealed to me. My emotions were mixed. On the one hand I still wanted to take Aldershot forward and I knew I was capable of doing it, but on the other hand an opportunity to manage my old club Colchester was very attractive. I didn't feel that I was being disloyal to Aldershot, just ambitious for my family. I had given several good years to the club as a player, physio, coach and manager and I now had an outside chance in my mind to progress into the Football League as a manager.

My next phone call was to Terry, our chairman. Somehow I felt that he was expecting my call even though I didn't mention my reasons for wanting a meeting with him. When we did meet up Terry was fantastic and said that he wouldn't stand in my way if I wanted to apply for the Colchester job, so I posted my CV to my old club and waited.

I received a reply within days inviting me to an interview for the vacant position. It was to be held at the premises of Ellisons Solicitors in the town centre, presumably because solicitor Peter Powell was on Colchester's board of directors. Anne and I hadn't returned to Colchester since 1984 when I was sold to Brentford, although I had been back to the football ground a couple of times to play in 'Vets' games for Aldershot (which we won, by the way!)

This was my first interview for a manager's position, as when I became the boss at Aldershot I was approached and offered the job without having to apply for it. So this time I had to sell myself as a manager and a person and I decided just to be myself. Gordon Parker, the acting chairman, knew me well from my days as a player at Colchester, so I was hopeful that he liked me. The interview seemed to go quickly and I felt that I had presented myself well. I shook hands with the board members and thanked them for their time.

Anne had gone down with me, as, unlike me (memory like a sieve!), she knew where to go in the town. She had been for a coffee and a walk down memory lane while I was being grilled. So we met up and drove back to Hampshire straight away. I just had to wait and see now.

When I went into my office at the ground the next day I must confess that I was in a bit of a daze. My mind was all over the place as I was trying to make plans for both eventualities. If I didn't get the job, what steps would I take to vamp things up a little for us, as we needed to improve our results quickly? If I did get the job, what would the reaction be towards me from both sets of supporters? We would have to move again and the kids were settled in school: Thomas was in the middle of his GCSEs, Jack was happy and Sally had just joined the Infants. Anne would support me whatever the outcome, but there was more and more to consider as my family matured. If I did take the job heaven knows what I was going to do during my first days at Colchester in the middle of the season when their manager had just walked out! There was a lot to think about.

A day or so later I got a telephone call inviting me to a second interview. This time I had to travel to Berkeley's Square in London. Mr Peter Heard, whom I later found out was the club's main financier, had his offices there and as far as I knew I was to go through the whole interview process again, but at least it showed that they were being thorough. Anne made the journey up to town with me. She knew London well seeing as we had lived in Ruislip for six years. She had taken the kids into the city on the tube back then, so she took the opportunity to visit some of her favourite places while at the same time being there to offer me plenty of moral support.

The offices were very impressive and, rather than being faced by the whole board again, when I was ushered into the room I discovered that it was to be a one-to-one interview with Peter Heard alone. He came over as a very articulate man who appeared to know exactly what he required from a manager. He complimented me on my CV, saying that it was one of the best that he had seen in some time. He was very quietly spoken and yet firm in what he actually said. From his questions, I could see that he liked to run a well-organised football club. He also told me that he was an ex-referee and expected the team and the staff to be well disciplined at all times.

I was very impressed with what I had heard in both interviews and I had made my mind up all ready: I wanted the job!

When I met up with Anne I told her that I definitely wanted to take the position as Colchester manager, whereas I had been quite philosophical about it all before. I would be very disappointed if I didn't get it, but had I done enough? Anne is very perceptive and when I told her how the second interview had gone she was very confident that I would get the job and we were on our way.

We liked it in Aldershot and so did the kids. In fact we had just had a large extension built on our house to accommodate two extra bedrooms and a dining room. We were quite happy to settle there for a while. It appeared that whenever we had made plans either to move into a bigger house or to extend, the chance of a new job would come up. Even though I had decided that I would like this new challenge, it was still going to be a wrench to leave everything behind and move on.

Colchester had an away game against Preston the following Tuesday, so I was eagerly awaiting the result. Since George's departure, his assistant Dale Roberts had taken charge and of the four games played by them only one had been a victory. I did some homework on the club and found out that the feeling in the dressing room was that someone should be appointed from within. That often happens and you can understand why: the players want to feel more secure. An outsider always causes concern for everyone, as nobody is sure what they are going to get. Some names that were suggested for the position were Russell Osman, ex-Ipswich, Mark Lawrenson, ex-

Liverpool, and Tony Pulis from Bournemouth. I was going up against men who had a bigger name than me in the football world. The one advantage that I had over them was that I had previously played for the club for seven years.

Late on the Tuesday evening after the Preston game the telephone rang. It was Gordon Parker and he didn't beat around the bush. He simply said that the board would like to offer me the job and they wanted me to start as soon as possible. I accepted Gordon's offer, so he asked me to go down to Colchester on the Thursday to be introduced to everyone as the new manager.

Anne and the boys were there listening in anticipation. Thomas was right in the middle of his GCSEs and he was training once a week at Southampton FC under Micky Adams, who was still a player then. Jack was on Swindon's books as a junior and was also well settled in school. The point that I am making is that the last thing the boys wanted to do at that time was relocate. However, when I came off the phone, Thomas was the first to congratulate me, which was very mature of him at 15 years of age. Jack also congratulated me in his own quiet way. Anne was her usual supportive self and just gave me a look that said, "I told you so." My whole family were behind me and I couldn't have asked for more. Sally was in bed but in the morning she was told that we were off again. This was her second move and she wasn't five years old yet.

I contacted Terry to give him the news and he was fantastic about the situation. After a couple of phone calls by him to his opposite number at Colchester, a compensation package was agreed. Terry didn't put any obstacles in my way, which I will always appreciate. Aldershot received a few quid as part of the agreement, so it wasn't all bad news for them and maybe some fans thought it was a good deal, who knows? One thing I did regret was that I didn't get the chance to say goodbye to all the players personally because it all happened so quickly. I have met most of the lads again in recent years and I don't think they have held it against me. It was just circumstances and there was no way that it was meant as a snub.

My first two-and-a-half years of football management could not have gone any better and I was proud of my achievements at Aldershot Town. I was leaving the club in a strong financial position and its structure was also sound. We had created a brand new club and put it on the road to where it deserved to be.

When we met at his house in June 1992, Terry told Graham and me that the new club could be back in the Football League in 10 years. Well, it took 16 years, but it was still a phenomenal achievement!

I am and always will be more than happy with my contribution in that fantastic journey.

CHAPTER 9

MANAGING A WEMBLEY DOUBLE FOR THE "U'S"

It was strange pulling up at Layer Road again. On the face of it nothing much had changed. Obviously this time I was turning up as the manager and I was excited at the prospect of being back in the Football League. Some great memories flooded back into my mind as I walked through the gates of the old ground. I had almost forgotten how compact the arena was after being at such an open space like the Recreation ground.

There were smiles all round when I met the club officials and the local press and media. Some familiar faces shook my hand and wished me well, which reassured me that I wasn't coming into a situation that was completely new. When the formalities were over I wanted to meet the players and staff as soon as possible.

The chairman had already briefed me about who was who at the club, so I had some sort of idea what to expect. Any thoughts I'd had of bringing in my own staff were not on, to start with at least. At Aldershot I had picked my own people and it had worked superbly. Colchester was an established club with people already in place and on contracts. I was on my own to a certain degree. Having said that, Mr Heard had told me that I would be the manager and the board would support me if I thought there needed to be changes. Even if there were to be changes it would not be straight away, as I needed to settle in and assess everything, from the playing budget down to how the kit was washed.

I was introduced to Steve Whitton, the player/coach. Dale Roberts, George's right-hand man who had been left in charge temporarily when he moved down the road to Ipswich, had now left and had joined his boss at Portman Road as coach. I didn't know 'Witts' personally but I had played against him once a few years earlier. I had been told that he was a good mate of my old friend Roy McDonough and I felt that wasn't such a bad thing. I was hopeful that Roy had given him the rundown on me, not as a manager but as a person. I knew that Steve would be a good asset on the pitch, so as far as I was concerned that was his first priority.

Brian Owen was the physio and a very experienced campaigner. His knowledge of the game and his connections would be invaluable to me. I hadn't met Brian before either, but he came over as very positive at our first meeting.

One member of staff that I did know was Steve Foley. 'Zora', as he was known, had been at the club for several years and had taken up a few roles during that time. We had played together during the seventies and I had chatted to him during the last Vets game a few years back. Steve wasn't in at the ground on my first day, so I asked Brian where he was. Brian hesitated slightly and then said, "Oh, he's not very well. He's at home." I found that a little strange considering it was the new manager's first day at the club, but I put it to the back of my mind and got on with meeting the players, who after all were the most important part of the club!

The team were lying in a reasonable position in the third division. George had put together a decent squad and by the looks of it there was a chance that a play-off place was attainable. Brian, the physio, clued me up as to what had been going on that season. He went over each player with me and gave me a short résumé of their abilities, character, etc. He also pointed out that we had a couple of injury worries and suspensions pending that month. He felt that these two problems might affect our results slightly over the coming games. Brian had been a coach in his earlier days and had worked with some very good people, so his knowledge and input would prove to be invaluable to me. When I spoke to Steve Whitton, I discovered that he was well and truly still a player. He was on the staff technically, but he came over very much as one of the lads.

I didn't know many of the players in the squad and I'm sure some of them didn't know me from Adam. That didn't bother me at all, however, having just put together a squad of players from scratch at my previous club. That it was a lower standard made no difference, as the principles are the same, and I was confident in my own abilities to assess these lads quite quickly.

I had a hundred and one jobs to do and I knew that it was going to be difficult in the early days in many ways. I had to cram in as much work as possible in a short a space of time. We had a home game on the Saturday, which was only a couple of days away.

I had sorted my contract out and I was staying at the George Hotel in the town centre. Logistically it was going to be a bit of a drag for a few weeks while Anne sorted out the domestic arrangements. We had decided to move to Colchester lock, stock and barrel, so Anne was going to have to deal with the house sale, schools, etc., while I was getting stuck in at Layer Road. I wanted my family in Colchester as soon as it was physically possible. The club had kindly organised my stay at the hotel - and very nice it was too! It was better than our last experience when Anne and I had stayed at the Peveril Hotel on North Hill when I was a player. The new owner of the George was Michael Slagle and he kindly left me a bottle of Glenlivet Scotch and a good luck card in my room on the first night. It was a nice gesture.

I was looking for as much feedback as possible as I was getting down to work. Some information that I received was that a few people from inside the club had also applied for the manager's position. One of them was Dale Roberts, who had left, the others being Steve Whitton, Tony English and Steve Foley. On hearing those names, a few little alarm bells started ringing in the old grey matter. Tony and Zora had accumulated many years at the club as players and, in Zora's case, he had occupied many jobs on the staff side. Witts was relatively new to the club but had a great pedigree as a player and had worked under some great managers such as Ron Atkinson and John Lyall. So you might say that they felt they had a genuine chance of landing the job and I already knew that those on the shop floor had favoured an internal promotion. Anything for an easy life, eh chaps? Well, they had me now and I was there to stay and do a good job!

I was aware that there might be a certain amount of dissent or resentment and that's not unusual when a new man comes in with new ideas or methods. That didn't mean that I was going to stand for it though. Anyone who didn't want to come to the party could do the other as far as I was concerned.

I wasn't going to uproot my family and give up a good job at Aldershot in order to fail. That wasn't an option for me. I intended to run the playing side of the club as I saw fit! Having said that, I had no intention of jumping in wielding a big stick. There was no need for that as it would be a gradual process. I would put into place the right players and staff to take the club forward and if people felt that I was stepping on their toes or maybe disrupting their nice little world, bad luck. I was now as competitive off the pitch as I used to be on it. In many ways it was others that needed to do their homework on me.

From the public's point of view a change of manager doesn't appear to be such a big deal. One out and one in, or two staff out and two staff in. That couldn't be further from the truth. The effect when there is a change of manager can be far-reaching depending on what the new man is coming into, as there can be major changes of policy, funding, targets, attitudes and jobs.

The directors on the board make the decision on the new man and have to back him as best as they can, otherwise there would be no reason to change the boss. In my case, it was slightly different as I replaced someone who had left of his own volition, but I was still going to get the backing of the board, as I was their choice to replace him. Behind the scenes there is a lot of activity when a new man arrives, but the supporters just want to see their team win. The peripheral workings of the club don't really matter to most fans. I would have to make changes, but I needed to get results as soon as possible as well.

My first game in charge of Colchester was soon upon me and our opponents were Barnet at home. As Brian had told me, we had some problems selecting our strongest side because of suspensions and injuries. The match finished 1-1, which was an okay start. I definitely hadn't wanted to begin with a defeat – well, who does? Ray Clemence, Barnet's manager, had also experienced a few selection problems, so he was pleased with their point. Barnet were up in the top ten with us, so it was probably everybody's banker for a draw in the circumstances. I was reasonably pleased with the players' response on the day, as they had been through an uncertain few weeks since George had left.

It felt fantastic to be back in professional football. The crowd were decent and the Layer Road atmosphere was nice to experience again. The media attention was much more than I had been used to as a manager at Aldershot and I immediately had to spend more time on interviews and the like. This gave me no problem at all.

I wanted everyone to settle down now and get on with the job in hand. I wasn't the 'devil', which I hoped the players had realised already. I was putting in long days in my office as well as getting out onto the training ground, which was my favourite part of the job. I was still very much a 'tracksuit manager' and I wanted to get my ideas over to the players as quickly as possible. I hadn't finished playing that long ago, so my energy levels were still very high at a sprightly 40!

Steve Foley, who had been off for a couple of days, came back to work as the club's youth coach. I hadn't had a chance as yet even to look at the youth side of things, so I called him in for a meeting in the hope that he could give me a brief rundown of our youth programme. Steve and I had known each other for many years and his association with the club was second to none. However, the moment he came into the office I could see by his body language that he wasn't totally happy. He had always been a bit of a joker and had loved the usual banter, but that day there wasn't much of that. I asked if he felt better and he replied that he did now. I didn't think that I needed to beat around the bush, so I asked him a direct question: "Do you want to work for me?" I told him that I had already asked the same question to Brian Owen and Steve Whitton. Both had given me a definite yes as their answer, which was good, as I just wanted to know where I stood and how they saw the situation.

Zora replied, "I work for the club." At first I thought I'd just misheard him, so I asked him again. It was a fair question, as I was the manager of the football club and my remit was the control of the complete football department as a whole. However, he repeated his previous answer.

I just looked at him and there was a short pause. I couldn't quite get my head around where he was coming from. Obviously he was disappointed at not getting the manager's position, but hang on a minute. He was in a nice little job coaching the youngsters and someone he knows and gets on alright with had just moved into the boss's seat. It didn't make sense, so I quite calmly asked the question one final time. His reply was just the same. I knew exactly where we stood then and anything that happened in the future would be totally his own doing.

Nobody on the playing side of the club is bigger or has more authority than the manager. No matter how long someone has been at a football club or how much they have contributed to that club, the manager is the person that determines the rules. Let's be honest, he is the man that gets the sack when things don't go well, so he expects all his staff to be with him. I was asked the same question every day by my boss Brian Talbot at Aldershot and had no hesitation in giving him my support. The fact that a member of my staff was unwilling to do the same for me spoke volumes!

I was forming a picture of what needed to be done at the club. Mr Heard had also given me targets to hit on the budget. Too much money was being spent in some areas, such as training kit, laundry and travelling, etc. We needed to trim things down. I looked at as many aspects as possible and came up with some ideas and procedures to save us some cash. I was invited to all the board meetings, which suited me. I had been used to attending meetings at Aldershot and I thought that it was a good thing for the manager to be present when important decisions were made. I was required to present a monthly report on football matters. At that time Gordon Parker, Peter Heard, Peter Powell and John Worsp made up the board and I found them all to be extremely thorough in every aspect of the running of the football club. We had some problems finding a suitable chief executive in the first couple of seasons, but eventually Steven Gage filled the role. He had extensive knowledge of running a football club after his involvement some years earlier with Wigan.

My old mate, Bobby Fisher, phoned me, as he had got involved with one-to-one mentoring, which didn't surprise me. Fish was a great lad to talk to and was very laid back on and off the pitch. I invited him for a chat and discovered that he was studying for the relevant qualifications in his field. I decided to employ him on a part-time basis to work with the senior players. They really took to his visits and opened up to him more than they would to coaches or a manager.

I received some valuable feedback from Bob, which helped me look at myself, my staff, our methods and, most of all, what made some of the lads tick. This was all done without betraying any confidences. Fish would only tell me what he thought was relevant, as he wanted to maintain a good relationship with the boys to help to improve them both as players and in character. Fish was a great help and definitely played his part in our success at Colchester.

We were employing the services of someone like Bob for some time before many lower league clubs were and it was done on a very small budget, so it makes me smile to hear top-level clubs using so-called 'pioneering methods' involving psychology, nutrition, fitness gurus, etc., all costing millions of pounds, when I used to do all that to a certain degree without a pot to pee in!

I was getting to know the players a little better and they were quite a talented bunch. I decided quite quickly that the team was not as balanced as I would have liked, but that would have to be addressed at the end of the season. Our home form was a major problem and in the end put paid to our play-off ambitions. The lads' away form was on a par with any of the main play-off candidates and we put in some excellent displays on our travels.

One such game that springs to mind was at Scunthorpe in February. I was still finding my feet a little, but this game was a turning point for me as a manager. Our results hadn't been great and we found ourselves 3-0 down after 18 minutes. I was frantically trying to get the players back into the game from the touchline, as I feared a rout was on the cards. Adam Locke and Tony English scored for us within the next ten minutes, which caused Scunthorpe manager Dave Moore to become just as frantic. At half-time I had to lay into a couple of the players. This would be my first rollicking of many, I suspected! I changed a couple of things defensively and I also had a few words with Gus Caesar. His performance in the second half was much better. Their lads seemed to be tiring as the game hit the 60-minute mark. I stuck Niall Thompson on and let him run about like the madman that he was. The lad was a revelation and scored two goals in the final part of the game. We had turned a 3-0 defeat into a 4-3 victory! I was pleased with the reaction of the players to some harsh words and I was pleased with myself as a manager. I had made a few calls as they say in Amercia, that had paid off. With a bit of luck, I may be taken seriously now, I thought. I didn't realise until someone told me that the match result was regarded as "The greatest escape in the 55-year history of Colchester United"!

Even though we had scored four goals at Scunthorpe, I knew we needed more firepower up front. I watched a young lad play for Brentford reserves called Carl Asaba. He was very raw but had loads of pace and strength. I phoned David Webb, their manager, and he let me have him on loan for a month. Carl was an instant success and scored on his League debut at Barnet. He went on to have a very good career, which did not surprise me one bit. All Carl needed was for someone to show some faith in him.

There was a fair amount of experience in the squad I had inherited. Trevor Putney was one of the most experienced but he was having lots of injury problems. When he was fit he was still a great influence on the pitch. Sometimes, when new managers come in, well-known senior players can be difficult to handle, but Trevor was first class and didn't give me an ounce of trouble.

I'm not sure that I can say the same for the 'big galoot' Peter Cawley! All 6 feet 4 inches of him could be a proverbial pain in the arse at times. Peter virtually ran the dressing room, or he thought he did. He was a very intelligent lad who for some reason wanted to do silly things a lot of the time. He was very influential over some of the younger lads and they looked up to him as the big bad rebel or the like! On a couple of occasions I had to put a couple of the lads in their place when they tried to push their luck in my presence. I'm not saying that Peter was responsible for their actions, but I could almost hear his words coming out of their mouths.

Peter was an excellent player who knew the game better than a lot of people gave him credit for. Most saw him as the big clown who was going to make them laugh and perhaps take the piss out of a member of staff. I saw right through that and, even though he was still a handful at times, there was definitely more to Peter than there appeared to be. He even cut up his tracksuit bottoms one day and turned them into Robinson Crusoe-type pants just to gain a reaction! There was one thing for sure: there wasn't any better big, strong, left-footed centre back in our League at that time.

When I eventually left Peter out of the side a year or two later his wife collared me at one of our functions and attempted to tear me off a strip. She was totally out of order, as I had looked after Peter on his final contract and had done everything right by him. I kept my composure and was as pleasant as I could possibly be. I saw Peter some years later on the other side of the fence when he was a coach at Wycombe. He was very pleased to see me and said in his own way how much he appreciated now how difficult it was in management and coaching!

I didn't have too many problems with the players in general. Just as in any job, people have to get used to one another. They definitely had to get used to me. I'm a bit of a perfectionist, which I think some people at the club found difficult to cope with at first. I was forever writing lists of things that had to be done. The first thing that I did when I got in each morning was sit at my desk and write a list on an A4-size piece of paper. Sometimes that list would fill the page from top to bottom, with anything from 25 to 50 items to be addressed that day. Then as they were dealt with I would tick them off. It could be anything from reminding the kit man of something very small to the signing of a new contract for one of the professionals. I had to be organised. My desk was immaculate with everything in its place. The pens were even in a straight line next to each other! That's the way I wanted the club to be run on and off the pitch. If I was walking from my office down to the dressing rooms and there was a piece of litter on the ground, then I would pick it up and take it with me. That was just my being tidy, even though some might describe it as obsessive.

I wanted my players to look tidy on the pitch and smart off it. For me, everything linked together on and off the pitch, and the demands that I put on the players were high. I liked a laugh and a joke as much as anyone, but I expected total concentration and application at the right times. Some of the players and office staff found my demands hard to accept at first, especially when results were still sketchy. I can just imagine them when I wasn't there saying, "Why are we doing this because nothing has changed on the pitch?" I could understand that to a point, but I knew that eventually the results would come if we stuck at it.

I put even more responsibility on the playing staff. All players now had to take their own kit home and wash it. They were given two sets so that they could alternate each day. This was a great money saver for the club in terms of the laundry bill and also meant that less kit would go missing, which was another saving. The lads weren't too happy to start with but they got over it. We also made a few quid in fines for the players' pool. Anyone who came in without a certain item of training kit was fined £1 per item.

I set down all the rules quite clearly in regard to timekeeping, going down to the kit room, which was now out of bounds, kicking balls about before an adequate warm-up, etc. If the rules were broken then a small fine was imposed, which again went into the players' pool. That pool would go towards some sort of recreation at the end of the season. It was self-governing, as the players loved catching the same old faces out and taking their hard-earned cash off them. It was a bit of fun but it worked and everyone knew where they stood. I also decided that any fines dealt out for offences on the pitch could also go into the same pool, with the permission of the board, of course, as I didn't want it to appear that we were rewarding players at the end of the season for any serious breach of discipline. I also worked very hard on each individual's discipline. Training sessions were quite strict as I wanted the players to get used to overzealous officials on match days.

I had read a lot about Mark Kinsella when I was at Aldershot, even though I hadn't seen him play, so it was pleasing for me when I worked with him. He proved to be everything that I had read and more. He was not the biggest or the quickest player, but he had a smart football brain and great technique. Even so, I had to ask questions of him on one occasion.

I noticed that there was a slight underlying atmosphere or maybe attitude coming from a few of the boys. I suspected that my appointment still niggled a couple of the lads that had been there a while, such as Mark Kinsella and Tony English. There may have been others but these two were well and truly entrenched at the club. There wasn't any open hostility towards me, and if there had been I would have kicked them out sharpish no matter who they were! I just felt it in my bones. In Tony's case, he had originally wanted my job, so it was probably difficult for him to hide every emotion. In Mark's case, I just think that he didn't really know me and I just had to prove myself to him.

We played away at Hartlepool in March 1995 and on the day they beat us 3-1. We were poor, especially in the first half. Mark usually played well in most of our games. He loved playing matches and his standards were very high. In this particular game he was well below his usual level; in fact at times he looked as if he was half cocked. Most of the team were poor but at half-time I dug Mark out and questioned his commitment. Some of the lads looked shocked that I would talk to him in that way, but I didn't give a toss! I just saw it as it was and dealt with it. Judging by the look on his face, Mark took my questioning as a personal affront. Who was I to talk to him like that?

Well, maybe it was about time that somebody rocked the boat to get a reaction!

Later on even John Schultz, Mark's father-in-law-to-be, came to see me! He told me that Mark was not very happy with the way I had spoken to him at Hartlepool and that a couple of the lads agreed with him. I had known John for years and liked him very much, so I didn't argue the toss with him and just told him that I heard what he was saying. Inside I was bloody steaming! Who the hell did these players think they were? Christ, we had just lost 3-1 to Hartlepool and I had players telling tales and whimpering! This was like a red rag to a bull to me and I was determined that there would be no let up.

Tony English was a very versatile player and he was vital to our squad at that time. He had also been at the club for a long time and had seen a few managers come and go. He would do a good job in whatever position I asked him to play. His performances were of a high standard and I had no complaints. He was also our skipper, but I still felt that he was distant at times. It was as if someone had bent his ear about me before my arrival. Even right up to the day he left, which was premature in my opinion, I don't think he liked me. I wonder why that was then?

I was getting the bit between my teeth and the job intrigued me more than concerned me now. I had been looking closely at our youth system while everything else was going on. We hadn't exactly produced a production line of players that would go into the first team over the years. With Ipswich and Norwich close by, it was always going to be difficult. My main remit was the first team, but I believed strongly that an effective youth and reserve set-up was vital to any club. We would often get the big clubs' cast-offs, but my vision was for Colchester United to produce players for the first team year after year in its own right. There was a distinct possibility that if I did manage to revamp that department somewhat I might not actually reap the rewards in the future, as it would probably take five years or so for it to bear fruit. However, I managed to persuade the board that a revamped youth system was the way to go and Mr Heard gave me the go-ahead.

On the domestic front we managed to get ourselves moved into rented accommodation while our house in Aldershot was sold. We were looking for a property to buy in or around the Lexden area of Colchester, which was only a ten-minute drive from the ground. Anne and I had wanted the boys to go to St Benedict's College, which was an excellent school, and Mr Whelan, the principal, made them very welcome. They settled well and, in fact, both Thomas and Jack went on to become deputy head boys in their final year there. Sally was accepted into St Teresa's Infants at the early age of four and a half years.

I couldn't confide in many people at the club yet, as to many of the staff in the offices I was still the new man on the block. I was getting on okay with Brian Owen and Steve Whitton, and even Steve Foley appeared to settle down and get on with the job in hand in the youth section. There was one person who would always give me an honest assessment of people and that was my old playing colleague Paul 'Sammy' Dyer.

Paul had been scouting on a part-time basis for several years, so I saw no reason to change that. At my request he would travel anywhere and either watch a team play or report on an individual player. His reports on the opposition were always spot-on and his knowledge of players all over the country was excellent. I liked to know as much as possible about our up and coming opponents, just as most managers do. I was a great believer in playing every game 'our way', but knowing the strengths and weaknesses of the other teams in advance was definitely important in planning an effective strategy.

Paul was well known in the town and at the club, so his feedback on many issues was very useful to me. I also trusted him to be honest and not just tell me what I wanted to hear. I felt that he took me on face value and had no hidden agenda or issues with me, which was a great relief. We hadn't always got on like a house on fire as players, but there was a mutual respect for each other and that was good enough as far as I was concerned.

Coming to a club without your own staff is always going to be difficult. The job itself is testing to say the least, so you need as much help as you can get. Brain and Paul were a hive of information for me, and Witts was a top-class player on the pitch.

I had imposed myself on the club and after three weeks or so I had sussed the place out. There was more work to be done than I had first envisaged and there were also more underlying problems at the club than I could have imagined. None of these things were serious, but they needed attending to and I was determined to sort them out.

The playing personnel had to change slightly, but most players were on contracts anyway for the following season so there wasn't going to be a clear-out. Trevor Putney was retiring, which was a shame as he was an experienced pro with great ability. I let Paul Stoneman go after his loan spell and released Tim Allpress and Niall Thompson. Steve Brown went over to Gillingham, with Robbie Reinelt coming the other way. I knew Robbie from his days at Aldershot as a youngster. The playing budget was limited and so most of my dealings were virtually one in, one out. I had done a lot of spadework over my first few months at the club, which enabled me to target a couple of players. Paul Gibbs came in from Diss Town, who had won the FA Vase at Wembley and were the team that beat Atherton L.R. who had knocked my Aldershot side out of the quarter-final stage of that competition. Michael Cheetham had come in from Chesterfield before the transfer deadline and stayed with us.

As the new season 1995/96 progressed, other players joined us. I brought back Tony Adcock, who had played with us previously and whom I rated very highly. 'Tadds' was a great signing for us and I knew that if I could keep him fit and free from injuries he would score goals again for Colchester. Tony McCarthy came in from Millwall. I had a good relationship with their manager Mick McCarthy at the time. My old mate Ian McDonald was still the reserve team manager at the 'New Den', so I had plenty of inside info on their players' availability. Steve Mardenborough also joined us on a short-term contract. I had to be so careful with the budget that I couldn't commit to long-term contracts for everyone. Wheeling and dealing had become an everyday occurrence for me now.

I had brought in players that in my opinion would improve the squad enough to go one better than the previous squad and reach the coveted play-offs. The final placing of tenth in the previous season was disappointing as we probably had enough talent to get closer to the play-off places. Lack of depth in the squad had restricted us at the turn of the year with suspensions, illness and injury. This wasn't an excuse; it was a plain fact.

One player that I had to make a difficult decision on was Steve Ball. I hadn't seen Steve play, as he had been out injured for the whole season with a ruptured hamstring. My spies told me that he was a fantastic footballer with a great pedigree, having previously been at Arsenal and Norwich. The easy way out would have been simply to give him a free transfer and use his wages to get someone else in. However, after having a long chat with him I decided to put him on a month-to-month contract, get him fit and then have a good look at him. The board were not particularly happy with the idea but reluctantly agreed.

I took to Steve as a lad and thought that he deserved a chance, but it didn't work out for him in the end, which was a pity. Some months later when I eventually had to give him the bad news he was not a happy bunny and let rip at me. He slaughtered my methods and virtually everything that I had done. He also had a go at Witts, who didn't take it too kindly, and at one point I thought there might be handbags at dawn! I eventually calmed them both down and explained to Steve that the decision had been made. The lad was distraught and I didn't see him again for a long time.

In fact it was years later when I had left Colchester United that I bumped into Steve in a shop. He came straight over to me, shook my hand and apologised for his behaviour on the day that I had given him the bad news. He said that it was only later, when he had experienced the difficulties and work involved in management first-hand, albeit at a lower level, that he had realised that I had done the best I could for him. It was just that his disappointment at the time was so acute that he had just wanted to offload onto somebody. I told him that I had fully understood his reaction on that day and he wasn't the first or the last to question my management skills!

Another couple of players came in: Joe Dunne, a young fullback from Gillingham, and Scott McGleish, a striker on loan from Peterborough. Both of these players would play a significant part in our success that season. I had seen Joe play for Gillingham reserves and, although he wasn't the most cultured of fullbacks, his determination and never-say-die attitude really impressed me. He was a typical Irish lad - a little rascal! Scotty was a real live wire with springs on his heels. He could be a little headstrong at times and I had to slap him down in training on a couple of occasions when he got out of his cage. He would show dissent towards me sometimes, as he did with anyone who went against his wishes. One thing was for sure though: he desperately wanted to play. I always liked hungry players and would put up with a certain amount of crap, but eventually they had to toe the line if they wanted to play in the side.

I personally wasn't a great fan of the loan system. I intended to use it only if I thought the player was definitely going to improve my team. To bring a lad in simply to make up numbers or as backup wasn't what I really wanted. If I had lads in the squad who could get into the team and do a decent job, I would try to do that instead as much as possible. Sometimes loans could disrupt the team spirit in the dressing room. All the lads in our squad needed assurance that they had a chance of playing in the first team and that I wouldn't just bring in a loan player every time we had a problem.

Some clubs had to use the loan system constantly because their budgets weren't high enough to have quality players on long-term contracts in their team. That's why a few teams' results would be okay while they had their full quota of loan players, but when these players returned to their clubs the results would fall away very quickly. Even though I did use the system sometimes, I liked to have players on contracts with a sense of team spirit and stability that comes with a squad that isn't being chopped and changed too much. Injuries, of course, would disrupt that ideal squad at times and that is when I mostly used up my loans.

I brought in David Greene on loan from Luton Town. David was a big strong centre back who was fantastic in the air as well as being technically very good. When I watched him play for Luton reserves he dominated in the air at both ends of the pitch. He headed nearly every defensive corner away and got on the end of most of the attacking corners and free kicks in the opponents' penalty box. I needed even more height in the side, so I took David after a long conversation with Lennie Lawrence, the Luton manager. Lennie was a little reluctant to let him out at first, but I reassured him that it would be best for both parties as first-team football would only improve his skills as a footballer and on his return to Luton he could well get into their first eleven. David did well for us but had to go back, but in view of his great performance I decided to sign him on a permanent basis the following season. He would turn out to be a real asset so long as he recognised his strengths and stuck to them. I had one hell of a job getting him out of some bad habits he'd picked up playing reserve-team football. David was a very effective player when he defended, but when he tried to bring the ball down in dangerous situations to try to play he gave us problems. I was always on

Greenies' back regarding his fitness, weight and general play. He probably hated me at times, but I helped him become a very effective centre back.

Carl Emberson was another big lump like David, and I was on his case too most of the time. Carl was a good goalkeeper but he had to be pushed in training. On Mondays and Fridays either Witts or I would weigh all the lads and log the details in a book. Certain parameters were set for each of them and if they were over their normal weight on these occasions they would be fined a certain amount per additional pound. Most of the lads didn't mind these weigh-ins as they didn't have a spare ounce on them, but the big lads such as Cawley, Greene and Emberson hated every minute of it. I wanted my team to be as fit as possible, so this procedure was an important element in my overall expectations of them. After some training sessions, if Carl and David had been up on their weight, as well as fining them I would do a 12-minute run around the pitch with them and if I beat them they had to do an extra lap of the pitch. They would be spitting feathers if I made them do this and the other lads used to wind them up about it. I knew which players needed to be dragged on to better things and which ones needed to be cajoled. My methods didn't go down well with some but they were effective in the end.

Tony English unfortunately played his last game in January 1996. It was exactly 12 years to the day since he had made his first-team debut as a teenager. He was having constant problems with his knee and he eventually made the decision to call it a day on his professional career. It was a great shame for him personally and a big blow for us. We would find it very difficult to replace him. I thought that he might seek out more opinions regarding the injury's prognosis, but he had made up his mind and I had to respect that; after all, it was his body and his decision.

As we went into February our results were very poor and I wasn't pleased with the commitment of some individuals. I called a meeting at the training ground and made my feelings known to the squad. I didn't pull any punches and actually insulted some of them. I wanted a reaction to kick-start our season. We had been knocked out of the FA Cup by Gravesend, which was a real sickener for me. We had bounced back with a great win at Oxford in the Auto Windscreen Shield, but our subsequent results were abysmal and something needed to be done.

Paul Abrahams had come back to us on loan from Brentford. 'Abes' had gone to Brentford the previous year for a decent fee and he had felt that the move would be beneficial for him at that time, but David Webb was a hard man to please and Paul had found the going tough. I had no hesitation in taking him back. He had many problems with niggling injuries but gave us good options up front or in wide areas with his pace and skill. Eventually I would buy him back for half the original transfer fee, so it was a good deal all round. I don't think that he saw me as quite the ogre he might have imagined after his Brentford experience.

David Gregory came onto the scene around this time, on Brian Owen's recommendation. Witts also knew him quite well from his Ipswich days. David was at Peterborough and going nowhere. When I first saw him he looked overweight and unfit. However, Brian insisted that if we got him fit he could be an asset as a goalscoring midfielder. I gave him a go and virtually told him that we were his last chance of saving what had been a promising career at Ipswich. He grabbed it with both hands and did a great job for me over the next few seasons.

Our results picked up in March even though we lost Carl Emberson to injury. His replacement, the young Canadian Garett Caldwell, was away on international duty, so I drafted in Andy Petterson on loan from Charlton. I got on well with Alan Curbishley, their manager, which links in with the Mark Kinsella connection and Charlton later that year.

Our form was good enough through March and April to propel us into the top ten and, with games running out, results became vital. The players had turned the corner and had started to perform more consistently. If we had picked up in February we would have been looking at going straight up. That was probably too much to have hoped for, especially with the injury problems we had.

One plus that had helped us that season was our fantastic defensive record. We had only conceded 51 goals. The club had only conceded less than 50 goals on four occasions during their 44-year history, so we were well up there in terms of holding one of the best defensive records. Looking back to season 1977/78, we only conceded 44 goals and I was one of the players in the back four that year, which had consisted of Micky Packer, Steve Dowman, Micky Cook and myself. My methods and ideas were working, which pleased me no end!

With just three games to go, we needed a minimum of seven points to give us a chance of making the play-offs. The first two games were away at Exeter and Mansfield and the last game was at home to none other than my old club Doncaster Rovers. We gained a draw at Exeter, which put the pressure right on as we probably had to win the final two games and hope for other results to go our way. The Mansfield game was almost a fairy tale come true for one player. The score was 1-1 with literally minutes to go when our fullback Joe Dunne popped up at the far post in free play to head a spectacular winner. It was a great turnaround for him, as he hadn't been in the side for long and already he was a crowd favourite.

I felt that I had silenced a few doubters in and around the football club up to that point. Now I needed to get the club into the play-offs for the first time in 16 years. Ironically, the previous time was the season in which I had gained promotion with Aldershot through the play-offs as a player.

The build-up to the final game was tremendous and the players looked very focused and relaxed. Joe's goal at Mansfield had been one of those defining moments that I mentioned earlier in the book and it had given us a feeling that it was our year to get into the top seven.

The game against Doncaster was a nervous occasion and we even fluked a goal to win the match. Gibbsy hit what looked like a cross from deep and it sailed over their keeper into the top corner of the net. This was just before half-time, which led to a nervy second half. News was filtering through that our rivals, Hereford and Wigan, were struggling, but I was reluctant to take too much notice as it could have been just a Chinese whisper. At the final whistle the 5,000+ crowd went mad. Maybe the news about our rivals was true? As it turned out, Hereford had won but Wigan had lost in the 86th minute at home to Northampton. Our win placed us just above that play-off line and our first game would be at home to Plymouth, who finished fourth, just one point off automatic promotion. We did a lap of honour and the crowd loved it. I felt as if it was somewhat premature, but why not? There hadn't been much to shout about at Layer Road for some time.

As is usual with managers, within hours I was planning how we were going to approach the Plymouth game. Their manager, Neil Warnock, was a playing colleague of mine at Doncaster many years earlier. Neil had a certain reputation as a manager and I was looking forward to facing him over the two legs, home and away. Neil always talked a good game as a player and nothing had changed now that he was a manager - he still liked to talk a lot!

I didn't have to say much to the players to motivate them for the home game against Plymouth. In training we went through how the opposition would play and then worked out our own formation. We had performed very well to get this far and I could see in training that the players had no intention of buckling, under to the opposition even though Plymouth had some very good players, as Neil had spent a fair amount of money on the squad. They were a bigger club than us and could attract up to 20,000 people on a good day.

The match was a sell-out and the atmosphere was just what I had hoped for. The crowd were right behind the lads right from the off and Layer Road was as lively as it could be. It was nip and tuck at times, but I felt confident in my players throughout the match and everyone did a good job. Mark Kinsella scored a fantastic goal for us and showed how much he had matured as a player with his overall performance. The opposition had a couple of good chances, which you would expect from such a good outfit. We also had a few other chances when we hit the post and bar and perhaps should have scored. However, when another chance dropped onto the crossbar from Robbie Reinelt I knew deep down that this might be the moment when our fate would be sealed. I wasn't being negative at all, but experience tells you that some incidents do come back to haunt you. In the event, we deservedly won the game 1-0.

Neil had his usual rant in the press about intimidation by our crowd - the usual dross! He was out of his comfort zone with us, as he knew we were one of the few sides capable of beating his club over the two legs. We already had done in the League matches, with a 2-1 win at home and a 1-1 draw at their place.

I would have been happier with a second goal going into the away game, but I was still confident in my team. I was sure that if we applied ourselves correctly the skills of the players would be enough to score an away goal and give Plymouth a mountain to climb.

The atmosphere was quite hostile on the night. There was a big turnout and their manager had done a job on the press and media to wind them up.

That was Neil; he had no qualms about telling 'porkies' to get the mood whipped up. He even said that missiles had been thrown at his players at the first game, which wasn't witnessed either by me or by my players.

In reality, all of this was irrelevant if we performed well enough on the evening. Unfortunately we didn't. Within minutes of the kick-off, Gus Caesar got on the wrong side of their striker Evans, who whipped a fierce shot over our keeper Emberson. All our hard work in the first game and all our preparation behind the scenes before this match was negated in a matter of minutes. Gus was a good professional and a very effective defender, but he was always prone to sleeping on the job at times. This was not the time for it to happen but it did and we were all square within three minutes in the Pilgrims' den!

The home crowd went crazy and you could see their players visibly grow in stature and determination. Neil was doing his usual jig while winding up the natives. I felt like running across to the dugout and putting my big toe up his backside!

We were still hanging on but looked a mere shadow of the team that had run Plymouth ragged at our place a few days earlier. They got a second goal and it looked all over for us, but we still had something left in the tank and Mark scored a spectacular goal for us from outside the box. We were back in it at 2-2. If it went to extra time and there were no more goals, then we would go through on the away goals rule.

Plymouth were visibly shaken and Neil got himself sent off for protesting to the officials too much. He thought that Tony McCarthy should have been sent off for a professional foul. He may have had a point, but as always with Neil he went over the top with his comments. He proceeded to stand behind our dugout in the crowd and whip up their supporters into a frenzy again.

Even though we hadn't played well, the game could have gone either way at this point. Then, just when it looked as though we were heading for extra time, they broke away down the left, sent over a cross and scored a third goal. There were less than five minutes to go. The referee had been under severe pressure, especially since the McCarthy incident, and he couldn't wait to blow up. Blow up he did, dead on time, and it was all over for us!

The feeling of disappointment was horrendous for everyone, although I tried my best to be a dignified loser. As we trudged off and walked down the steps to the dressing rooms, Neil came running after me, shook my hand and said, "Bad luck, Wiggs," and then he was back out on the pitch to celebrate with his team. I just accepted his comment and got back in the dressing room as quickly as possible.

Everyone sat down and all the staff just stood around. There was complete silence. We could hear the crowd in the stadium and I noticed a couple of chins quivering. I stood in the middle of the room looking around at the players and I wasn't sure where to start or what to say. Then we heard all their lads coming down the steps, shouting and whooping it up. They had to go right past our door, which made it even worse! The room was still silent. When the noise outside had died down, I decided to begin.

I had no intention of raking over details about our performance as a team or as individuals. Now was not the time for that. What I did say was that they should all remember how bad they felt at that moment, so that the next time the team were in that position of importance – We were not going to feel that way again. They would be motivated to go one step further and be winners and there would be a next time. That was about it from me.

The season was over for us and it had been a great experience for the players and me. I felt that I was a proper football manager now and I was confident in my own ability. I had been reasonably successful for four consecutive seasons. It hadn't been a flash in the pan, as I had worked at two completely different clubs with different staff, players and directors, and yet I had still managed to get results consistently on the pitch. We had just failed at the final hurdle, so I would look at the reasons for that over the summer. I would analyse my staff, all the players and my own contribution. Some tough decisions were necessary if we were to improve again in the 1996/97 season. One tiny consolation concerning the play-offs was that Plymouth went on to beat Darlington at Wembley to clinch their place in the second division, so at least we had lost to the winners!

Decisions on players' futures had to be made and after long consultations with my staff I called each lad into my office to give them the news, good or bad. That aspect of management is definitely the most difficult. In some cases you are putting a man out of work and he might never get another job at that level again. Looking into the eyes of a player that may well have given everything physically and having to tell him he is not wanted is very difficult.

I had done it before, of course, but the task never became any easier over time. In the end I released Tony Dennis, Michael Cheetham and Gus Caesar.

We had some good young lads coming into the squad that year in the shape of Nicky Haydon, Tony Lock and Karl Duguid. Karl had already been included in some games during the previous season. These three lads were a real bonus for me, as I could see all three of them playing in the first team in the not too distant future. Credit must go to Steve Foley who had nurtured these boys through the youth system.

Talking of Zora, he decided that his future was away from Layer Road and wanted to link up with our old colleague Micky Walker at Norwich. Steve had just got on with his job that previous season and I hadn't interfered or made it difficult for him. I felt that I owed him some respect for the job he had done at the club over the years and also we had been teammates back in the seventies. Overall, however, I was disappointed at how it had turned out. I was aware that he had wanted a go at the main job and unfortunately he had let the disappointment of not getting it cloud his views of me. His obvious snub to me at our first meeting had made the outcome inevitable.

Not long after I had taken over as manager, I went into the commercial department and my old mate Roy McDonough had called in for a visit. He hadn't changed at all - still having a laugh and saying exactly what he wanted! He had become more outspoken following his experiences as a manager, which I can fully appreciate. He was still raw after his sacking from Colchester United, which again was understandable. However, he was pleased that I had got the job as we had always got on very well.

Roy also felt that he should 'mark my card' on a few things within the club, for old time's sake perhaps! He mentioned Zora in despatches and he also said that he had a bit of a problem with a bloke called Neil Partner who was a close friend of Zora's. I didn't recognise who he was talking about at first and then he explained that he was involved with a junior side and that he sometimes played in the Vets games for Colchester. I now vaguely recalled whom Roy meant and asked if it was the geezer who kept kicking the ball into the stand nearly every time he got it. "Yes, that's him!" Roy laughed. Apparently Roy and Neil had nearly come to blows at one point, when Roy had called him into his office to question him about certain rumours.

I took on board what Roy had said, but I also realised that he was very disappointed at the way he had lost his job and felt that I had to take people on face value. Roy's contribution as a manager was fantastic and I think that he was undervalued by many people. In fact I think lots of them took the pee behind his back but rarely said anything to his face.

There were going to be changes at youth level and I interviewed some candidates for the jobs available. I felt that we needed a youth development officer to co-ordinate things from junior level up to the youth team. I gave the position to a local lad who knew the club and the town inside out. Geoff Harrop used to be an apprentice professional when I was a player back in the seventies and eighties and he was ideal for the post. I liked him, he had the club at heart and I thought that he would bring a certain enthusiasm to the job.

We also needed a youth team coach after Steve Foley's departure. I interviewed a few people for the position, one of whom was Adrian Webster. Adrian had been at the club for years in one capacity or another and had a very impressive CV. In the event, he came a close second to the man that I eventually picked for the job. I appointed Micky Cook, another ex-player who had been around the club since the days of the Leeds United game in the early seventies. Mick was working for Football in the Community at the time, so it was a natural progression as far as I was concerned.

I knew that these two appointments might cause a few waves in certain parts of the club, as often people within clubs and on the fringes don't like change; they don't like their little world to be disrupted or altered. However, I intended to do what I thought was right to improve the football club. It would have been easier if I had been able simply to sit in my office with my list of pros and not bother with any other aspect of the club, but that wasn't my way. I was going to do it correctly and lay down a solid foundation that could be built on in the future. Whether it would be under my guidance or someone else's remained to be seen.

I even took an interest in the much younger players and went down to see how things were going. Geoff was there and I knew he was finding his new role quite tough to start with. I was confident that he would cope with it and tried to give him my support whenever possible. When I arrived there were coaches and kids milling around, so I just walked up to say hello. It had been unusual for the first-team manager to be seen at these sessions in the past, so it was a bit of a surprise to some of them. As I greeted them, most of the coaches, such as Steve Dale who did a great deal of work at youth level, were very pleased to see me there. However, Neil Partner, the coach that Roy had mentioned, blatantly blanked me by deliberately turning his back. Was I missing something? The coach of one of the junior sides was showing total disrespect for the manager who had taken time out to come down and look at the kids!

I saw red and tore him off a strip, although I can't remember what I actually said. Everything that Roy had told me came flooding back. Who did he think he was? He obviously felt confident enough to show that he didn't give a toss who I was! He wasn't happy with the situation and he was going to make sure I knew about it, which was a big mistake in my books.

I received a phone call at home from Marie Partner, Neil's wife. She told me that he was upset and had been up late discussing the matter with her. Marie worked in the offices at Colchester United and she wasn't happy that he had brought home matters concerned with the club. From what she said, I don't think she was given an accurate account of events. It was Neil who had the problem, not me! The bottom line is that he was a junior coach at the football club and, although his role was no less important than that of any other member of my staff, I was not going to be blanked by him and nor did I expect him to go bleating to his wife! I have no idea why she phoned me rather than Neil coming to see me in person, but he didn't.

I have only mentioned this because the public have a right to know that at clubs like Colchester there are people who think for some unknown reason that they are fireproof. New managers will always come up against opposition that may not be personal to start with but if confronted will become just that. I had no intention of ducking issues that needed dealing with, whether it was with junior or senior staff.

Neil's young son, Andy Partner, was a pro at the club at this time. Unfortunately he had a knee problem and, although it was bad enough to keep him out for some time, I stuck with him. We helped him back to fitness and kept our faith in him for as long as possible, but he wasn't going to displace the likes of Peter Cawley or Tony McCarthy so in the end I had to let him go. I didn't have a minute's trouble with Andy and he was a good lad with an excellent attitude.

Changes were made that were beneficial to the club on and off the field. Three new players came in: David Greene, Richard Wilkins and David Barnes, my old playing mate from my Aldershot days who signed from Watford. David Barnes, who came as a free transfer, was probably the best left back in our division by far but unfortunately his stay with us went pear-shaped quite quickly.

Colchester old boy Richard Wilkins was a massive coup for me, as he was a very talented footballer who could perform in a few positions. I had always liked him even when I played against him. I actually signed him while I was holidaying in Swanage, Dorset. Anne and I had taken the kids on a camping holiday, which they loved, and the campsite was an old favourite even though it was pretty basic. There was an old telephone box there that only took coins and I can remember speaking to my contact regarding the deal between us and Hereford while worrying that I didn't have enough change! I agreed a fee of £17,500 for his services, even though an erroneous figure of between £30,000 and £50,000 was bandied about in the press. The cost would turn out to be an absolute snip over the coming seasons.

Our pre-season went well, especially our victory over Blackburn Rovers at Layer Road. The late Ray Harford had brought his team down for what they thought would be a routine game. We played very well and deserved our 2-1 victory. The only player missing from their star-studded line-up was Alan Shearer, who had moved to Newcastle. Ray wasn't over happy about the result but congratulated us on our win. Ray knew me quite well from his coaching days at Colchester when I was a player, but on that occasion he didn't have a lot to say to me. For some reason, he had turned into a man of few words since becoming a manager.

We needed more quality in the side if we were to emulate the previous season's results. Our early League form had been average, but the team was looking quite well balanced now.

We lost 3-2 at home to West Bromwich Albion in the first leg of the Coca Cola Cup and nobody gave us a cat in hell's chance of winning the second leg at their place. Against all the odds, however, we went into a 3-0 lead, but we also lost our keeper Caldwell due to a thigh strain. Steve Whitton replaced him in goal at half-time and we went on to win the game 3-1! It was an exceptional performance by us, and their manager at the time, Alan

Buckley, was very complimentary. He was under pressure because of their poor results, so for him to speak to me after the game in such a genial manner impressed me.

Our performances against higher opposition were commendable, but we needed to win the bread and butter games if we were to climb the League.

I knew that Mark Kinsella would probably go to another club. His contract was coming to an end and he didn't really want to sign another one, which was his prerogative. After our little spat earlier on when I hadn't been at the club very long, he had appeared to accept me more readily, and I even sent out videos of Mark's performances on the pitch to other clubs. I wanted to help him achieve his ambition, which was to play for his home country, the Republic of Ireland. To some people that dream might have seemed a little ambitious, but not to the lad himself or me. I had to do what was best for the club, but at the same time he deserved to be treated correctly. He originally went down to Southend FC and trained with them. Coach Theo Foley kept phoning me and asking more and more questions about him and I told him that Mark was easily good enough for them. "Make us a firm offer," I said, but he didn't respond with one. He just wanted to know how good he was without the ball, i.e., his defensive qualities. I couldn't see where he was coming from and so I was relieved when Mark came back to us. It wasn't a good move for him anyway. Then Charlton had a look at him and Alan Curbishley liked him. They didn't have pots of money but they had enough to offer a decent fee for the lad. To start with nothing was forthcoming and Mark had to come back and play for us, which was difficult for him. He was totally professional but at the same time very frustrated about the situation.

Eventually an agent representing Mark telephoned me and declared, "Charlton will pay £60,000 for him and that's it."

I politely responded, "No deal. He's worth a lot more than that."

The agent saw his backside and said, "If you don't do the deal I'll take him off abroad and you won't get a penny!"

Those were the rules then, so he did have a point, but I wasn't happy with his attitude or tone so I basically told him, "F*** off and do what you want!" Neither the club nor myself would be bullied into a deal that wasn't suitable.

His indignant response was, "You can't talk to me like that!"

"I just have, mate," I said. "You go and do what you think is best, old luv!"

And I put the phone down.

Within weeks Charlton came up with an offer of £160,000 with extras after he had made a certain number of appearances. I was happy for Mark and the club was happy with the money. In reality he was probably worth more, but in the financial climate of the time it wasn't a bad deal. I had lost a fantastic player, but I hoped that I had replaced him with someone who would also do a good job for us, 'Wilks'.

Even though I had added physical strength to the side, some teams such as Lincoln were still bullying us. Their manager, John Beck, had his own way of approaching games. His philosophy was to get the ball forward as quickly as possible and get free kicks, corners and throw-ins. Then he would load all his six-foot troops into the penalty box and, as they say, 'put it in the mixer'! It wasn't great to watch but it was very effective at times.

We had height and strength in our side but I wanted to mix things up a bit more and basically play decent football. We lost 3-2 at Lincoln in late October but by the return fixture in November it was a different story. It was sweet revenge in some ways but more of a vote of confidence for playing the game in the way it should be played.

John had all sorts of tricks up his sleeve from physical to psychological. When you played at Sincil Bank in Lincoln the radiator in the dressing room would be on maximum with no valve to turn it down. If you played there in warm weather it was like a sauna! On one occasion we found salt in the sugar bowl served up with the tea. Your warm-up footballs would be like concrete blocks and filthy. So generally you weren't made welcome and, if you were lucky, you wouldn't get a good kicking on the pitch!

He was still up to his old tricks at our place. During the warm-up he put on a crossing and finishing session in the Layer Road end penalty box. The pitch was damp and so it was cut to pieces even before the game started. Our lads were already warming up when I came out and saw what was going on. I collared Dave Blacknall, our groundsman, and told him to get them the hell out of it. Dave was a lovely lad but could be too polite at times, so he probably didn't like to say anything to their hairy-arsed players and staff!

I was steaming and part of my team talk was about the Lincoln lot taking the piss out of the club and us. It must have had some effect as we ran out 7-1 winners. We totally humiliated them with some quality football. After our seventh goal went in they kicked off and laid the ball back to a midfielder who smashed it 60 yards down the pitch into the corner. They stuck to what John Beck had told them, no matter what the score. It was a one-dimensional outlook that would be effective but almost turned players into robots. John Taylor, whom I had just taken on loan, and Richard Wilkins had both played for John Beck when he was most successful. Both respected what he had achieved but preferred our type of football and philosophy.

The Lincoln victory was our biggest League win in 35 years, so it was a great achievement by the players, especially against the big bullies of the division.

I was still frustrated with our lack of back-to-back wins, but that was to change at the turn of the year. In January 1997 I was lucky enough to be chosen for the Manager of the Month award. We had beaten Fulham, Exeter and Torquay with draws against Doncaster and Carlisle and we had also beaten Brentford and Millwall away from home in the Auto Windscreens Shield. It was quite a month for us. The last time a Colchester United manager had won such an award was back in 1987 when Roger Brown was the recipient.

I had added another player to the ranks, Paul Buckle, who was a free agent from Wycombe. Bucks was a lad who at one point thought he was on his way out of the professional game. I decided to take a chance on him, as he seemed to be desperate to do well if he was just given the break. He joined us in November and did well enough, but he really came into his own when he scored some vital goals for us in our Shield run.

We had played the first three rounds away from Layer Road. Our 1-0 win at Cambridge was followed by the two victories that I mentioned above. The semi-final was against our old rivals Northampton, who were managed by the ex-Colchester boss Ian Atkins. They were a strong, physical team who prided themselves on grinding the opposition down; in fact they could be a little dour at times. Ian liked his teams to play that way. So long as they didn't concede any goals then he was happy. If they managed to get their noses in front they would just hang on; he loved a 1-0 result.

The game itself was different to many others I had experienced as a manager. Our keeper was sent off after 20 minutes for a professional foul and so Richard Wilkins went in goal. At half-time we put Peter Cawley in goal and Wilks went back out onto the pitch. The players were unbelievable. Even with a man down we still managed to outplay Northampton and win 2-1, with Paul Buckle scoring a late winner!

We were through to the two-legged area final against Barry Fry's Peterborough United. Our victory at West Brom earlier in the season without a regular goalkeeper had been a fantastic performance, but this was even better with only ten men on the pitch.

The competition had become serious stuff at that stage and we were now two games away from a possible Wembley appearance. After our match with Northampton our League results suffered, which was of great concern to me. The team were capable of getting into the play-offs again, as we were definitely one of the top six sides in the division. We had proved that by beating two clubs from the next division up away from home in the Shield. We had also outclassed some teams in our run of results at the turn of the year.

Our first leg of the area final at Peterborough was a disaster, or so it appeared. We lost 2-0 and it looked all over for us. We had our chances but, on the night, they deserved to win. I had my work cut out lifting the players, as it was vital that we regained our confidence quickly. A victory in our next League game helped to do this and we were ready to go into the second leg against Peterborough with nothing to lose.

There was a rumour that the opposition had already ordered suits for their players as though winning was a formality after their first-leg victory and a trip to Wembley was a dead cert. Rumour or not, I used it as part of my motivational talk to wind the lads up a bit. I also instilled into the players that we would start on the front foot and avoid taking a backward step as much as possible.

On the pitch the players were like lads possessed and Peterborough didn't know what had hit them. We managed to level the scores at 2-2 and the game went into extra time. We had already experienced the golden goal rule, which basically means that the first team to score in extra time wins the game. Paul Buckle had smashed a 30-yard screamer for the winner at Millwall in a previous round. This time the hero was Paul Abrahams, his 25-yard dipping shot flying over their keeper to clinch the game. The whole place exploded! Even I got off the bench and ran on the pitch, though it was only a couple of yards over the touchline.

Barry and his team were devastated. It must have been heartbreaking after having a 2-0 advantage and then eventually losing 3-2 with a Wembley appearance at stake. Was I really bothered though? I think not!

I had experienced quite a few ups in my career as well as many downs, but this was something else. This achievement was special from my point of view. We hadn't won anything yet, but getting to Wembley as a manager was another dream come true. Taking into account the resources we had and the opposition we had overcome, in difficult circumstances at times, this was a major achievement. The players had applied themselves magnificently and whatever happened in the future I would always look back on them with respect.

All the usual hype and distractions came along. I tried to get the players focused on our up-and-coming League games, which wasn't easy. We actually won our next League match but unfortunately we then lost our following three. Two of those scores were 1-0 and that had probably lost us a play-off place. Even though we still had a couple of games left to play after the Wembley final against Carlisle, it was a long shot.

In the build-up to the big game our commercial department had been very busy promoting the whole occasion. The sale of replica shirts was something that came to my notice more than anything. I had seen more people in the blue and white in and around the town for as long as I could remember. It was nice to see kids in Colchester United shirts instead of West Ham, Arsenal or Tottenham ones. Even our son Thomas, who worked in the club shop with Maureen Dale on match days, joined in the spirit of the occasion. He is a very talented artist and had drawn caricatures of the players and me to sell. I believe the prints of Peter Cawley were the best sellers! This game really had caught the imagination of the supporters and I hoped that we could make it a special day rather than just a good one.

The big day arrived and I wasn't particularly nervous. A lot of the hard work had been done and the lads had proved that they were more than capable of putting in a performance when needed. My intention was to enjoy the whole experience as much as possible and I also wanted everyone working on the football side of things to be involved in the preparation for our prestigious match, from Kelvin Wagner, our kit man, to Paul Dyer, our scout. Everyone had contributed to the success of the side, so why shouldn't they also enjoy the trappings?

Everybody looked very smart in their navy blue suits and we even managed to get one made for big Mark Sale - all 6 feet 5 inches of him! Mark had not been with us long but he had settled in well and gave us a different option up front from our usual format. He was a much better technical player than he was given credit for. Some years later he contracted a cancer similar to that suffered by my old colleague Colin Smith at Aldershot. Thankfully Mark also fought it and survived.

The actual game wasn't a classic as both defences were well organised and very strong. We cancelled each other out for most of the game. Half chances fell to both sides and just one goal was probably going to win it. However, that didn't happen and we were set for a penalty shootout. I gathered the players together with my staff and went through who would take the first five penalties. The lads were absolutely shot physically, as were the Carlisle boys, so any pre-match list went out of the window. I looked into the eyes of some of our players and there weren't many looking back with an eagerness to take one of the kicks. Consequently I had to ask who was up to the task. There was no shame in saying no, as we needed lads who felt comfortable, physically and psychologically, taking a spot kick in front of thousands of people.

Peter Cawley put himself on the line, which was typical of the big man. At times he could be a clown off the pitch, but you would always want to stand alongside him on it. Young Karl Duguid, who had only come on as a sub, put his hand up before some of the senior players, many of whom had looked at the floor when I had asked the same question. From that moment I knew that Karl would make a living in the game. He could sometimes be a rascal, opening his mouth and putting his foot in it at times, but now he was showing me that he had the bottle.

It was a tense finale but unfortunately Karl and Peter's kicks were saved and Carlisle came out the winners on the day. We were all disappointed, but technically we had not lost the game against one of the best sides in the division as we had more than matched them in every department in free play.

The reason that I've mentioned Peter and Karl individually is that I want to explain how some supporters' minds work. I used to receive letters and faxes, some saying how well we were doing and others telling me how I should pick the side, who I should play and in what position! It was all the usual stuff. A couple of blokes used to fax over all sorts of comments from their local business. Some of the content was less than complimentary even when we were winning on a regular basis.

I must have had a rush of blood to the head and invited the two 'supporters' (I use the word tongue in cheek) to my office for a chat. In my mind I had formed a picture of these two men: young and a little headstrong. However, I was wrong as they were both in their fifties and very conservative looking. I welcomed them in and they were very pleasant and thanked me for inviting them.

I brought up one of their criticisms about our penalty takers at Wembley. They had wanted to know why I had chosen a centre back and an 18-year-old to take such important spot kicks. They suggested that a good manager would 'demand' that certain players take the kicks. I explained the situation regarding fatigue and how some players just hadn't fancied the task and pointed out that it wasn't as cut and dried as they thought. They listened but I don't think they really took it in.

They also brought up several issues about why certain players had left. I explained that personal information couldn't possibly go to press because it was private. They listened and said that they hadn't known the facts when they had sent the faxes. I told them that was the reason I was explaining that not everything was as straightforward as it might appear. They said all the right things and thanked me for taking the time to speak to them.

After they left, I thought: that's put a couple of cynics in their place! Well, not on your nelly! Within a few weeks, exactly the same criticism about other situations came through on the fax machine from the same blokes. What a pair of noodles!

I had already been treated to that delightful ten-page letter at Aldershot, criticising everything I had done after a championship-winning season, so perhaps I shouldn't have bothered trying to educate a couple of fans. I decided that I would never ever invite another supporter into the club to explain anything, as it would just be a waste of time. My apologies to any supporters who do actually 'get it' in terms of the difficulties of a manager's job.

The party after our Wembley appearance was held at the Hilton Hotel in London. Mr Heard did us proud, with a wonderful meal in the restaurant on the top floor overlooking the city. Our table was in the bay window and the whole setting was magical. It was a pity that we hadn't won the Trophy but everyone enjoyed the fabulous food and drink. This was a taste of success for the players and I was hopeful that it would spur them on in the future for more of the same.

As a manager I definitely wanted more, but unfortunately we only managed to win two of our final four games, with a draw and a loss in the other two. Consequently we missed out on a play-off place by one point. There was no doubt in my mind that our Shield achievements affected our League results. Just one more result would have seen us into those big games again. Overall, however, we drew too many games throughout the season, which cost us in the end.

I knew I would have to tweak the squad again to give us that extra ingredient needed to get us out of that division.

Gordon Parker was acting chairman and he did an excellent job over the seasons that I was there. Our post-match shindig was a classic example of the generous input of our main benefactor, Peter Heard. Peter was the man who stumped up the majority of the cash needed to offset any shortfall in funds at any given point. Our success had taken the pressure off his purse strings a little, but we still couldn't compete with some of the richer clubs in our division. As I have already said, I attended most board meetings and I can count on one hand the number of disagreements that I had with Mr Heard. If there were a point of conjecture I usually came off second best, as if he felt strongly about something then you wouldn't shift him, even if it only cost a fiver! On the other hand, he was one of the most generous and considerate men I have ever worked with. The other board members all played their part and were fantastic, but Mr Heard was 'the man'. At times he appeared to know what I was going to say before I even said it. I sometimes wondered whether he had a spy in the camp, but I think he was just such a perceptive person and sussed out a lot more than some people gave him credit for.

On a couple of occasions the board suggested that we should dispense with the services of Steve Whitton. Steve had been involved in a couple of scrapes or problems off the pitch. I was well aware of these, but Mr Heard and the board knew most of the details better than I did. The initial information was not passed from me to them; they presented the facts to me at meetings. I have always been a very loyal person and so I headed the "Injuns" off at the pass and kept Witts in a job. I have never spoken to Steve about this to this day; in fact I haven't told anyone how close he came to the sack. The board had their reasons for airing their displeasure and if I had been in their shoes I would probably have said the same thing.

Another player whose name cropped up in the boardroom was David Barnes. Barnsey was at Watford before I took him on and I think that Mr Heard had done his homework on him. When I told him that I intended to sign David he advised against it. I reassured the board that I knew about his reputation as a bit of a handful but I felt that he would toe the line for me because of our playing days together. I said that he would be a revelation for us if we could keep him free from injuries. There was no fee involved and his wages were within our parameters.

How wrong could I have been? Within a few months he was gone!

David had started playing up in training, as basically he didn't want to do as he was told. Eventually I had to dig him out in front of the other players in a session. I gave him the option to do things properly or go in. He chose to go in and that was about it! I'm sorry to say that he let me down big time, as I went over a barrel for him and he just took the piss! David was a quality player, but he made me look a prat in front of the board. He even had the audacity to phone Micky Cook afterwards and ask if he could do some coaching at our School of Excellence to obtain his coaching badge. It appeared that he only wanted to get back to the Ipswich area with his family at the club's expense. I vowed that I would be more wary of supposed mates next time.

My second full season was over and, although there was a feeling of disappointment, there was also still a large amount of satisfaction in what we had achieved. Most of my new signings had done well and the squad was looking good. I had made fewer errors than in the previous season from a manager's point of view. These were only mistakes in my mind and not visible ones as such. More tough decisions had to be made. Garrett Caldwell had gone and I let Chris Fry go. Paul Gibbs and Adam Locke also joined them on the free list.

Adam was the big surprise for everyone, as he was an immensely talented player and I could put him in a few positions. He wanted to play as a central midfielder all the time, but I utilised him as a wing back on some occasions, which didn't please him too much. Ironically, when he left us and signed for Bristol City he played in that position regularly and gained promotion with them.

I liked Adam a lot but he could be a right scatterbrain at times. He was forever forgetting his training kit or his boots. His timekeeping was poor and he always had a different excuse every time. The amount of money he contributed in fines to the players' pool was incredible! As we organised a trip abroad with the proceeds at the end of the season, at the airport most of the lads raised a glass to him to thank him for the holiday! He had probably paid about a third of the total amount put aside for it. He took it all in good spirit though.

I found it hard having to give Adam the bad news that his contract would not be renewed. The board had decided that they were not prepared to help out with any more over Adam's personal problems, as they had been very good to him already, especially Peter Heard. So they basically felt they had to call time on the situation. I had lost a quality player, which was a blow, but I just had to get on with it.

A few people also questioned my decision to free Chris Fry, who had done a decent job for us. The problem there was of a financial nature. I couldn't justify paying him what he wanted in signing-on fees, etc., in his proposed new contract. I didn't feel that it was correct to make such details public, so I had to take some flack for that decision as Chris was a bit of a favourite with the fans.

Scott Stamps came in from Torquay. Scotty was another scatterbrain but I saw more in his all-round play than Gibbsy, who went the other way to Torquay. Paul had done well but had struggled defensively at times. Steve Forbes came to us from Millwall and he would give us more physical strength than Chris. He could also play in central midfield. Aaron Skelton joined us from Luton Town. He was having problems with injuries but I knew that if I could get him fit he would be a great asset with his capability for scoring goals from midfield and general all-round ability on the ball.

Our trip away to Spain in the summer of that year was a reward in part for the players, but technically it was paid for out of their own pockets by the fines imposed on them throughout the season. I had experienced these types of jaunts before at Aldershot as manager and I wasn't completely comfortable about it. I needn't have worried as the players and staff conducted themselves well and there were no problems. Witts, Paul Dyer and Geoff Harrop were in attendance, so at least I had staff to talk to. The players didn't really want to socialise with the manager - and who could blame them? At Aldershot the players had seen me in a slightly different light, which was understandable. The full-time lads, however, saw me as the boss and that was how it should be. They also called me 'boss' or 'gaffer', but not for any egotistical reason. It's just so that everyone knows where they stand and it's traditional in football to address the man in charge that way.

One night Witts, Geoff and I went for a walk down the road to where all the bars were situated. It was quite early so there weren't many people about. We plonked ourselves down at a table in an open-air bar with what looked like a small stage, as we thought there might be some entertainment to watch while we had a drink. Sure enough, after a short while there was some movement about the place and a few people wandered in and sat at the other tables. At the back of the small stage a woman started to set up what appeared to be a sound system. She had her back to us as she pulled the speakers out from behind a curtain. She had long black hair and was wearing a very short dress. Her legs were as perfectly formed as you could get and seemed to go on forever, and it was rather difficult not to look as she bent over to attend to her equipment! Geoff's eyes nearly popped out of his head. It was definitely a sight for sore eyes! He kept nudging us and saying, "Bloody hell, what's this?" For a moment I thought we might have happened upon a strip joint - but surely not? After all, it was open air and right next to the main road. She disappeared behind the curtain and we ordered another drink as our curiosity had got the better of us by now.

The place filled up quickly and we had pride of place in the centre of the bar right in front of the mini-stage. Many of the other bars weren't busy at all, so we thought we'd picked the right place – or had we? The background music was turned off and everyone shuffled in their seats in anticipation of a grand entrance on the platform. The curtain flew open and out strode this girl. She was immaculately made up with a perfect tan, great figure and what a mover! Everyone in the place broke out into simultaneous applause as she reached the front of the stage, which was about 12 feet from us, much to the delight of Geoff.

I suddenly sensed that something wasn't quite right. I thought: it couldn't be, could it? It bloody well was - it was a GEEZER! Jesus, what the hell was I doing there? I caught Witts's eye and he caught mine; within seconds we had both come to the same conclusion. However, Geoff was completely oblivious. He was totally engrossed and thought that 'she' was great! 'Her' voice was terrific as she blasted out a few songs to a very appreciative audience. We managed to get Geoff's attention and tried to put him in the picture. He was having none of it, however, and even when we left the bar after the cabaret he still wasn't convinced that the object of his adoration was a transvestite! Witts and I were in hysterics at his protests and pulled his leg unmercifully on the way back to our apartments.

The next day we told 'Sammy' (Paul) Dyer about the place, but we didn't give the whole story away. We wanted to see his reaction when he clocked him/her. That evening we all descended on the same bar early enough to get a ringside seat. As Paul was never short of something to say, I was looking forward to his comments. The show started and straight away Paul eyeballed the 'crumpet' and batted a few harmless comments in Geoff's direction! Then, to my horror, the singer came down from the stage to mingle with the audience while he sang. He was making a beeline for us; I just knew it! I could feel my knuckles whiten as I clutched the edge of the table. He waltzed around us as everyone looked on, and Sammy said something under his breath as the singer put his leg up on an adjacent chair. Quick as a flash, Witts pointed at the revealing pose and exclaimed, "I can see the Elastoplast!" Oh my God, I thought.

All of a sudden the singer slapped Sammy on the shoulder as if to chastise him! Paul had burnt himself badly in the sun the day before and had huge blisters all over his chest and shoulders. The smack burst a large patch of them and parts of his nice white shirt became soaked in the fluid oozing from the burns. Paul was in agony but we nearly fell off our chairs with laughter as the 'cross-dresser' copped the needle. We left soon after, when he had paraded off to a reasonably safe distance. Geoff had been forced to agree with us by then, and Paul giggled even though the offending slap had ruined his holiday shirt!

The next evening we walked straight past the bar as our curiosity had been well and truly satisfied. Believe it or not, the singer spotted us from the stage and came running towards, weaving frantically between the tables. We got on our toes and scarpered! He clearly wasn't happy with us for some reason and we had no intention of hanging around to find out why!

The trip was good for team morale and everyone had managed to let their hair down a little with no harm done.

My third full season, 1997/98, started with a decision by Tony McCarthy, one of my regular centre backs, to go back to Ireland. He wanted to study and play for Shelbourne in the Irish League again. I was disappointed but understood his reasoning. I had enough cover initially, but later on in the season I brought in Guy Branston, a young defender from Leicester, who were in the Premiership at the time. Martin O'Neill, my old colleague from Notts Forest, was in charge there and he did me a favour.

My head had been spinning in the close season as usual. Although in many people's eyes managers are on holiday at that time, in reality they only have a window of about two weeks when they can switch off fully - if they're lucky! I had been in the management profession for five years by this time and I had probably had less than ten weeks' holiday away from everything in total. Even then, when you're away you still have to deal with important phone calls.

I answered my phone to one such call while I was visiting my parents-in-law in North Wales in the summer of 1997. It was David Webb from Brentford Football Club, whom I knew from my dealings over Paul Abrahams. He was very forthright and very rarely minced his words, and so he came straight to the point and asked me if I was happy at Colchester. I told him that I was very happy and that I was working with good people. He reiterated that by telling me that he knew Peter Heard and Gordon Parker. He then asked me if I was on a contract and I told him that I was. Basically David wanted me to take over from him at Brentford so that he could 'go upstairs'. I would be in total control of the playing side of things and he would look after the rest, i.e., the board etc. He had no intention of asking me to walk out while I was on contract, as he wanted to do everything correctly. David asked me to talk to my people about the situation after he had officially approached them.

The Colchester board refused Brentford permission to speak to me unless their compensation figure was agreed. This was fair enough, especially after the farcical situation with George Burley and Ipswich just before I joined the club. The only problem was that Colchester slapped a £300,000 compensation package on my head!

I understand that the club wished to protect their assets as they saw fit, but the figure was somewhat unfair in my mind. Although I was very happy at Colchester, I must admit that I saw the possibility of a move to a London club as a great opportunity for me to further my career. I am a loyal person and never for one minute would I have considered walking out on the club as the previous manager had done. However, looking back on these events a little further down the line and with the benefit of hindsight, one could ask the question: who made the right decision, George or me?

Brentford withdrew their interest after the large demand, which disappointed me. The paper talk was plain enough for everyone to see and that probably unnerved some of the players. A couple of them probably wanted rid of me, but they would have to hide their feelings for now. I brought them all together and told them that I was going nowhere and that we were going to get out of that division this season by hook or by crook.

One thing that did irk me about the whole affair, however, was the lack of communication from the board. No one had pulled me in to explain in detail their reasons for the 'no deal' or to ask me how I really felt about the Brentford situation. Eventually I received a call from Peter Heard after it had filtered back to him that I was not over pleased, so I went into London to meet him at his office, followed by a meal at Langan's where he had his own table – very nice too.

The meeting was a little strained to begin with as I was obviously not happy, but he didn't see it as such a big deal. Deep down, I probably saw the Brentford offer as another of those defining moments for me and so no matter what came out of that meeting or whatever happened from then on I still had a gut feeling that I might regret not going, under whatever circumstances. Anne thought it was an opportunity that I should take and friends and people in the game had phoned me and told me to go for it no matter what, but in the end I couldn't be disloyal and David Webb probably wouldn't have wanted to go to court over me, which was understandable.

As the meeting went on Mr Heard eventually said, "Well, how long a contract do you want - two, three, four, five years?" I knew he was desperate for me to stay and he didn't want to lose another manager again under similar circumstances. I accepted a new four-year deal and Mr Heard was happy, so there was something positive to come out of the whole affair. I had secured the immediate future for my family, which was always one of my aims throughout my career as both a player and a manager.

The meal at Langan's was superb and there were a few familiar faces in there as usual. On one occasion, Mr Heard took Anne and I for lunch there and, while I was visiting the loo, Will Carling was making eyes at my missus and chatting her up, the cheeky beggar! Mind you, he had good taste, and it worked when he made eyes at Lady Diana so why not try my squeeze?

That was it, drama over, and I had to refocus again. The first League game was approaching. The season started slowly but gained momentum in September and October.

At one home game in October, possibly against Scunthorpe, we drew 3-3. We had thrown two points away at the end of the match and I was livid! I was having a go at a few people, David Gregory being one of them. I cannot recall the exact content of the conversation, but basically he came back at me and I reacted to his comment. I walked over to him and laboured the point and he responded in the same manner as before. In a nutshell, I lost it and went for him. I had completely gone and had to be held back by some of the lads. Even then I kept struggling to get at him. It was something and nothing that had tipped me over the edge and I can't even recall why it happened. Maybe other peripheral matters were on my mind, or perhaps it was due to the festering frustration of losing an opportunity to better myself, I don't know. What I did know, however, was that no matter what the circumstances were I was out of order and if I had assaulted a player I could easily have found myself out of a job. It took me a while to calm down, which is also unusual for me, as although I can lose my temper I usually settle in no time at all. This had clearly got to me and I think that some of the players were shocked by my actions too. Later that week I spoke to David and apologised. I wasn't sorry for the rollicking that I had given the players, just my conduct towards him, and he accepted my apology. David had done well for me in a few positions and he would continue to do so.

The job itself wasn't getting any easier, and it never would, but I was still confident that I could improve on the previous year's League finish. I was managing the club better all the time and I was keeping more balls in the air than I had done before. It was still a fantastic learning curve and I certainly didn't know it all and probably never would! As a manager you can take on board as much or as little as you want. There are certain aspects of the job that are set in stone but there are some that you can duck if you want. When I used to speak to more experienced managers than myself, some of them came over as quite cynical about everything. Some didn't speak to youth team lads, supporters, club peripheral staff or the like, they just put all their efforts into the first team and they weren't interested in anything else. Other duties were delegated to their own staff.

In contrast, I wanted to be involved as much as possible as that was my way, and even though it brought me more hassle than I needed I tried my best to be approachable from all quarters. Witts was different from me, as he didn't really want to get involved with fringe issues, which was just his way. So when we had to give the news to the young YTS lads that they were not being taken on, Steve preferred to give it a miss. Unfortunately for him I insisted that he stayed in the room as the news was given out. Telling a young 18-year-old boy that he wasn't going to make is one of the hardest things I have ever done; it was horrible. Some of them would break down in front of you, which was horrendous. As I had young lads of my own, I could also feel for the parents at that time.

The boot was on the other foot in a way with a young lad called Daniel Slatter. Danny was on schoolboy forms and my staff rated him very highly. Danny was a pleasant lad, very lightweight but with a lot of skill and overall ability. We wanted him to sign as a youth trainee but his dad saw it differently. Wanting to be involved, I spoke to Micky Cook about the situation and invited Danny and his father into my office to discuss the situation.

At the meeting the reaction of Danny's dad to everything I said was very indifferent and I think he had made his mind up that the lad was going to sign for Chelsea. In fact his attitude was so flippant that he kept glancing at his watch. Eventually I'd had enough and so I asked him why he kept looking at the time when his son's future was at stake. He saw his backside a bit and tried to get out of my office ASAP. Before they left I told them that Danny would never play a League game for Chelsea and, by the time he'd come to realise that, lots of other players at lower League clubs would have overtaken him and clinched a League career. I pointed out that if he stayed with us he would have a greater chance of playing League football, although I obviously couldn't promise that I would put him in the team. His father dismissed my comments out of hand as he left. I shook Danny by the hand, looked him in the eyes and said, "Good luck, you'll need it." That was the last I heard of Daniel Slatter until a few years later when I read his name in the non-League paper. I hope that his dad has no regrets.

The season was well under way and we had done okay, but over November and into December we lost four out of five League games and after 20 games we were 13th in the table and going nowhere. I had to shake things up and, against the advice of some of my staff, I decided to work the players even harder. I had them up hills at Spring Lane and put them under more physical pressure. There was always the danger of their picking up more injuries but I didn't care, as something was needed to reignite our season.

I signed Isaiah Rankin from Arsenal on loan. He was a quick-footed centre forward with lots of potential, although he found our training regime really tough. In fact at times he just couldn't keep up with the lads. I told this to Pat Rice, the coach at Arsenal, when he phoned to see how Isaiah was doing and Pat wasn't very happy with my comments! The lad was probably struggling because he had played too much reserve-team football and also he hadn't been pushed in training enough. It wasn't a criticism of Arsenal, just an observation, but I think Pat took it as the former! I was only being honest and, after all, he did phone to ask!

Later on that summer Paul Jewel, the manager of Bradford City at the time, phoned me to ask about Isaiah as he was thinking of buying him. I told him what I thought regarding his fitness levels, but I also told him that I knew he would get him goals.

If I'd had £200,000 the previous season we probably could have had him, so it's food for thought that in the end they paid about £1,300,000 for his services. Strange how the price went up so quickly!

By late January our results were still inconsistent, but after our home defeat against a poor Swansea side we kicked into gear, losing only two of our final 15 fixtures. Within this run one of our defeats was away at Chester. Our home game with Hull City the Monday before was a fantastic 4-3 win for us, which meant that if we could win two of our last three matches there was a very good chance that we could go straight up. With this in mind, I decided to speak to our chief executive, Stephen Gage.

What I wanted was for us to go to Chester on the following Friday and to stay overnight so that we could be nice and fresh for the game on the Saturday. Our overnight trips were kept to an absolute minimum because of the cost, but I felt that if we could win at Chester there would be no stopping us. Steve got back to me and said that the answer was not favourable - in other words, no! I couldn't believe it, as I felt that everything could ride on this match and thought that they would back me at this stage of the campaign if I thought that the best preparation was an overnight stop. I was both confused and annoyed, so I set out to find someone who would sponsor the trip. I found somebody prepared to cover the expenses in no time at all and I presented the idea to Steve and the board. To my astonishment, the answer was still no! This was pure intransigence and I simply couldn't figure it out. The players had come to me asking if they could make it an overnight trip and some had even volunteered to pay their own bill. I could feel a big row developing so I nipped it in the bud and toed the line.

We made the four-hour journey to Chester on the morning of the match and in the end we lost the game 3-1. There was no way that I could blame the result on our long journey, as we played poorly in the first half and couldn't recover sufficiently in the second to get anything out of the game. The mood on the coach on the way home was pretty sombre, as the wrong message had been sent out to us - but for what reason? I struggled to understand why Mr Heard had stuck to his guns over something that wouldn't have cost the club anything. The whole promotion race could now be in jeopardy because of a principle.

My job was to get the lads back on track, which wasn't that difficult. They knew what was at stake with just two games to go. One of them was a home game against Leyton Orient and a local derby was probably the last thing we wanted at that stage of the season. As we all knew, League positions usually counted for nothing in derbies. In the event, we didn't manage a win and had to settle for a 1-1 draw.

For the last game we had to play away at my old club Doncaster Rovers, who had already been relegated to the Conference. It was another of those ironic situations in football and I found it sad, as I would see a lot of very disappointed faces at Rovers. Their club had been run into the ground and there were genuine concerns for its future. I had been well versed in that sort of scenario with my experiences at Aldershot, but it hadn't got to that point yet at Doncaster. It needed someone to take control as soon as possible.

On the day of the game, Belle Vue was almost like a wake. Some supporters even carried a makeshift coffin into the ground, representing the death of the club. It was all a little dramatic and the mood of the place wasn't the best. I had to remind my players that if we won this match and the results went in our favour we could technically still go straight up. We needed to concentrate on the job in hand and ignore the peripheral goings-on around the ground.

Donny were a poor side but they gave it everything in front of a crowd of 3,500, which was a pretty decent turnout considering their relegation. Neil Gregory, my record signing from Ipswich, got the deciding goal and we ran out 1-0 winners. Neil had done the job that I had brought him in to do and that was to score vital goals for us. When I had handed over £50,000 for him a few eyebrows had been raised, but it was money well spent as far as I was concerned, especially if he helped us to gain promotion. I also quite liked to see brothers playing alongside each other in the same side. David seemed to do even better for me when his brother Neil arrived before the transfer deadline that March. The 15 goals that they scored between them probably spoke for themselves!

Doncaster's ground looked very sad and rundown as we left on the coach. I had mixed feelings as we pulled out of the car park where we used to play behind the Rossington end stand back in the seventies. I'd had some great times there back then, but now, 25 years later, I was the manager of a team that had just beaten Donny's first team. It only seemed like yesterday that Terry Curran, with his white headband on, was being booted all over the place by the senior pros and I was picking the cinders out of my bum cheeks after trying to slide-tackle someone!

The results had filtered through and to our surprise, as well as disappointment, we had been closer to promotion than we had thought. Torquay and Barnet had lost, Scarborough had drawn, but unfortunately Lincoln had won. Lincoln had pipped us by one point, so a draw at Chester would have seen us through. We had scored more goals than them, 72 to be precise, which would have put us in third place instead of fourth. Now we would have to play Barnet, who finished in sixth spot, home and away in the play-offs.

On the journey home I didn't analyse the game we had just played as I usually did, I reflected on the season as a whole. I didn't harp on many negatives, even though we had come so close to clinching it on the last day of the season at my old club. We had achieved so much, yet again, and with some style!

The previous season we had drawn too many games and we had improved on that by only drawing 11 and winning 21 this term. We were the second-best scorers next to the champions Notts County and we were on a good run of results going into the play-offs. I was reasonably happy with myself and with the previous experience of losing out to Plymouth in the season before last. I was confident that I could take the team one step further this time.

We had a few days before our first Barnet game, so I needed to get my thinking cap on regarding the preparation needed for such an important match. I was happy to have our first leg at Barnet's ground. If we needed to have a little help in the second game I knew that our supporters would be up for it, as they had been in our previous big games against Plymouth in the play-offs and Peterborough in the Auto Windscreens Shield. John Still's Barnet (or lack of it in 'baldy' John's case - sorry John!) were a very strong outfit. Up front they had Sean Divine, who was one of the best strikers in the division. Our old player Scott McGleish was also in their line-up, which brought even more spice into the contest.

The game at Underhill was a tight affair, which was to be expected, and when Carl Emberson made a hash of a punch early in the second half their centre back, Heald of all people, cracked in their goal. We had a few chances but had to settle for a 1-0 defeat. Towards the end of the game, Guy Branston got tangled up with Divine over something and they were both sent off. This was a blow for each side, as both of these players were key men at that time.

In some ways that little spat livened things up for the second game, as there was a little ill feeling but not in a nasty way, just enough to get the sap rising somewhat. I wanted to wind the tempo up and that is exactly what I did. Neil Warnock did it the wrong way in my opinion, but he did have a point!

A full house was just what we needed and we had a great start with an early penalty from David Gregory, but they went 2-1 up on aggregate just before half-time. We still had to chase the game in the second half, so the tempo was even higher. Howarth, their centre back, was sent off and that provided the break we needed. David Greene put us level at 2-2 on aggregate immediately afterwards. Now we had a game on our hands. In extra time David Gregory hit a shot with his left foot from the edge of the box, taking us to 3-2 up, and Wembley beckoned. The next 25 minutes seemed to go on forever. It was frantic stuff, but this was what it was all about and these were the days you live for in football. I had played in such games and now I was managing in the same pressure cooker. It was superb!

John Still must have felt gutted, but no more so than I felt when Plymouth had beaten us at their place in almost identical circumstances.

The feeling after the game was indescribable. We were going to Wembley again! You couldn't have written a better script for us and I didn't want the evening to end. I cast my mind back briefly to some of the players' faces when I was on the warpath at the turn of the year. I had turned the screws on them back then, but looking at their faces now I could see more teeth than a dentist working in the National Health Service, especially David Greene's as they were massive! Richard Wilkins used to slaughter him about them and would say on a cold day in training, "Bloody hell, Greenie, your teeth must be freezing"!

Tony Locke, Karl Duguid and Nicky Haydon had come through the ranks under Steve Foley, which was good news. Tony and Karl had already featured in the first team and Nicky was to follow. Eventually Tony would succumb to a serious knee injury, which was a shame as he had real pace with the ball and had an eye for a goal. Karl was here to stay as I had predicted after he volunteered to take the penalty at Wembley. We all thought that Nicky had the most potential, but after a very good start he went backwards and appeared to lose heart, or perhaps he couldn't cope with League football week in, week out. Only he knows the reason, but he faded out of the game at a reasonably young age.

All three of these lads were good at heart, but I had a few problems with their discipline at first when they became young pros. They showed some belligerence towards me when I first arrived as manager and it appeared as if someone had marked my card to them. Sadly this meant that I had to come down on all three of them on separate occasions for different breaches of club rules. As they became more integrated into the first team squad they settled well and contributed to the team's success.

While I was tending to the first team throughout the season, Micky Cook and Geoff Harrop were quietly getting on with their jobs in the youth department. Little did we know at the time, but the new youth system we had established would reap more benefits than we could ever have imagined. Geoff was always talking to me about finding little nuggets of gold locally that we could sign on and he was always optimistic, which impressed me. Mick was very experienced with youngsters and got on very well with Geoff. This meant that as a pair, with the help of Adrian Webster, I had a good team.

As is normal at every level of football, Geoff would bring in lads and have high hopes for them. Some wouldn't last five minutes, some would stay the pace for a while and some would hang on for a little longer. Then, if they were decent (for example, Daniel Slatter), they would sod off to a bigger club! It was a difficult job, especially at a club like Colchester.

One lad that appeared on the scene was a 17-year-old straight out of college football. Geoff had seen him play for his college and invited him in for a trial. Even though he was nearly a year older than most of the other boys vying for a YTS place, if he was good enough there was no reason why he couldn't join us.

Anyway, this young fella turned up for his 'big chance' with no boots and no shin pads, so our son Jack, who was by now a youth trainee, lent him some boots and pads to enable him to play. He came on in the second half of the trial match and proceeded to score a hat-trick! Mick and Geoff knew that they had someone here who was very different from anyone they had seen for some time and they couldn't wait to show him to me.

Geoff was his usual bubbly self when he described the boy to me, but I looked to Mick for a more reserved assessment and he nodded his approval. So we invited the lad in for training so that we could all have a butcher's.

When I first saw him I certainly wasn't impressed with his haircut, as it looked as if someone had run a mini-lawnmower all over his bonce in different directions, forming a weird pattern. However, on the plus side he did look strong and well developed for his age. I stood and watched him in a small-sided game. He had a different running style to any of the other lads, as he held his head back, almost akin to when you're struggling to read something up close and you withdraw your head to see it clearer. However, within minutes he had done more on the ball than any of the other players on the pitch. His strength and awareness overall were exceptional for his age and I didn't feel that I needed to see much more, so I let Mick and Geoff get on with persuading him to sign on as a second-year YTS. Oh, and the lad's name was Lomana Tresor Lua Lua.

Lomana found the whole change of lifestyle difficult to begin with. Although he could speak several languages, he was just beginning to learn English. His timekeeping wasn't the best and his application in games left a lot to be desired at times. I used to try to see our youth team play as much as possible, so if we were at home on a Saturday afternoon I would pop up to the Garrison to watch our lads in the morning at 11 o'clock.

On this particular day I arrived about 20 minutes late and, as I walked to where Cookie was, I noticed Lomana wandering around in the trees by the side of the pitch. I thought that he must have picked up a knock or another injury. I asked Mick what the problem was and he said, "I've taken him off because he didn't want to do what he was told"! I didn't question the decision as Mick was top-class at his job and I trusted him implicitly.

There was no doubting the lad's ability, but they were having a few problems with him. There was nothing serious, but we had to be sure that he would knuckle down and work hard day in, day out. Mick, Geoff and I had a meeting to discuss Lomana's future and, to be honest, it was touch and go whether we kept faith in him and gave him another chance or let him go. We chose the former, and it turned out to be one of the best decisions we had made that year!

I integrated Lomana into the first-team training sessions and he didn't really look back. His English skills improved at an incredible rate and within 12 months he was taking the pee out of the lads in the dressing room! He and Jack became good friends over this time, but the fact that Jack was at the club was always going to draw the odd derogatory comment from some quarters. Geoff and Mick had originally taken him from Swindon's books when we moved, because they thought he was good enough. He wasn't the biggest at 16 years old, but within 18 months he had grown to 6 feet 2 inches and was captaining the youth side in one of our best ever FA Youth Cup runs.

After the Barnet game the smiles on everyone's faces over the next few days didn't really fade. The suit-fitting day was a good one and we plumped for a lighter material this time. It wasn't my choice I have to say! The players were given a large input in terms of the whole design of the outfit - and why not? I reckoned I was going to look like the man from Havana, but I would even have been prepared to wear a Mr Blobby outfit if they could guarantee me a victory!

The final was to be played on a Friday night because of England's game against Saudi Arabia that weekend. Talk about princes and paupers! Unfortunately the timing of the match meant that some of our supporters were going to miss one of the biggest games in their club's recent history because of work commitments, etc. It was a joke really, and I am sure that if the match had been between Man United and Arsenal the FA would have found a way around it. England were in preparation for France '98 and learnt very little from the Saudi game, which ended in a 0-0 draw.

I got everyone involved with the big day just as I had done when we played Plymouth. As always, it wasn't just about the players and me. I had to tweak the team a little tactically because of the way I knew Torquay would play. Rodney Jack was their main danger, but I thought Richard Wilkins could deal with him in a big match like that. I reckoned that our former player, Paul Gibbs, at left back could cause us a some grief if we let him get on the ball too much, so I pushed Stephen Forbes out wide right to give Gibbsy a problem. Stephen was big and strong with fantastic pace.

I felt confident in my players and they appeared to be very focused and determined to finish the job after three hard seasons of trying. The team had changed substantially since our heartbreak in the previous play-off game against Plymouth. Simon Betts and Carl Emberson were the only ones left in the side from that day, but all the staff were the same and that defeat still hurt, so we had no intention of experiencing it again. This team was virtually my team now as I had signed 90 per cent of the players, which was what I had wanted. I was going to achieve something off the back of my own decisions and that gave me tremendous satisfaction.

Travelling to the stadium and seeing all the families there with everything that went with an appearance at Wembley was fantastic. There was something magical about the old Wembley Stadium that gave you goosebumps when you pulled up in the coach! We definitely looked the part in our light-coloured suits and blue shirts. I wasn't sure about the multi-coloured tie, though - I think that Abes and Peter Cawley must have picked that!

In big games such as this I tried not to give the players too much information in my team talk. We had done our preparation for the game already, so it was basically just little reminders to everyone. I knew who needed a quiet little reminder in their ear and perhaps who needed a gee-up in front of the other lads. On such important occasions some of the boys tend to glaze over a bit anyway, so you can end up talking to yourself to a certain extent. Players react differently to certain pressures and I think good managers can spot who needs reassuring or reminding and who needs to be left alone. I had to make good decisions in the dressing room and I needed the right help from my staff.

Brian Owen had been priceless at times, especially when I first arrived at the club. He advised me on many issues and, although I didn't always run with them, they gave me food for thought. Witts also played his part after his experience at the top level of football. Along with Paul Dyer and Micky Cook, whose opinions I respected, we had a winning combination at the club.

We were in better form than Torquay as far as recent results were concerned. They had just missed out on the final day of the season, as they could have gone straight up if they had drawn their last game. It was going to be interesting to see how that disappointment had affected them. They had a very experienced outfit with Watson, Gittens and McCall in their line-up and they had all played at a much higher level.

The game was, dare I say it, not a classic! The two teams were quite well matched but I felt that we were in control for much of the first half. Stephen Forbes did a great job on Gibbsy and even got on the end of a ball in the box, which John Gittens handled. The referee gave a penalty, which in my opinion was the correct decision. The centre back probably thought it was harsh, but it definitely struck his hand as Forbsy tried to flick the ball over the top of him. It was only 20 minutes or so into the game, so I didn't get too excited about it.

David Gregory took a textbook penalty into the bottom left-hand corner of the net to give us a lead. There was plenty of commitment from both teams, as you would expect, but it didn't look as if there were going to be many clear-cut chances. I was happy to go in 1-0 up at half time and we didn't change much tactically as I still felt reasonably comfortable with our performance. I would describe it as professional rather than inspiring - but who cared? We were there to win the game and collect the prestigious prize of promotion to the next division!

The second half was much the same as the first. There had been a few bookings in the first half and there were more to come in the second as Torquay saw time was running out. We had a few chances to seal the game that went begging. They had very few sniffs at all until very late on when the ball broke on the edge of our box. One of their lads hit a snapshot through lots of bodies in the penalty area, but our keeper Carl Emberson dived full length along the ground and tipped the ball round the post. This was probably the only vital save that he had to make in the whole game! Their bench thought it was in and were on their feet. I just sat motionless, but when the ball was tipped past the post I knew deep down that we were there and that my team would not throw it away now. All the players had played well enough, even though we had not sparkled. It just wasn't that sort of match, but we had been well organised, brave and confident in our system and method of play.

Within minutes the referee blew his whistle for the end of the game and everyone leapt off the bench! Cookie jumped all over me and the players were running all over the place on the pitch. I didn't do a David Pleat at Luton though! I admit I was wearing a similar suit, but I did try to keep my composure! I remembered to shake their manager's hand, which I thought was important. In all the mayhem it can be easy to get carried away with your own team's celebrations. Kevin Hodges was polite but couldn't wait to get out of the way - and who could blame him?

I walked onto the pitch to congratulate my players and noticed that Gibbsy was on his knees, obviously distraught. I patted him on the head to acknowledge his disappointment. It had been a bad day for him, especially as he had been playing against his old club with the manager who had let him go the previous season.

It was a shame that the crowd only numbered 20,000, as it would have been nice to celebrate that moment with all the Colchester United supporters. At least they saw it on SKY TV that evening. When I watched the game a few days later on video I was disappointed that Barry Fry and Sam Allardyce thought that Torquay were unlucky not to win the match. Maybe Barry was still smarting after our semi-final win over his Peterborough side a year or so back? In Sam's case maybe it was because we took four points off champions Notts County that year when he was their manager? Or maybe I was watching a different game at Wembley!

While everyone was celebrating on and around the pitch, our chairman, Gordon Parker, grabbed my wife's hand and led her down from the royal box and along the tunnel where all the dignitaries usually emerge to be presented to the teams before games. He ushered her onto the pitch by my side, which was a great gesture, and it was wonderful to have her there after her continuing faith in me as both a player and a manager.

It had turned out to be a perfect day. Both our sons, Thomas and Jack, were there of course, but our daughter, Sally, not being a football fan, had decided to "come next time"! My brother, David, had brought my parents down to the game too and it was fantastic to see them all.

Gordon had done a good job as chairman and had dealt with the press and all the media very competently. He had also always given me his support where possible. Gordon had been a supporter of Colchester United for many years and was the father-in-law of Roy McDonough and Tony Adcock, so his connections with the club were long-standing.

I did all my media interviews and then stood and watched the lads go up the famous Wembley steps to collect their medals and Play-Off Trophy. When Richard Wilkins held that silver trophy above his head I felt a real calm and sense of achievement inside. I know it wasn't the FA Cup or the Champions League Trophy but it was still a major achievement for us, everything considered. Our preparation over the season would have been very similar to any successful side in all of the divisions. I was confident that if I were given the chance in the future I could achieve success at any level. I wasn't being arrogant or egotistical just realistic.

I mentioned Sam Allardyce earlier. Well, his career went into overdrive once he went to Bolton, which eventually took him to the shortlist for the England job. At the time I considered myself to be as good if not better, as I had fewer resources by far compared with those available to him at Notts County.

An interesting fact from the season was that we only used 23 players that term, which was exactly the same as Torquay. Most teams in our division used 30+ and even Notts County used 29. So there's another little point just to show how well we had done!

When we got back into the dressing room it was strangely calm. I think all of the lads were more exhausted than they thought, and after all the dancing and jigging about on the Wembley turf they probably needed five minutes of normality before the post-match celebrations got under way. All the kit went AWOL, which was understandable as it had been monogrammed especially for the final so all the players wanted a souvenir. One of the staff managed to find me an unused shirt, which I have kept to this day.

Mr Heard and the board had arranged a tremendous victory party at the Hilton Hotel. We couldn't get the room on the top floor that we'd used last time, but needless to say it was a great bash! The food was top class and we even had entertainers mingling amongst the guests and showing off their skills. Everyone found their second wind and just went for it! The place was jumping and I enjoyed watching the most unlikely of people really letting themselves go. Even Witts and Brian were up on the dance floor throwing shapes all over the place. I think Cookie did some tap-dancing, which he later insisted he taught to my daughter to help her gain a scholarship to the performing arts school! Another person gliding across the floor with the greatest of ease was Mr Heard; he loved it! We'd had very few differences of opinion over the previous three seasons and that was almost unheard of in professional football. The board at Colchester United would turn out to comprise the best people that I would ever work for as a manager.

Anne and I sat at our table watching everyone enjoying themselves for the whole night. I felt absolutely mentally drained, as if all the pressure and tension of the whole season had just been exhaled from my body. I had a few drinks but it didn't seem to affect me apart from sending me into some sort of smiling stupor! As for Anne, she was in agony, as on the morning of the game she had slipped on the stairs at home and twisted her ankle, or so she thought. It turned out that she had in fact broken the fifth metatarsal in her foot. That is actually the dreaded football injury of the modern era, which many people think is down to the new blade-type boots. She could hardly put her foot down on the ground never mind have a mad half-hour on the dance floor! Some of the lads might have thought that I was being aloof, but I can assure them that I wasn't. I was in a coma and Anne was on the injured list! I don't think anyone wanted the night to come to an end, but by the time everyone had filtered out onto the coach for the journey home some of the lads were definitely running on empty.

The following day I was down at the football club for a photo shoot with the chairman and the trophy. My old mate Francis Ponder, a journalist from the Evening Gazette, never forgave me for not phoning him, as the exclusive pictures went to the East Anglican Daily Times. I genuinely didn't know who was coming to the shoot as the club had set it up. I did try to explain this to Franny, but I don't think he believed me. I'd had a good relationship with him over the seasons and I had confided in him certain things that were not for publication. To be fair to him, he didn't let me down on that score.

Franny always came on the team coach with us on away trips and I didn't have a problem with that. The club and the newspaper needed each other, so I was always confident that he would produce an accurate account of events and his reporting was always well balanced. Over my seasons as manager of Colchester there were many good times to be written about, which probably made Franny's job a lot easier!

Some years later, during the tenure of manager Phil Parkinson, I noticed that he was not permitted to travel on the coach with the team, which I thought was a strange decision, but everyone to their own choice. Something I had always tried to do during my management career was to form some sort of relationship with the local media, although I was also well aware that once a journalist, always a journalist! So long as that fact is always in the back of your mind then you shouldn't slip up too many times.

On the Monday after the game Gordon resigned as chairman. After five years he was standing aside for Mr Heard to take over, although he would continue as a director at the football club. One of his quotes in the press was: "The last three years under Steve Wignall's management are the best in the U's history and I am very proud to have been part of it." Considering the number of years that Gordon was involved with the club, he couldn't have paid me a better compliment

Mr Heard vowed to spearhead the club, in conjunction with Colchester Borough Council, in terms of building a new stadium. In previous board meetings I had personally encouraged Mr Heard to pursue the idea of a new ground. Gordon had tried his best, but I was confident, knowing Mr Heard as I did, that if anyone could succeed then he could, even if it took him several years and I was long gone as the boss. I knew it would give the club their only realistic chance of progressing any higher and staying there. And Mr Heard did just that - eventually!

We all went away again for a week in the sun and the players more than deserved it. The destination this time was Porto Banus on the Costa del Sol, just up the road from Marbella. On this occasion I took Anne with me and we stayed in a separate hotel from most of the boys. It was a great holiday. We had champagne on the flight out and the whole works, as we felt that we had earned it!

Anne's brother Philip and his wife Lynne had retired out there, so we had the pleasure of meeting up with them again. Their beautiful villa located just up the coast overlooked a golf course and lake and really was a little piece of paradise.

At our hotel I met David Pleat, who was sitting in the sun studying the teams and names of players for his commentary work on the up-and-coming World Cup in France. He congratulated me on our promotion and was very complimentary about my team.

When we returned from the trip I had to get to work on planning for our biggest challenge yet. Our new division included the likes of Manchester City, Stoke City, Fulham and Reading, which were just four of the clubs that would probably have quadruple the money in their playing budgets that we had in ours. I was under no illusion what was in store for us. I knew that I couldn't possibly make wholesale changes to the squad even if I'd wanted to, as the playing budget simply wouldn't stretch to that and, anyway, I was confident that the majority of the players were quite capable of playing in the next division.

What I decided would be beneficial, however, was a couple of players who had played at an even higher level, just to give us a little more quality and experience when we needed it - and we were definitely going to need it! So I drafted in Geraint Williams from Ipswich and also Jason Dozzell, another ex-Ipswich player who had also had a spell at Tottenham.

'George', as everybody called Geraint, was a good mate of Steve Whitton, so that helped to persuade him to come over to us. He was a quality midfield player with a winner's pedigree and when I first spoke to him he was very modest. He told me that he wanted to play for a season or so and then get out of the game. He'd had a good career with Derby and Ipswich and felt that a couple of seasons at our level would be enough for him. As for Jason, he was a local lad from Ipswich and so a move to Colchester made sense for him. Again, he was a very good player with top-class experience.

Both players fitted into the club's strict wage structure and if they hadn't we wouldn't have signed them, simple as that. I had managed the budget as well as I could over the seasons, which had proved difficult but that's the way the club had to be run. Mr Heard had financed any losses up until then and fortunately we had done well in easing the burden on his input. I knew that in order to gain promotion we would have to increase the budget, and the board sanctioned some extra cash. Realistically, however, it was not going to be enough to make an assault on the division. To be honest, my feeling was that if the club stayed in the second division that season then it would be an achievement. I hoped that we would be able to surprise a few teams and gain a good start, which would then give us both the confidence and some points to see us through the inevitable difficult stages of the season. All these mixed thoughts were in my mind at that time, but I wasn't prepared to go to the press with any negative stuff at all. I was just being honest with myself, as always. Although we had been very successful, I wasn't going to look at things with rose-tinted glasses or with my head up my backside!

I released a couple of players to make way for new blood. Ian Hathaway, who had been signed from Torquay, left for Aldershot Town. Their manager, George Borg, had phoned me about him earlier in the season and I had given him a good reference. Ian had a wonderful left foot and could provide quality crosses into the penalty box, but he couldn't get up and down the pitch as much as I would have liked for Football League matches. Peter Cawley also left us, which was unfortunate as he had been a very effective player for the club over several seasons. I'd had my ups and downs with Peter, but he was always a winner and in his own way he was a professional, even if he didn't necessarily want you to know it!

As a manager you always have to make difficult decisions about other people's futures, whether YTS players or professionals. Sometimes those decisions are more painful to make when the club has been successful, especially if the player you're releasing has played a part in that success. Unfortunately sentiment doesn't breed success, so you just have to do what is required.

At this time I was definitely flavour of the month, or season if you like! Everyone in the club and the town was very positive and so we all enjoyed it while we could. I was also lucky enough to win the Sports Personality of the Year award from BBC Essex Radio. With the likes of Frank Bruno winning the honour on previous occasions, I was proud to be the latest recipient.

The 1998/99 season got under way and we came up against Chesterfield at home for our first game in the new division. They were pretty negative and appeared happy with a 0-0 draw. Mark Sale scored our first goal of the season in the last minute to win us the match. It was a good start but right from the off I had noticed how resilient the opposition seemed. Even though they were quite dour in their approach to the game, they still had more quality throughout their side than most of the teams that we had played in the previous season.

The following week we travelled to Wrexham, who had beaten Reading 3-0 on the first day of the season. It was a very warm day and we played very well, taking a 3-0 lead. Young Nicky Haydon scored his first League goal and looked a good prospect for us, but as I mentioned earlier it didn't quite work out for him. We ran out 4-2 winners and found ourselves lying second in the division with six points after the first two games. This was just the start that I'd been looking for, but reality was to kick in very soon. Fulham, managed by Kevin Keegan, were our next opponents at home. We lost in the dying minutes after Richard Wilkins was fouled on the edge of our box. The referee waved for us to play on and they punished us. We learnt a harsh lesson, as we deserved at least a point from the match.

What interested me was a press report on the game, which described it as a "battle of the second division heavyweights"! That was a great compliment aimed in our direction, but in the real world it was as far from the truth as possible. Not only were Fulham managed by Kevin Keegan, but the players included the likes of Peter Beardsley, Gus Uhlenbeek, Paul Bracewell, John Salako and Paul Peschisolido in their ranks, to name just a few! Their budget was massive and their aim was to win the division.

Having said all that, I think that with a tiny bit of luck we could have won on another day and it showed how far we had come, but in the end we had lost the points and we were disappointed. I watched the Fulham team closely as a unit and listened to what Kevin had to say. Nothing changed my mind and, just like many of the other lower league managers, I still felt that I was capable of managing at a higher level.

By the time we had played ten games we were sat just above the halfway mark in the division and we were only a point behind Manchester City, who were attracting crowds of 30,000+. This constituted a good start so far as I was concerned, but I knew that we needed to add to the squad. However, I had no intention of bringing in players that were no better than those that I had already.

I had targeted a couple of players that could come into the side and improve it and I decided that it was the right time to do it rather than wait until we were struggling, which I felt wasn't far away. I wasn't thinking negatively. My assessment of the side was that some players were playing out of their skins just to survive at that time. We were getting away with some decent results, but I was certain that we needed more quality to keep those results coming in.

Football had changed very quickly with the Bosman ruling and the big money filtering into the game. I hardly ever spoke directly to a prospective player anymore, as everything was usually conducted "through" his agent. The player only became involved once he came to meet me, again accompanied by his agent. The figures I was being quoted were ridiculous. Players who were available on a free transfer were demanding colossal wages compared with what we paid our lads. If there was an initial transfer fee involved then they were probably completely out of our reach. As an example one player, who shall remain nameless, was willing to join us from a club similar to ourselves and in the same division if we offered a package that was twice as much as any player on our books was getting. Apparently his present club were paying him not far off that amount already.

I couldn't see how we were going be able to add to the squad. The new loan agreements were all very well, but you still had to persuade the top managers or players to sanction a move. The writing seemed to be on the wall and I was becoming very frustrated. There was no point in my going to the board and requesting that they start almost doubling the players' wages, as it just wasn't going to happen.

At the same time as I was attempting to improve our squad our luck on the pitch seemed to run out. We only took two points from our next six games and the concerns that I'd had were becoming a reality. In one of those games we lost 4-0 at home to Burnley and it was probably the first time in my managerial career that my team had been totally outclassed from start to finish. I was so disappointed that I found it hard to have too much of a go at the lads. This was also the first time at Colchester that I'd got absolutely slaughtered by a fan walking past our dugout with his kids. He called me for everything. I turned around to look at him as he started and he gave me both barrels. It was also the first time that I didn't respond to personal abuse! I think during his tirade I felt great empathy towards him. All the plaudits had come my way on promotion night and I had felt ten feet tall, but in those few moments I felt as low as a snake's belly.

Our luck, or whatever you want to call it, didn't improve. We lost to Preston away and then it got even worse in our home game against Bournemouth. We were desperate for a result and I was confident that we could win that game.

Just before the match was due to start, the rain had been horrendous and the pitch was becoming waterlogged. Dave Blacknall, our groundsman, did his best to fork the puddles so that the game could be played. About 45 minutes before kick-off I met with the referee, Lee Cable, whom I'd known for a few years as he had refereed and assisted in the Hampshire area when I was at Aldershot. It was still tipping down and there was an element of doubt as to whether the match would go ahead. Lee ran around with the ball and did all the usual checks and he decided that the pitch was playable. I was pleased, as we wanted to get on and play. I raised my concern with Lee that the match might be halted halfway through due to the conditions and his reassuring reply was, "Definitely not. If we start it we'll finish it."

Once we were on the pitch, we took to the conditions and tore into the opposition. They didn't really fancy it and their manager, Mel Machin, was constantly on at the referee and his assistant after our second goal went in. We finished the first half 3-1 up and we were flying. We had played the conditions extremely well, much better than they had.

I was in the middle of my team talk when there was a knock on the dressing room door. It was the referee. "Can I have a word with you, Steve?" he said, as he sheepishly popped his head inside. As I didn't think for one minute that there would be a problem with the conditions, I thought there must be another issue. He pulled me to one side and said, "I'm calling the game off as the conditions are too dangerous."

I went ballistic with him and reminded him of his pre-match reassurances about finishing the game. However, he just dismissed my comments and went back into his own room. He had been got at by Mel and his lads and had bottled it! Lee was a nice lad and was on the way up as a referee, but after that day I lost all respect for him. To make matters worse, by the time the lads had showered and changed the rain had completely stopped and the pitch was perfect. In my opinion Lee should have been dealt with severely by the powers that be, what were the assessors thinking of? Not a thing was done. I wonder if, in the same circumstances, he would have called the game off at Manchester City, with their huge crowd? I think not!

Our next game was in fact away at the City ground. This was a real tester for us. In comparison to their lads on thousands of pounds a week, we had young players like Karl Duguid on about £300 a week. They had top players in most positions and a top manager in Joe Royle.

We more than held our own in the first half, as we were well organised and competitive, but it was all too good to be true. Within a couple of minutes of the restart, the referee gave a really soft penalty against Greenie. He assured me after the game that it was never a spot kick. They had their tails up at 1-0 and then a couple of minutes later scored a second goal from a corner. It was harsh on the lads, as the game was very close. At that point everything could have gone against us, but my players bounced back and Jason Dozzell scored with a header. We made it very uncomfortable for them in the last 20 minutes and with a little luck we could easily have scored an equaliser. It wasn't to be, but it was a gallant effort and I was very pleased with the players if not the result.

I spoke to Joe Royle after the match and he was sympathetic, which I suppose was easy for him seeing as they had taken the three points, but he was a nice bloke and he appreciated how difficult it was for us to cope with some of the bigger clubs in the division.

At the press conference, which was totally different to the ones I was used to at Colchester, I sat in front of several journalists and one of them, who was from our own area, asked, "Where do you go from here after that performance?" I was totally gobsmacked! Basically he was criticising a team that included mainly free transfers, a couple of youngsters and around £70,000 worth of transfer fees and who had just taken a massive club like Manchester City to the wire. I didn't give him a sensible answer, as he didn't deserve one. After all, we now had some people thinking that we should be competing with the likes of Man City on the pitch as if we were equals.

I couldn't believe that anyone would have a go at us after a brave effort like that and I was really starting to get pissed off! The expectation levels had become silly, but unfortunately that is football and I had to be prepared to take more criticism even if it was totally unwarranted at times.

Further severe criticism was to follow, but this time it was deserved. The FA Cup had not been a great hunting ground either for the club or for me. Three times over the last five years Colchester had been knocked out of the competition by non-League opposition. So when I heard that we had been drawn against a team called Bedlington Terriers away I wasn't over pleased. For a start, I didn't even know where Bedlington was. but I was to learn soon enough and I would never forget. It was some miles away in Northumberland.

Our League form was going okay at the time, and although I was disappointed with our League position I was still confident that we could consolidate ourselves in the division by the end of the season.

We beat Northampton at home midweek and then travelled up north on the Friday for the FA Cup game. Even though I knew very little about them, I was confident that the players could cope with anything that awaited us. Two of the lads reported that they had injuries after the midweek game and told Brian that they couldn't make the trip to Bedlington. I asked Brian about the severity of their problems and he said that they were not too bad at all and suggested they could possibly have fitness tests up there if needed. My view was that we needed all hands on deck and so I decided to ask the players to make the trip.

The two players concerned, Paul Abrahams and Neil Gregory, were not very happy with my decision, so I got the hump with them and told them that they were going and that was that. I found it hard to fathom out why players would prefer not to go even if they only had the slimmest chance of playing. Perhaps I made myself unpopular at times because of my direct attitude, but I didn't care if they saw it that way! For me, there is only one way to do things in life: with full commitment.

The weather in Northumberland was at its usual 'best' in November. It absolutely peed it down all night and it continued into the morning. When we arrived at the ground I think that some of the lads were shocked to see how small and run-down it was. Nothing surprised me, however, after my experiences with Aldershot Town at places like the Old Spotted Dog ground in Clapton. The ground and changing facilities were irrelevant in my opinion, as my biggest concern was the state of the pitch. When we went out to warm up I couldn't believe that we going to start the game. It was still raining and the ground was completely saturated, so much so that the pitch itself had become a bog! When you put down your boot, your foot sank almost ankle deep.

No officials came to speak to me about the conditions or announced a pitch inspection as such, so it appeared that the game was going ahead and that was that. I had to accept the situation and get on with motivating my players, who incidentally seemed very quiet and fragile.

I cast my mind back to my non-League days with Aldershot Town and what I had said to the players then when they were faced with poor conditions away from home most weeks. Any sort of passing game was going to be difficult, so I attempted to get the players into a 'win at all costs' frame of mind. It would have to be man-to-man physical stuff if we were going to win or get something out of this game. If they did take on board what I said it didn't work, as Bedlington outfought us and outplayed us for a large part of the match, eventually running out 4-1 winners and deservedly so!

Our travelling supporters, who were well and truly soaked and frozen to the bone, showed more than a little displeasure towards me, which was completely understandable in the circumstances. It was a small ground and the fans were just within touching distance as we literally trudged through the mud back to the changing rooms. I felt so embarrassed by my team's performance that I couldn't look at anyone, neither the players nor the staff. The dressing room was completely silent and there wasn't even an air of anger or frustration just plain defeat. Inside I was screaming but on the outside I appeared quite calm. I walked out and left everyone to get on with it while I faced the media. I had no intention of hiding away or taking the gloss off their great win by sulking. I complimented them on their performance and meant it. After managing at a similar non-League level I knew how their lot felt and just thought good luck to them.

As we walked out of the ground I glanced back at the pitch and it looked like the something you would see after a battle, never mind a game of football. There was hardly a blade of grass left on it!

I wasn't looking forward to the long journey home, as by the time we were on the coach I was starting to come round from the shock of losing and I was getting my angry head on! I told Witts that there would be no beer or anything else for the players. In my mind I would analyse my own performance and that of the players, but at that moment I was not happy with them at all!

There was a case of 24 bottles of beer at the front of the coach and Witts very sheepishly asked if I wanted one. "Sod it, yes I will!" I said. We sat there and polished off the lot between us on the long journey home. For most of the trip the players sat in silence. I don't think they even dared let out a titter. Then eventually one of the lads bravely asked my permission to put on some music or a video. It had been one of the worst days in my managerial career and I knew that I would wake up with a sore head in the morning, but that was nothing compared with what had been done to my pride.

The fallout in the local press was inevitable and we all took a bit of a pasting. Most players will tell you that it's a crap feeling going to training on the Monday morning after a defeat the previous Saturday, but it's even worse when you've lost to a lower league outfit. The nature of our defeat was of great concern to me as not only were we out of the FA Cup but we had been publicly humiliated too!

I had mulled over the whole trip to Bedlington in my mind. Had I prepared the team correctly? Was the hotel suitable? Were the players motivated the right way? I went through everything on the Sunday and satisfied myself that there was no significant reason why we should have performed so poorly. We had beaten Northampton only days earlier and had played very well, so I had no intention of changing my thoughts on the preparation for our next game at Notts County, the previous year's champions, where Sam Allardyce was manager. What I did do, however, was rehash our set pieces because that had been one area where I felt we could have given Bedlington problems and it just didn't happen. I didn't slaughter the players that week, I just stuck to the task in hand and that was to turn things around in three or four days before we travelled back up north to Nottingham.

Lo and behold we totally outplayed Notts County on their own patch and beat them 3-1. We scored two goals from the set pieces we had worked on. David Greene put two headers away from corners and David Gregory scored one in free play. I gained a lot of satisfaction from that result and in my own mind took much of the credit for the outcome. I had learnt more than I thought from football management after that week.

A year or so earlier I might well have carpeted the players all week for their diabolical showing on the previous Saturday, but I had tried to see it differently. It still hurt as much, but I needed to keep my head and point the players in the right direction even if I did feel like kicking a few of them up the backside!

After our win at County, Sam Allardyce received some horrendous criticism from the crowd as he was walking off. I later found out from someone I knew in the area that he was very close to getting the dreaded sack, which seemed ridiculous after his team had won the title in the division below about seven months earlier. He survived and the rest of his career is well documented.

Even though we had turned it around after our nightmare, deep down I was becoming more and more frustrated with the situation of bringing in some better players. I spoke to Steve Gage, our chief executive, on a regular basis and he was very sympathetic. Steve had been involved in football at Wigan with Brian Hamilton, so he knew exactly what I was going through. The bottom line was that we couldn't afford or were not prepared to break our wage structure to attract better quality players to the club. I felt as though I was in a straitjacket and I couldn't see how we could progress or how much further I could take the club under those circumstances. We were now struggling to score goals, which any manager will tell you is a major problem. In fact I think we only scored four goals in the next seven games. One of those goals was scored by our young debutant, Lomana Tresor Lua Lua. We needed something different in the final third of the pitch and young Lomana had been showing incredible skills in the reserves. We were away at Chesterfield and two goals down, so I threw the youngster on and within minutes he had poached a goal to put us back in the game. Alas they went straight down the other end and scored a third and it was over for us. But the one bright spark was Lomana's debut!

When you take a youngster on and give him a pro contract, no matter how well he has done in training, youth or reserve games, you are never quite sure if he is going to cope with first-team football. The first team, whether in the Premiership or the third division, is a big jump from reserve-team football. Some lads appear to have everything but when they venture into the real stuff it just doesn't happen for them. I have also seen other boys who looked average in training or nothing special in reserve games blossom when thrown into the first eleven!

Lomana had most attributes and was always going to play in the first team at some point. What I hadn't anticipated was how he would blossom so quickly. He thrived on first-team football and in the short space of time he was on the pitch at Chesterfield I knew that Colchester had a gem on their hands! He was always going to be unorthodox at times, but that is what made him that little bit special. He would frustrate you in training at some point but he had so much talent that it didn't matter. My youth staff were delighted with Lomana's progress and it was a feather in their cap to have played their part in helping with his development, not just as a player but also as a young man.

Mick Cook had signed some decent-looking lads on the new three-year scholarship or apprenticeship as it used to be called. The youngsters could stay on for an extra year, which was equivalent to a first year professional. This didn't cost the club any additional money so it was a better deal all round. My son Jack was also signed on this scheme and had opted to live in digs with the other lads, so he was part of the club in his own right. They played in the Combination Reserve League, which was good experience for all the young players that had become too old to play in the youth side.

Our home game against Wrexham in January 1999 turned out to be my last game in charge of Colchester United. We lost 3-1 and the mood in the camp had changed dramatically since facing Wrexham in our first away game of the new season. That 4-2 victory seemed a million years away. I felt completely drained and somewhat disillusioned. I had been the manager for four years almost to the day.

I went to see the chief executive and told him that I was not happy with the way things were going and that if he felt it was appropriate he could have a word with the board to relay my feelings. Perhaps they needed to do something to change the situation? Looking back, perhaps it was a cry for help. I don't mean that I was feeling sorry for myself, it was just that I couldn't take the club any further. The feedback wasn't quite what I had expected, as there was a certain amount of "if that's what you want" about the answer. In fact, I don't think I knew what the feedback should have been. I was floundering and I needed good advice, which I didn't seek. In hindsight that was a big mistake. I was physically and mentally tired after seven years of constant work, travelling and pressure. My actual time off during that period had been minimal and I was definitely running on empty!

Anne urged me to talk to an independent person and I don't know why I refused. I had made up my mind and it looked as if the club weren't going to twist my arm to carry on. I negotiated a settlement on my contract and the club were very professional and fair in their dealings, which was par for the course as that was the way Mr Heard worked. Everything was done properly. I went to see Peter Powell, the club's solicitor, to finalise the details and he tried to make me think again about my decision. Peter is a very nice man who has served the club fantastically well over the years and so I felt a twinge of guilt for a second, but I had made my decision and that was that. When the news went to the press I received several phone calls asking the usual questions. I met Stewart Houston and he questioned my actions and told me that I should have spoken to him before making my decision. Bryan Hamilton said the same, but the deed was done and there was no turning back.

Witts wasn't very happy, which was understandable as technically I was putting everyone's job in jeopardy. Brian Owen asked me if I had another job lined up and I told him categorically that I had not. Then it dawned on me that the board probably thought that I might have something in the pipeline too. If they did, they couldn't have got it more wrong as that wasn't my way. Friends in the game all told me that I shouldn't have left before fixing myself up with something else, but that idea just hadn't entered my head as I was a totally loyal person. In hindsight they were all proved right, as I was out of work for 12 months. Unfortunately loyalty and ethics don't necessarily get you a job or keep you in one!

In all honesty it wasn't my original aim to go straight into another job, as I was looking forward to a rest and spending time with Anne and Sally. Our boys were living away from home, Jack in the YTS digs and Thomas at the University of Hertford.

When Anne and I drove away from Peter Powell's office I felt as though a huge weight had been lifted from my shoulders. I had made the decision, rightly or wrongly, and I intended to make the most of the opportunity to relax.

CHAPTER 10

NEXT STOP STEVENAGE, ALL CHANGE FOR DONCASTER

Not driving into Layer Road every morning seemed strange for a while, but my head was totally clear of any sort of conjecture or problem.

Before I had completely cut my ties with the club I had spoken to a couple of the players, including Richard Wilkins, my skipper. Wilks had done a magnificent job for me and I couldn't thank him enough for his contribution. He voiced his concerns to me about who would be taking over the manager's position, and I am sure all the players shared his sentiment. However, I told him that I was confident that the board would make the right decision, or at least I thought they would. I took all my own staff out to dinner to thank them for their support. It was a very relaxed affair and they all appeared in good spirits, but I think they were genuinely disappointed that I was leaving.

One big regret that I did have was leaving Jack at the club in his first year as a trainee. I needn't have worried as he made his debut for the first team at Bristol Rovers after coming on as a substitute for David Greene in December of that year.

Anne and I enjoyed our new freedom and I hardly looked at the football results in earnest. I still took an interest; it would have been impossible not to do so after being involved in the game for so long. Colchester were doing okay and I was pleased about that. I didn't know the new manager, Mick Wadsworth, at all but Jack told me that he was good with him personally so that was positive. After a few months Richard Wilkins phoned me to air his concerns, as the new man didn't seem to take to him at all. I found this very strange, as Wilks was an excellent professional and was easily good enough to play in the Colchester team. I tried to reassure Richard that things would work out for him and advised him just to keep his head down and do his talking on the pitch.

I was feeling reasonably well rested and, slowly but surely, over the coming weeks I started to get my appetite for the game back. It was around this time that I received a phone call from a journalist in Southend. He asked me if I would be interested in the Southend manager's job if it became available. I was reticent to commit myself to any sort of answer, as the position wasn't vacant as yet. Alvin Martin was still in charge as far as I was concerned and the last thing that I wanted was to be named as a contender when the man was still in the chair. The conversation turned more hypothetical so I admitted that I might be available if the situation arose. A week later my telephone rang again and the same journalist informed me that Alvin Martin had left Southend and the chairman John Maine would like to meet me with a view to offering me the manager's position.

I had a long chat with Anne and she said that I should do what I felt was right and that she would support me once again if I went back into the 'madhouse'. I felt quite excited about the prospect of a new challenge - and that is exactly what it would be! Southend and Colchester were big rivals, but I didn't feel as if I was being disloyal to my former club because it was right on their doorstep. I just saw it as a new problem to be solved.

I spoke to John Maine and agreed to meet him at a hotel on the A12. He came over as a really nice man, maybe too nice to be a chairman! We had a good chat and I think I asked him more questions than he asked me. We talked about budgets and he appeared visibly shocked to hear what budget I had at Colchester after we had gained promotion to the second division. The Southend playing budget was bigger and they were in the third division. I assured him that it would be possible to control their budget and still improve things on the pitch. He even talked about my salary, which was also substantially more than my Colchester remuneration.

Before I left the meeting he told me that Southend would be playing at Rochdale on the following Tuesday evening and he suggested that I take the opportunity to see the team play. That way I would be better prepared for the local derby at Leyton Orient on the following Saturday. I agreed and drove up to Rochdale on the Tuesday afternoon. What a journey that was! It took me about four hours to get to Spotland, which isn't the most salubrious place to find yourself on a cold Tuesday night. As I had gone incognito, I sat in the stand behind the goal. Both teams were poor and the "Shrimpers" lost 1-0 and faced a long and agonising journey home to the south coast. I got home at about 2.30 a.m. and was absolutely knackered. At the time I thought that I was back in a job so I felt the trip had been well worth it.

John had told me that he would phone me on the Wednesday once he had informed the relevant people that I was going to take charge. So I waited for his call, but it never came! I was totally confused. By Wednesday evening I knew that there must be a problem, but I had no intention of phoning John myself. Everything had gone quiet, with no calls either from the journalist or from the club!

Eventually John called me on the Thursday evening and said, "You're going to hate me, Steve. I've given the job to someone else!" I can't remember exactly what I said to him but I was polite and wished him good luck. I was very disappointed and a little confused, especially as I had been approached about the vacant position. The journalist had assured me in the first phone call that the job was mine if I wanted it. It was all very strange and to this day I never found out what made John Maine change his mind. The job went to Alan Little, the brother of Brian Little who had offered me the physio/coach's job when he was at Leicester. I felt a little paranoid over that decision and wondered if someone had put the knife in for me. Who knows? Only John and that person, I suppose.

Southend continued to struggle, which gave me no pleasure as I saw it as a missed opportunity to turn Southend around as I had done with my previous two clubs. John was a nice man, so I decided that going public in order to have a go at him wasn't an option. Anyway, my sources told me that he was stitched up himself eventually! That's unusual for our beautiful game, isn't it?

That was as close as I came to landing a job for some months. I did some scouting for Spurs and I enjoyed that. I also went to plenty of games at all levels to keep my hand in. This was my first period out of work for a long time and I seemed to meet more managers and coaches in the same situation than I had before. Maybe because I was not in employment I spent more time talking to people at matches, whereas when I was a manager I tended to keep myself to myself more. All the unemployed tended to have the same or very similar stories to tell regarding their demise. One thing was for sure: no matter how tough your job is, you're better off in one than trying to land one!

It had been my decision to leave Colchester, so I wasn't feeling sorry for myself. I was facing up to the gravity of my decision and had to stay positive and look forward. It became crystal clear that the people I had worked for at Colchester were in a different class to some of the ones described to me by many of the lads who were out of work. Many of the stories would make your hair curl in terms of the way some chairmen and directors behave towards managers and coaches. Thankfully I hadn't encountered that - YET!

I knew a lot of people in the game and they used to keep me updated on who was getting the sack next week or who had three or four games to save his job. It was a joke really! Those managers were probably working their nuts off to try to turn things around and yet outsiders knew that their time was up before they did. Out of work managers were forever seen at matches when the present incumbent was on thin ice. I found this quite distasteful but that's life unfortunately. I didn't do this as I didn't want to appear to be the man in a vulture suit sat in the stand waiting to pounce. In many cases it was already a job done anyway! I found out on lots of occasions from agents and journalists that an appointment had been made behind closed doors before the present manager was dismissed, stitched up, hung out to dry or flayed, or whatever you wish to call it. So getting a new job was extremely difficult even if you had a reasonable CV as I did. You had to be one step ahead all the time. Having inside information was essential as your application had to be in sharpish and it had to go to the right person. The reason I say that is because you were never really certain if your CV actually arrived on the main man's desk!

Mr Heard telephoned me to let me know that he had put my name forward for the vacant manager's position at Blackpool FC, as Nigel Worthington had resigned. He had spoken to Mr Karl Oyston, their main man, and had suggested that I would be a good option for them. He told me that he had received a favourable response and that I should get my CV off to them as soon as possible.

I was quite excited at the prospect of moving back up north. The north-west coast is a great area and with most of our family living within spitting distance it would make linking up with them much easier after such a long time away. It would mean leaving the boys behind but they were capable young men who were already making their own way.

I submitted my CV and received a reply within the week inviting me up to Bloomfield Road for an interview. Anne travelled up with me as usual to share the driving, as it was such a long haul. The meeting was to be held at the football ground, so I dropped Anne off at one of the seafront hotels. It was out of season and so the place looked pretty desolate. The 'golden mile', although something to behold at night when illuminated, looked very average on a cold, wet and windy day.

I wasn't particularly nervous going into the interview as I felt as though I had done it all before and I didn't expect to face anything more difficult than in my interview for the Colchester position. I was shown into a rather dark room, possibly their boardroom or a visitors' lounge, which looked as if it hadn't changed in 50 years. It was all a little run-down, as was their ground, which had been ravaged by the sea air for years. The whole place looked rusty and corroded and exactly how I had remembered it from playing there.

When I walked into the room there was only Karl Oyston, one other director and a lady secretary waiting for me. It was all very informal and if anything they appeared to be more nervous than me. The whole interview wasn't really structured and I ended up asking more questions than I would have liked. I felt comfortable with them but got the impression that the club was being run by very few people. It was a reasonably big club with a decent history but it didn't come over that way in the interview. Their main theme on the agenda was that they were going to develop the ground over the next couple of years, which was a real positive for me. That was one thing that was an absolute necessity if they were serious about moving forward. I came away from the interview reasonably confident, but I knew that there would be some big hitters throwing their hats in the ring.

Blackpool's location in the north-west presented a good opportunity for a manager to establish himself in that area and open bigger doors if he was successful. I always felt that many people saw Colchester as the back of beyond. You were out on a limb slightly, as you were with Norwich and Ipswich to a certain degree. So many clubs are close to one another in areas such as the north-west, Yorkshire or the Midlands, so managers tend to hop on and off the bus as there are more jobs available. It was a little bit like being 'out of sight, out of mind' down in Essex.

I discovered that Steve McMahon had been interviewed for the Blackpool position but he was also in line for another post. I didn't know the identity of the other club but apparently if he received the thumbs-up for that job then he wouldn't be going to Blackpool. The feedback that I got from another source was that it would be either Steve or me for the Tangerines.

A few days later I received a call from the director who had been present at the interview. He informed me that I had not been successful in my application for the management position. He was very pleasant and thanked me for my time. The next day Steve was announced as the new manager. It was a close thing but it wasn't to be! I now had my appetite back and I wanted to get back into work as quickly as possible. Anne and I were both disappointed, as it would have been a good opportunity to take on a new challenge and get ourselves back north of Watford!

Steve Gage was good friends with Bryan Hamilton and had previously introduced me to him at Colchester. Bryan had been Wigan's manager when they played against Brentford at Wembley back in the eighties, so I already knew him from a distance you might say! Bryan and I got on quite well. I remember once I phoned him on his mobile and he answered in a whisper and sounded quite sheepish, as if he didn't want anyone else to hear him. I asked if I had called at a bad time and in his soft Irish brogue he replied, "Well, yes, I'm really sorry but I'm in church at the moment"! I felt terrible but he always found time to speak to me and so he called me back later! In my mind I could picture the phone ring piercing the godly silence and him ducking down between the pews to take the call as quickly as possible! He is such a nice man.

When I was out of work Bryan invited me to a match at Norwich, where he was assistant manager to Bruce Rioch. Bruce had his own private room for his family and friends where you could have a nice meal and relax before the game. I had only met Bruce on a couple of occasions at Colchester and he came over as a very modest and genuine man. He had a fierce reputation as a strict disciplinarian, which went down well with me. He and his wife would often chat to Anne at Colchester home games and he suggested that we go out for dinner with Bryan and his wife, which was nice of them. True to form, Bruce had arranged for us to be his and Bryan's guests at a Norwich game and afterwards we all went out to dinner at a fantastic restaurant in the country. He and Bryan were very supportive and they both gave me some sound advice on how to get back into work. Bryan also gave me a telling-off for leaving Colchester without talking to him first. So two very experienced professionals had let me know that I hadn't played my cards right!

I continued doing some scouting but I was becoming more and more frustrated with being out of the game. On the way home in the car after games on Saturdays, I used to listen to the football scores and reports. I found myself wishing that teams would lose so that a job opportunity might crop up. It wasn't a personal vendetta against any individual managers, just a survival instinct coming out in me I suppose! I would also study all the match results and League positions in the Sunday morning sports papers to get an idea of which jobs might be coming up that I could have a realistic chance of getting.

As time went on, however, my 'realistic' chance began to descend the scale and I was looking at Conference jobs, but I needed to get back in the industry somehow. I had been unemployed for about 14 months, which was a much longer rest than I had originally anticipated. A job in the Conference became available at Stevenage Borough when Richard Hill left. Stevenage was one of the better non-League clubs with good facilities for that level of football, a fair fan base and great potential. I phoned around to find out what the situation was at the club and much of the feedback was positive. The chairman, Phil Wallace, was only young but he was very ambitious. The structure of the club was geared for League football if only they could get themselves out of that division. The downside for me was that, like my former club Aldershot, they weren't full-time yet, which wasn't ideal, but they were a good club and so I put my CV in the post and kept an open mind.

Phil contacted me and asked me to go to the ground for a meeting, so I drove up the following day. The journey took me just over an hour, which wasn't too bad. If I got the job I would be doing the trip on a regular basis and it didn't appear too daunting. As I have already mentioned, I wasn't one for travelling great distances to work.

As I pulled up in Broadhall Way's car park I spotted Terry Brown, another prospective candidate no doubt, coming out of the main entrance. He was the manager of Wokingham when I was at Aldershot so I recognised him straight away. He caught sight of me even though I had tried to be discreet and remain in my car until he had disappeared. I wouldn't have thought that he was particularly pleased to see me turning up for an interview. I think that he was the manager of Hayes at the time so at least he was in a job of some sort.

When I met chairman Phil Wallace he came over as very thorough, almost too thorough. He wanted to know the ins and outs of a dog's behind about me! He even gave me one of those 'multi choice questionnaires' that supposedly profile a person. He tried to make light of it and I knew that he wanted to be absolutely sure of every detail, which was commendable, but this appeared a little worrying from my perspective. According to reports, there had been 50 applicants for this position, so Phil must have been pretty busy if all his interviews were as intense as mine! It was a plum job for many people in the non-League, so I have no doubt that there were many applicants for the position, but I reckon that 50 might have been an over-exaggeration on Phil's part in order to get publicity for his club, which I suppose was understandable to a certain degree.

Phil called me back again for a 'chat', as he described it, and when I returned I was confident that he was going to offer me the post. I had decided that I also needed to test him out if I was going to work for him and get the club into the Football League where they belonged. I say that because they had been denied entry a few seasons earlier on a 'ground technicality' when Paul Fairclough had been their manager. Phil produced a list of their current playing squad, handed it to me and said, "How many of these players are good enough to get us out of this league?" I had already done my homework on the team and so I took about 30 seconds to look at it and then replied, "None of them. No, sorry, maybe Mark Smith as he was in the team the last time they won this division"! Phil's face was a picture and there was a short silence as he retrieved his jaw from his chest! "Right!" he said. "We have some work to do then!"

I presumed that as he had said "we" the job was mine and that was proved right as he went on to offer me the manager's position. The salary wasn't the best and I told him so. He said that it would be reviewed later on if I were successful. I accepted the job but in my mind I was in no hurry to sign a contract on that salary! Phil wasn't that bothered about my signing a contract immediately either.

I got stuck in to the job straight away and they provided me with a club car, which was very handy as I had such a lot of travelling to do. The team was very average, so I knew I had my work cut out. I was putting plenty of miles on the car watching as many games as possible to spot any prospective new players. I only needed about eleven! The office staff and others at the club were fantastic and made me very welcome. As I was employed full-time I saw them a lot and they were a tremendous help in terms of getting my feet under the table.

However, early doors into the job my initial worries began to surface! Phil was never off the phone to me. He wanted to be involved in and informed about everything. I'm sure that he meant well but he only had a 'little' knowledge about football at that level, which can be dangerous at times. I was beginning to feel stifled and I had only been the manager for five minutes! I feel sure that Phil had his finger on everything that was going on in every department of the club and spent a lot of time and effort on Stevenage, so heaven knows how he ran his own business as well!

About four weeks or so into the job, I still hadn't signed a contract or even discussed it again with Phil in any depth. I received a phone call from a friend up north asking me if I would be interested in taking the Doncaster Rovers job. I was surprised to say the least, as I had been after a position for months and now I had finally found a job at Stevenage another opportunity had come my way within weeks. I initially didn't know what to say but I couldn't dismiss it out of hand.

When I told Anne she was as surprised as me but said, "You are going to take it, aren't you?" She knew me better than myself! It would be a massive opportunity for me to manage one of my old clubs again and I had already done a good job at Aldershot and Colchester. It also gave me a great confidence boost. When you have been out of work for a long time your confidence definitely takes a tumble no matter who you are. Anne said, "You must have done something right in your career as you have an opportunity of managing a third club, fourth if you include Brentford, that you played for and you were also the captain of all of them at some time too."

I followed up the phone call and arranged to go up to Cheshire to meet with the co-owners of Rovers. I must admit that I felt quite awful inside, as I had never been disloyal to anyone in my life. I still hadn't really, as technically I wasn't being disloyal in this case. For a start, I hadn't signed a legally binding contract. If Phil had originally come up with a decent package then I would have been tied up by then and wouldn't be talking to anyone.

I drove up to Cheshire the following morning to meet chairman John Ryan and Peter Wetzel. The information I had received about John was that he was a local Doncaster man and was the owner of Transform, one of the biggest cosmetic surgery companies in the country. Peter, another businessman, was a close friend of his.

Anne kept me company on the long drive and adopted her usual role of navigator as my sense of direction is hopeless! We were both met at the door and within a few minutes the receptionist led me to John's private office while Anne was well looked after and pampered in the plush entrance lounge. There were a few people milling about but I didn't see many 'customers'. Call me sad or naïve but I'd been half expecting to see people wandering around with tight faces or huge boobs! John had told me that one of his main clients was Melinder Messenger and she definitely wasn't there! Mind you, when Peter Wetzel came in he looked at Anne and complimented her on her neat little nose, so she was quick to inform him that it was her own, as well as everything else! He was very charming and he was also rather late, which was about right for him on both counts.

John's office was more of a plush boardroom. John was sitting at one end of a huge table in the middle of the room and in front of him was a silver tray containing peeled fresh fruit. The whole atmosphere smelled of quality and the room oozed opulence. From the window you could see John's Bentley parked in a solitary parking space. This was a man who meant business.

John stood up to greet me with the biggest smile ever. He was a loud, enthusiastic man with an infectious demeanour. Peter came in soon after and said something about this gorgeous woman he had just met in reception! "Oh, that will be Anne," I said calmly. That definitely broke the ice. We had a long chat and John told me about his reasons for financing the club, which he had supported all his life. He was a Donny lad through and through, almost a fanatical supporter. He knew more about me than I had anticipated and he had also seen me play for Rovers years earlier. He wanted his beloved club back where it belonged in the Football League.

Peter was a more reserved man but he was equally as determined to take the club forward. They had both been involved with the club in a lesser capacity before, but they were in total control at that time so far as I could see.

They left the room for a few minutes for a private discussion and then they came bouncing back in and offered me the job! I couldn't possibly refuse. We sorted out the finances and virtually every other detail in no time at all. I would obviously have to move up to Yorkshire with Anne and Sally, but John and Peter were very reassuring. My big problem would be informing Phil at Stevenage. John said that he would talk to him and put across the club's point of view, which put my mind at rest to a large extent in terms of any conjecture, but I would still have to tell Phil personally about my decision.

The journey home with Anne was both sweet and sour. We were delighted that I had managed to land what appeared to be a good position at one of the biggest clubs in the Conference and it was an exciting prospect, but I had never let anybody down in this way before and so the thought of telling Phil the bad news wasn't sitting well with me.

When we arrived home I didn't waste any time and I phoned Phil immediately. I told him what I had done and that I had made a decision. He was more than shocked and asked me to reconsider several times, but there was no way that I was going to change my mind. Phil was clearly upset but remained reasonably controlled. However, I knew that there would be some fallout following my decision. I didn't feel much better after the phone call but at least I had done it and I also had the full support of John and Peter should there be any legal ramifications. My solicitor had told me that without a contract at Stevenage I was technically a free agent, so I was confident that there wouldn't be any problems on the legal front. Obviously Stevenage would demand some sort of compensation from Doncaster for my services, but that was up to the two clubs to sort out.

While we were away in Doncaster Phil phoned our home and Jack answered. He was clearly upset about the situation and vented his anger on my son. He may have thought that he had the moral high ground, but I felt that approaching a manager's family in that way was totally unacceptable. However, he didn't get the better of Jack, who handled the situation well coming from a football background!

A few days later a figure of £50,000 was mentioned, which was ridiculous. An agreement was eventually made, but I wasn't privy to the details so the matter was closed as far as I was concerned. I did have another rather embarrassing problem. I still had to return my Stevenage club car to the ground. I couldn't very well ask them to come and pick it up, as that would just add insult to injury, so we decided that I would drive the club car back to Stevenage and Anne would follow in her car. I needed to be in Doncaster quite early that day, as it had been arranged for me to be officially introduced as the next manager, so Anne and I arrived at Broadhall Way at around 7 a.m. I parked the car by the main offices and pushed the car keys through the letter box in the front door. I then quickly scurried back to Anne's car, jumped in and we shot off up the A1 to Doncaster. I felt a bit of a prat but it seemed the best way to do it. Feelings were running quite high and I just wanted it to be as civilised as possible.

The plan was that I would stay up in Doncaster and Anne would return home to Sally the next day to set things in motion for yet another move. Anne already knew where she wanted to live and so we took a little detour off the A1 through Bawtry on our way up. It was a nice little area and we knew it quite well from our days living in Armthorpe back in the seventies. Anne had always liked it there and we felt that it would be an ideal place for us to settle. As we approached the high street we passed a large wooded area with a wonderful carpet of bluebells in bloom.

Anne was happy and we were both looking forward to living in Yorkshire again.

CHAPTER 11

MANAGEMENT DAYS AS A ROVER WERE NOT TO END IN CLOVER

Anne and I were booked into the Earl of Doncaster Hotel just a stone's throw from the ground. I had been to Belle Vue a couple of seasons earlier with Colchester. That was a sad day for Rovers as they were relegated to the Conference and they were finding it tough to climb back out of it.

The club had appointed the Snodin brothers, Ian and Glyn, to run affairs in their first season in the Conference. These two lads were regarded as icons in Doncaster as they were local to the town, had both played for the club and had gone on to have excellent careers in the game. I knew Glyn quite well as he used to come in and train with us when I was a player back in the seventies. He was only about 14 years old then and he used to have a kick about with us, but he showed tremendous skills for his age. Ian was younger and so I didn't see much of him in the early days. It was a difficult job for them as it was their first crack at management and coaching, so it was definitely a case of being thrown in at the deep end. For whatever reason it didn't work out and, even though they did well in the Nationwide Trophy Cup competition, in the two seasons that they were in charge it had been a struggle for them in the League.

I realised how well thought of the two brothers were after I had finished my hour with the press. A supporter who had attended the meeting with the media approached me and asked in quite a terse manner and a strong Doncaster accent, "Tha's betta na yoo've got a hellava act ta folla wiv Snodins!" I just smiled politely, said, "Thanks for that" and walked away. When I had digested properly what he had said I couldn't quite work out what he meant. In terms of the results the club was nearer the relegation zone than promotion. I knew that the brothers were adored as players but it didn't happen for them as managers and so that was the end of that, or so I thought. Other people spoke to me in a similar way about the previous regime being a hard act to follow and I was a little confused about it all. Was there a core of people who didn't want a new man in charge? I don't mean any disrespect to Ian and Glyn, who had given it their best shot in difficult circumstances, but football just doesn't work that way. You get even less time now to succeed, so two seasons of struggle usually results in a change of some sort.

During the first few weeks the brothers filled me in on a few things that they thought I needed to know. Once again there were snakes in the camp, which was par for the course! Just how many they numbered and how venomous they were I would have to find out for myself!

I had come to the club completely alone, as I couldn't bring in my own assistant or coach. John and Peter had already appointed an assistant, Alan Lewer, before I took the helm. I knew absolutely nothing about Alan apart from reading in a paper that he was Telford's manager a while earlier. John told me that they had taken him on because of his connections with and knowledge about all levels of non-League football. I didn't have a problem with that at all as I always took people at face value at first. Alan had also come into the club 'blind' as he didn't know anyone else, so we were thrown together if you like! I hoped that the mix would work and when I was introduced to him he seemed a nice, open sort of chap who spoke very well and I took to him straight away. In fact when I first saw him he reminded me of Uncle Fester in The Addams Family: with his bald head, lack of height and penguin-like walk, he was a real ringer! I don't think that the players noticed the similarity immediately – it probably took a couple of seconds! Alan wanted to do well and I was confident that he would work hard at the job in hand. He had found himself a place in Rotherham, which was about eight miles away. His partner Ann was living there with him, which I was pleased about, as I liked my staff to be happy and reasonably local. I was going to demand a lot from him, so it was important to me that he was settled.

Logistically, Anne and I had a lot to sort out. I was totally committed to the job, so we decided to buy a property in Bawtry as soon as possible. We had not long bought a bungalow in Lexden, Colchester, so we decided to keep it so that Jack could live there with his mate Andy Taylor, another YTS lad with Colchester United. We were confident that Jack would be okay there. Thomas was in his second year at university in Hatfield and could be in Bawtry in about an hour and a half, which meant that we could see more of him.

Anne and Sally moved up the A1 and we all lived in the Earl for some weeks, which was a strange sort of existence. Sally even helped on reception sometimes, which she thoroughly enjoyed and all the staff were fantastic to us. Anne had been as well organised as usual and had managed to place Sally in the Mayflower Junior School in Bawtry, so they had to travel each day from Doncaster initially. As the weeks passed it was becoming very expensive for the club to continue to put us up at the hotel and they found us a bungalow to rent in Barnby Dun, which backed onto a canal. The owners of the property also had a longboat and they would take off on that and let out their bungalow while they were away. It was a great setting as you could literally fish in the canal from your back garden. Thomas visited us on many a weekend to take advantage of this 'perk' and the three of us were always glad to see him. It wasn't the most luxurious of places but it was adequate for us.

On our first night in the bungalow we were sitting watching the television when all of a sudden we were jolted from our relaxed state by a dreadful clattering and whirring noise. A massive shutter had started its descent down the exterior of the panoramic window in the living room and we were quickly plunged into complete darkness. We all just sat there in shock as the iron curtain clanged shut. It was like some sort of lockdown and felt as if the house had descended into a bunker! It felt very surreal, almost as if you were on a film set or in the middle of a siege! Anne didn't look too happy with the situation and Sally's lip was looking a little square. I wasn't too keen myself! We discovered that the shutter had been set on a timer to close on an evening and open again in the morning, but no one had shared that little snippet of information with us, and, as we weren't going to be there very long, we decided not to meddle with it. In fact after that we used to joke about this nightly event: "Colditz, you will not escape"!

We had found a nice place in Bawtry and the purchase was going through reasonably quickly as we had nothing to sell. The previous owner was a builder and he had done an excellent job of extending and renovating the property to a very high spec. We loved it and so did Sally, who still talks about her own room there. Once we had moved in we were able to send for Ralph who had been staying with Jack. The poor old dog's exciting days at Rickmansworth Lido were well behind him by then. His legs were bent, his teeth were falling out and his coat was matted, but apart from all that he was well loved and he had a massive garden to stumble around in.

My first game in charge was at my old mate's club, Rushden and Diamonds. Brian Talbot had taken charge there after coming back from Malta where he had managed a team called Hibernian. We had kept in touch, so I knew a little about his new club and he'd had a lot of input in terms of the new ground and the facilities. It was one of the best set-ups outside the Football League. In fact it was better than many in the first, second or third divisions. Brian had a fantastic budget and was destined to get them in the Football League.

I was quite pleased with my team's first showing. It wasn't a great match but some decent football was played and we had a good competitive edge to our game. On reflection the 0-0 scoreline was just about right and I was probably the happier of the two managers on the day. I had a good chat with Brian afterwards and he was confident that Rushden would be up there the following season. He also thought that we would be a force in that division, although he felt that it would be difficult to win it in my first season as it was such a tough league. I did agree with him but I had no intention of going public with that one! The Doncaster supporters, who were fantastic on that day, would only accept the championship from what I had heard.

Dave Penney and Mark Atkins had taken the team in the interim period between the Snodins leaving and my taking over. Alan and I spoke to them in depth about our present squad. Alan had seen most of the lads play before and I had watched some of them. We had also looked closely at them in training for a few days but Dave and Mark's input was vital, as we needed to make some harsh decisions in a very short space of time. I went through all the players' contracts, many of which were up at the end of that season, 1999/2000. Some were being paid a lot more than I had expected and some a lot less. The main thing was that there was an opportunity to revamp the squad by releasing some lads to bring in new blood. I had to be as ruthless as I could to improve the squad and a lot of unpleasant decisions had to be made by my staff and me.

We still had the final of the Nationwide MacMillan Trophy at home against Kingstonian before I could finalise my retain list. Ian McDonald, who was the coach at Kingstonian, had done a great job there in getting them to the FA Trophy final, which was to be played the following Saturday after our game. I also knew their manager Geoff Chapple quite well from his days at Woking. There was a great turnout by our supporters and we won the game with some style. Alan and I were pleased with the outcome because it gave all the fans something to cheer about and we could all go into the summer break in a positive frame of mind.

After a final meeting with Alan Lewer and Dave Penney, who was to become player/coach, we came up with a retain list. Several players whose contracts had expired were released: Jason Minett, Dino Maamria, Tommy Wright, Scott Maxfield, Lee Warren and Glen Kirkwood. I hadn't known any of them personally but that didn't make the task any easier. Scott took the decision badly. He was a local lad with a big heart and he loved playing for the club. Seeing him visibly upset wasn't pleasant and in those instances I sometimes wished that I had chosen another career after I had finished playing. My conscience was clear, however, as the decisions had been made after advice from and consultations with other staff members who knew them much better than I did.

These players had to be replaced and Alan already had one lined up. Jimmy Kelly came in from Hednesford Town. He was a fellow Scouser so he couldn't be all bad! The chairman forked out £15,000 for him, which I felt was a little steep. However, we were known as a reasonably well-off club at that level and players didn't come cheap to us, as other clubs saw it as an opportunity to up the ante!

At this time my workload appeared enormous, as it was evident that there needed to be changes in many areas. The training facilities were poor, the training kit looked scruffy, and even the general look of the dressing rooms and boot room was unkempt. Just as with my previous clubs, all the fringe problems needed to be corrected if we were to become a decent outfit on and off the pitch. I also had to deal with the on-field indiscipline, which had got out of hand. The chairman had informed me that Doncaster were required to go before an FA Disciplinary Committee to face charges for being one of the worst disciplined teams in the country, meaning a possible fine of £5,000. I represented the club at the hearing and managed to persuade the panel to suspend the fine on the back of my discipline record at my previous clubs, which I told them I intended to mirror at Doncaster. John was delighted with the result of the hearing and thanked me for my input.

Another player who was going to join us for the next season was a lad called Colin Hawkins. Peter Wetzel had sung his praises and said that he was the best centre back in Ireland. A fee had been agreed for him and he had signed a contract for us. I knew absolutely nothing about the boy but Peter and John assured me that he was 'top drawer'. However, when I saw him play I was not sure at all. He appeared to have a lot going for him, as he was tall, quick, had decent feet and looked brave enough, but in games he couldn't produce it week in, week out. I played him in the middle of the park as a ball winner and he did okay but not great. When I played him at centre back he either made a mistake or got caught out of position too much for my liking. To be fair to him, I think that he gave his all but he looked at odds with himself over his performances.

John and Peter were being railroaded into some deals and were paying over the odds for average players. I told them that I would like to be consulted about every deal in the future, although as it was their cash any final decision was theirs.

I was feeling good about the job but there still seemed to be an undercurrent at the club. I couldn't put my finger on it and neither could Alan. At least everyone was pleasant to my face, but I had the distinct feeling that people knew something that Alan and I didn't.

During the first few months that I was there, my office and others in the block were broken into on several occasions. Nothing major was taken but everything had been rifled through and thrown about. I had organised a new kit cupboard in the main stand and had a new room created just for that purpose. Only half a dozen people knew about it but within 24 hours someone had smashed through a wall into that particular room and all the kit had been stolen. I wasn't at all happy as I suspected that it was an inside job and I had enough to contend with without worrying about silly pilfering or wanton damage!

I had this horrible feeling in my bones that all was not right at the club. Although I was enjoying the challenge of creating a new team and all that went with it, I always felt that there were other problems brewing, some of them possibly serious. John and Peter were fantastic towards me and Alan supported me to the hilt, but I still didn't feel totally comfortable. Ian McMahon, our chief executive, tried to be very positive but sometimes he looked as if he was on the brink of a nervous breakdown.

Joan Oldale, our football secretary, was the complete opposite, however. She was so incredibly laid-back that she reminded me of a female version of 'Uncle Arthur' from Dad's Army. All the office and commercial staff at the club tried to be helpful. Alick Jeffrey Junior, who was a real character, worked in the commercial department and he and his pal Miles Cartwright were a great double act. Alick had been an apprentice with my brother Dave when I was a player at Rovers and he was a tough little beggar who was always going to be in the shadow of his famous father Alick Senior. I also knew big Alick from my playing days when he attempted to make his comeback. Alick Senior was the president of the club and he pulled me at the end of season do to tell me that I had his support. He also told me that there were a few people who were a problem in and around the club but that I should ignore them and that if I could get some success on the pitch then they wouldn't matter anyway! I appreciated his taking time out to talk to me. I got on well with young Alick too, which was a bonus. He really looked after Anne when he showed her around the best places in the area to look for furnishings for the new house.

There was a lot for me to think about both on and off the pitch but our next move was to get some quality players in for the next season. Alan spoke to me about a player called Carl Alford, who was at my last club Stevenage. He asked my opinion but I said that I hadn't been there long enough to judge, although I did think that he was overweight and looked a little lazy. Alan told me that he knew him well and thought that if we could get him in, with the benefit of full-time training, he would score us a hatful of goals. I spoke to Brian Talbot about Carl as he had paid £85,000 for him at Rushden. Brian wasn't totally complimentary about him but agreed with Alan's assessment. John sorted out the deal with Stevenage, which was in the region of £50,000. To me that was a big fee considering that it was the same as the record fee I had paid out for Neil Gregory when I was at Colchester a few seasons earlier. The main thing was that we had a recognised goalscorer and Carl's record was second to none in the non-League.

We went for two other players of very good quality at that level, Jamie Patterson and Stephen Halliday. Jamie, a left-sided player, came in from Halifax. He'd had the chance to go to League clubs but we persuaded him that Doncaster was the place to be over the next couple of seasons. Rushden had been willing to pay £200,000 for him the previous season but Jamie had turned them down. We had managed to get him on a free transfer, which was a good bit of business. Stephen Halliday came to us from Motherwell and was a centre forward with tremendous ability. I had seen him play on several occasions at Hartlepool and Carlisle and he always looked like a player who could play at whatever level he wanted if he put his mind to it.

I also brought in Tim Ryan, a left-footed defender from Southport. Tim was a very competitive lad who could play at left back or centre half. Mark Wright, Southport's manager, was furious with Tim for leaving them. Mark seemed to lose it over many things, especially on the touchline on match days!

Barry Richardson came to us to fight it out with Andy Warrington for the goalkeeper's jersey. Barry used to be at Lincoln in the John Beck era and I was always impressed with him, especially his kicking ability. He was probably one of the best with the ball at his feet in the lower divisions. He was also a winner and I had a lot of respect for him. In addition Michael Stone, a young defender, came down to join us from Rangers' reserves in Scotland.

So I now had eight very good players on the books that were of a better quality than those I had released, which on paper looked exciting!

A couple of other aspects that needed addressing were the training facilities and the reserve side. We entered a team in the Avon Insurance League, which was essential as far as I was concerned. The reserves were an important part of development and rehabilitation for any club. I also pushed for a new training facility and received the club's backing.

We developed a site over at Cantley Park, which brought back great memories for me, as that was where I had made my debut as a youth team player for Rovers. I wanted a totally independent training ground where we could train, play practice games and youth matches, and also eat together. As it progressed we would also have video equipment installed to go over games and discuss tactics, etc., with the players.

I was knocking the club into shape quite quickly and I had changed a few people's attitudes and outlooks towards preparation and professionalism. As usual some players were finding the going tough, especially my weekly weigh-ins. I even joined in with a few of the morning exercises in pre-season training and at 45 years old I surprised some of the lads with my fitness. At first they probably thought: look at that silly old git! However, I forced them to think again when I kept up with their groups on a couple of 200-metre runs around the track! I didn't expect a player to do something in training that I couldn't do at their age, so I put myself through some pain to show them that I wasn't all whistle and no trousers!

The physiotherapist at the club was ex-Oldham player Jon Bowden. Jon was a forthright sort of character who didn't suffer fools gladly. I could relate to some of his frustrations with the players, as I had been the physio for a short while at Aldershot. Being an ex-player, he often saw straight through some of the lads if they tried to swing the lead. He was very good friends with the Snodin brothers, which couldn't have made it easy for him to accept me - and I am not totally sure that he ever did. He applied himself well and was very much part of the camp when our backs were against the wall in some competitive games. Some of his comments from the bench on match days could be very cutting towards either the players on our team or on the opponents' side. I had to tell him to curb it a little on numerous occasions, but to be fair to him his judgement was usually correct!

Another member of staff that had been at the club a little while was Micky Walker. He looked a little like Norris, the character in Coronation Street! Micky was one of the first people to greet me when I turned up at the ground on my first day. I didn't know him but he knew of me by association after playing with my brother David at Gainsborough Trinity some years earlier. When he told me this I was straight onto my brother to get the low-down on him and Dave told me he was a decent bloke but in his words: "a bit busy"! As we all know, youth team coaches tend to know everything about a club, so I tapped into him as often as possible.

I also appointed Andy Mutch as our chief scout as he could expand our network through his own contacts. Alan introduced me to Mutchy as he used to work with him at Telford. He didn't realise the connection between us at first, until I reminded him of the Wolves v. Aldershot play-off final back in the eighties. He didn't know what to say initially but he soon got into some banter with me. "You were lucky," he said, so I replied, "Very lucky ... it was only 3-0 over the two legs"! He was a great asset and worked very hard looking at players all over the country as well as doing match reports for me.

Soon my first full season, 2000/01, was under way and I was pleased with the squad. Alan was still networking to try to find players that we could nick or take on loan in the future. We had five new players in the starting line-up for our first game with Nuneaton at home, but we always felt that if we were able to improve the squad even more then we would.

We had a slow start to the season but for most of September we picked up and won four, drew two and lost one of our matches. The unfortunate loss was against Yeovil, who were flying and sitting at the top of the Conference. We knew that they were genuine contenders for the title and so it was a vital game for us. We travelled down to Yeovil on the Friday before the Saturday fixture. The preparation had to be right, which I insisted upon. We were starting to put a run of results together and I didn't want us to lose any more ground on the top two teams, the other being Rushden. We had prepared fully on the training ground, everyone was confident and I felt that the team was starting to gel a lot better. My only concern was that Carl Alford hadn't scored a goal yet. His striking partner, Stephen Halliday, was just the same. Neil Campbell had forced his way into the side and had scored three in only three starts, which was a real bonus for us.

The players knew the format on overnight stops: dinner together and then back in their rooms at a reasonable hour, the only restrictions really being no alcohol or going out of the hotel. I always tried to treat players like adults and expected them to behave responsibly.

I was sitting in the hotel lounge area with Alan after our meal, putting the football world to rights, when I noticed a waitress walking past us with a couple of pints of beer on a tray. She went through some double doors that led to the hotel bedrooms. I didn't give it too much thought and continued with my conversation. About half an hour later the same waitress went past again with another couple of pints on a tray, taking the same route.

I turned to Alan and said, "Did you see that?"

He said, "Yes boss!"

"You don't think that the beer is going to any of our lads' rooms do you?" I said.

"It better bloody not be! No it can't be!" Alan replied with his eyes widening anxiously, as if it were true then he knew I would go apeshit!

We just sat there and didn't mention to anyone else that we had our suspicions. After the third tray of beer had made its way through the double doors I just had to make some enquiries at the bar. I had a room list for the players, who were all paired together, so I politely asked the bartender the destination of the liquid refreshments. He gave me the number of the room and I scanned down my list, hoping against all hopes that it didn't match up with any of my players. However, I was to be disappointed. My finger stopped at the number of Jimmy Kelly and Jamie Patterson's room. The two idiots were drinking pints of beer the night before our biggest game of the season. I thanked the barman but didn't say anything else to him. I just walked back over to Alan, sat down and gave him the bad news. He wanted to go up and confront them there and then, but I told him that we would sort it out in the morning because I didn't want the whole squad disturbed. If we had collared them then the players would all be phoning each other, so I decided to let sleeping dogs lie as I watched the fourth shuttle run of beer float past.

I was steaming inside! I couldn't believe that any of the players would disregard a rule that was crystal clear to everyone. Not only that, did they think that they were dealing with some sort of muppet who would just turn a blind eye, or were they just plain thick? I didn't sleep well as I was pondering about what action to take.

In the morning I got myself down to breakfast quite early and I saw Mark Atkins. He was the PFA representative as well as being one of the senior players at the club. When I told him what had happened he wasn't happy at all and his reaction was something along the lines of, "Oh dear, what a pair of silly fellows" - I don't think! I told him to inform the two players that were impersonating professional footballers to get themselves out of bed and meet me in the foyer immediately. I asked Mark to be present as their representative so that there could be no misunderstanding about what was said.

Five minutes or so later the two boys strolled into the foyer with Mark just behind them. I tore into them straight away and gave them very little chance to answer back until I had finished. To my horror, Jamie tried to say that he didn't see anything wrong with having a few pints the night before a game. Jimmy didn't say anything and just looked at the floor. Jamie was a cheeky little git and I was livid with him! Jimmy was usually a great lad but I had obviously paired him up with the wrong roommate this time. Mark couldn't believe his ears at Jamie's comments either. His retort had tipped me over the edge. Had he shown some shame over their actions my decision might have been different. I told the pair of them to pack their gear and get out of the hotel immediately. They tried to come back at me but I was having none of it and walked away, leaving them with Mark.

The local press were accompanying us in the hotel, so I had no option but to come clean and I thought it was only right to do so. Usually I would back my players to the hilt, but on this occasion these lads had taken the piss, not just with me but also the club and its fantastic supporters, and they deserved to face the fallout.

Needless to say, we lost the game 2-0. The whole incident affected the camp and I couldn't get my head around why any professional would behave in that way. The two cabbages came to see me separately on the following Monday. Jimmy was very remorseful, as he felt that he had let me down when I had given him a chance to get his career back on track. Jamie was still on the defensive and said that he wasn't happy with the press coverage about the incident. He said that he didn't see why the media had to know. I explained that the press were in our bloody hotel, for God's sake! If it had been reported that I had tried to sweep the incident under the carpet then I might well have found myself out of work! He reluctantly accepted that he was wrong and promised that it wouldn't happen again. "I know it won't," I said. "Next time I will sack you."

We played Hednesford Town on the Tuesday after Yeovil and Jamie scored two of the goals in our 3-1 victory. At least that was a positive response and it got the fans back on his side. Despite the problem at the hotel, I genuinely felt that we had a side that could compete near the top of the division.

Only one team could win the Conference, which was ridiculous in my eyes, as it put undue pressure on managers after only a couple of months of the season. The expectations at Doncaster were very high, but even with John and Peter's input it would have been unrealistic to expect a team that had flirted with relegation the previous season to win it.

To emphasise my point, we played our next game away at Boston United, who were managed by a very strange little Scotsman called Steve Evans. I didn't know him at all but Alan marked my card about him. Apparently he wasn't a very pleasant character and to say he was outspoken on the touchline and in the press would be an understatement. When I actually saw the man I wondered how somebody so fat and ugly could have the gall to give others stick! The 'cheeky weeble' even had the impudence to phone my chairman, John Ryan, and tout for my job when I was still in possession! That wasn't my concern at the time, as there was plenty of rivalry between the two clubs anyway and it was going to be a tough game on what was usually a poor pitch.

At Boston you came out of the dressing room and emerged from behind one of the goals, which was quite unusual. As I came out of the tunnel I was met with a torrent of abuse from a supporter, and this was only for the warm-up. I didn't take any notice initially, but obscenities were still being hurled when I reached the edge of the pitch. I glanced around expecting it to be a Boston supporter and to my surprise I discovered it was the Doncaster supporters' end! The abuse was so personal that I reacted and told the bloke where to go! He went ballistic and shouted that I couldn't speak to him like that.

I couldn't work it out; it almost seemed like a wind-up. We had just played well and won a game on the previous Tuesday, so it didn't make sense! Barry Richardson, our keeper, also heard the 'escaped inmate' and asked me what the hell was going on at the club. He was a very experienced player and had heard both abuse and praise before in his career, but even he was mystified by some of the comments and behaviour. Things got worse as we lost 3-1, which wasn't on the agenda. The abuse towards me as I walked off the pitch was some of the most vitriolic and nasty that I have ever heard. It wasn't just directed at me either. Chairman John Ryan and his daughter copped for it as well. Barry had it for the whole of the second half of the game and they absolutely slaughtered him even though he hadn't done anything wrong. John had put fortunes into Doncaster Rovers over the previous few seasons and without him and Peter Wetzel there wouldn't have been a club. He literally had saved them from going into liquidation and he certainly didn't deserve what was handed out to him at Boston that day.

When I got home after the game I told Anne what had happened and she was equally confused as to why things had got out of hand so quickly. The players were also feeling the pressure. Even though the abuse was directed at their manager it still affected the team. Some of them became very angry and reacted by putting themselves about on the pitch. In some cases this wasn't a bad thing as I wanted commitment, but it became misdirected at times when we needed clear heads. Other players went into their shells and adopted self-preservation mode, which was understandable. Every player had a different character and acted accordingly in pressurised situations.

I brought in a couple of new players to freshen things up a bit. Centre back Barry Miller came on loan from Gillingham and centre forward Mike Turner joined us from Barnsley. They both did okay and the crowd took to them. Stephen Halliday had gone back to his old club Carlisle and poor Carl Alford was struggling all round with injuries and illness. His goalscoring touch had deserted him completely, which was a total mystery to him and everyone else.

The abuse calmed down somewhat but there was no margin for error from anyone. It didn't take much for the natives to become restless but thankfully we didn't have a repeat of the 'Boston episode' for a while.

By December 2000 we were fifth in the table and on the face of it that wasn't too bad to most people in football. However, you had to win the division to get promoted and Yeovil were 12 points ahead of us. Rushden were five points behind them and had played two games more than Yeovil. It was the halfway stage of the season and in my head my report read: "Doing better than last year, could still do better, needs to do what he knows is right and not listen too much to others ...". If the play-offs had been in place, our position would have been viewed from a completely different perspective.

We were settled in Bawtry and our life was very enjoyable. Sally was attending school there and we had successfully transferred her dance training to the Riley School of Dance in Doncaster. She had also won a place at the Louise Browne Ballet School for a year's part-time training in York and had won second place in the South Yorkshire Junior Ballet Championships for 2001. Anne loved the new house and we were within walking distance of several restaurants and shops and our life was very enjoyable. Thomas was able to visit often from university and we had swapped Rickmansworth Lido for Clumber Park! We made some new friends as well as reacquainting ourselves with some old pals from my playing days nearly 20 years earlier.

I mentioned previously that Alick Jeffrey Senior had been very supportive when I had spoken to him earlier in the season, so it was as a huge shock when the news came that he had died suddenly. Alick was a true legend at Doncaster Rovers. At his funeral, John Ryan described him as one of the best footballers that he had ever seen. He was even revered above the likes of Kevin Keegan, who was also a local lad. The funeral was held at Belle Vue and it was a very emotional affair.

That wasn't to be the only sadness for the Jeffrey family, as Alick Junior was attacked in the town one evening. I didn't get to know the exact circumstances, but he ended up in hospital and nearly died from head injury complications. He had to undergo brain surgery in Sheffield and it really was touch and go at one point. Anne and I went over to see him in hospital and although he was very ill he was still trying to have a laugh and a joke with us, which was typical of him. It was through great luck and immense determination on his part that he made a full recovery and was eventually able to return to work. We were all pleased to see him back!

The pressure of the job was greater than I had expected but that wasn't a problem as I had confidence in my own ability to get it right given enough time. We couldn't make up the lost ground behind the top two teams and I just had to soldier on and try to finish as high as possible in the division. I was assessing my squad all the time and planning for the following season earlier than I had done in my previous jobs.

My assistant Alan appeared to be feeling the pressure, or so I thought, as he seemed to be a lot quieter than he usually was. I did all the coaching and Alan was always there to talk to the players and add his own little bits and pieces of knowledge. He also went to lots of games, perhaps two or sometimes three a week. Maybe he was just physically tired but I was sure that there was something troubling him.

Early one morning Dave Penney, who was still playing well for me, came into my office to discuss what players he had for an up-and-coming reserve game. He was taking the reserves, which was good experience for him, as he wanted to go into management or coaching in the future. Alan was usually punctual but I hadn't seen him, so I asked Dave if he knew where he was. "Funny you should ask that," said Dave. "I've just seen him driving the other way on the motorway. He usually comes in from the other direction of Rotherham, where he lives." I was puzzled but didn't think any more about it. Alan came in half an hour or so later and apologised, saying that he had been delayed in traffic. In hindsight, I was a little slow on the uptake, especially as Dave had been only too happy to mention Alan's strange route to work on that day! I knew that Dave was ambitious and there was nothing wrong with that. He had obviously been disappointed when overlooked for the assistant's position or even the main job when Alan and I had come in. He was still a player and a very effective one, so in my opinion player/manager wasn't a realistic option for him at that stage.

A few weeks went by and Alan seemed to become more and more distant. There wasn't the same sparkle and enthusiasm in his demeanour, which was a concern to me. Then one of the directors, Stuart Highfield, pulled me. Stuart had been very helpful when Anne and I were looking for a rental property and I got on very well with him. He told me that he had heard that there was a problem with Alan Lewer. I listened to what he had to say but I didn't make any comment. He didn't go into any specifics but it was something that the board were concerned about and they wanted me to deal with it. I was surprised to say the least by what was said. Even though Alan had appeared to be behaving differently, I hadn't guessed that it might be a major problem. I decided to try to nip it in the bud immediately as I was never one to dodge an issue that needed my attention.

I asked Alan to meet me at the Earl of Doncaster Hotel the following afternoon for a cup of coffee. I liked Alan and so I felt that I owed it to him to give him the chance to come clean if there was a problem. I told him that a member of the board had suggested that he was not doing his job properly, or that is how it appeared, and I asked him if there was anything that he wanted to tell me, making it quite clear that it would be in total confidence. He assured me that there wasn't a problem and that there was nothing untoward going on. I pursued the subject and this time explained that the matter might be taken out of my hands if I didn't sort it or at least attempt to do so. Alan was having none of it and he repeated that nothing was wrong. We finished our coffee and I shook his hand, saying, "I hope that you're being straight with me." He said that he was and he left.

A week or so after this, my wife received a phone call from Alan's partner Ann and she was querying why I was sending Alan all over the place to watch games, as he was coming home at all hours. She wasn't over happy with me, which was understandable, but the fact was that I had only asked him to go to the same grounds we always visited. Obviously I was right in the middle of a domestic situation, which technically was none of my business, but if the board wanted me to take action then it looked as though I didn't have a choice, for now at least.

My head was spinning with all these issues when I got out of my car at the Cantley Park training ground one morning. A voice that I recognised called my name across the car park. I turned around and straight away saw my old mate Gary Booth. Gary was the young lad who threw the cricket ball a mile when we were at the back of the church hall some 30 years earlier. I had last seen him at my wedding in the seventies and so this was a real bolt out of the blue! I asked him what he was doing with himself and he told me that he was the head greenkeeper at the local Bawtry Golf Club. I couldn't believe that we now lived within spitting distance of each other after all those years of moving around the country. Anne and I got together with Gary and his wife Lynne for a meal. He also had a couple of teenage sons, so we had a lot of catching up to do and it was great to see him.

I hadn't had much contact with my old club Colchester at all, but I had spoken to Cookie on a couple of occasions to check out how Jack was doing. My son had said that he was doing well, which I didn't doubt because our boys were realists. That is how they had been brought up - there was no bullshine in our house! We had been involved in sport for too long to try to kid ourselves.

Jack made his first-team debut coming on as a late sub in an away game at Bristol Rovers in December 1999. He had just turned 18 years old at the time so his football appeared to be on track. He continued to be involved in the first-team squad and he eventually got his chance away at Swansea in the Auto Windscreen Shield. He replaced Alan White after half an hour, which meant he had played a good 60 minutes of first-team football. Jack got rave reviews from the press and the staff at Colchester, with manager Steve Whitton even singling him out for special praise in his programme notes and newspaper column. He said that Jack was their best defender when he went on the pitch and that it was nice to see young players emerging from the youth team. Jack had also been put on standby for the Welsh U21 international squad that season. He was eligible because Anne was born in Wales. So it was looking very promising for him and we were very pleased bearing in mind that we had left the club so suddenly. He had worked very hard to get as far as he had.

However, in February 2001 he telephoned me to say that he had been released from his contract, just three months before his three-year scholarship was due to finish. I was dumbstruck! I couldn't understand why he wasn't given a chance as a young professional at what would be a minimum cost to the club. He told me that none of the young players were taken on as professionals that season even though Micky Cook, the youth team coach, had recommended that at least two or three should be awarded contracts.

Many people reading this may think that my feelings were just 'sour grapes' because I am Jack's father, but that was not the case. My question was: what is the point of having a youth system and a youth team coach who was there to recommend players to the manager if those recommendations are completely ignored? That group of young players had gone very much further in the FA Youth Cup than other groups in previous years, so what incentive was there for the youngsters and the youth staff if one of the best intakes of boys all ended up out of the door? Even if there were doubts about their final pedigree, they could always have been loaned out to other clubs to cut down any salary costs to a bare minimum.

Jack was devastated and didn't want to talk about it too much, which was understandable. Sean Hillier, one of the other lads, was released at the same time and the rest of the boys were released at the end of their scholarships. My initial reaction was that of a typical parent I suppose, as I was annoyed and disappointed for Jack. I knew that he had wanted it badly and my natural reaction was to phone Steve and ask him why. Steve had been my assistant for four years so he must have known that I wouldn't be happy, but I was probably just another parent with his head up his backside to him. Obviously the decision had been made and so there was no point pursuing it with him, but I felt that he could have given me a bell sometime beforehand just to give me the nod. After all, I had more than looked after him on a couple of occasions! In fact if I hadn't done so who knows what might have happened to Jack or the other boys?

I spoke to Cookie to check that nothing untoward had happened and he told me that everything seemed fine and he was certain that some of the boys should have been taken on. He was in an awkward position. Although we were old mates, he was employed by the club and quite rightly had to toe the line. To make matters even worse, Jack told me recently that when he found a new club, Dagenham, after his release in 2001, Gary Hill the manager said that he had phoned Steve Whitton in December 2000 to try to get Jack on loan. Witts had refused and had told Gary that Jack was part of the first-team squad and in his future plans! So what on earth happened in the following six weeks before Jack's release? At a later date I offered Jack the opportunity to come to Doncaster as a young professional. However, he declined, as he preferred to remain in the south and play semi-professional football.

It wasn't a good February for Rovers as our home game against Kingstonian turned out to be a nightmare. Ian McDonald, their coach, had been onto me regarding players, as they were struggling near the bottom of the table and needed a striker desperately. A couple of months earlier I'd let him have Ian Duerden, who couldn't get in our side and, Sod's Law, he came back to haunt us as is usual in football and scored one of the goals in our 2-0 defeat. Kevin McIntyre was sent off, so we had to play with ten men for much of the game. The crowd got onto me big time. They were chanting "Wignall out" amongst other things. The abuse was back to its 'best' and I even had to be escorted off the pitch. One fan threw his replica shirt at me and I threw straight back at him. Anne and Sally took some stick and Sally found the fact that people wanted to attack her father all a bit too much to take.

In the press John Ryan gave the abusers an ultimatum: if it didn't stop he would withdraw his financial support and the club would be shut down. He felt the same way as I did in as much as people were entitled to their opinion but outright abuse and intimidation was unacceptable. I had no intention of quitting so long as I had the support of the chairman and the board. The supporters were creating an atmosphere that was very difficult for the players on the pitch. Some of the lads were relieved to play away from home at times - Boston excluded, of course! I had never experienced anything like it before as either a player or a manager. At a couple of home games some tough-looking blokes came to the back of the see-through dugout and hammered on the perspex with their fists, and this was before the kick-off. The young subs used to crap themselves, but if they thought I peed a bit then they had to be joking. They were prats and I hoped their donkey died!

The dressing room was starting to adopt a siege mentality, which isn't a bad thing at times but a happy dressing room would have been preferable. I didn't want it to seem like a battle against our 'fans' as well as the visiting team. The opposition were all tough enough as it was. All that shite also gave the other side a massive boost!

The situation with Alan Lewer raised its head again. This time Joe Hoggins, our new chief executive, came to me and spelt out the problem: Alan's private life was a concern to the club. I was disappointed that he hadn't come clean to me previously but it was now out of my hands and the club had decided to dispense with his services. Joe and I called him into the office to give him the bad news. Alan still denied everything, which was embarrassing, as I had been told all the facts and knew that he was out on a limb. We made him an offer on his contract and after some wrangling we came to an agreement. It was a sad affair for everyone concerned really because Alan was an inoffensive man with a nice demeanour. Joe was reasonably new to the job but he didn't shirk his responsibility and dealt with the matter well. I had lost my assistant within the season, which wasn't ideal, so I decided to promote Dave Penney as he was the obvious choice and he was "more" than happy to take over the role.

We had a decent run of results towards the end of the season, the abuse eased off and we finished a disappointing ninth in the League. Compared with the previous season we definitely looked more likely to break into the top four of the division. Our major problem was scoring goals, especially away from home. Our general play was as good if not better than most teams in the division but it was goals that counted and our two main hopes, Alford and Halliday, hadn't produced.

My old mate Brian Talbot at Rushden and Diamonds had done a great job in overtaking Yeovil to win the championship. At one point Yeovil had looked the odds-on favourites. We took four points from the champions that season, which proved that on our day we could be up there with the best in that division.

There had been some good news in December, as the club had been given the green light to draw up plans for a new stadium just a mile from Belle Vue. If everything went to plan there was a possibility that the new ground could be in place for the 2002/03 season. Also, our reserves had been promoted in their first year and our youth team had finished top of their league. This was just how I liked it, as I wanted Doncaster Rovers as a whole to regain its credence as a football club. I wasn't there just to run the first eleven; I wanted every team in the club to be in the highest position possible within their leagues. That may sound like the bleeding obvious, but I knew a lot of managers who didn't give a monkey's about how the other teams did within their club.

John and Peter had backed me to the hilt all through the season and I was determined to get them to where they wanted to be. They even gave me a new contract, which ran for two years. My eyes had been opened to many things that first full season. In my opinion this job was the toughest in the division by far. The expectation levels were ridiculous but I couldn't change that. I felt that if I could cope with the abuse and hostility that I had already faced I could cope with anything in the future. My staff had all worked hard. Dave, Micky and Jon Bowden were not my men but they were in place and I thought that if results went well in the future I hopefully wouldn't have any problems.

It had been a very serious season but there were some lighter moments, for instance when John invited Anne and me to a Manchester United game one day. He was a season ticket holder; in fact I think he had about four as we all had a seat! We were invited up to John's house in Cheshire for the weekend. It was a fantastic place, with an indoor swimming pool and a beautiful Japanese garden. Before the game we had lunch at Old Trafford, where John had his own table that looked out over the stadium. It was tremendous. John loved to treat people and he was a great host. The game itself was a classic for Manchester United fans as they hammered Arsenal 6-1. It was one of the most one-sided premiership games I have ever seen. On that day some of the Arsenal lads threw in the towel. At the time I could only dream of managing a club as big as Arsenal or Manchester United. Thinking with my manager's head, I would have liked to be a fly on the wall in the Gunners' dressing room after the game. I know what I would have said, but I wonder what the Arsenal boss Arsene had to say to his lightweights that day?

John also organised a table for us at a celebrity charity auction that was also taking place at Old Trafford. It was a black tie do and John took us in his Bentley. When we pulled up, the paparazzi were everywhere, and as we went through the main doors I noticed Royle Family actor Ricky Tomlinson leaning against the wall outside having a sly fag! Typical of a Scouser, he asked Anne how she was doing as we walked past. His character Jim Royle in the TV series is the spitting image of my brother-in-law, whose name is also Jimmy! Some of his sayings are identical. Years before the programme was on the box, Jimmy used to say to my sister Lorraine, "Get us a cuppa cha, Lor, me mouth's as dry as Ghandi's flip-flop!" So we laughed when we heard the exact saying used in the script.

There were plenty of celebrities knocking about from soaps such as Coronation Street and Emmerdale, as well as several Manchester United players. At our table we had Steve Smith, the ex-England rugby union international, and his wife. He was a friend of John's and was another of his guests. Plenty of wine was flowing and Steve was partaking of the grapes quite liberally. He was a great laugh and we got on really well.

The auction started after our meal and all the punters were pretty well oiled, as the organisers had planned, so a few quid would definitely be changing hands. On each table there was a metal stand about two feet high bearing the table number and if guests wanted to make a bid for an item they would raise the stand. Steve was on great form entertaining us with rugby stories and generally being outrageous. Anne and I were in pleats but a couple of people on our table didn't see the funny side of some of his antics, which made me laugh even more. Carol Vorderman was the auctioneer and she did a good job, raising the bids on some of the items to between £5,000 and £10,000 at a time. She loved all the banter with all the Manchester United stars, who were readily putting their hands in their pockets.

Out of the blue and for reasons unknown to us, Steve Smith shouted out, "Who's giving Carol one these days?" I nearly choked on my Cabernet Sauvignon! It got even worse when some comedian at the back retorted, "Dwight Yorke"! I don't know if Carol herself heard the comments but a lot of people did and the conservative couple on our table didn't know what to do with themselves. Anne and I just stuffed our napkins in our mouths and then smiled nicely at people on the surrounding tables!

Steve's wife wanted to bid for a few items and kept raising the numbered stand, followed by Steve wrestling it off her, especially when really expensive items were involved. Most of the time she was just teasing him for a laugh and it all got a little boisterous. Finally Steve pulled the stand from her hand and threw it up the table. The quiet couple that were not overly impressed with the lively atmosphere were sitting opposite him and it bonked the wife right on the head! That was it, I nearly wet myself and I had to turn away, and Anne almost suffered a coronary stifling her laughter with the napkin! Steve got up and went over to the couple to offer his apologises. You could tell that the husband was dying to give Steve a tongue-lashing but had thought better of it; after all, Steve was an ex-rugby player and not exactly a pencil-neck pushover. Obviously Steve had no intention of hurting anyone when he lobbed the stand, it was just high jinks with about four bottles of red wine mixed in!

It was a fantastic evening and one of our fonder memories of my Doncaster reign.

The season had come to an end and not before time. It had been an eventful few months and definitely not for the faint-hearted. We had fallen short of what everyone would have liked, but John and the board had shown great faith in me. We needed to add to our squad again and show some players the door. I didn't shirk putting my decisions into action and released Simon Shaw, Mark Barnard, Mark Atkins, Carl Alford and Dean Walling. I felt particularly sorry for Carl, as he had worked so hard to get his weight down and improve his fitness. It was unbelievable that his goalscoring ability had dried up after all his success in previous seasons. He finally signed for one of our main rivals, Yeovil, but he didn't hit the heady heights of his 25 goals in a season again.

In readiness for our new season, 2001/02, I added some very good players to the squad. In came Kevin Sandwith, a left back from Telford; Paul Carden, a midfielder from Chester; and Gareth Owen, another midfield player from Wrexham, who was an ex-Welsh B international as well as having played for the Under 21s some years earlier. I also took a chance on Francis Tierney, who had lost his way a little, as he could play wide on either flank, and big Mark Sale left Rushden to come to us. Mark had done exceptionally well for me at Colchester and at 6 feet 5 inches tall he would be a handful for anyone. You could also call Dean Barrick a new signing, as he came to us late the previous season from Bury and had done well at left back. My ace in the pack was Paul Barnes, or Barnsy, a very experienced centre forward who in my opinion would definitely score goals on a regular basis in the Conference.

We were raring to go and I was confident that the squad was even stronger with more quality than the previous season. Our pre-season went okay and all the new players had appeared to settle reasonably quickly. Joe Hoggins, the chief executive, had also settled in and we got on very well. Joe lived in Northamptonshire and was commuting backwards and forwards at weekends, which wasn't easy for him.

Even though I had been at the club for a year by now and had settled in nicely at Bawtry, I still felt that not everybody involved with the club had accepted me. I had some problems with a man called Dave Parker, who was the club's 'media manager', whatever that was. He lived in the Halifax area, so I didn't see a lot of him. However, when I had first arrived the Snodins had told me to keep my eye out as they'd had a few ups and downs with him. My immediate reaction was to take note of the advice, but at the same time I couldn't understand why any manager would have problems with their own club media manager. However, I soon found out, as stories were escaping from inside the club to the new Non-League Paper. Not all of them were positive and the paper chose to latch on to the more negative issues surrounding Doncaster Rovers. I'm not suggesting that all the reports were untrue but some items were not for public consumption, especially if they were blown out of proportion and created any negativity for the club.

I spoke to Colin Maffam, who worked for the Non-League Paper and he confirmed that many of the stories had come from within the club but declined to reveal the source. You hardly had to be a genius to work out the origin of the information. I spoke to John and Peter about the problem and they said they would address it, but for one reason or another nothing changed. I was disappointed with the outcome, as it was difficult enough to run the team without a national paper stirring things up. The rag was published each Sunday and it was great for the lower levels of football, but during the time that I was with Doncaster Rovers I could probably count on one hand the number of positive articles that were printed regarding the club.

I was very confident about our new campaign after our showing in pre-season. The only downer was an injury picked up by Barnsy. We played a strong Manchester United eleven in late July and gave them a hell of a game, drawing 2-2 and putting a smile on the supporters' faces. My front two on the day were Neil Campbell and Paul Barnes, who gave centre backs John O'Shea and David May a torrid time. Just before half-time a chance fell to Barnsy in the United box. He lashed at the ball at the same time as David May launched himself into the tackle to block the shot. Barnsy kicked the bottom of May's boot and went down clutching his foot. Maybe it was experience on my part, but I just knew that he was hurt and it wasn't just a knock. I was proved right eventually, as basically that injury ruined his season! He had it scanned and although it originally highlighted nothing serious he was still finding it difficult to twist and turn at match pace several weeks later. A second scan revealed some sort of stress fracture, which meant that he needed more time for the injury to heal. It was a nightmare scenario for him and for the club, as we missed his goals desperately.

We had entered a pre-season competition in the north-east in early August and we were all set to go when something happened that would change our life as a family. The day before our departure I had got out of bed at about 8 a.m. as usual and I was in the en-suite bathroom of our bedroom having a shave. The door was open and I was talking to Anne, who was sitting on the edge of the bed. I was rambling on about something and nothing and she was answering me when suddenly it went quiet and I heard a thump on the bed. I poked my head around the door to see Anne lying flat on her back looking up at the ceiling. She said anxiously, "There's something wrong. I felt something go in my head. Oh my God! Everything is moving all over the place!"

I wasn't sure if she was joking at first, so I walked over to her and asked if she was okay. She didn't answer me properly and then I could see that she was struggling and couldn't sit up. I went very cold and didn't know what to do; it was as if everything had gone into slow motion.

Anne started to panic a little, as she seemed to be losing control in some way. I walked around the bed a couple of times like an idiot before deciding that I had better phone an ambulance. Sally had woken up by now and wanted to know what was happening to her mum. I tried to reassure her and, although she was only eleven, she appeared to stay calm as events unfolded and she held her mum's hand. The ambulance arrived within 15 minutes, during which time Anne hadn't moved off the bed. She had the mother and father of all headaches and was lying as still as she could. I let in the two paramedics, a man and a woman, and tried to explain to them what had happened as they walked up the stairs. The woman appeared to recognise me and then went on about how lovely our house was. I was trying to be polite but I felt like saying, "F*** the house, just deal with my wife, she might be dying!" The paramedics secured Anne in one of those upright chairs and carried her down the stairs, out of the house and into the back of the ambulance. She was in agony, her skin looked a pale putty colour and her lovely brown eyes had a look of panic in them as she looked at me trussed up in the chair. She was still looking at me as they closed the back doors of the vehicle.

Sally saw exactly what I saw and started to cry as she nestled up against me on our front drive. I reassured her again as we went back indoors. It was almost surreal and my priority was to follow that ambulance to the hospital. Everything regarding my job just went out of my mind. My first priority was to find someone to look after Sally, so I phoned a friend who lived close by and she came to help me out. I got myself to the hospital, which was about nine miles away, and when I arrived Anne was still sat upright in a wheelchair. She couldn't focus or think straight and had a horrendous headache. She also looked like shit!

I asked a nurse what she thought was wrong with Anne, but she couldn't give me a straight answer. After a while they wheeled her downstairs to a small room where a young male nurse checked her vital signs: blood pressure, heart rate, etc.

When the nurse had finished and Anne was just propped up like a corpse, he said, "You can take her home and come back tomorrow if you like."

I replied, "What did you say?"

He repeated his response and so I retorted, "Are you taking the piss? My wife can't even stand up; in fact she can't even move her head. Can we see a doctor now please?"

The colour drained from his face pretty quickly because I think he thought I was going to slap him one!

"Oh, we had better get her back upstairs then," he responded.

"I think that's a better idea, mate!" I said sarcastically.

That didn't bode well and my worry turned to anger, as they appeared to be dithering about what to do with Anne. There was no neurological ward at Doncaster Hospital at that time. Eventually they decided to put her on a ward in a private room, as any noise or light of any kind troubled her terribly. I sat with her and all she kept saying to me was, "Get me out of here. Please get me out of here!"

For maybe the first time in my life I felt absolutely helpless. I know that a lot of people say that they would swap places with a loved one who is ill or worse, and at that moment I would have done anything to change places with her and take her pain away. I just wanted that scared, agonised look on her face to go away. It was like a bad dream for us all.

I eventually had to leave Anne to sort out a few things. I phoned the boys to let them know what had happened and Thomas travelled up the A1 the next day, which was a real boost for Anne. Jack's football commitments meant that he wasn't able to come immediately but I reassured him that I would ring him daily. I then phoned Dave Penney at the club to let him know that I wouldn't be making the journey up to the north-east on the following day. I told him to carry on as we had planned and keep me informed of the team's progress or if there were any problems. I also phoned Joan, Anne's mum, who kindly came over from North Wales to help look after Sally for us. We had some good friends in and around Bawtry and they were a fantastic help to us as well.

The doctors at the hospital were still a little sketchy in terms of what exactly was wrong with Anne, but one specialist was quite forthright and said that her symptoms were a classical indication of a brain bleed. All I knew was that she was in a terrible state and I wanted something done for her. The following day they took her down for an MRI and a CT scan. The results confirmed that she has what is called a cavernoma, meaning a malformation of blood vessels within the brain. It had haemorrhaged and that was why she was in such a bad way. I asked if it was life-threatening and they were somewhat non-committal. They said they would be keeping her in for the foreseeable future, so I had to get myself organised.

My head was all over the place and I needed to speak to the chairman, John. I telephone him and he was fantastic as usual and told me to take as much time off as I needed. I told him that wouldn't be necessary as Anne was staying in hospital and that as long as I could get to see her each day I would still turn in to work. John and Peter both sent gorgeous bouquets of flowers to the hospital for Anne. John's were so exotic that some of the nurses came into her room just to admire them. There were even jewels woven into the arrangement. The club also sent her a floral gift on behalf of all the playing staff.

I decided that I would go to see Anne first thing each day before training and then return again in the afternoon after training. I would then go home to have dinner with Sally before taking her to see her mum in the evening. I was determined not to miss any training sessions or games. This wasn't just my decision; Anne insisted that I carry on as normal at the club. It was a hectic time and, thinking back, I was probably wandering around in a bit of a daze. I was so worried about Anne's health but I was trying not to show it to the players and staff. I expect the players were walking on eggshells for a few weeks, but I like to think that I was totally professional in my approach to everything at the club during that time. Joe Hoggins was fantastic; he didn't bother me with trivial matters, he just dealt with them.

I was still looking forward to a successful season and thought that my luck had to change at some point, but there was to be another sad twist to the tale. My old mate Mick Hughes, whom I knew when I was at Doncaster in the early seventies, went to bed one afternoon for a nap and passed away in his sleep. He wasn't an old man and was looking forward to his retirement with his lovely wife Eleanor. I couldn't believe it and I was gutted. He had been to our house for dinner only a few months earlier with Pat and Walter Elwiss. I had to tell Anne, which didn't go down well at all as she thought a lot of Mick and Eleanor.

What was on the agenda next, I wondered? If I only knew!

The first game of the season was at Farnborough Town, which was near to my old stamping ground. I wasn't exactly flavour of the month there because of my connections with their bitter rivals Aldershot. Farnborough's manager, Graham Westley, was a strange kettle of fish as he was forever making outrageous predictions and quotes in the press. He also had a habit of talking out of his bottom on the touchline from what I had heard. The combination of all these factors was like a red rag to a bull for me. I loved all that stuff because it livened up the fixture. I would have preferred to play in it, but I was only a few years away from a Zimmer frame so I had to settle for the banter on the sideline.

The changing rooms entrance, which led out onto the pitch, was a little tight so you had to squeeze past anyone else standing in the corridor, and that is exactly what Westley did as our lads filed into the away dressing room. When they walked past him he said, "No point turning up today, you're not going to get anything here." Tim Ryan came and told me this and as he could be a bit of a rum lad at times he didn't exactly mince his words: "Who is that knob in the tunnel?" That was the perfect wind-up for us and it helped with my pre-match talk no end. We won the game 1-0 and basically put him and his team in their place. It was a good start and I had learnt something else that day: how not to shout stupid things from the touchline! And, yes, Tim was right: Westley WAS a knob!

After four weeks into the season we were sitting third in the division with ten points from five games. As usual I felt that we could have had more points if we had taken our chances. We were a decent side but still lacked the cutting edge that Barnsy might have given us.

I had a phone call from Brian Talbot at Rushden to say that his top striker, Justin Jackson, was available. I spoke to John and he said that he was interested in buying him. Justin had been the top striker for Rushden the previous season and his pace and goalscoring ability were admired throughout the non-League. Joe Hoggins set up a meeting with Justin and his agent at a hotel a few miles down the A1. Joe intended to liaise with John over the phone regarding Justin's financial package. The two clubs had apparently agreed a fee for his services estimated at £100,000. To be honest I was thrilled to get someone with his ability but I had reservations about the figures involved. The meeting seemed to go on forever before we got down to the nitty-gritty of wonga. Justin left all that to his agent, a scenario with which I was never that comfortable. I preferred to sit down with a player face to face and discuss his contract. Justin, however, didn't even stay in the room, insisting on going outside while an agreement was reached. Joe did a lot of the talking and I must admit when I heard the salary that he had been earning at Rushden I cringed inside. I was not being disrespectful to the lad but it did seem excessive for that level of football. Considering what my players at Colchester had been earning a few years earlier in the second division, it was outrageous. I was starting to feel that I should have pulled the plug on the whole idea but it had gone too far. Joe spoke to John on the phone and the deal was done; the chairman had come up with the finances again. I was almost speechless and just hoped that Justin would produce the goods in return. I felt that if he did we would take some beating but if he didn't we would be 'also rans' once again. Justin appeared quite a shy or nervous sort of lad and not a bit like I had imagined after seeing him play. There would be big pressure coming his way.

Anne had not improved much but I was getting in to see her as often as possible. I even managed to sneak in very late one night after an away game. The place was deserted and I just took a chance. I was wearing a suit so perhaps anyone who saw me thought I was staff! When I got to her room I poked my head around the corner. She was laid on her side with her eyes wide open looking straight at me. She said, "I knew it was you. I can tell that stride anywhere. I heard your footsteps from the entrance of the ward." She was feeling very lonely and emotional and so even if I only got in to see her for a few minutes it gave her a lift.

Anne was having episodes when her body would shake uncontrollably and the doctors recommended that she have a lumbar puncture, which would mean transporting her to Sheffield Hallamshire Hospital where there was a neurological team. Anne's physiotherapist called to tell me that they were going to send her in a taxi on her own for the procedure and she thought it wise that I discussed it with the nursing staff. I couldn't believe what I was hearing and I went straight over to the hospital to speak to the nurse in charge. I told him there was no way that my wife was getting in a taxi on her own to travel to Sheffield for a lumbar puncture! For a start, she couldn't yet walk more than the few yards she needed for her en-suite toilet, she had no balance or co-ordination, she was having major problems with the shaking episodes and she was also distressed. I was steaming. I queried why she wasn't going in an ambulance and the nurse insisted that there were none available at that time, hence the taxi. I became quite irate at this point and he finally admitted that he hadn't read her notes properly and had misjudged Anne's predicament. He studied her records and suggested that a nurse should travel with Anne in the taxi. It was still a crap idea as far as I was concerned but I had little choice. The lumbar puncture had been booked and I didn't want her to miss it. The procedure isn't very pleasant, as it involves drawing off some spinal fluid from the lumbar region and this actually causes the brain to drop slightly, resulting in the headache of all headaches afterwards.

It really was like comic cuts in the hospital at times and nobody ever actually took me to one side to explain exactly what was happening to Anne apart from the initial brain haemorrhage.

On the day of the transfer Anne was taken down to the main entrance and a nurse helped her into the cab and accompanied her on the 15-mile journey to Sheffield. When they got there, the nurse realised that she had left Anne's notes on a chair in the main entrance of Doncaster Hospital! Could it have got any worse?!

The outcome of all the tests that Anne had sadly revealed that she had epilepsy, which had been triggered by the haemorrhage. It was decided that Hallamshire Hospital would take over her care when she was well enough to be discharged from Doncaster and an appointment was made to see a surgeon about the cavernoma. While she was still in hospital she had a few other visitors, including Mick Elwiss's parents, Pat and Walter, and Eleanor Hughes, which was of great comfort to her.

Anne was discharged from hospital at the end of the first week in

September and she continued to have physiotherapy at home. She needed it, as she couldn't even walk up the stairs. Her brain had to retrain itself to do the most menial of tasks and it was going to be a long haul, but Anne was really relieved to be out of hospital and I was so chuffed when I went to pick her up!

Thankfully I didn't really have many problems with my own health over the years that we were in Doncaster, but during the first 12 months I did contract a virus that hit me pretty hard. I thought I had the flu at first but it developed into something worse. One of the by-products was a urine infection, which was the most painful experience you could imagine. It was like peeing razor blades, hot chilli sauce or barbed wire! It was horrendous and something that I wouldn't like to go through again. I also contracted food poisoning for the first time in my life when Anne, the kids and I went for dinner at a local hotel for Sunday lunch. I chose the salmon, which was accompanied with a sauce. I wished I'd chosen the bloody pork afterwards! When I was eating it I noticed that the some parts of the sauce were a little on the cold side, so fortunately I didn't eat it all. That evening my stomach was in a terrible way. Although I wasn't sick I had to run the ten yards to the loo in record time to prevent an accident. Over the next few days the whole world fell out of my bottom and the barbed wire and chilli sauce feeling that I'd had with my urine infection had taken up residence in my bum and I lost a load of weight. I suppose it made a change from doing the 12-minute runs each day after training to keep myself in shape! I did see the doctor, of course, who noted where and what I had eaten over the previous 24 hours and took samples, which confirmed food poisoning. The doc suspected that it probably was that bit of 'Lillian Gish' that had done the damage!

On the pitch we were playing some excellent football, but once again another striker was finding it very difficult to reproduce his goalscoring achievements at previous clubs. Justin was finding it hard as he was picking up niggling injuries that didn't help and his confidence was wafer thin at times. The team had turned the tables on our home and away results. In the previous season we had struggled to get the results right away from home whereas this term we had only lost one in ten games away from Belle Vue by November. At home we had won three, drawn three and lost three whereas at the same point the previous year we had won six, drawn one and lost two.

There was no obvious reason for this but it looked as though the players were feeling the pressure of playing at home. The expectations of the season were affecting the players more than I had hoped.

The whole atmosphere at the club changed quite suddenly. Trevor Milton joined the board from Scarborough. He had been on the board there, so he was reasonably experienced at running a football club at the lower levels of the Football League and the Conference. He came over as a very amiable sort of chap. He was getting on a bit but he still appeared to have an enthusiasm for the job. John had decided to step aside for his own reasons, and I wasn't totally privy to these, and as far as I understood Trevor was our new chairman. I hadn't seen Peter Wetzel for some time but he was still involved as far as I was aware.

Trevor told me a few stories about Scarborough's struggles. One related to a past manager called Mick Wadsworth, who had been on his way out when Colchester approached them regarding his availability for taking over at Layer Road. Trevor was delighted with the compensation package that Colchester offered for his services; in other words, they snatched Colchester's hands off! Colchester had done the job for them and they had also received some dosh!

We were not going to win the division unless we put together a fantastic run of results, which was possible but not likely. The squad was very strong and we had only lost four games out of 20 by November. However, we just couldn't score enough goals to turn our draws into victories. I was at a loss as to why, over the one and a half seasons, four top strikers had not managed to score ten goals between them. Alford, Halliday, Jackson and Barnes were excellent at that level but it didn't happen for one reason or another. We dominated many games, so it wasn't as if they were in a struggling side. We also passed the ball around quite well and created good chances in most matches. We had to spread our goals around the team, with Campbell and Patterson contributing well.

After one home game Trevor came into my office to speak to Dave Penney and me. He sat down and the first thing that he said was, "John Ryan isn't very happy with you, Steve." I was surprised as John hadn't been at the game, but Trevor had apparently spoken to him to give him the low-down.

"Why is that, Mr Chairman?" I asked.

"Because you said to me after the game that John wouldn't give you more money for some better players," came back the reply.

Dave and I couldn't believe our ears. I hadn't said anything of the sort to Trevor. What I had said, and Dave was present at the time, was, "Some of these players are not good enough under this pressure and I may have to change a few." We had underperformed again at home and I was being honest with the chairman. I hadn't once mentioned money or John!

Dave Penney actually stated to Trevor, "That's a lie, Trevor. He didn't say that!"

I was steaming and also called into question his integrity. Trevor got the old red face on and tried to justify the comments that he had relayed to John. I wasn't happy and told Trevor that he was out of order and that I would speak to John myself. Trevor left the office with a flea in his ear and Dave looked at me in disbelief. I didn't say much more about it to him, as I was deeply concerned about my future from that moment on. The instant someone of any standing at a football club starts telling porkies about you, then alarm bells start to ring. I tried to contact John as soon as possible but couldn't get hold of him for a few days. When I did eventually speak with him, he appeared to be okay after I explained what was actually said. However, he seemed to want to skirt the issue and change the subject. I feared that the damage might already have been done.

Peter Wetzel put in an appearance the following week and I collared him to explain everything. Peter knew that I was straight down the line and his words to me were, "This seems to be the start of a witch-hunt!" He wasn't happy and said that he would look into it. I didn't see much of Peter again after that.

Trevor came to me and said that the finances at the club were under pressure and we would have to trim the wage bill by letting a few of the players go. Colin Hawkins was sold back to an Irish club and I was informed after the event. I didn't have too much of a problem with that, as Colin had struggled and hadn't lived up to his billing. He wasn't one of my signings and so I had a pretty clear conscience on that one. That had been a first for me, as even though the deal sat well with me I had wanted to be involved and had been excluded. There didn't appear to be any immediate threat to my job but something wasn't right.

The team were playing okay and we did well against Scunthorpe in the FA Cup at home, outplaying them for large periods of the game. They pipped us 3-2 but we had proved that we could compete with teams in the Football League. It was getting out of the bloody Conference that was the problem! The word was that the play-offs would be put into place the following season. That would transform the division and it would also provide a little more security for the managers of the teams competing at the top end of the table. Finishing in the top four and reaching the play-offs would be seen as an achievement. With a second team being promoted with the champions it would invigorate many fixtures right up to the last day of the season.

Unfortunately I was not going to get that chance! The culling of the squad went ahead, with Paul Carden leaving along with Barry Miller. Barry Richardson was also targeted around that time. I wasn't sure where it was all leading but it didn't look good. I was determined not to miss any training sessions at all, as I hadn't when Anne had been in hospital for those four weeks or so. She was still not very well but I could leave her at home for a few hours at a time and the physiotherapist from the hospital would pop in to see her for her rehabilitation. I didn't tell Anne too much about what was going on, as she needed to avoid any sort of stress or upset at any cost. Even though she wasn't great she would have sussed it all out, so I kept the details to myself.

There was already another sadness for the Wignall household to cope with that winter when our dog Ralph became ill and passed away. He had enjoyed a very happy 16½ years as part of our family and was a well-loved, loyal dog.

Going into December the situation appeared to deteriorate. The results were decent but everything was being cut back. After one home game I walked into the boardroom and to my surprise Anne and Sally were sitting there. Anne hadn't been to a game since her illness; in fact she had not been out on her own at all. Her physio had said that it would be okay for her to get a bus with our daughter so that she could go to her dance class. Unfortunately, the return bus was full, so they had decided to walk to Belle Vue and wait for me until after the match. Anne looked terrible, as her exertions had obviously taken a lot out of her. It was freezing and she had walked a fair way from the bus stop. I didn't wait around too long and got them both into the car and back home. When we got back Anne asked me what was going on, so I asked her what she meant. "When Sally and I walked into that boardroom you could almost hear a pin drop! They seemed more than surprised to see me," she explained. "And only John Ryan's partner came over to enquire as to how I was. Trevor Milton commented that I didn't look very well at all."

That was just about it for me and I knew my days were numbered but I wasn't sure why and I wasn't sure when. I decided to go and see John at his offices in Cheshire, although I wasn't certain what I was going to say to him. He had backed me all the way in the past but now there seemed to have been a total shift in the way that the club was being run. John was his usual welcoming self but it seemed as if the spark had gone from him. We didn't really talk candidly about the situation and I presumed that I might be the next casualty. I still had 18 months left on my contract, which I did mention and John said that he was well aware of that. I didn't at any point suggest that I would resign or anything of that nature; I didn't need to, as the script had already been written.

I left feeling sad but nothing specific or concrete had been settled. John gave me a bottle of champagne and shook my hand as I went. He was always giving me gifts, as he was one of the most generous men I have ever met. As I shook his hand and looked at him I knew that it might be the last time I would see him for some time, if ever. I wasn't far wrong either, as the last time I did meet him was when I was manager of Southend a couple of seasons later. My mind was all over the place. On the one hand, I felt secure in the knowledge that I had a contract but, on the other, many of the noises coming from the club were not positive, especially on the financial front. I was desperate to stay in the job but I knew that wasn't on the agenda at present.

I went with Anne to see the neurosurgeon in Sheffield and we were hopeful that he would give her some positive news about her cavernoma. Unfortunately, however, the news wasn't good. He said that they couldn't operate to remove it because of its position in the brain and the best course of action would be to monitor it regularly for further bleeds or changes and control the seizures with drugs. It was a bitter blow for her. She could no longer work as a nursery teacher and she would also lose her driving licence.

When she came out of his consulting room she was devastated at the news; we both were. It felt as if there was no way out of that crappy situation. She was taking so many drugs for her epilepsy every day.

Even though my thoughts were with my wife, I didn't stop doing my job to the best of my ability and the team did well, scoring eight goals in my last two games in charge against Scarborough and Leigh RMI.

I gave the players a Wednesday off in early January, as a couple of games had been postponed and we had been training reasonably hard. I took the opportunity to take Anne on her first shopping trip in about five months and we drove down the A1 to a shopping centre. This was a big event for her with so many people about and the noise and general movement gave her major problems. We did have a laugh as well though, especially when her leg just would not step onto the escalator as it was moving and she remained frozen at the bottom with me trying to cajole her into some sort of manoeuvre! It was the first time in many weeks that I had heard her giggle and it was music to my ears even though her difficulty was tragic to me deep down. Luckily, because she found it hard to get her credit cards out of her handbag, we didn't spend anything! We just had a cup of coffee in the cafe upstairs as a reward for finally negotiating the escalator!

As we were leaving the store my mobile rang and it was Joe Hoggins. He cut straight to the chase: "You had better come in immediately, Steve." I didn't labour the point and told Anne that I had to go to a meeting. After dropping Anne off at home I drove to the ground. Joe assured me that Trevor wanted to see us both. He didn't have to say any more and I didn't say anything to him.

Trevor came in and sat down and then he looked at me and said, "You've already sorted everything out with John Ryan."

I replied, "No I haven't, Trevor. I don't know what you mean."

"Well that's what I've been told," he said. "Anyway, the club can't afford to pay you. You're both having your contracts terminated."

Joe had not long since signed a long-term deal and bought a house. We were both speechless. That was about it really and we were to leave as soon as possible! But had we been sacked or had we been made redundant? We weren't sure, but in reality was there a difference?

I spoke to all the players the following day and remained reasonably calm as I shook their hands. In fact I even had a smile on my face as I had no intention of showing how I really felt. There was no point kicking and screaming, as the decision had been made and I couldn't change that. What I did do was ask the LMA (League Managers' Association) to assist in sorting out my contract with the club.

I spoke to Anne at length and even with her problems she was still very philosophical about it all. She thought that I had done my best and that luck had not been on my side over the 18 months. She had a point I suppose. We had only been in our house for less than 18 months too and Sally had been in secondary school for only four, so the thought of moving again wasn't pleasant. Logically it would have been prudent for us to stay where we were and for me to look for another job in football around the Yorkshire area, and we did consider that option. However, after a second appointment with the consultant in Sheffield we decided that it would be better to move nearer London and its National Hospital for Neurology and Neurosurgery, which apparently offered the best facilities in the country. As Anne's health was paramount and we still had our house in Colchester, moving back there seemed the best course of action.

It was tough on Sally again but she understood. Even though she had made some good friends in the Doncaster area, she also had lots of old friends that she could link up with again in Essex. In addition, she would be able to see more of her brothers and we would be more of a family again. So, although we loved our house in Bawtry, we had to sell it. We put it on the market with a local estate agent but before they'd had chance to put the sale board up a lady knocked on the door and asked if she could buy it! We couldn't believe it when she said that she was representing her father and that she only lived at the rear of our property. She had admired our house for years and her father was going to move into it so that he could be near to her. The lady didn't quibble over the cost and gave the full asking price, so the deal was done. I had to get my skates on as I had about six weeks to get our other house ready for our arrival.

I kept my hand in by going to games at Scunthorpe and Sheffield, as it was hard for me to switch off completely. Just after I left Doncaster, a local paper phoned me up for a statement regarding my departure. I was reluctant to say too much as words can be taken out of context at times. The club had said that Joe and I had left because of financial problems or cutbacks at the club. What I did say was that I had been sacked, as there was no other way of saying it because I wasn't in my office at that moment and I hadn't asked to leave. When the newspaper article was published I received a phone call from Trevor saying that he wasn't pleased with my comments, as I hadn't been sacked. I told him that I had and that I had done nothing wrong at any time. His reply to that was, "I'm sure we can find something"! I went ballistic with him and suggested that he should be careful what he said or suggested.

That left a really nasty taste in my mouth. I couldn't grasp what his problem was with the newspaper article. He couldn't have it both ways. Relieving me of my position and then not wanting to take responsibility for it wasn't on. The impression that they had given me was that the club was on the back foot and going backwards, yet they were reasonably close to securing permission to go ahead with the new ground. I didn't get it at all and something wasn't right, but I was out of it. The LMA sorted out the finances, for which I was grateful.

Joe Hoggins was very disappointed after committing himself to the club. He told me that he'd had a few strange phone calls a few weeks before leaving. Some of them had told him to pack his bags and get himself down the road to Northampton. He hadn't taken much notice at the time, but bearing in mind that he was the chief executive this was all very odd. It was as if someone knew that he was on his way out, but why that was I would never know.

I had to get myself up and down the A1 over the coming weeks to sort out our bungalow in Colchester. It needed complete redecoration after Jack and Andy's 18-month occupation. I couldn't leave Anne overnight because of her seizures, so I had to make the three-hour journey first thing in the morning, do whatever work was necessary and then drive back in the evening. I did this for about a week, which left me absolutely knackered! I eventually found a local decorator who was willing to do the work immediately and set him on to do the necessary work on the whole of the inside of the property. However, I still had to travel down a couple of times a week to check on progress.

To this day Anne and I miss our place in Bawtry. We had a good life there until the circumstances changed dramatically, but it was totally out of our hands. What an 18 months! More strange and tragic things happened in that short time than in any other period in our lives. I can recall back in the early seventies, as an impressionable 17-year-old, having a conversation with good old Jackie Bestall. He used to tell me some weird and wonderful stories about Donny Rovers and Belle Vue. One of them was that there was an old gypsy curse on the ground that went back years! I wonder ...?

We left Bawtry and settled into our bungalow and Anne managed to place Sally in St Benedict's College where Thomas and Jack had been pupils. Mr Whelan, the principal, was very understanding about our situation and because of our family connections he found room for her. She later went on to become head girl at the college, which was one hell of an achievement considering her upheavals and experiences during the early parts of her education.

I found myself deliberately not looking for Doncaster's results in the papers to begin with, as I couldn't bring myself to think about what was going on there. Eventually I did succumb, however, because I had started to do some scouting again. I always listened to the sports results on the radio in the car on the way home from games and on one particular Saturday a piece about Rovers came on. It mentioned that Dave Penney and Mickey Walker had been given new contracts as manager and assistant respectively. Also the new stadium had been given the go-ahead.

I wasn't really surprised by what I heard, but I was gutted that I wouldn't be part of it all. I spoke on the phone to a few friends in Doncaster and they told me that I had been a dead man walking for longer than I had thought. I wondered if any of my staff knew that. It would have been nice if one of them had tipped me the wink; after all, I had been as loyal as I could have been to them.

I must have had my eye off the ball more than I thought while my wife was ill.

CHAPTER 12

YOU DO RANT RON RON, YOU DO RANT RON!

I was out of work again but for a different reason. I had been sacked for the first time in my life. I hadn't even been given a free transfer in my 20 years as a player.

Trevor Milton had begged to differ as to the reasons for my departure from Doncaster, but whatever the wording I had still been relieved of my position!

We were glad to be back in Colchester even though we had been happy in Yorkshire. We could see Thomas and Jack more often and Sally was back with all her friends and returned to her old ballet school, Showcase Dance Academy. Anne's health was still a major problem but at least we could travel to London on a regular basis without too much hassle.

I was doing some part-time scouting for an old mate of mine, Ray Train, at Middlesbrough, which sometimes took me on scouting missions to Colchester. I also worked for BBC Essex Radio, doing assessments with Neil Kelly on the commentary. I really enjoyed the radio work and it gave me an insight into the other side of football. I tried to be impartial but my association with Colchester United probably showed on occasions! If I just fancied going to a home game at Layer Road totally independently, then I would phone up and they were very accommodating. They would provide me with two seats in the directors' box if I wanted them. Whenever I attended home matches everyone was always very nice to me, from the man on the gate to Mr Heard the chairman. It was a very friendly club and that is how I had always remembered it as a player and as a manager.

However, one Friday when I phoned up as usual to ask for a ticket for the Saturday match I was informed that there was no room in the directors' box but I could sit in the stand with the supporters. On the face of it there was nothing wrong with my sitting in the stand, but I was a little confused as to why the directors' box would be full. After all, it wasn't a big game with a full house expected. I thanked the ticket office and said that I would make my own arrangements.

I telephoned Mr Heard and he was his usual polite self. In fact he invited me as his guest, which was very kind of him. When I went to the game and sat down at the back of the directors' box with Mr Heard I counted probably a dozen or so empty seats in the box, which was pretty confusing seeing as I had been told the day before that there was no room. I didn't make a big thing of it, enjoyed the match and thanked Peter Heard for the invitation. I was never invited to Layer Road again, and approximately six years elapsed before I was invited to another match. Although I have worked for the radio, I have never phoned up to ask for a ticket, as I wasn't prepared to request something that the club didn't want me to have. Even after I had left Southend and the new ground at Cuckoo Farm was developed, I wasn't invited to anything concerning the old club.

The last game at Layer Road was a very emotional affair for many people. I would have loved to attend, especially after being a player there for seven years and manager for four. As for the new stadium, I had not been and had received no contact from anyone at all until a call that came totally out of the blue. At the end of November 2008 my old friend John Schultz got in touch and invited Anne and me to a game in December as one of the past legends of the club. We were also asked to attend a meal before the game, which was a pleasant surprise. We had a wonderful time and John was the perfect host. We met many old friends, including Peter Heard, Peter Powell and John Worsp. I remember when I was still manager of Colchester United, after we had won at Wembley, I was speaking to Peter Powell at a board meeting about the possibility of a new ground, which was exciting for everyone even as long a go as that, and he said to me in jest, "Maybe they will name a room after you, Steve!" I laughed and said, "I doubt it!" But I wasn't far off, was I? However, having lived in the Colchester area with my family for over 30 years, I found it quite sad that I'd had no contact from the club until John's call. Just before the arrangements were made for our visit to the new stadium we saw on the news that in November Marie Partner had left the club as chief executive.

The last six months of 2002 went quickly and it was my intention to get back into the game as soon as possible. Anne was still finding life difficult, as she wasn't permitted to drive and had to make frequent trips to London, so I had certain responsibilities regarding Sally in regard to school and her dancing, etc. Once again, Anne was incredibly supportive and encouraged me to apply for jobs in football. Our trips backwards and forwards to the hospital weren't really reaping any benefits, as the doctors couldn't quite put their finger on Anne's problems, which had been going on for over a year now. However, she told me that she thought I had unfinished business in football and that I should go for it again.

I did just that and applied for the vacant Southend United position, as I thought perhaps it might be second time lucky. Rob Newman had just left and the chairman, Ron Martin, had brought in Stewart Robson as coach, so he took over as caretaker manager. I didn't really know Rob but I had played against him a couple of times. I decided to phone him to try to find out the situation at the club. The conversation could have gone one of two ways. He could have told me to bog off and tap into someone else or he could have been very helpful and honest in his assessment of matters. I am glad to say that his reaction was the latter of the two. Although he was gutted at the way things had gone and he didn't want to give me many details, he did give me the low-down on the players in the squad. He also told me a little about Ron and Stewart. He was quite rightly reticent about saying too much to me, as he didn't really know me, and I thanked him for his time and his opinion.

My interview went well and Ron Martin came over as very professional and forthright. Geoffrey King, the deputy chairman, appeared to be a very nice man and straight away I saw him as a calming influence on Ron. The remainder of the board didn't have a great deal to say and it was quite obvious to me who were the main men.

I didn't know the identities of the other candidates, except for one: Steve Whitton. He was in for the job after leaving Colchester. I had bumped into Witts at one of Southend's games and we actually sat together and watched the match. We didn't discuss the vacant position, as there was no need: we both knew the score!

For reasons unknown, Ron didn't make a decision for some weeks, which gave the incoming manager even less time to assess the squad and act accordingly. I don't know why he waited for so long, but perhaps he was giving Stewart a shot at it to see if he was suitable. I think that Stewart wanted the job but his experience in management was limited. Eventually, however, I was offered the job and I was delighted, as I felt that it was a great opportunity to progress at a good club, with a big fan base for that level. The club had been in free fall for a few years and the downward spiral needed to be stopped as soon as possible and turned around. It was going to be a huge task, as the playing squad was poor and wholesale changes were needed. By the time I was appointed it was mid-April and so there were only four games left, leaving me limited time to look at all aspects within the club. On top of that, once again I was going into a new club without any of my own staff. I obviously wasn't over keen on the situation, but it was made quite clear to me that Stewart Robson was already installed as the coach. If I had demanded that I bring in my own man then I wouldn't have landed the job.

I had already phoned around various people that I could trust and that might have some useful information on the club and they had clued me in as to what was going on behind the scenes even before I went for the interview. The feedback that I received was that the place was in a bit of a mess on the playing side. The people upstairs were getting things together with a reduced budget, which was the correct way to go at that time.

I spoke to three people in football about Stewart and I got virtually identical answers from them all. The main theme was that he was a good technical coach but that I should be careful with him, as his reputation as a 'team player' wasn't great. He had been a top-class player at Arsenal and West Ham, meaning that he would have high standards, which pleased me. However, I needed to be able to trust my staff completely, so there was a concern there for me before I had even taken over. I had always taken people on face value initially though, so I intended to do the same with my new staff.

I knew John Stannard, the physiotherapist, from the time when I attended the FA course for the treatment of injuries some years back. He was a very straight lad and I felt very comfortable with him. Steve Tilson, the youth team coach, was virtually part of the furniture at Roots Hall even though he had been away at Canvey Island for some time. The feedback that

I had on Tilly was that he was in the comfort zone at Southend and was tootling along nicely. I even made enquiries about the youth team and the feedback on that wasn't very positive. The words "lack of discipline" and "disorganised" were among those that came back to me.

I knew that it was going to be a big task but it's the same with every new job at first. When I spoke to Ron and the board about the size of the venture they were very supportive and said that they realised that success would take time. I was as impatient as anyone to bring progress to Southend United and it wasn't my intention to take a couple of seasons to build the team. However, there was a distinct possibility that was how long it might take considering the lack of quality in the squad at that time.

I watched a couple of games before I actually took charge and I wasn't particularly impressed, but at least Stewart had got the players trying to pass the ball about. It all looked a little lightweight to me: pass and move. It made for decent football but with very little end product and without any real physicality in the side. The games that I saw only reiterated that a lot of changes were needed. I spoke to Rob Newman again and he told me more about the players, which helped me to form a picture of what was needed: unfortunately the majority of the squad had to go!

I did know someone quite well at Southend, but he was not involved in the football side of the club. His name was Brian Wheeler and he worked in the commercial department. He was at Colchester United when I was the manager and had done a good job there during our successful period. I used to call him 'Munson' after Woody Harrelson's character in the film Kingpin. He had loved the banter and all that went with it at the U's. His nickname hadn't travelled with him to Roots Hall, so when I called him Munse in front of the other staff in his department I don't think he was too pleased! That was tough luck, as when I told them where it came from they loved it. Brian was a good lad and he was very supportive of me during my stay at Southend.

My first day in the job was quite interesting. I was introduced to Stewart Robson in Ron and Geoffrey's office at the club. Stewart shook my hand and came over as very confident and sure of himself. He seemed to have a certain familiarity with Ron but not so much with Geoffrey. That was only my first gut impression during the first few minutes of the meeting but it was quite significant in my mind. I was introduced to Steve Tilson later that day and he appeared as quite servile and reserved.

Ron had told me that he wanted a review of the youth system and the merits of the coach as soon as I had the time to do it. Ron had shown quite openly that he wasn't over happy with what was going on in that department! I had enough on my plate initially, so that had to go on my list of 'things to do' after I had sorted out the first team.

I had a staff meeting with Stewart, Steve and John the physio within days. Straight away I could tell that Stewart and Steve were not exactly bosom buddies! There was nothing said in the meeting to support this, but my experiences over the years had left me reasonably perceptive. I told them all what I expected of them in their roles and responsibilities and it went as well as could be expected. I informed them that a lot of decisions had to be made on the future of players during a short space of time and it was important that they were completely honest with me in their opinions of players whose contracts were up in the close season. I intended to watch everyone closely in training and the final few games and formulate my own opinions before cross-referencing with all the staff. The final decision on each player would be mine alone but their input was essential, as they knew everyone much better than I did. I also had the input from the previous manager, so I was confident that no mistakes would be made.

I left all the coaching and prep work to Stewart to start with so that I could overview everything. He was an excellent technical coach and initially I was very excited at the thought of working with him. Many of the players were struggling with some of his expectations on the training field, which I could see frustrated Stewart at times. This wasn't too much of a worry to me, as I had hoped that we could sign some better players that would be more comfortable with the sessions. I had been used to doing most of the coaching and preparation myself, but it was so obvious that Stewart was an out-and-out coach that I needed to give him his head to a certain degree. I couldn't have him just picking up the cones and passing the bibs out. Ron had already put him on a contract so I had to use him, whether I wanted him or not! Some of Stewart's sessions were as good as I had seen at any standard. His passing drills were impressive, if not a little complicated at times, and his general coaching was top class.

The season was coming to an end and the results were meaningless in so far as we were not involved with issues at either end of the table. The players themselves were in some cases playing for their contracts, so there was no lack of application or effort on their part, which was as it should have been, particularly as there was a new manager to impress.

Technically my first game in charge was against Torquay at home and we came out as easy winners 3-0, which was a nice start. However, our second game on the Monday at Boston United wasn't such a success. Their pitch wasn't the best - in fact it was crap - and my team talk was pretty basic. I knew exactly how they would play, which was very direct and physical. Boston knew that it was very difficult to pass the ball on their surface and didn't mess about trying to do so. My advice to our players didn't go down well with Stewart, as it appeared that he was itching to jump in and contradict me. Stewart had played at the highest level and at much more salubrious places than Boston United. He looked like a purist to me but this was lower division professional football and you needed to be strong and resilient before you looked to play. I had played at that level long enough to know what was needed. The lads gave their full effort and did all that was asked of them but in the end lost to a very late penalty. We had struggled to match Boston physically at times, so that was something that I needed to look at.

The coach had picked some of us up at the motorway services at Stansted. It took me about 45 minutes to get home and after about another half an hour my telephone rang. It was my friend Ian McDonald and he had just been talking to one of my players, Mark Beard, on the phone. Ian said to me, "Watch your back, mate. Your coach has just slaughtered you to Mark"! Apparently Stewart had collared Mark as we got off the bus at the services and had asked him what he thought of the new manager. The lad had tried to be as diplomatic as he could, seeing as I had hardly got my feet under the table. Stewart had gone on to say that he thought that I had no personality and just wanted to play the long-ball game all the time. Needless to say, I wasn't happy at all - my manager's chair wasn't even warm!

I thanked Macca for his tip-off and wondered what Stewart was thinking in saying that to a player. He must have had his head up his arse if he thought that it wouldn't get back to me somehow, or was he so arrogant that he didn't care? Maybe he hadn't done his homework on me, because all my teams had played a high-tempo game, passing long and short, and we had been very successful doing so. I got the impression that Stewart lived in "Stewart's world" where nobody else was as clever or as knowledgeable as him!

I was in a quandary about what to do. On the one hand, I wanted to sack him as soon as possible; on the other, I had only been there a couple of weeks and Stewart had just signed a new two-year contract. Ron was not going to be a happy bunny if I went in with all guns blazing and demanded that they bin him! In the end I decided that I would have a quiet word with deputy chairman Geoffrey King, and he wasn't completely surprised when I told him what had happened. I don't know why that was the case, but perhaps there had already been feedback before my arrival? He took note, echoed my concerns and asked me to keep him informed if there were any more problems. I did tell him that Stewart had his merits and that I would try to work with him if I could.

I took one step further and invited my staff into another meeting in which I spelt out that I expected total loyalty from all of them. I didn't want a sycophantic set of robots, just honest people who wanted the same outcome for the team as me. I made it clear to them that if I didn't get that then I would replace them. That is how I felt after Stewart's little powwow with one of my players, so I probably sounded a little harsh!

The whole job was like a bag of monkeys, as there seemed to be factions all over the place. The people in the downstairs offices didn't seem to stop moaning about what was going on upstairs, my two coaches couldn't stand each other and my main coach was stabbing me in the back! On top of that, my office was a mess and the reception just outside it was even worse! All sorts of stuff had been left lying around and it was doing my head in, so I collared Munson to get it shifted so that people waiting to see me could sit in some comfort and perhaps take me seriously when I was able to see them. To be honest the whole place appeared to be a bit of a joke. It had been on a slippery slope for some time and a lot of things seemed to be sloppy to me. To be fair to Ron and Geoffrey, they knew what they wanted but I wasn't sure if they knew how to get it.

The difficult task of telling the unfortunate players that their contracts would not be renewed came around at the end of the season. The cross-referencing had been done and there was virtually 100 per cent agreement on who should go. Some of the lads that we wanted to stay were offered reduced terms on new contracts because I had to keep to the budget set by the board. To be frank, some lads were earning more than they should have been for the return that the club was getting from them. In my opinion the club was paying average players above-average wages. I had always handled budgets efficiently, which stemmed from my experiences at Aldershot as a player and a manager. Ron had set a budget figure and I was determined to keep within it if at all possible.

In all we let 13 players go and I brought in 11 in close season. Bringing in so many players in such a short time was the most difficult task I had ever done. My job at Aldershot, where I had started with no players at all, was difficult but this was different in as much as these lads were full-time professionals on contracts rather than part-time, non-contract players. This amounted to a big commitment for the club. Ron had left me very little time to sort this out but I gave it my best. Most clubs don't even bring in five or six players in close season and they definitely don't let 13 go, but the cull was essential for the future of the club. Getting rid of players is much easier than recruiting, especially during a matter of weeks, but that is what the board wanted and I think in theory they were right. All the staff also agreed, including Tilly who knew the club better than all of us.

One of the players released was Darryl Flahaven, the goalkeeper, who had been with the club some time and was a very competent player. However, Stewart told me that he was struggling and that we needed a more dominant keeper. I hadn't seen a lot of Darryl but had kept an open mind about him. He didn't do himself any favours with anybody prior to his release when he got pissed at a club function and started shouting out from his table. I was sat on the next table to him with Geoffrey King and he was not impressed at all as there were sponsors, supporters and dignitaries present. I pulled one of the lads and suggested that he have a word to try to settle Darryl down. I was uncertain why one of the players was behaving that way, especially in front of the new manager at his first public appearance at the club. At the end of the evening I approached Darryl and suggested to him that it might be a good idea for him to phone Geoffrey King to apologise, as the deputy chairman had been left a little red faced. He did so and I later found out that Darryl had suffered a family bereavement sometime earlier and that it was still affecting him. I sympathised with him, of course, but he still needed to behave correctly when representing the club.

Apparently, before I took the position of manager, Darryl had made it clear that he had a club lined up for the following season and didn't appear to be overly concerned if his contract wasn't renewed. This seemed to be confirmed when we called him into my office to tell him that he was being released, as he sat down long enough for us to give him the news and then stood up and simply said, "Okay," before walking out and leaving the door wide open! Stewart and I just looked at each other and shrugged our shoulders, as he didn't seem to give a jot! Everything wasn't as it appeared though. A couple of months later when we had injury problems with our goalkeepers I found out that 'Flavs' did not have a club at all! So I got in touch with him and invited him back in for a chat. When he came to see me he looked like a different lad. His old sparkle had returned, he was apologetic about his past behaviour and overall he looked much happier. He was very keen to give it another go and I was only too pleased to oblige him, and he did very well on his return.

A little while ago I happened to read a newspaper article about Darryl's success at Southend after my departure. I was disappointed to read that he said that the manager at that time, meaning me, hadn't shown enough understanding towards him that season. He obviously had a short memory, as it was me who actually did try to show some understanding. Darryl had chosen what route to take that year and I had welcomed him back into the fold!

In the close season the free transfer list of players, containing hundreds of names, is compiled by the PFA in Manchester and sent out to club managers in the form of an A4 book. If you want to be ahead of the game and contact players before other clubs get the chance, it is possible to visit the headquarters in Manchester to have a sneak preview. That is exactly what I decided to do. I took Anne up with me so that she could copy out all the names and phone numbers as I went through the 'tome'. Mick Maguire at the PFA was very helpful and left us alone in an office for as long as it took to gather the necessary information. I asked if I was the first boss to make the trip and was informed that I was the second, as my old mate Brian Talbot had left just before we arrived.

I was determined to contact as many players as possible before they went on holiday or were snapped up by other clubs. Without being disrespectful, there were many names that were nowhere near good enough for our needs. There were also names that we couldn't afford in a million years. We came away with about 50 names of players at different levels of ability and salary. I phoned one lad, who shall remain nameless, and firstly enquired about his salary at his last club. On receiving an answer of £2,500 per week, the conversation didn't go any further, but he was genuinely pleased that I had shown some interest in him before the general release of the list. He probably didn't command that wage again, but even half that amount would have been beyond our budget. In my opinion he was a good player but not of a standard that would command that sort of salary at Southend. Wages had gone through the roof further down the soccer pyramid, but some of my prospective players would have to settle for £300 to £400 a week.

Within my budget I had to fashion a squad with as much strength and quality as possible to compete in our division and when I took the job it was obvious that there wouldn't be a great deal of money to spend on transfer fees. Consequently, all my signings would be free transfers, except for one: Mark Gower. I had seen him play several times and felt that he hadn't fulfilled his potential yet. Although he was one of Barnet's best players, I knew that he had more in his make-up than Conference-level football. Ron agreed the deal and we brought Mark in for about £20,000. It turned out to be a good signing for the club even if it did take him a while to adjust. I had a good knowledge of players at the lower-league level, but getting exactly the right players at such short notice was a big ask. When I was at Colchester I had the time to watch players several times in all kinds of different situations and conditions before making a decision on them. At Southend however, it was totally different. Stewart knew very few players at our level and so most of the lads that I brought in were totally unknown to him. Tilly knew a few of them but he had been out of the Football League for a while so his knowledge of players was also limited.

The goalkeeping situation needed addressing and so I brought in my old keeper from Colchester, Carl Emberson. Carl had done well for me for four seasons at Layer Road and he had also gained promotion a couple of seasons later with Luton Town. I felt that his experience would be important to us, but unfortunately the crowd didn't take to him from the off! Every little mistake he made seemed to get blown out of proportion by the fans and his confidence suffered somewhat. Maybe his Colchester connection had something to do with it or perhaps it was just that Flavs was the fans' favourite!

I brought in three defenders - ex-Wimbledon Duncan Jupp, Jamie Stuart from Bury and Mark Warren from Colchester United to play alongside Leon Cort; three midfielders - Jimmy Corbett, Jamie Fullarton and Leke Odunsi; and two strikers: big Drew Broughton and young Michael Husbands. Also Che Wilson joined us from Cambridge City when he came in on trial for pre-season. After Che had impressed me in a few positions I decided to speak to one of his old managers, Ian Holloway. Ian and I went back a few years, so I knew that he would give me a genuine assessment of Che. Without hesitation he told me to take him, as he was a great professional and would do a decent job wherever I asked him to play. So I squeezed Che into the budget on low wages with some appearance money. I remember a few months later, after a defeat in which Che had played, a director at the club said to me, "He is one of the worst players I have ever seen play for this club!" I replied, "I don't think so. Especially when he's only on £300 a week." If my memory serves me right, in the not too distant future following that conversation Che went on to play his part in a very successful promotion season.

We only had one goalkeeper as the budget didn't stretch to a second, so I needed a backup. Ian Miller, an old playing colleague of mine, then at Blackburn Rovers, recommended a young goalkeeper that they had just released. His name was Ryan Robinson and, as with Che, he would have to be on a low wage. However, he saw the offer as an opportunity and he gratefully accepted. As it often is with young keepers, fortune can quite easily go either one way or the other. In Ryan's case it started quite well for him in pre-season, but unfortunately it all went pear-shaped when he was given his big chance in the first team.

Stewart mapped out most of our pre-season training and it went reasonably well. This was a first for me, as I usually did this entire organisation by myself. Maybe some delegation was the right way to go - it kept him happy anyway! We had a few trialists in along the way but we finally settled on about 18 senior professionals with the addition of young Michael Kightly. 'Kites' was a really likeable lad and after training he used to challenge me to a game of hitting the crossbar with the ball from 30 yards away. He couldn't manage to beat me but he kept on trying. He was quite physically lightweight but had a lot of potential as a player. A few months into the season I eventually put him in the team and he showed some great touches, which did him no harm at all in my eyes. In my opinion he wasn't quite ready to play regularly in the first team but he was definitely destined to have a Football League career. After I had left Southend I couldn't understand the reasoning behind letting him go to Grays in the Conference. Someone with a white stick could have seen that Kites had a chance! Mind you, it's all about opinions, isn't it?

Our pre-season games went quite well even though we didn't produce great results. We virtually had a new team, so it was always going to take time to gel. Some of our football was very good, which is common for teams in pre-season on nice pitches in warm weather. We gave my old club Colchester a real test in a 1-1 draw and should have beaten them. Brian Owen, who was still on the staff with the U's, thought that we had potential as a squad.

Our game against local rivals Canvey Island had some history to it and so it was always going to be a tetchy affair. It was a local derby, so it wasn't ideal preparation from my point of view, but it had already been arranged and therefore had to be played. We lost the game 1-0 but we'd had enough chances to win it, especially in the second half. What stuck in my mind more than anything, however, was the behaviour of one of my own staff.

The game nearly boiled over on a couple of occasions and the opposition's bench had plenty to say for themselves. Glen Pennyfather, their coach, was never short of a word or two and, rightly or wrongly, had words with big Drew Broughton once or twice from the touchline. I had no intention of getting involved; I wanted to keep myself to myself and any comments I made were to my staff close by. Tilly usually stood or sat in our dugout for games but on this occasion he was standing just outside the box in the tunnel entrance. As words were being exchanged between Glen and some of our players, Glen turned to Tilly and made some derogatory comments about

Drew and another of our players. Tilly laughed and appeared indifferent to the outburst! I knew that Tilly had spent some time at Canvey as a player, but as far as I was concerned his loyalties now lay at Southend. I was already wound up inside, seeing as they were giving it the big 'un because of their 1-0 lead, so I didn't need one of my staff turning a blind eye when it was all getting a bit naughty. I shouted over to him, "Tilly, I think you need to realise on which side your bread is buttered, mate!" He just looked away and visibly shrunk a little. The next time I looked around he had moved, which perhaps was the best course of action having been caught out! I didn't broach the subject of that incident again with him, but now I felt as if I had two disloyal people in the camp.

The season got under way and we had a good start with a win at home against Cheltenham. Two goals from Mark Gower showed what he was capable of even if one was a penalty. I think that was the only penalty we scored out of several other opportunities while I was manager. We lost the next three League games, one of them being at my old club Doncaster Rovers. Rovers had gained promotion back into the Football League and that was their first home League fixture of that season. Ironically I was manager of Colchester United, as I have previously mentioned, when they played their last match at home before dropping into the Conference. It was a strange feeling for me, as I had left Rovers in difficult circumstances, but I was still pleased that they had made it. I had played some part in their successful climb back into the League and the smile on John Ryan's face was still as big if not bigger than I had remembered it when I shook his hand on the pitch before the game. On the day we were no match for them and although we had some good chances we rolled over too easily for my liking. I didn't want to hang about too long after the game for obvious reasons, but I did meet a few of the real Donny diehard staff and they were great to me. However, I didn't want to chinwag with some people who may or may not have contributed to my demise at Belle Vue.

We lost the following two games to Mansfield and York, which meant that, including our League Cup defeat to Swindon Town who were managed by my pal Andy King, we had lost four games on the bounce. I think that was a first during the whole of my managerial career and the team weren't reflecting me at all. We were quite enterprising at times and were moving the ball about well, but we had a soft centre and weren't making it difficult for the opposition to play against us. I spoke to Stewart about my views and used words such as "basics", "closing down" and "rolling our sleeves up". He listened but asked me what I meant by "basics". He knew exactly what I meant but didn't agree. He thought that technical coaching with good passing and movement would turn things around. Although I liked his ideology, I thought that they belonged at a younger and higher level of football than we were at. In my opinion he would have made a good FA coach, perhaps taking the U18 England side, with even a progression from there. His methods just didn't work at our level and he also found it hard working for someone else who was picking the side – something that was obvious to almost everyone! However, I stuck with him for a few more games.

We beat Bury at home somewhat fortunately but then we lost at Oxford. The away game at Oxford became an eye-opener for me in terms of my relationship, or should I say lack of one, with chairman Ron. We lost 2-0 and Oxford went to the top of the division. I wasn't happy and kept the players in the dressing room longer than usual, as I needed to have my say. I was starting to lose patience with the whole situation and felt that I needed to take more control of just about every aspect of managing my side. I spoke to them and everyone listened. They obviously did take some notice, as our performances did improve over the next few games even though it wasn't reflected in the results. We all got straight on the bus afterwards, as I had taken quite some time with my rollicking of the team!

When we were sailing down the motorway back to Southend my mobile phone rang and it was Ron. He asked me where I was and when I told him that I was on the coach on the return journey home he demanded to know why I hadn't gone upstairs after the game. I told him that my place was in the dressing room and that I had a job to do there. His voice was already high-pitched but then he became quite patronising. He bellowed that there were people up there who had wanted to "see" me and "wanted explanations". The tone of the whole call was unbelievable. I felt like a chastised naughty little boy who needed to report to the headmaster's office! I replied, "Who do you think you're talking to? I'm not some young kid. I had a job to attend to and that's that!" The conversation didn't go much further and after I rang off I thought: what the dickens is going on here? Ron had gone from a very organised, intelligent man to a silly arse shouting down the phone at me and we were only six League games into the season!

We lost two more games on the trot, at Hull and at home to Lincoln. We should have got a draw at Hull after missing a last-minute penalty to make it 3-3. We also missed another penalty at the home game against Lincoln, which cost us the match! We were still not performing how I would have liked, but we were still having no luck at all with injuries. As for the penalty situation, it became ridiculous. Although we tried different players for the penalty kicks, we still couldn't stick the ball in the net! The Hull City result was a travesty as we had played well. This time Ron came into the dressing room after the game and, although disappointed, he was very complimentary towards me and the team. Neither of us mentioned the post-Oxford phone call, but I knew that I was dealing with someone who was very much a 'knee-jerk reaction' kind of person and that worried me.

Our home game against Carlisle was a turning point for me. We were 2-0 up and cruising at half-time. Carlisle got back in it with a goal and then we missed another penalty to clinch the game. It was Sod's Law when they equalised late on and more points went begging. I was furious and went home that evening with a lot to think about. I decided that there were going be changes and that I must be in charge of my own destiny.

I met with Geoffrey and Ron in Chelmsford at their business premises and I told Ron that we had to release Stewart. I would manage alone until I could find a suitable replacement. The decision had been coming for some weeks, as some of the senior players had pulled me to vent their concerns regarding Stewart's methods and behaviour. They told me that he wasn't behind me and that the players were getting mixed messages. From their point of view there could only be one boss and as far as they were concerned that was me. I thanked them for their support and explained that I wasn't blind to what was going on and that it would be dealt with in due course.

My old confidant Bob Fisher had joined me to help out, as he had done at Colchester United. When Bob first arrived and I had introduced him to Stewart the look on my coach's face was a picture; it was as if he had lost a fiver and found a shilling (5p to you young 'uns)! I suspect that he wasn't happy because I had brought in one of 'my men'. Bob also gave me some feedback from the shop floor and it wasn't exactly glowing about Stewart.

Ron was pretty shocked but Geoffrey didn't appear surprised at all about Stewart, as the coach was really Ron's man. However, I had put him on the line and had explained exactly what had been going on and Ron agreed. He set about writing a letter to Stewart almost immediately, as I wanted it done as quickly as possible. I thanked them for their support and, although part of me regrets not telling Stewart myself, I didn't really owe him that since he wasn't my appointment. So Ron could do the necessaries as far as I was concerned!

When I went into training the day after Stewart had left, the lads were in high spirits. I wouldn't go so far as to say they were glad that he had gone, but there seemed to be a lighter, more open atmosphere in the place. As I walked up the stairs to the treatment room where John Stannard was sorting out some of the lads, I saw a three-foot-high picture of a snake pinned on the wall that looked as if it had been cut from a magazine or something similar. At the bottom of the picture in big letters was the word "ROBBO" and it was quite obvious to whom it referred. I left it there for the time being and went into the physio's room. Several of the professionals were there and in unison they all said, "Morning boss!" I replied, "Morning!" but I didn't make any comment about the poster. They were obviously waiting for a reaction of some sort, but I didn't give one immediately. I can't say the incident made me happy, but they do say in life: "If you make your own bed, you have to lie in it". Nobody owned up to the prank and I didn't push it!

Stewart went on to coach at Rushden and Diamonds but experienced similar problems in so far as they couldn't win games on a regular basis. After I had left Southend I did some work for BBC Essex radio, assessing a Cup game between Rushden and Colchester United, and I predicted on live radio that Colchester would win the game comfortably at Rushden. In the event, they stuck four goals past them to win the match. The home side looked tidy and well drilled but there was no steel and determination in the team, allowing Colchester to roll them over at three-quarter pace.

That was just how it had been earlier in the season for Southend, and it was my fault for letting it continue for the first ten games rather than taking over the reins sooner. It probably killed our season and eventually maybe even cost me my job!

After Stewart's departure I took the helm completely, with Tilly helping out if I needed him. He appeared happier in himself, perhaps because of the coach's exit, as the two hadn't got on well. To be fair to Stewart, he hadn't really hidden his intentions whatever they were. With Tilly I struggled to suss out what his thoughts were at times - if he had any, that is. One such example happened one day at 'Boots and Laces', our training ground. I had just finished with the first team and I sat down to have a roll and some fruit with everyone. Geoff Pike from the FA came over to sit at the staff table next to me and he had a face like thunder. Geoff had come to take the YTS lads for their coaching certificates.

I asked Geoff if he was okay and he replied, "No, I'm not taking those lads this afternoon, they're are a disgrace!"

I wasn't best pleased and asked, "In what way?"

"They're just taking the piss, messing about and showing me no respect!" he replied.

I couldn't believe my ears. This had never happened before at any club I had managed. I was embarrassed and asked if Geoff would reconsider if I had a word with them. He agreed and so I pulled the lot of them immediately to speak to them outside. Even as they filed outside they were having a laugh and a joke. I went into one and threatened them with the instant sack if there wasn't a great improvement with Geoff and there would be no reprieve if he gave me any names at the end of the afternoon session. From what I can remember, youth team coach Tilly was not there at the time. Thankfully, Geoff reported that there had been no problems during the session and I apologised to him for their earlier behaviour, which he accepted. He was perplexed, however, as to why the group would want to behave like that. From my point of view the youth team coach's outlook should be reflected in the young lads' behaviour. I told Tilly about the incident and he was somewhat reticent about responding. Perhaps he just wanted an easy life but that wasn't my way; I wouldn't stand for indiscipline at my club. I wanted visiting coaches or officials to go away with a good impression of what we were trying to do. To me the whole place had been riddled with problems and there were too many people doing their own thing throughout the club. I wasn't interested in politics or egos, I just wanted to build a successful side and expected as many people as possible to hop on board for the benefit of the club.

My first game in total control was our 1-1 draw away at Scunthorpe. Southend hadn't gained any points away from home for some 13 games, which included nine games that were played before my arrival. In fact we took eight points from our next four away games, including the Scunthorpe match. We drew at Darlington, won at Kidderminster and won at Macclesfield. That was promotion form away from home but our home form still suffered. Leon Constantine, whom I had picked up from Brentford on a free transfer, scored our goal at Scunny in the 1-1 draw. He later went on to score plenty of goals for the Shrimpers. When he smacked in the equaliser he ran from the far side of the pitch right over to our dugout and jumped all over me, followed by several other players. I was somewhat taken aback by this, but it was obviously the players' way of saying that they were pleased for me and they were right behind me. That was a nice feeling and I felt at that moment that I was back in the role I enjoyed. It was 'MY' team now and everyone was going to know exactly what their job was on the pitch. It wasn't going to be complicated, just basic stuff with a lot of heart behind it.

It was like a fresh start for me, but I was still short of an assistant and that was where I made my mistake!

Originally after my interview for the manager's position it had been my intention to ask Stewart Houston to join me, but unfortunately Stewart Robson was already in place. I should have got straight onto Mr Houston immediately after Robbo's departure and heaven knows why I didn't! Instead, I approached Geoff Wood, an ex-goalkeeper who was at Colchester for a while when I was a player there. Geoff had good experience in coaching and managing at Brighton, he was local and he was also someone that I could trust. For one reason or another, Geoff was encountering problems with the coaching school that he was attempting to set up in Spain, so I wasted a couple of weeks waiting for him to sort out his affairs. Eventually he had to turn down my offer because of his commitments abroad.

I then contacted Ian McDonald (Macca) to see if he was interested and, to my surprise, he was as keen as mustard. I had thought that he wouldn't want to move up from Hampshire but I was wrong and he said that if he were offered the job he would come to Essex with Glenis ASAP. That was great news, as I was close to putting in place my own man, whom I knew would break his neck to do right by me and the team. I even recruited my old 'pineapple-catching mate' Gary Phillips as the goalkeeping coach on a part-time basis. By getting Ian, Bobby Fisher and Stig on board I would essentially have staff that knew exactly what was required and what made me tick.

Ron agreed to meet Macca before our home game against Boston in late October 2003 and I had primed Ian about Ron and the way he worked. I had also told him about the budget and what sort of salary he could expect. It wasn't going to be great but it would be a good opportunity for him. We had been extremely unlucky in our previous two home games against Leyton Orient and Huddersfield, but I had turned the team into a much more resilient unit away from home as the results had proved. It was going to take time to turn our fortunes at home around, but we were not that far away from doing so. Unfortunately your home games are very important to the fans, which goes without saying.

The Boston performance was probably our worst in the last six games and the supporters vented their frustrations at me in no uncertain terms. Calls for "Wignall out" were quite clear! Ron also came in for some stick, which he struggled to cope with. We lost the game 2-0 and deservedly so, but I was still confident that we were moving in the right direction and could consolidate our performance when some of our injured players returned. Near the end of the game, however, Ron marched down the steps in the directors' box, leant over the dugout wall, pointed his finger at me and said, "I want to see you after the game." The substitutes and some of the players sitting in their seats just below him gazed up in amazement. I just looked at him with contempt and turned back to the game. Mark Warren, our centre back, who wasn't playing that evening, told me afterwards that he felt like standing up and punching Ron in front of everybody. He thought it was the most embarrassing display by a chairman that he had ever seen in professional football. It looked as though Ron had gone into 'Oxford phone call mode' again!

After the game I went up to the directors' lounge and bar where Anne was waiting with Bobby Fisher and Ian McDonald. I asked Macca how his meeting had gone before the match and he was very positive, saying that

Ron had been very professional and had told Ian that there was only the salary to sort out after the match.

Macca was desperate to talk about the game and what we needed to do to turn results around, but his first comment was, "What was Steve Tilson doing down there?"

"In what way?" I said.

"You clearly needed some staff support on that bench when everyone was having a go at you, but he kept his head well below the parapet!"

"Did he? I hadn't noticed!" I answered. "But that sounds about right!"

Fish and Anne didn't say a lot, they just had a wide-eyed look on their faces. Ron was prowling about waiting to speak to me and so I went straight over to him. His face was as red as a beetroot and his hair in his frustration looked like Beethoven's! His eyes were pretty wild and he asked me in a ferocious manner, "What are you going to do about this situation? I want answers NOW!" I looked down at him and said calmly, "I have no intention of going into details now, Mr Chairman, as this is the wrong time and place to hold an inquest." Feelings were running high, so I thought that the best way of settling him down was not to rise to his bait. He wasn't happy with my answer at all and continued to pace up and down with rage! He was the chairman and was entitled to ask whatever he wanted, but experience told me that he needed to calm down before I could talk to him sensibly. However, he was having none of it. There was a door leading to the supporters' bar opposite the directors' room and some of the fans in there shouted something to Ron, but he just slammed it shut as he walked out.

When Ron had left I spoke to another director who was much more composed and I said to him, "Ron must do what he feels is right but I am doing my best. I will definitely get there in the end if I am given the time."

It had been six weeks since the post-Oxford conversation with the chairman when he had phoned me on the bus with his 'knee-jerk reaction'. I was fearful that he would go down the same road again after his dreadful behaviour in the directors' box and lounge. He didn't seem to be able to control himself in high-pressure situations, or ones he perceived that way. On the way home from the Boston game Anne told me that Ron had spoken to her before I had come upstairs, asking what I was up to. Fish had tried to talk calmly to him but he was also bemused by Ron's overreaction!

The next day Ron contacted me to tell me that Ian was not suitable for the position as my assistant. He also commented on my lack of explanations in the face of his questions following the game. I rang Macca immediately to tell him the bad news. He wasn't at all surprised after seeing Ron's reaction at first hand.

"You're not going to be there much longer then?" he asked.

"I don't think so, mate. Sorry about the job. We could have given it a right go!" I replied.

"That's true, but something's not right with him," said Ian.

"I've thought that for the past six weeks!" I responded.

It was a farce. I was a dead man walking yet again and it was a horrible feeling! I had only been solely in charge for a total of eight games. I knew that I would get it right and the squad wasn't bad considering the short time that I'd had to put it together.

Our game at Macclesfield on the following Saturday was to be my last away game, although I didn't know it for certain at the time. I was just hoping that Ron had put his sensible head on and would be willing to stick with me.

Before we went up to Macclesfield Anne said that there was something she needed to tell me. She hadn't mentioned it to me before but now felt that I was entitled to know as much as possible about what was going on. She had been standing amongst a group of people at the Boston game and Helen Giles, the club secretary, was chatting to them. Helen must have forgotten or not noticed that Anne was in the company, as she started speculating about the possibility of Stan Collymore returning to the club as the manager. He had been at Southend previously as a player. She was clearly excited at the prospect of him coming back when in full flow she spotted Anne out of the corner of her eye. Her face flushed, there was a short, embarrassing silence and then she changed the subject! Anne wasn't naïve but this came totally out of the blue, as it didn't make sense at that time, and to be so matter of fact about it in front of people in the lounge was totally out of order. Helen had been helpful and welcoming to me when I had arrived as the new manager, so I was disappointed with her but I didn't really know her so perhaps it was par for the course. Maybe she was just another snake in the grass at Roots Hall?

The Macclesfield game was a success and we played very well away from home again, winning 2-1, although it could quite easily have been three or four goals. Ron was sitting in the stand with a bloke I hadn't seen before. Even though we had won well, Ron didn't show any expression on his face at all. In my mind I had been saved from the gallows for the time being and still desperately wanted to carry on. I felt that we would probably finish in mid-table by the end of the season and we were still in the old Auto Windscreen Cup competition. That was no great shakes but, bearing in mind all the upheaval, a solid foundation had been laid on which a team could be built up in the coming months. Realistically, if we had lost at Macclesfield I would have been sacked on the Monday. The pressure was silly. It was like treading water in the middle of the ocean but knowing that eventually you are going to drown. Unless there was a miracle, of course!

We lost at home to Northampton on the following Saturday, although we actually played okay. However, that was irrelevant, as Ron did what he thought was right and within days I was sacked!

Ron called me into his office and with just the two of us present he gave me the bad news immediately. He said that our season would be over if we lost the following Saturday in the FA Cup. I told him that it was the wrong decision and I was the right man for the job. He was obviously panicking about our impeding FA Cup match and couldn't take the pressure, so the easy solution was to dispense with my services. I had no intention of grovelling or pleading for my job, as Ron had made up his mind. It was all quite civilised, as he was calm and in control of himself when there was no heckling or abuse bearing down on him from the fans. I kept my dignity but I can honestly say that if he had tried to speak to me in the manner in which he had previously on a couple of occasions, I would have pulled his tongue through his arse and left him on his desk to think about it! I shook his hand as I left and he assured me that my contract would be sorted out. Even though it had 18 months to run, I had agreed to just six months' pay on dismissal. I had never been a money grabber and I would have preferred to earn the remainder of my salary.

I drove away from Roots Hall feeling totally deflated but at the same time with a certain amount of relief because Ron had become a nightmare to work for. From the moment I had let Stewart Robson go I felt that the chairman had changed towards me. I may have been wrong, but after thinking about it I came to the conclusion that my future may well have been decided much earlier than I had realised.

Geoffrey had been good to me, although he may have been different behind my back. I found him to be intelligent, thoughtful and even-handed. Therefore, I had no reason to think that I would have any hassle over my contract being honoured. Ron had appeared genuine when I left his office - but how wrong could I have been? The whole affair turned into a nightmare for me and my family!

There was no early response from the club regarding settlement of monies owed. I had arranged collection of my club car with Brian Wheeler as soon as possible. I was trying to be proactive but they were not for some reason. I had hoped that the matter could be settled quickly but that wasn't the case. I had to inform the League Managers' Association again and John Barnwell dealt with the issue on my behalf.

In a nutshell, Ron acted like a 'lupin'! I even received a letter attempting to sue me for £50,000 for allegedly signing poor players! The LMA had not come up against anything quite so ridiculous before. What was being suggested was that managers who sign players that are not up to scratch in the chairman's view could be sued for large amounts of money. That is equivalent to suing a top premiership manager for millions of pounds because one of his big name players didn't quite perform well enough. You could go to every club at every level and sue the manager every time a player didn't quite cut the mustard in the chairman's opinion! What a ridiculous man Ron was and still is!

Ron even went as far as hammering me in one of the match-day programmes at a home game. A friend of mine posted it to me to show me what Ron was up to. Part of my dressing-down was when he suggested that I wasn't what I seemed to be once the veneer had been stripped away. In reality, I was exactly what you saw and he was the one that was nothing like the person he appeared to be! I'm proud of my reputation in the game. How is Ron's? I couldn't get another position without forfeiting any money that was owed by Southend and Ron was making it as difficult as possible for me, so I had the hump for months until the LMA eventually managed to sort everything out.

I was having my usual haircut at North Hill Barbers in Colchester when I got a call from Geoffrey King. I agreed to meet him at the Marks Tey Hotel, ironically where Anne and I spent our first night when we arrived in Colchester in 1977. Geoffrey was so respectful and almost apologetic and we agreed on a settlement fairly quickly. Why Ron had been so vindictive after I had left was beyond me. I had clearly upset him by not bowing down to him, but I had always been honest and hard working. I am a good manager and, given the time, I have no doubt that I would have succeeded. I certainly did not deserve to be treated like something you wipe off your shoe! In my conversation with Geoffrey I suggested that if he had been in total control I could still have been the manager of Southend to that day. He didn't disagree but wouldn't say any more about the whys and wherefores of what had gone on, but I didn't expect him to. Business is business and he was heavily involved at Southend and that was his priority.

The whole affair had taken about 15 months to resolve. That was 15 months of stress for all the family, especially for Anne who was supposed to be trying to lead a stress-free life! Unbelievably, I actually received a letter from Ron Martin after the club's final payment saying that he hoped there were no hard feelings and it was just business. He also said that if I needed a reference for any future position he would be delighted to oblige! I didn't know whether to eat the letter, frame it, or wipe my backside with it! I still have it, filed away and kept for posterity. Mind you, I will always be able to look at myself in the mirror; Ron won't – well, he will I guess if he stands on a box! 'Little man syndrome' is a sad affliction for those that have it!

I was more than disillusioned by now. Anne's health and Sally's welfare became my total priority. I stopped applying for managers' positions and just took time out with my wife. We still had to travel to and from London to see her specialists and in all honesty she was having problems with her condition. The Southend experience had done her no good at all as she was supposed to avoid stressful situations at all costs, so it was my aim to help her do just that. I consciously made a decision to come out of the professional game until Anne was much better and Sally was 18 and hopefully well on her way towards her chosen career path.

Managing football clubs is becoming more difficult by the day. The experiences at my last two clubs made it obvious that you need to try to surround yourself with staff that you know and trust. The job is nigh on impossible at times without having people working against you. You must have so many strings to your bow just to give yourself half a chance of being successful. Some people are up to the task and some are not. That is the same in any walk of life. Getting the best out of everyone involved around you is a skill and in my opinion you either have it or you don't. The methods used to bring out the best in a person may well differ greatly between individuals, but however it is done it is a bloody marvellous feeling when your method works and you gain success.

Sally auditioned for and was offered a place at London Studio Centre to study for an honours degree in Theatre Dance. Jack is now married to Kristi. He works in the health and fitness industry and continues to play semi-professional football. He even has thoughts of joining the 'madhouse' of management and coaching! Thomas has worked in the film industry as a prop modeller for such films as Charlie and the Chocolate Factory, Wimbledon and the Bond productions. He now owns his own creative design company called Face Fracture, which includes special effects, models and props. He lives in Rochford with his partner Louise. Ironically, Thomas played in the college football match against Lomana on the day he was spotted by Geoff Harrop for CUFC. However, Thomas now prefers to play with a different shaped ball and turns out for Welwyn Rugby Union Club most Saturdays.

I have kept involved with football by doing some part-time coaching, which I have enjoyed very much. Through keeping in contact with the LMA I have been involved on work permit panels for foreign players entering this country. I have found that interesting and hope to do more in the future.

Anne's health seems to be much improved and now that the children are more independent she has been encouraging me to look for a more demanding role in football. My appetite for the professional game has never diminished and I would go back into it tomorrow given the chance – not as a manager, but an assistant's or coach's job would suit me down to the ground.

New young managers need as much help as possible. They have lots of drive and energy, but they also need good quality advice from somebody who is not going to nick their job. They can benefit from having someone on their staff that has been there and done it with no ego to massage. It is still important to bring in people that you know, but it is also important to recruit people who know what they are doing.

There are many such people out of work and out of the industry at present, which is a real shame, as there is no getting away from the fact that experience will always count.

I have enjoyed writing this book and it has been very liberating for us! I say 'us' because Anne's input has been invaluable. I always thought that I had a poor memory and now I know that I have. Anne's recall is definitely better than mine. We have laughed, cried and cursed as the chapters unfolded!

I have done more in my years in football than I thought, and although I didn't reach the top in my trade I gave it a damn good go and I enjoyed NEARLY every minute of it! I always felt good inside after a hard day's work and after penning this book I feel good inside again after 35 years of hard work.

After the final words for this book were written, I decided to treat Anne to a meal out. As we pondered over the menus, I couldn't decide what to have. Anne peered at me over the top of her specs. The sparkle had returned to those lovely brown eyes and grinning cheekily she said:

"I'll have the pasta, you can have chips!"

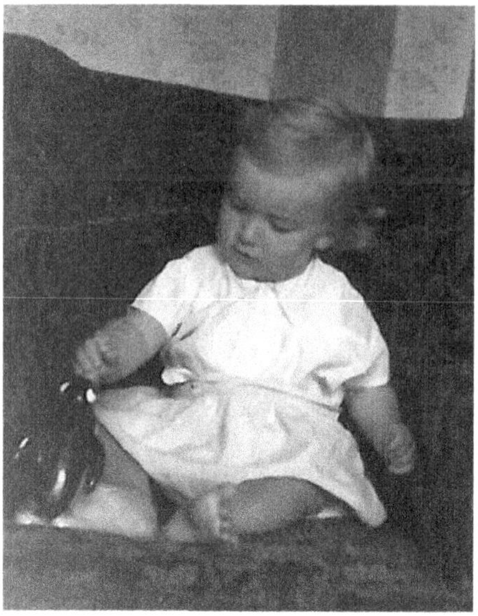

It's NOT a dress! They're football shorts!

Above: Hard luck little bruv, I got what I wanted from Father Christmas!

Left: My mate Gary and I at Boys Brigade "Boot" camp!

Above: Anne and I modelling the latest jackets for an advert in the 1970s

Left: "Socks?"

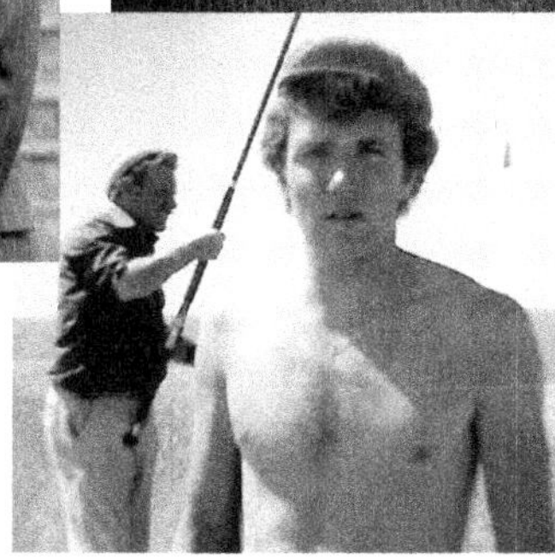

Top left: Our wedding day in the hot summer of 1976

Top right: Ralph in rehab after the "Rickmansworth Incident"

Above: They are both bad hats but at least mine is not a tea cosy dad!

Above: Me, Anne and Sally. An uncanny resemblance to our ancestors!

Right: The family on our return to Colchester in 1995

Top: The kids and us

Left: My Mum and Dad on their 60th wedding anniversary

Bottom left: Dad, Lorraine, Mum, Pauline, Carol and me. No brother just yet!

Below: The three kids, Jack, Sally and Thomas, our pride and joy

Top: Boys Brigade team, I am front row in the centre. My brother David is the little'un on my left

Left: Aldershot Football Club, just weeks before their demise from the Football League in 1992 (I am back row on the left)

Below: Me on tour in Germany with Nottingham Forest in 1976

Above: Bobby Roberts and Ray Harford with a great Colchester United squad

Left: Nottingham Forest squad during the 1976/1977 season. I am second row, third from left

Right: It wasn't me ref! it was him! (David Hurst, playing for Sheffield Wednesday)

Bottom left: Celebrating with Tony Adcock and Stewart Houston after scoring a goal at Chesterfield.

Bottom right (top): An ariel challenge for Aldershot against Cambridge. (Lyndsey Smith, ex-Colchester United player in the centre of the shot)

Bottom right (bottom): Getting a piggyback against Plymouth

Top left: Holding the Championship Trophy at Aldershot Town in 1993

Above: It can be a lonely job as a manager

Bottom left: Getting started as the "Boss" at CUFC

Below: Attending a Christmas Ball at the Town Hall in Colchester

Top: With Sir Alex Ferguson and others at the Rothmans Awards

Left: Champagne for "The manager of the month!"

Below: Tarzan impression after reaching Wembley with Colchester United!

Top: Leading the Colchester United lads out at Wembley Stadium

Middle left: The smile that says it all at the final whistle!

Middle right: Proudly lifting the trophy with David Gregory, the scorer of the goal that gained us promotion

Left: On the balcony of Colchester Town Hall celebrating promotion!

WORDS OF SUPPORT FOR STEVE WIGNALL AND HIS BOOK:

"Steve was an excellent professional and an honest no nonsense performer. I had no hesitation in making him captain at Brentford as he had the full respect of all the staff and fellow players. Therefore I am sure his book will prove to be an excellent read with his professionalism and honesty showing through."

- Frank McLintock

"Steve Wignall boasts the rare distinction of both playing for and managing Colchester United. As a stylish yet combative central defender he made more than 350 appearances as a player and enjoyed the kudos of two Wembley finals and a promotion as one of the club's most successful managers.

Steve's enthusiasm to pen his autobiography without the usual ghost writer shines through in his honesty, thoroughness and attention to detail and makes the life and times of this ultra professional footballer, coach and team boss a compelling read from cover to cover."

- Francis Ponder, Colchester Gazette

"Even the title 'You Can Have Chips' is intriguing and typical of the many interesting anecdotes told by Steve. The book is very much a reflection of the man, fascinating and told with intelligence and dry humour. He is so right - it is not just the big names who have a interesting story to tell. A great read that all football fans will enjoy."

- Derek Davis, East Anglian Daily Times

WORDS OF SUPPORT FOR STEVE WIGNALL AND HIS BOOK:

"It is great to have an incite to Steve's background as Steve was the man that turned me from an amateur footballer to a professional with Colchester United, it's also good to see that Steve and I have not only travelled and played for the same clubs but Steve has been through many of the same ups and down's in football as I have. I owe Steve for giving me "my chance", for that I am forever grateful!"

- Paul Gibbs

"I am really pleased that Steve has put pen to paper and I found it a very easy read with lots of interesting stories. When you don't want to put a book down it tells you all about people involved in the stories and so much about Steve himself. A book about a football man, from a football city that reminded me so much about my own past. I enjoyed working with and against someone who was looked upon as a good and very honest professional. Steve had both of those very admirable qualities. My very best wishes and thank you for the memories."

- Bryan Hamilton

"As a lifelong resident of Colchester, I welcome Steve's warm and informative book. His memories of arriving in town, to meet a "young-looking" Bobby Roberts, make interesting reading as he anxiously joins the team he was destined to manage. All U's fans will enjoy this entertaining autobiography, laced with Liverpool humour and great memories - from the pitch, and beyond the touchline."

- Liz Mullen, 107 Garrison FM

WORDS OF SUPPORT FOR STEVE WIGNALL AND HIS BOOK:

"A true football story from a true football man. This is not a story of ferraris, glamour models and oodles of cash. But here is a story of a determined man, working his way up the football ladder. There are tales of joy, laughter and tears. An absorbing story of life as a jobbing footballer, manager and coach, warts and all."

- Glenn Speller, BBC Radio Essex 103.5 & 95.3 FM

WORDS OF SUPPORT FOR STEVE WIGNALL AND HIS BOOK:

"Steve Wignall is a somewhat rare figure in professional football - he is a "gentleman". I have no idea what he is like in the confines of the dressing room, mind you, but I have no knowledge of him as being anything other than a thoroughly decent guy.

I saw him play for the U's, and I appreciated his time as the Club's Manager several years later. He was a stylish player, who gave 100 per cent at all times, and he brought the same qualities to his time as Manager. On and off the pitch, he was a perfect ambassador for football in general and Colchester United in particular.

During his playing career for the U's, along with other players, his kit was sponsored by a local business - the season in question, by H. Gunton and Son, of Crouch Street. They had sponsored players' kits for several years, but I recall Mr Keith Gunton telling me how pleasantly surprised that he had, for the first time, received a letter from the player thanking him for the sponsorship. The player was Steve Wignall.

I remember, as the Town's MP, having the honour of being in The Royal Box at Wembley when the U's won the League Three play-off final against Torquay. It was a very proud Steve Wignall who led the U's onto the pitch, and I can still see him looking up to the Box and giving a lovely smile and wave to his equally proud wife. This was a very special day for both of them.

And then I recall another side of Steve Wignall. Away to non-League Gravesend and Northfleet in the FA Cup (a game where the U's were humbled 0-2), there was the Manager lugging the wicker case containing the players' kit from the coach to the changing room. To me, that showed him to be someone who was prepared to get stuck in - he did not stand on ceremony, and was happy to get involved as both an individual and as a member of the team.

The above give a flavour of Steve Wignall, and the fact that I can fondly recall these incidents perhaps confirms that he is someone very special in the world of football."

- Bob Russell, MP

www.apexpublishing.co.uk

Lightning Source UK Ltd.
Milton Keynes UK
UKOW04f0506231117
313152UK00003B/470/P